INDIVIDUALS, INSTITUTIONS, AND MARKETS

Individuals, Institutions, and Markets offers a theory of how the institutional framework of a society emerges and how markets within institutions work. The book shows that both social institutions, defined as the rules of the game, and exchange processes can be analyzed along a common theoretical structure. Mantzavinos's proposal is that a problem-solving model of individual behavior inspired by the cognitive sciences provides such a unifying theoretical structure. Integrating the latest scholarship in economics, sociology, political science, law, and anthropology, Mantzavinos offers a genuine political economy showing how social institutions affect economic outcomes.

C. Mantzavinos teaches economics at the University of Freiburg and the University of Bayreuth and is a visiting faculty member in the Department of Political Science at Stanford University.

POLITICAL ECONOMY OF INSTITUTIONS AND DECISIONS

Series Editors

Randall Calvert, Washington University in St. Louis
Thráinn Eggertsson, Columbia University

Founding Editors

James E. Alt, Harvard University
Douglass C. North, Washington University in St. Louis

Other books in the series

Alesina and Howard Rosenthal, *Partisan Politics, Divided Government, and the Economy*

Lee J. Alston, Thráinn Eggertsson, and Douglass C. North, eds., *Empirical Studies in Institutional Change*

Lee J. Alston and Joseph P. Ferrie, *Southern Paternalism and the Rise of the American Welfare State: Economics, Politics, and Institutions, 1865–1965*

James E. Alt and Kenneth Shepsle, eds., *Perspectives on Positive Political Economy*

Jeffrey S. Banks and Eric A. Hanushek, eds., *Modern Political Economy: Old Topics, New Directions*

Yoram Barzel, *Economic Analysis of Property Rights*, 2nd edition

Robert Bates, *Beyond the Miracle of the Market: The Political Economy of Agrarian Development in Kenya*

Peter Cowhey and Mathew McCubbins, eds., *Structure and Policy in Japan and the United States*

Gary W. Cox, *The Efficient Secret: The Cabinet and the Development of Political Parties in Victorian England*

Gary W. Cox, *Making Votes Count: Strategic Coordination in the World's Electoral System*

Jean Ensminger, *Making a Market: The Institutional Transformation of an African Society*

David Epstein and Sharyn O'Halloran, *Delegating Powers: A Transaction Cost Politics Approach to Policy Making under Separate Powers*

Kathryn Firmin-Sellers, *The Transformation of Property Rights in the Gold Coast: An Empirical Analysis Applying Rational Choice Theory*

Clark C. Gibson, *Politicians and Poachers: The Political Economy of Wildlife Policy in Africa*

Ron Harris, *The Legal Framework of Business Organization: England 1720–1844*

Continued on page following index

INDIVIDUALS, INSTITUTIONS, AND MARKETS

C. MANTZAVINOS

CAMBRIDGE
UNIVERSITY PRESS

PUBLISHED BY THE PRESS SYNDICATE OF THE UNIVERSITY OF CAMBRIDGE
The Pitt Building, Trumpington Street, Cambridge, United Kingdom

CAMBRIDGE UNIVERSITY PRESS
The Edinburgh Building, Cambridge CB2 2RU, UK
40 West 20th Street, New York, NY 10011-4211, USA
10 Stamford Road, Oakleigh, VIC 3166, Australia
Ruiz de Alarcón 13, 28014 Madrid, Spain
Dock House, The Waterfront, Cape Town 8001, South Africa

http://www.cambridge.org

First published 2001

Printed in the United States of America

Typeface Sabon 10/13 pt.   *System* MagnaType™ [AG]

A catalog record for this book is available from the British Library.

Library of Congress Cataloging in Publication data
Mantzavinos, Chrysostomos.
Individuals, institutions, and markets / C. Mantzavinos.
p. cm.
Includes index.
ISBN 0-521-77358-X
1. Institutional economics. 2. Social institutions. 3. Economic development. 4.
Organizational change. I. Title.
HB99.5 .M36 2000
306.3–dc21

00-37940

ISBN 0 521 77358 x hardback

To the memory of
Alfred E. Ott
my teacher in Tübingen

Contents

Preface   *page* xiii

Acknowledgments   xvii

I Individuals

1. Explaining Individual Behavior: The Problem-Solving
   Framework   3
   1.1. Explanation of Individual Behavior as the First
        Analytical Step   3
   1.2. Individual Behavior as Problem-Solving Activity   7
2. The Motivational Aspect: The Striving for Utility Increase   10
   2.1. Psychological Approaches to Motivation   10
   2.2. General Motivation and Individual Behavior   12
3. The Cognitive Aspect: The Theory of Learning   16
   3.1. The Evolutionary Perspective   16
   3.2. The Theory of Learning   22
   3.3. Old and New Problems   34
4. The Choice Aspect   43
   4.1. Choice as a Reflection of Alternatives   43
   4.2. Imagination and the Creativity of Choice   46
   4.3. The Theory of Rational Choice   50
   4.4. Beyond *Homo oeconomicus* and *Homo sociologicus*   54
   4.5. Epilogue: Individual Problem Solving   59

II Institutions

5. Shared Mental Models: Emergence and Evolution   65
   5.1. The Issue of Social Order   65
   5.2. The Emergence of Shared Mental Models   67
   5.3. The Evolution of Shared Mental Models   69

Contents

5.4. Cultural Evolution as Collective Learning? 73

6. Explaining Institutions 83
    6.1. Institutions: Introduction 83
    6.2. Why Do Institutions Exist? 85
    6.3. How Do Institutions Emerge? 90
    6.4. Why Do Institutions Persist or Change? 94
    6.5. How Are Institutions Adopted or Enforced? 99

7. Informal Institutions 101
    7.1. Conventions 101
    7.2. Moral Rules 106
    7.3. Social Norms 118
    7.4. Order without Law 126

8. Formal Institutions 131
    8.1. The State as an Enforcing Agency 131
    8.2. The Enforcement of Property Rights 147
    8.3. Law and Social Order 149
    8.4. Social Institutions: Open Issues 152

III Markets

9. Institutions and the Market: The Aggregate Level 161
    9.1. The New Institutionalism and the German
        Ordnungstheorie 161
    9.2. Market Evolution within Institutional Constraints 164
    9.3 Institutions as the Selection Environment of
        Evolutionary Market Processes 167
    9.4. The Metaphor of "Artificial Selection" 172

10. Institutions and the Market: The Microeconomic Level 178
    10.1. How Stable Is the Selection Environment? 178
    10.2. Learning and the Relative Stability of Institutions 181
    10.3. Old Problems, New Problems, and the Channeling
        of the Market Process 185

11. The Theory of Evolutionary Competition 188
    11.1. Evolutionary Economics, German
        Wettbewerbstheorie, and Austrian Market Process
        Theory 188
    11.2. The Supply Side: The Problem-Solving Entrepreneurs 193
    11.3. The Demand Side: The Selecting Consumers 197
    11.4. Exchange and Communication between Supply and
        Demand 203

Contents

11.5. The Driving Forces of the Market: Arbitrage,
Innovation, and Accumulation   208
11.6. The Market as a Selection Order I: The Issue of
Coordination   214
11.7. The Market as a Selection Order II: The Emergence
of Technologies   218
12. An Application: Institutions, Markets, and Economic
Development   227
12.1. Two Types of Theory for Explaining Development   227
12.2. Interpreting the Evidence   232
12.3. The Four Elements of a Wealth-Creating Game   235
12.4. Which Institutions Permit a Wealth-Creating Market
Game?   240
12.5. Credibility and Commitment   241
12.6. What Informal Institutions Foster Economic
Growth?   248
Concluding Observations: Unified Social Science as Political
Economy?   257

References   259
Author Index   303
Subject Index   311

Preface

This book offers what may with reservations be described as a theory of how the institutional framework of a society emerges and how the exchange processes within this framework take place. We already possess a wealth of theoretical knowledge concerning the emergence and functioning of social institutions, as well as numerous fully developed theories explaining how markets work. The main purpose of this book is to show that both social institutions, defined as the rules of the game, and exchange processes can be analyzed in terms of a common theoretical structure. We propose that a problem-solving model of individual behavior inspired by evolutionary epistemology and cognitive psychology may provide such a unifying theoretical structure. A problem-solving model based on solid experimental findings from the cognitive sciences provides a synthesis of the two basic models currently employed in the social sciences: those of *Homo oeconomicus* and *Homo sociologicus*. This model, in turn, is the key to incorporating issues relating to institutions and institutional change and issues relating to the functioning of the markets in a genuine political economy.

Such a political economy can be understood as a transformation of neoclassical economic theory into a discipline that seriously considers the issue of institutions. In fact, the thrust of our argument is that any serious student of economic phenomena must pay attention to the institutions framing these phenomena. Although economists often pay lip service to the importance of institutions for economic and social life, they construct theories as if institutions were somehow given or even optimal. Instead, a theory of political economy must integrate systematically the study of the institutional framework and show how it affects economic outcomes.

Obviously, such a theoretical enterprise can be accomplished in different ways. Since sociology, political science, and anthropology have provided important insights in explaining institutions, a theory of political economy can be successful only if it can consistently integrate the different disciplines of social science into the general project of the study of institutions. In such a project, neoclassical economics must change and take institutions seriously. Neoclassical economics can be transformed into political economy only if one seriously reconsiders the behavioral foundations of the discipline. The fascinating developments in cognitive science provide rich empirical material one can draw from in order to revise the predominant behavioral assumption of utility maximization. Our view is that such a richer psychological model can provide the basis for a successful integration of institutions in the economic theory.

This revision of the behavioral assumptions of economics goes hand in hand with a shift of theorizing toward evolutionary arguments. Cognitive psychology teaches us that individuals actively interpret their environment and always act pragmatically, that is, in relation to a problem. This cognitive activity is responsible for the generation of novel behaviors and therefore for indeterminacy as well. The possibility of novelty implies the historicity of the evolutionary process and greatly complicates the theoretical attempt to come to grips with socioeconomic change. Despite the fact that the open-endedness of the evolutionary process dramatically reduces the possibility of predicting the exact forms of institutions that will be created in a society, the given institutions, once created, will act as the selection environment for the market processes that unfold within them. This means that institutions decisively channel the behaviors tried out in the given market arena.

Institutions, thus, matter for economic outcomes. This conclusion is common in every theory of political economy. What we want to state in addition in this book is that institutions come first. When theorizing about markets, one must first examine the prevailing institutional framework and then draw conclusions concerning market patterns and economic outcomes. This is not a methodological postulate. And though empirical evidence (for example, the failure of socialist economies) verifies this simple contention, it does not provide a substitute for a theoretical explanation. Such an explanation can, in our view, be provided only by consistently employing the cognitive-evolutionary model of individual behavior. Institutions are, from an internal point of view, nothing more than shared problem solutions that individuals have acquired while interacting with their environment. People proceed in exchange acts in markets on the basis of their existing knowledge of how to solve problems of social conflict. Institutions come first because they are already anchored in the minds of the people before they start exchanging in markets. The channeling of market processes by institutions exists and is effective only insofar as it has its counterpart in the minds of the interacting individuals.

Because this causal relationship linking institutions and market outcomes is founded on cognitive path dependence, the feedback mechanism concerning entrepreneurs or organizations that try to change the institutional framework motivated solely by the effects of the distribution of wealth that the institutions have caused in the first place must be relativized. The distributional effects of market processes (i.e., the economic gains and losses that individuals or groups of individuals realize while participating in the market game under the given institutional constraints) do not automatically lead them to modify the rules in order to improve their competitive position. Whether such a step will be undertaken and who will undertake it depend on how the agents subjectively interpret and perceive their own position in their social setting; since their choices depend on their learning histories, the feedback mechanism is extremely difficult to explain and sometimes even to describe ex post. Therefore, our more modest claim in this book is to show that the direct causation linking institutions and market outcomes is valid.

Finally, we should remark that the focus of this study is positive rather than normative. Considerations of optimality and efficiency are systematically avoided so that the discussion of the issues can remain positive and therefore open to critical appraisal.

Acknowledgments

Many people helped me, each in his or her own way, while writing this book, and it is a pleasant obligation for me to thank them.

Peter Oberender offered his decisive support at a moment when I thought that I was the only one who believed in the ideas presented in this book. His thoughtful suggestions helped me to avoid many errors, and his constant encouragement motivated my further work on the manuscript. He is the person to whom I owe most thanks.

In November 1996 I spent two fascinating days in St. Louis discovering that Doug North was working on the same issues as I was. I am grateful to him for all the wise support he has offered me since then.

I thank Bernhard Külp for his unfailing help and his valuable comments on an earlier draft. I am also particularly grateful to Egon Görgens and Helmut Gröner for their support of my work.

I owe particular debts to Wolfgang Kerber and Ulrich Fehl, who read and commented copiously on drafts of this study. My intellectual debt to both of them extends far beyond what is indicated in the text.

I owe special debts to Petros Gemtos, my teacher in Athens, from whom I have learned throughout the years more than from any other person. For his constant willingness to help and many valuable discussions I want to thank my fatherly friend, the philosopher Tassos Bougas.

I have profited greatly from helpful discussions with Raymond Boudon and from his written comments on the first draft of the study. Thanks also go to Pavel Pelikan for his written comments and helpful suggestions.

I owe thanks to Manfred Tietzel for a letter he sent to me in 1994. He was the first to recognize, in the sketch that I sent him, my real intention and the scope of my project, and he encouraged me to work on it.

For profitable discussions I want to thank Rolf Ackermann, Peter Boettke, James Buchanan, Susanne Cassel, Günter Hesse, Ernst Heuss, Her-

Acknowledgments

bert Keuth, Lambert Koch, Richard Langois, Olaf Prüßmann, Mario Rizzo, Karen Vaughn, and Viktor Vanberg. I also thank Jörn Sideras for many discussions and moral support.

I would like to thank the German Marshall Fund of the United States for Grant No. A-0375-09.

My dear friend Dimitris Vassiliou has helped me many times during the different stages of the preparation of the manuscript. In addition, his penetrating questions helped to clarify my thoughts on many issues relevant to this book.

My beloved family in Greece helped me in many ways during the long gestation period of this book. I want to apologize if the work on the book often prevented me from showing the care that they certainly deserve. Lastly, I am grateful to my wife. Without her love and care I never could have finished this book.

Freiburg i. Br.
July 2000

PART I

INDIVIDUALS

I

Explaining Individual Behavior

The Problem-Solving Framework

I.I EXPLANATION OF INDIVIDUAL BEHAVIOR AS THE FIRST ANALYTICAL STEP

Disentangling the mystery of human nature is the most difficult task for anybody who aspires to deal with human affairs. It is this great difficulty that social scientists often try to surpass by not analyzing individual action and behavior directly, but instead by focusing exclusively on aggregates or collective schemes. This technique often proves to be impossible to use consistently, though, since at some stage of analysis the author is forced – by the nature of the subject – to refer, in a direct or indirect way, to assumptions of individual behavior. These assumptions are then made in an unsystematic and often ad hoc way.

Since sooner or later every analysis of society and economy must use explanations of individual activities, it is preferable to start explicitly with the observation and explanation of *individual* action and behavior. One can hope, then, that more clarity in this manner can be provided. It is better to handle an issue, however difficult, directly and with all available means than to try – in the end unsuccessfully – to avoid it. Because, if this issue is important for the study, then it will appear in another form later in the analysis and will lead to complications or theoretical mistakes.

This methodological doctrine of starting any social analysis with the individual, known as *methodological individualism*,[1] has so far proved to

---

[1] Schumpeter (1908) was the first who explicitly stated the principle and gave it a name. See ch VI: "Der methodologische Individualismus" of his Habilitation-thesis: *Das Wesen und der Hauptinhalt der theoretischen Nationalökonomie.* See also Arrow (1994, p. 3): "The starting point for the individualist paradigma is the simple fact that all social interactions are after all interactions among individuals. The individual in the economy or in the society is like the atom in chemistry; whatever happens can

---

be successful. All of the great achievements in the explanation of social phenomena are due more or less to the predilection of the authors to argue in individualistic terms. In particular, the acknowledged progress of economics among the social sciences is, to a great extent, the result of following the individualistic method. And in sociology and political science, those branches of research that have employed the method of individualism have led mainly to successful explanations of social and political phenomena.

Starting with the explanation of individual action and penetrating to the social phenomena to show that they are the result of interaction between individuals who follow their own interests according to their beliefs is, though, by no means a program equivalent to that of the *rational choice* theory. The rationality postulate is, either in its form as an internal consistency of choice or in its identification with the maximization of self-interest,[2] different from methodological individualism in two ways. First, methodological individualism clearly operates on the level of meta-language, suggesting how good theories of social phenomena can be attained. Rational choice theory, in contrast, is designed to offer explanations of the actual behavior of the individuals. Second, methodological individualism is a heuristic principle of a more general nature than rationality: it contends that the analysis of individual behavior as the starting point is most important, regardless of its *concrete form*.

One can explain individual behavior on different levels of generality. It depends only on the explanandum phenomena how detailed the explanation must be. In other words, it is the pragmatics of the explanation that define the degree of specificness necessary for an adequate explanation. If, for example, the fact to be explained is the individual behavior of a mentally ill person who thinks himself to be Napoleon, then a set of general propositions must be employed to account for the abnormal behavior of this specific individual. If, on the other hand, social phenomena are the explananda, then it is obvious that another set of proposi-

---

ultimately be described exhaustively in terms of the individuals involved. Of course, the individuals do not act separately. They respond to each other, but each acts within a range limited by the behavior of others as well as by constraints personal to the individual, such as his or her ability or wealth."

[2] Cf. Sen (1987, p. 12): "How is rational behaviour characterized in standard economic theory? It is fair to say that there are two predominant methods of defining rationality of behaviour in mainline economic theory. One is to see rationality as internal *consistency* of choice, and the other is to identify rationality with *maximization of self-interest*." See also Walsh (1994).

tions must be employed in order to explain the action and behavior of individuals.

The so-called problem of the realism of the behavioral assumptions in economics and social theory must therefore be put in a pragmatic setting. It is only the explanatory needs that define how realistic these assumptions of individual behavior should be. The debate on how realistic statements on individual behavior must be cannot be settled without taking into consideration what the purpose of the whole analysis is.

The analytical goal of this book is to explain how institutions structure social life and particularly how they constrain market processes. In Part II of the book the emergence of different types of institutions and in Part III the functioning of the markets within the institutional framework are explained. A proper description and explanation of individual behavior must thus be offered in Part I of this book so that adequate explanations of the different social phenomena can be attained. This first step of analysis, that is, the explanation of individual action and behavior, is thus of crucial importance for the analysis of social and economic order.[3] An adequate explanation requires that certain criteria be fulfilled.

The first criterion is that the explanation of individual behavior and action be a genuine one. In other words, any analysis of behavior should be of nomological character with empirical content rather than a presentation of a pure logic of choice.[4] A genuine explanation of behavior involves subjecting the observable behavior to general laws. This contrasts to both a pure decision logic of exclusively formal nature and to a prior-

---

[3] It seems that in the last several years, social scientists have increasingly acknowledged the importance of appropriate models of human behavior in order to explain social phenomena successfully. See, e.g., the presidential address of Ostrom (1998), who pleads for a more behavioral approach. See also Soltan, Uslaner, and Haufler (1998, pp. 9ff.), Lindenberg (1998, p. 721f.), DiMaggio (1998, p. 701), Korobkin and Ulen (1999), Drobak (1998), and Thaler (2000).

[4] Hans Albert was the first to differentiate explicitly between "market sociology" and "pure logic of choice," insisting on a research program of economics that is based on empirical psychology. He summarized the purely formal models generated by the neoclassical research program of economics under the name "model-platonism" (*Modellplatonismus*) and showed their methodical deficits, mainly in the form of their tautological character. See Albert (1967/1998, p. 254): "the neoclassical market sociology is much more concerned with a logic of decision than it is with a genuine behavioral, that is, nomological reduction of the social facts of the issue under consideration. In any case, it should not prove at all easy to interpret a model of calculation of the pure economy as a true nomological hypothesis for the purpose of explaining the market behavior of either the economic subject or the quasi subject. Moreover, it appears that among a large number of market theorists the provision of such an interpretation is not the goal." (Translation by C. M.)

ism. The former is mainly concerned with models of choice that are logically inherent and incontestable but empirically irrelevant. Much of rational choice theory, game theory, linear programming, and so on belongs to this tradition of logical models that have no counterpart in reality. A genuine explanation of individual behavior also has nothing to do with a prioristic reasoning. Individual action is not just a concept from which the whole system of a praxeological science can be deductively reduced without any empirical test.[5] This a prioristic praxeology, inspired by Ludwig von Mises and retained by a minority of economists operating in the Austrian tradition, cannot serve as a theoretical foundation for any empirical social science (Albert, 1967/1998, pp. 90ff.). For a successful explanation of human behavior, one should, therefore, draw from the empirical results of psychology. The methods of experiment employed and the testing of hypotheses of human behavior as performed by modern psychologists have led to a valuable corpus of knowledge on the way people think and act. Only a dogmatic attitude toward the findings of other disciplines would prevent a social scientist from paying attention to the results of psychological research. Although a number of those findings are obtained in circumstances created artificially in the psychological laboratory, anyone who is interested in explaining human behavior should not neglect them (Rabin, 1998, p. 41). Therefore, throughout Part I of this study, careful attention will be payed to the psychological research.

The second criterion for an adequate explanation of individual behavior serving the analysis of social phenomena is that it should take into consideration dynamic aspects of behavior. Since individuals are the bearers of social and economic change only if changes in their behavior can be accounted for, the interaction between them can also generate a socioeconomic change. Understanding individual action in a specific time and space is of importance for many issues; but it is mainly the fact that individuals are constantly making choices or are faced with new problems that they then try to solve that sets social and economic processes in motion. This dynamism of behavior is of great importance to understand the flow of social and economic reproduction; therefore, a proper explanation of individual behavior must consider both the static and dynamic aspects.

---

[5] As Mises (1940, p. 19) observes: "A priori science is purely a conceptual science. Thus, it can do nothing other than yield tautologies and analytical propositions. All of its pronouncements are derived from purely logical means out of the terms themselves and the definitions of terms. What is gained then is nothing other than that which was already evident in the presuppositions." (Translation by C. M.)

The third criterion of modeling individual behavior is that it should take into consideration the differences in behavior among individuals. This is the issue of subjectivism: Every person possesses a uniqueness manifested in his individual history, deeds, and thoughts. The character and qualities that make one person different from all others is to be stressed. But is it possible to explain individuality adequately? Does an account of genuine individual action belong to the domain of predictive science? Is it not perhaps impossible to state general laws of human action given the creativity, complexity, and uniqueness of every individual? In a sense, this is the central question to be answered. The main aim of this book is to balance between two extremes: to give an explanation of social phenomena based on some psychological laws that predict human behavior while, at the same time, allowing for creativity and freedom of choice, which diminishes dramatically the possibility of applying general laws.

1.2. INDIVIDUAL BEHAVIOR AS PROBLEM-SOLVING ACTIVITY

These three criteria for the adequate explanation of individual behavior can be attained if we treat individual behavior in a problem-solving framework. The main contention is that the whole range of human activity can be viewed as problem-solving activity. People are continuously confronted with problems, and they mobilize their energy in trying to solve them. Problems arise from the environment of an individual, and each solution to a problem generates new problems. But what is a *problem?* In their classical treatise entitled *Human Problem Solving*, Allan Newell and Herbert Simon give the following answer (1972, p. 72):

A person is confronted with a problem when he wants something and does not know immediately what series of actions he can perform to get it. The desired object may be very tangible (an apple to eat) or abstract (an elegant proof for a theorem). It may be specific (that particular apple over there) or quite general (something to apease hunger). It may be a physical object (an apple) or a set of symbols (the proof of a theorem). The actions involved in obtaining desired objects include physical actions (walking, reaching, writing), perceptual activities (looking, listening), and purely mental activities (judging the similarity of two symbols, remembering a scene, and so on).[6]

[6] See also Albert (1978, p. 23), who argues in a more philosophical manner: "The point of departure for an analysis of human action . . . can be the view of behavior in various situations as a more or less consistent and successful attempt involved to

Problem solving is then a process of searching through a *state space.* A problem can be defined by an *initial state,* by one or more *goal states* to be reached, by a set of *operators* that can transform one state into another, and by *constraints* that a solution must meet (Holland, Holyoak, Nisbet, and Thagard, 1986, p. 10).[7] The procedure of problem solving can be perceived as a method of applying operators so that the goal states can be reached. The set of operators are information processes, each producing new states of knowledge (Newell and Simon, 1972, p. 810).

This problem-solving framework is thus appropriate when accounting for individual behavior because of its *general applicability.* Problem solving covers both syntactic and pragmatic aspects, thought processes and behavior, statics and dynamics. It thus covers a wide range of phenomena and prescribes the way people solve their problems without specifying narrowly what they see as a problem and what their motivation is to solve it. These issues will be discussed in subsequent chapters. The point here is that viewing individual activity as problem solving offers a proper modus to understand human behavior in its great variety. Primarily, then, the problem-solving framework has great integrative properties: Many issues such as the interpretation of reality, learning, motivation, and so on, can be easily incorporated as subaspects.

In the following chapters, these subissues will be analyzed with reference to the problem-solving framework. The main idea is that all phenomena of the mind, such as cognizing, learning, and so on, are handled properly theoretically if one views them in the context of problem solving. Human beings are primarily concerned with solving their problems; they perceive reality, they learn from their environment, and they choose and act according to their problem situation. There is no perception per se, but always perception in relationship to a problem.[8] And there is no learning per se either, but always learning about ways to solve problems. In Chap-

---

capture and solve problems. These problems can be of extreme variety – the fundamental problems of life which are involved in the maintenance of naked human existence (e.g., making provisions against hunger and cold, seeking protection against enemies, providing for group security) to the most subtle problems of art, science, and religion." (Translation by C. M.)

[7] See Holland, et al. (1986, p. 10): "Problem solving methods are procedures for selecting an appropriate sequence of operators that will succeed in transforming the initial state into a goal state through a series of steps. Some methods are highly specialized for solving problems within a particular domain (for example, a procedure for solving quadratic equations), whereas others are generalists that can be applied across a broad range of problem domains."

[8] Albert (1978, p. 23) speaks of the "Kontextabhängigkeit des Problemlösungsverhaltens."

ter 2, we will argue that the foremost problem of every individual is to increase his or her own utility. This is also to be understood as the general motivational assumption. In Chapter 3, we will discuss the problem of perception, interpretation, and learning of the individual. In Chapter 4, the issue of choice will be analyzed and the dichotomy choice versus rule-following will be shown to be false.

2

The Motivational Aspect

The Striving for Utility Increase

2.1. PSYCHOLOGICAL APPROACH TO MOTIVATION

Motivation is one of the main domains of modern dynamic psychology. The main problem with motivation is that it is an abstract concept and is not directly visible. To explain behavioral changes that are observable we must, according to dynamic psychology, make inferences about the underlying psychological variables that influence these changes. These inferences about an individual's intentions, goals, needs, and purposes are formalized in the concept of motivation.

There are various theories on motivation, ranging from instinct theory to drive theory and sexual motivation. From the great spectrum of theories that account for motivation we will discuss paradigmatically only one: the humanistic theory of growth motivation of Abraham Maslow (1970) because of its wide acceptance among psychologists. He contrasted deficiency motivation, in which individuals seek to restore physical or psychological equilibrium, to growth motivation, in which individuals seek mainly to realize their fullest potential. Maslow constructed a needs hierarchy that consists of the different types of human needs as well as their order of importance. In a bottom-to-top hierarchy Maslow differentiates between biological needs (i.e., for water, oxygen, etc.), safety needs (i.e., for comfort, security, etc.), attachment needs (i.e., to belong, to love, to be loved), esteem needs (i.e., for confidence, respect of others, etc.), cognitive needs (i.e., for knowledge, understanding, etc.), esthetic needs (i.e., for order and beauty), self-actualization needs (i.e., to fulfill one's potential and to have meaningful goals) and transcendence needs (i.e. spiritual needs for cosmic identification). At each level the need is inborn, and an individual moves from the bottom to the higher levels of the needs hierarchy only when the lower needs have been satisfied.

From our perspective, there are two arguments against this motivational hierarchy. The first one concerns the empirical content of Maslow's theory: It presupposes a rather optimistic view of human nature. Humans strive, according to Maslow, not for their utility as they themselves perceive it, but rather for a predetermined course that aims at their self-actualization and transcendence. Irrespective of the empirical question of whether this view of humans is valid or not, there is a second argument of a pragmatic nature: For the purpose of social theory, Maslow's theory explains too much. Since we are concerned here with how individuals behave and interact with their social environment, we need a view of humans that is abstract enough to allow for generalizations in social reality. Maslow's theory is thus not operational enough to be adopted by social and economic sciences.

The same is true for a variety of other motivation theories that dominate the field, such as the theory of cognitive dissonance[1] arousal theory[2] and the achievement theories.[3] For our purpose, that is, the exploration of individual behavior within its social setting, accounts of motivation must remain very limited. As we shall see later, human behavior is influenced by culture and institutions, and in this sense, human actions are often dominated by external rather than internal factors. Therefore, it is futile to give a detailed account of motivational forces per se without taking into consideration the cultural and social environment of the individual.[4] Hence, for our purpose, a general motivation that is empirical and operational enough to be employed in social theory will suffice. We therefore adopt the following hypothesis: Every individual strives for an increase in his own utility.[5]

[1] See, e.g., Festinger, (1957), who developed his theory of cognitive dissonance based on ideas of his teacher, Kurt Lewin, (1936). An attempt to formalize the theory and put it in a utility-maximization form has been made by Akerlof and Dickens (1982).
[2] Murray (1938) was the first to postulate a need to achieve. McClelland et al. (1976) developed a method for measuring the strength of the need for achievement. Röpke (1977), based on the theories of McClelland (1961) on the motivation of the entrepreneurs, tried to incorporate the achievement motive in his general theory of innovation (see especially pp. 136–173).
[3] Arousal theory is mainly associated with the so-called Yerkes–Dodson law, which contends that performance of difficult tasks decreases as arousal increases, while performance of easy tasks increases as arousal increases (Yerkes and Dodson, 1908). See Kaufman (1999).
[4] For a discussion on the cultural consequences of markets and other economic institutions on preferences, see Bowles (1998).
[5] The Scottish moral philosophers of the eighteenth century postulated a general behavioral disposition in human nature according to which people generally aspire to better their condition. Ferguson sketched this universal tendency in his classical

2.2. GENERAL MOTIVATION AND INDIVIDUAL BEHAVIOR

The explanation of individual behavior requires, first, a motivational hypothesis and, second, a cognitive hypothesis. The cognitive hypothesis is dealt with in Chapter 3. This chapter gives a more detailed account of our statement on motivation and examines how it fits into our problem-solving framework.

The motivational system is perhaps one of the least understood aspects of human existence. Although psychology has made progress in researching human motives, the exact mechanism by which a certain action is initiated and a certain choice is made is still unknown. The only relatively safe conclusion that one can reach is that the motivational system possesses a certain preeminence in regard to individual action and choice. Our faculties of reasoning and imagination are mainly in the service of what our motivational system considers important. We act and behave as directed by our motivational system, presumably inherited from our animal ancestors.

As Selten (1990, p. 653) puts it: "The power of imagination and reasoning is a later addition to our biological heritage. Probably the human brain evolved as an instrument to create substitute experiences by imagination and reasoning to be processed by the motivational system in a similar fashion as real experiences. This means that rationality is in the service of a rather unsophisticated higher authority." In other words, Hume's ideas are still with us, and reason is the slave of the passions. In view of our ignorance regarding how our motivational system functions,

---

formulation (1767/1966, p. 6): "He [man] is in some measure the artificer of his own frame, as well as his fortune, and is destined, from the first age of his being, to invent and contrive. He applies the same talents to a variety of purposes, and acts nearly the same part in very different scenes. He would be always improving on his subject, and he carries this intention where-ever he moves, through the streets of the populous city, or the wilds of the forest."

Smith stated (1776/1976, p. 362f.): "But the principle which prompts to save, is the desire of bettering our condition, a desire which though generally calm and dispassionate, comes with us from the womb, and never leaves us till we go into the grave. In the whole interval which separates those two moments, there is scarce perhaps a single instant in which any man is so perfectly and completely satisfied with his situation, as to be without any wish of alteration or improvement of any kind."

This postulated tendency of aspiring to better one's condition is compatible with the dynamic aspect of the attainment of happiness. It is part of human nature always to seek to improve one's position and never to be satisfied with one's achievements. What is important is the fact that the Scottish moral philosophers interpreted the striving for happiness as a dynamic process and explicitly used this assumption of human behavior to explain social phenomena in a positive way.

the hypothesis of individuals striving to increase their own utility seems to be reasonable. This hypothesis, which is consistent with utility theory, can easily be incorporated into the problem-solving framework: Utility is the ultimate problem of humans. All their efforts are concentrated in the attainment of utility, that is, in the solution of this prime problem. Different people have different problems according to their genetical equipment, their cultural background, and their individual history; however, they all share a common problem, which is also their most important one: how to increase their utility.

The thesis that the attainment of utility is the ultimate problem of the individual does not, however, define exactly what the concrete content of this utility for every individual is. Every person considers and pursues utility in a different way. The observable diversity of lifestyles and behavioral patterns suffices to prove that all individuals attain a contented life in their own personal manner.

But does this mean that, apart from the common very general motivational characteristic of striving for utility, all deeds, choices, and behaviors differ among individuals? Is it really true that, except for the objective aspect of general motivation, all these other characteristics of individual behavior are radically subjective? And if this is so, where does all this diversity come from? Is man really the initiator of his own life, untouched by the influence of other men?

Humans are massively influenced by culture. This mechanism involves mainly learning cultural rules (see Chapter 5). But, although individual behavior is largely a product of culture and thus in a way is homogeneous, it is still the individual who determines his own life. The individuality of man is reflected in the personal way he makes choices, acts, and behaves. In terms of our framework, this individuality is interpreted as the way in which man perceives the future and the current state of his environment as problems. In other words, the uniqueness of every human being is manifested in the way he imposes self-created problems upon himself.[6] The inimitable originality of every person is hence to interpret particular states of the world as a problem and then to try to solve it in his own way.[7]

---

[6] Frankfurt puts the issue in another way, but he means, we think, the same thing when he identifies a "person" as a creature that can have second-order desires. See Frankfurt (1971, p. 7): "Besides wanting and choosing and being moved to do this or that, men may also want to have (or not to have) certain desires and motives."

[7] In the different setting, on the theory of knowledge, Polanyi addresses the issue of how a researcher can see a "problem" as such. See Polanyi (1966/1983, p. 21): "It is a common place that all research must start from a problem. Reasearch can be successful only if the problem is good; it can be original only if the problem is original. But

As humans create their own social environment by interacting with others, they also create their own lives and their own future. But this creation does not need to be consistent with any external standards. The problem of assessing the consistency of one's choices and life plan by using standards of rationality is not relevant for our purposes. As we shall see in Section 4.3 of Chapter 4, rationality of action is a different kind of problem; it is one of a mainly normative character. Thus, the issue of whether humans bring their preferences into a consistent order, that is, whether there is a well-defined structure or hierarchy of problems, is also not interesting from an external point of view such as that of rational-choice theory. It is rather the factual issue that is important, the empirical case that people often fail to face and solve their problems according to their importance. Although they acknowledge first that problem A is more important than problem B; second, that the solution of problem A will increase their utility more than the solution of problem B; and, third, that the solution of B will prohibit the solution of A, they nevertheless devote their energy to the solution of B. This is the classical problem of the "weakness of the will" which has concerned moral philosophers for centuries. Elster (1979/1984) discusses the problem in his classical treatise in the form of the allegory of Ullysses and the Sirens.[8] He shows that people,

how can one see a problem, any problem, let alone a good and original problem? For to see a problem is to see something that is hidden. It is to have an intimation of the coherence of hitherto not comprehended particulars. . . . To see a problem that will lead to a great discovery is not just to see something hidden, but to see something of which the rest of humanity cannot have even an inkling."

The German anthropologist Arnold Gehlen formulated the issue splendidly in his classical treatise *Der Mensch* (Gehlen, 1962, p. 32): "Man is the acting being. He can not be defined more precisely than this, i.e. man is then, in and of himself, a purpose (*Aufgabe*). One could also say that man is that being which takes up a position. The act of his taking up a position is what we call action and to the extent that man is himself a purpose (*Aufgabe*), he can be said to take on a purpose (*Aufgabe*) himself and 'make something of himself.' This is not a luxury which could also be omitted, but the 'state of being without completion' belongs rather to man's physical requirements, to his very nature. . . . To the degree that man, based on his own, can also miss those life-sustaining tasks, he is also an endangered being, one who is bound to live with a constitutional chance of failing prey to some fatal misfortune. Finally, man is a *planning being (vorsehend)* . He is a Prometheus dependent upon that which is distant or remote, upon that which is not of the present in time and space. In contradistinction to animals, man lives for the future and not in the present." (Translation by C. M.)

Further discussion of the definition of individuality is not relevant for this study. It is only important that – for our purposes – this individuality is defined as the human interpretation of a problem as such. On this, see, e.g., Williams (1973).

8 See the passage from the Odyssey of Homer (Book XII, lines 39–54, trans. Richard Lattimore: "You will come first of all to the Sirens, who are enchanters of all mankind

both in their individual and in their collective behavior, are conscious of their weaknesses and try to overcome them by means of precommitment. In decision terms, precommitment involves a certain decision at time t_1 that secures that one will make another decision at time t_2.[9] This whole issue of binding oneself involves fairly complicated problems that need not concern us here. For our current purpose, it suffices to remember that individuals often do not resolve their problems in a structured way. They sometimes make choices that are inconsistent, but they are conscious of this inconsistency and they then try to overcome it.

To summarize, we have tried to show in this chapter that the motivational issue is perhaps the most difficult one to understand. Since our ignorance of the motivational system of humans is great, and since for purposes of social and economic analysis we need an operational assumption, we have adopted the hypothesis that the ultimate motivation of man is to increase his own utility. This hypothesis is equally supported by the history of ideas and by modern psychology, although psychologists offer more detailed theories on motivation than are needed for social and economic analysis. Increasing one's own utility can be easily incorporated into the problem-solving framework if it is considered as the ultimate problem of man. It is important that the individuality and uniqueness of humans is stressed: Man is, albeit massively influenced by culture, the creator of his own life. Sometimes he is inconsistent when structuring his problems, but he also possesses the means to overcome this inconsistency.

and whoever comes their way; and that man who unsuspecting approaches them, and listens to the Sirens singing, has no prospect of coming home and delighting his wife and little children as they stand about him in greating, but the Sirens by the melody of their singing enchant him. They sit in their meadow, but the beach before it is piled with boneheaps of men now rotted away, and the skins shrivel upon them. You must drive straight on past, but melt down sweet wax of honey and with it stop your companions' ears, so none can listen; the rest, that is, but if you yourself are wanting to hear them, then have them tie you hand and foot on the fast ship, standing upright against the mast with the ropes' ends lashed around it, so that you can have joy in hearing the song of the Sirens; but if you supplicate your men and implore them to set you free, then they must tie you fast with even more lashings."

[9] Elster (1979/1984, pp. 37–47) enumerates five requirements of a complete definition of precommitment: (a) To bind oneself is to carry out a certain decision at time t_1 in order to increase the probability that one will carry out another decision at time t_2. (b) If the act at the earlier time has the effect of inducing a change in the set of options that will be available at the later time, then this does not count as binding oneself if the new feasible set includes the old one. (c) The effect of carrying out the decision at t_1 must be to set up some causal process in the external world. (d) The resistance against carrying out the decision at t_1 must be smaller than the resistance that would have opposed the carrying out of the decision at t_2 had the decision at t_1 not intervened. (e) The act of binding oneself must be an act of commission, not of omission.

3

The Cognitive Aspect

The Theory of Learning

3.1 THE EVOLUTIONARY PERSPECTIVE

The first condition necessary for an adequate explanation of individual behavior is an account of motivation that was given in the preceding chapter. The second necessary hypothesis refers to the cognitive content of the individual brain. Traditionally, philosophers have devoted much ingenuity to understanding how people perceive, but it was the Lorenz (1941) interpretation of the a priori categories of Kant that caused a radical change in epistemology and laid the foundation stone of evolutionary epistemology. For Lorenz, our a priori categories are nothing more than a natural vessel that has been formed, like our organs, in the process of biological evolution, and these categories have remained with us because they secure our existence and our adaptation to the environment.[1] The main contention of Lorenz was, hence, that human categories of thought have not existed a priori, but phylogenetically a posteriori and they are to be viewed as successful, species-specific information systems.[2] The hypothesis of Lorenz is thus that a distinction between phylogenetic and ontogenetic learning potential must be drawn. Phylogenetic learning is

---

[1] See Lorenz (1941, p. 102) where he says that Kant's a priori categories are "thoroughly natural and, like every other organ, phylogenetically evolved vessels for the reception and retroactive processing of those law-governed effects of the 'an sich Seiendes,' which we must face, if it is our desire to remain alive." (Translation by C. M.)

[2] (Ibid., p. 96). See also Campbell (1974/1987, p. 79), who interprets the Kantian categories of perception in the same evolutionary way: "Though we reject Kant's claims of a necessary a priori validity for the categories, we can in evolutionary perspective see the categories as highly edited, much tested presumptions, 'validated' only as scientific truth is validated, synthetic a posteriori from the point of view of species-history, synthetic and in several ways a priori (but not in terms of necessary validity) from the point of view of an individual organism."

species specific, and sets the framework of possibilities within which every member of the species can acquire his learning history, that is, ontogenetic knowledge.

Lorenz's distinction between phylogenetic and ontogenetic knowledge was much more than another interpretation of Kant's a priori categories. It signaled a new era in the theory of knowledge: the era of evolutionary epistemology. Under this general heading, a number of theories are summarized that originate in different domains: biology, philosophy, ethology, and so on. The main argument of evolutionary epistemology is that the process of knowledge growth is Darwinian. In Campbell's classical essay (1974/1987), the evolutionary perspective on human knowledge processes is carefully constructed.

Campbell's thesis is that a blind-variation-and-selective-retention process is the fundamental mechanism for every increase in knowledge. He finds this thesis substantiated at every observed level of knowledge retention, varying from the nonmnemonic problem solving of unicellular organisms to the activities of scientists. In this blind-variation-and-selective-retention process there are three essentials (Campbell, 1974/1987, p. 56): (a) a mechanism for introducing variation, (b) consistent selection processes, and (c) a mechanism for preserving and/or propagating the selected variations. "The many processes which shortcut a more full blind-variation-and-selective-retention process are in themselves inductive achievements, containing wisdom about the environment achieved originally by blind variation and selective retention" (ibid., p. 56).

Even the simply-structured organisms such as the unicellular organisms are endowed with hypothetical knowledge, although they have no memory. For example, they are able to stop their random movements, which is a case of blind variation of locomotor action, when a nourishing setting is found (ibid., p. 58). But apart from direct search processes, vicarious search processes also function according to the same principle of the blind-variation-and-selective-retention model. Campbell gives the example of a blind man's cane. "The less expensive cane movements substitute for blind trials and wasted movements by the whole body, removing costly search from the full locomotor effort, making that seem smooth, purposeful, insightful" (ibid., p. 60). Biologically higher organisms also learn by the same process: after the creation of a blind variation, organisms apply their hypotheses to their environment, and according to which selective criteria prevail in this environment, a selection process of the best-adapted hypotheses takes place.

Campbell thus composes a global biological theory of the evolution of knowledge that operates on all levels of nature, that is is valid for all organisms. His "Nested Hierarchy of Selective-Retention Processes" gives an account of how knowledge is created (by blind variation), and how it is selected and retained. The evolutionary epistemology is thus, in general, the discipline that interprets the findings of the different sciences such as biology, psychology, and linguistics through the glasses of the theory of evolution.[3] Evolutionary epistemologists argue that the same process is at work with regard to the growth of knowledge at every level; this is the process of variation and selection.

Popper described the issue in his classical formulation that from the amoeba to Einstein, the growth of knowledge is the same (Popper, 1972/1992, p. 261). He stressed the importance of the environment in selecting perception organs in the case of animal evolution and theories in the case of human evolution.[4] Instead of speculating along traditional philosophical lines on whether reason or senses are the primary spring of our knowledge, Popper emphasized the importance of the emergence of mind in an evolutionary process that is avowedly the source of our knowledge.[5] The cognitive apparatus of humans is the result of a process of natural selection in which the human brain has been selected because of its capacity to solve successively the problems of the environment.

Given the evolutionary epistemology of the caliber of Lorenz, Campbell, Popper, and the newest contributions, it is important for us to keep in mind that the human brain has evolved in a long evolutionary process of variation and selection and thus is "designed" to solve the specific problems of its environment. The way in which the brain functions is thus the main constraint to all of our learning efforts as human beings. Of course,

[3] Apart from the classical treatises of Konrad Lorenz, one of the fathers of evolutionary epistemology (such as Lorenz 1943, 1959, 1965, 1973), see also Riedl and Wuketits (1987), Wuketits (1984), Radnitzky and Bartley (1987), Irrgang (1993), and the standard work in the German-speaking world, Vollmer (1975/1994). Popper's works, especially of his late period, also belong to this tradition, although Popper himself rejects the label "evolutionary epistemology" for his own approach. This quite strange remark is found in Popper (1987, p. 32). On the convergence of the ideas of Lorenz and Popper, see Popper and Lorenz (1988, pp. 11–43).

[4] See Popper (1972/1992, p. 238): "*Animal evolution* proceeds largely, though not exclusively, by the modification of organs (or behaviour) or the emergence of new organs (or behaviour). *Human evolution* proceeds largely, by developing new organs outside our bodies or persons: 'exosomatically', as biologists call it, or 'extrapersonally.' These new organs are tools, or weapons, or machines, or houses."

[5] Popper regards the emergence of the human mind as the third great event in the recent evolution of the universe, after the emergence of consciousness and previously that of life. See Popper (1956/1982, p. 122): "A third great miracle is the emergence of the human brain, and of the human mind and of human reason."

we cannot be assured that the present genetically predetermined structure of the brain will not evolve in the future. Obviously, this will be the case. But for our present purpose of examining how human beings learn and behave in their social and cultural environment, it is unimportant to examine further how our genetic equipment will affect our way of thinking and acting in the remote future. All of these issues are irrelevant for an account of social interaction and social evolution. Thus, it suffices to stress that *Homo sapiens sapiens* has possessed the same genetic characteristics for the last 30,000 years. (On these grounds the insights of sociobiology are irrelevant, since human intelligence is so dominating that no considerable selective pressure from the natural environment can affect the genetic structure of human beings. At least not in the near future.[6])

Regarding its origin, the knowledge of every individual consists of three parts: (a) genetic knowledge, (b) cultural knowledge, and (c) atomistic knowledge.[7] Genetic knowledge is incorporated into our sense organs (i.e., dispositions are built into the sense organs that are helpful in distinguishing certain typical situations),[8] cultural knowledge is transmitted

---

6 For a critical discussion of sociobiology, see Koslowski (1984/1989). See also Witt (1987a, ch. III, 3), where he states on p. 110: "At first, one must bear in mind that in the sociobiological model prolonged behavioral adaptations only ensue from genetic means. Genotypically fixed modes of behavior underlie such adaptations through the reproduction of manifest variability through mutation and genetic drift. If behavioral variations appear as well and the pressure of selection is sufficiently great, then these new adaptations can be disseminated after some generations throughout the population through the higher reproduction rates of its carriers. Such a mechanism of behavioral adaptation is equivalent to a trial-and-error method that generates new purposeless variations. Measured in human categories, an extremely long period of time is required to discover improvements, to successfully enforce them, and finally to achieve an optimal level of adaptation. For this reason alone, an unlimited transference of sociobiological argumentation to the realm of observable human adaptation must be ruled out. Large portions of the latter are taking place in the modern industrial society in a particularly dramatic fashion within a single generation, far too quickly, one might add, in order that it be founded upon a genetic basis." (Translation by C. M.). See also Hayek (1979/1982, pp. 153–5).

7 I use the curious word "atomistic" for lack of a better term to designate the part of the knowledge of the individual that has been attained during his life and is not shared with other individuals of the same culture or society.

8 See Popper (1972/1992, p. 71f.): "Because all our dispositions are in some sense adjustments to invariant or slowly changing environmental conditions, they can be described as *theory-impregnated,* assuming a sufficiently wide sense of the term 'theory.' What I have in mind is that there is no observation which is not related to a set of typical situations – regularities – between which it tries to find a decision. And I think we can assert even more: *there is no sense organ in which anticipatory theories are not genetically incorporated.* The eye of a cat reacts in distinct way to a number of typical situations for which there are mechanisms prepared and built into its struc-

through culture to the members of a cultural community, and atomistic knowledge is obtained by the individual through his "history" and is not shared with the rest of the members of the culture or society. About the categories of cultural and atomistic knowledge we will have to say more in later chapters. But the issue of genetic knowledge must be dealt with here. We have two lessons to bear in mind. The first lesson, that of evolutionary epistemology, is that the brain is the product of a long evolutionary process during which our cognitive apparatus has adapted to its environment. The brain can thus solve problems inherent in the environment in which it exists and is forced to survive. The brain is, hence, constructed so as to solve *adaptive problems*. We have thus learned from evolutionary epistemology and biology that the brain consists of behavioral programs and that, in contrast to computers, the brain is not programmed but is rather self-programmed. The fundamental genetic self-program is coded in the DNA tape (Popper, 1978/1987, p. 151). With Mayr (1976, p. 23), then, one can distinguish between closed and open behavioral programs. A closed behavioral program is characteristic of animals and prescribes their behavior in great detail. An open behavioral program is the differentia specifica of humans; it does not determine all steps of behavior but leaves open certain alternatives, that is, *the possibility of choice*. (This very possibility of choice is the creative element in human behavior, which we will discuss later in more detail.)

Following the same line of argument, the discipline of evolutionary psychology offers a new view of the architecture of the human brain (Cosmides and Tooby, 1992). By focusing on the simple fact – borrowed by evolutionary biology – that form follows function, the hypothesis is made that "the properties of an evolved mechanism reflect the structure of the task it evolved to solve" (Cosmides and Tooby, 1994, p. 328). Thus, the second lesson that we have to learn is from evolutionary psychology and is a delicate one. It consists of the new hypothesis put forward that the human mind is not similar to a general-purpose computer, as is traditionally assumed in psychology. The mind is, on the contrary, to be understood as a kind of multimind consisting of many computational devices that are specialized to solve specific problems. "Because biological evolution is a slow process, and the modern world has emerged within an

ture: these correspond to the biologically most important situations between which it has to distinguish. Thus the disposition to distinguish between these situations is built into the sense organ, and with it the *theory that these, and only these, are the relevant situations for whose distinction the eye is to be used.*"

evolutionary eye-blink, these devices are inherited from the past and remain functionally specialized to solve the particular distribution of problems that were characteristic of humans' hunter-gatherer past, rather than those of the modern world" (ibid., p. 329). Human reasoning is functional rather than logical (Ortman and Gigerenzer, 1997, p. 707), and therefore the social context matters when individuals solve problems.

The mind as a system of specialized problem solvers is apparently an optimistic point of view. Cosmides and Tooby speak of "reasoning instincts," that is, quasi-automatic circuits that can solve specific problems without any conscious effort and that are applied without any awareness of their underlying logic. The obvious conclusion they then draw is that, in terms of rationality, the human mind is not worse than rational (because of processing constraints, e.g., boundedly rational) but rather better than rational.

The dichotomy between perfectly rational and boundedly rational as well as all the connected definitions of irrational, nonrational, and so on, do not need to concern us here. We shall discuss the issue in Section 4.3. From evolutionary psychology we should keep in mind that the brain consists of more than one problem-solving device: It is a network of problem-solving circuits employed to solve specific problems. The mind is not a one-dimensional but rather a multidimensional problem solver. But how is this problem-solving process to be analyzed in more exact terms?

Popper's simplified scheme can give a first tentative account of the process. This can be described as followed:

$$P_1 \rightarrow TS \rightarrow EE \rightarrow PP_2$$

Starting from some problem P_1 we proceed to a tentative theory, a tentative solution TS. This theory is, in the case of human problem solving, a product of our faculty of imagination (Popper, 1972/1992, p. 148) and is always conjectural in character; therefore, it is always submitted to a critical and experimental discussion in the case of scientific conjectures or in any other case to an error-elimination process taking place in the human brain (we will specify this later as a competition of rules employed by the human mind when exploring its environment and solving its problems). This error-elimination process is formalized as EE in the preceding scheme. New problems P_2 then arise from our own creative activity; they are the result of the new situation that has arisen from the conjectured solution and the error-elimination process (Popper, 1972/1992, p. 243).[9] And the cycle of problem solving starts anew. In the meantime, the individual has learned the solution to a specific problem, has thus enriched his behavioral repertoire, and may in the next cycle, when the same kind of problem reappears, solve it with the aid of the already learned tentative solution.

Popper developed this problem-solving mechanism in order to account not only for human learning but also for the learning of all organisms in the setting of an evolutionary epistemology. The intuitive power of this simple schema is great, so that we can employ it as a first approximation to our issue, that is, of the learning behavior of individuals. Based on the results of evolutionary epistemology and evolutionary psychology regarding the cognitive architecture of the mind, we can now give a more detailed account of exactly how this learning takes place. The first issue of genetic knowledge can thus be closed with the general statement that *in this period of evolution all humans learn in the same way based on common genetic equipment.* Hence, our brain sets the limits of our learning capability that is common to all humans. Our next step is to give an account of how this learning potential is developed, that is, of the mechanism of learning.

3.2. THE THEORY OF LEARNING

In giving an account of the learning mechanism, we shall follow the recent empirical research on human knowledge of the cognitive sciences (e.g. Gardner, 1985; Thagard, 1996; Wilson and Kehl, 1999). We shall base our account mainly on the pioneering book of Holland, Holyoak, Nisbett, and Thagard (1986), which presents a very interesting synthesis of cognitive theories and is closely related to our problem-solving framework. The primary interest of Holland et al. is to study induction in a pragmatic context, that is, in relation to the problem-solving activity of the individual organism. To avoid possible misunderstanding, by *induction* they do not mean the usual logical procedure of the generalization of single events leading to general laws. They define the study of induction, in contrast to the procedure discussed in logic, as "the study of how knowledge is modified through its use" (p. 5). Hence, induction is the

---

[9] As Popper formulates it (1972/1992, p. 119): "and these new problems are not in general intentionally created by us, they emerge autonomously from the field of new relationships which we cannot help bringing into existence with every action, however little we intend to do so."

name of the dynamic process of learning.[10] The theory of learning that we are going to adopt consists of the following eleven theses:

1. *The Pragmatic Aspect.* Humans perceive and learn only in regard to a problem situation. We do not perceive reality in any direct way, as traditionally described by the philosophical subject-object relation, with "object" signifying the external world as a whole. Instead, we form internal representations of reality in the form of "problem space" (Newell and Simon, 1972, p. 59). In other words, humans perceive and learn pragmatically.[11] This pragmatic aspect is very broad though. Scientists, for example, try to solve theoretical problems, which, of course differ from the problems confronting persons who act. But even in science there is no pure contemplation, but always contemplation in relation to a problem. Although the action of a scientist consists mainly of thinking (and experimenting), that is, his problem is of a theoretical nature, it is always thinking of something that takes place. Thinking itself is thus also a goal-directed activity.[12]

---

10 It is, perhaps, unfortunate to handle the cognitive aspects of learning under such a title, since induction is intuitively associated with the philosophical debate. Since the time of Hume, and more recently of Popper, we know the logical invalidity of generalizing from the particular to the general. And any trained philosopher of science is bound to react allergically to any defense of the logical process of induction. It is therefore important to stress that the purpose of Holland et al. is not to deliver any new support to the obsolete logical "induction," but rather to *give a psychological account of empirical processes of inference and learning*. To avoid any confusion when discussing the theory of learning of cognitive psychology we shall thus try to avoid, as far as possible, the use of the term induction.

11 Tamborini (1997), who suggests the adoption of a similar theory of human knowledge for economics under the name "constructivism," also holds that the "representation of the cognitive subject as an intentional system" (p. 55) should be the starting point of the analysis.

12 This is one of the rare points on which Popper and Kuhn agree, perhaps because the empirical evidence is convincing on this issue. See, e.g., Kuhn (1962, p. 122): "[T]hose examples typify the overwhelming majority of research. In each of them the scientist, by virtue of an accepted paradigm, knew what a datum was, what instruments might be used to retrieve it, and what concepts were relevant to its interpretation. Given a paradigm, interpretation of data is central to the entreprise that explores it."

Although the starting point of Popper is different, his famous *Transzendenz der Darstellung* in the *Logik der Forschung* (1934/1971) leads to the conclusion of the theory-impregnated experience. (See also Popper, 1972/1992, pp. 341–61, as well as his first work, *Die beiden Grundprobleme der Erkenntnistheorie* (1979, p. 45), and his comments on the Immanenzphilosophie of Slick.)

2. *Rules as Elementary Units of Knowledge.* The most basic epistemic building block is a condition-action rule, which is of the form "IF such-and-such, THEN so-and-so" (Holland et al., 1986, p. 14). The mind can be conceptualized as a rule-based system that can be described, according to Holland et al. (p. 15), "in terms of a cycle with three steps: (1) matching facts against rules to determine which rules have their conditions satisfied; (2) selecting a subset (not necessarily a proper subset) of the matched rules to be executed, or 'fired'; and (3) living the selected rules to take the specified actions." As examples of an "IF-THEN" rule, one can give the imperatives, "IF you want to loose weight, THEN you have to reduce the quantity of the food you eat" or "IF it is raining and you do not want to get wet, THEN use an umbrella." These rules are, of course, very general. Our mind consists of rules that vary from very limited statements to very general imperatives.

These rules are not to be understood as categorical imperatives, though. Rather, they are suggestions that propose the classification of environmental messages or internal information of the organism in a certain way. They specify that if certain conditions hold, then certain changes in the environment will take place (Holland et al., 1986, p. 15). This purely *suggestive character of rules* implies that at any given moment, many rules can compete in offering a suggestion of classification, action, and so on; there is thus a *parallelism* of rules, that is, more than one rule can describe the situation of the agent's environment. Each rule hence predicts what will happen under certain circumstances, and the important characteristic here is that our mind avails itself of many rules that may make predictions simultaneously. The fact that a parallelism of rules can exist means that different rules can either be bound together in order to form a suggestion or they can compete with each other to form different suggestions. There are, in other words, two elemantary relationships that can prevail between these elementary units of knowledge called rules: rules clustering or rules competition.

3. *The Mind as a System of Classification.* Hayek, in his neglected work *The Sensory Order* (1952), presented a view of the mind as a relational order based on the nervous system, as an *instrument of classification*. The mind is conceived as an active interpreter and at the same time as a classifier of physical events. It is not necessary for our purposes to discuss the neurophysiological process of classification that takes place when the nerve fibers are stimulated by external events. *It is only important to view*

the mind as a classification authority operating in order to solve the problems of the organism.[13]

The classification of events and their interpretation in the light of a current problem of the organism takes place according to classifier rules. Hence, the rules of the general type IF . . . THEN that we have described have an essential classificatory function. Every cognitive act can thus be conceived as a rule-based classification in relation to the current problem. The main characteristic of the human mind is then its infinite potential to create new rules, that is, to group together events in classes. (Knowledge representation in the form of mental models, which we will discuss later, can also be conceived intuitively as the creation of classes of events. Hence, the picture of the mind as a classification system is suggested as a first general approximation to how our mind works, before we proceed to a more detailed analysis.)

4. *Clusters of Rules.* "Rules that often are activated together in the system's attempt to model its environment will eventually become associated" (Holland et al., 1986, p. 17). A set of interrelated rules employed together by our brain forms a cluster of rules. *Many elementary perceptual rules together form a cluster of rules which is called a category.* Natural categories, for example, as are known from philosophy (Quine, 1969), which emerge from everyday experience (e.g., dog, sea) are a set of rules that provide expectations concerning the perceived object. For example, when I identify an object with four legs moving before me, some rules are activated, for example, "IF the object has four legs, THEN it is an animal" and "IF the object is moving, THEN it is an animal." The two rules combined give a more secure prediction about what the moving object before me is, as opposed to the employment of every single rule separately. Therefore, the synthetic rule composed of the two single rules is then "IF the object has four legs and is moving, THEN it is an animal." This new rule, although more certain than any single one, does not offer a definite conclusion about whether the object is an animal. Although this expectation is prima facie justified, the object could still be a small child crawling before me. In other words the following rule also exists: "IF the object has four legs and is moving, THEN it is a crawling child." Therefore, the elementary cluster of two rules does not form a category yet.

[13] In artificial intelligence, the simulation of the mind as a classifier system is a common enterprise (see, e.g., Holland, 1986); obviously, these classifier systems, like all computer simulations of the mind, suffer by not accounting satisfactorily for creativity. In Section 4.2, we shall discuss how creativity can be best handled in our context.

More characteristics of the object must be available in order for it to be classified as an animal. If, for example, I hear the moving object barking, I can add to the rule cluster the following rule: "IF the object is barking, THEN it is an animal." The new rule cluster, "IF the object has four legs, is moving, and is barking, THEN it is an animal" (which still possesses only a hypothetical character) is closer to the category formation "animal."

Many rules together thus form categories that are higher-order knowledge structures. The categories are not definite classification schemes, but they always possess a hypothetical, expectational character. Obviously, rule clusters that consist of a large number of rules are better classifiers in the case of natural objects than rule clusters that are poorly specified. The uncertain nature of the classificatory power of these rule clusters is best illustrated by the notion of a default hierarchy.

5. Default Hierarchies. "Rules and rule clusters can be organized into default hierarchies, that is, hierarchies ordered by default expectations based on subordinate/superordinate relations among concepts" (Holland et al., 1986, p. 18). Because rules and rule clusters can be more or less general, it is obvious that they form hierarchies consisting of different levels of generality. At the top of a hierarchy are the more general rules or rule clusters, and the degree of specificity is increased from the top to the bottom. Since at every level, though, the character of rules remains purely conjectural, the hierarchies are to be understood as default hierarchies, that is, prone-to-error-hierarchies. To give an example, knowing that an object lying on my desk is a book produces certain default expectations about it, such as that it is a philosophical treatise, a guidebook on Freiburg, and so on. These expectations can be put aside, though, by more specific information produced by evidence from a rule of a lower order. The book can then be identified as a dictionary. But even this expectation can also (following the default hierarchy) be put aside by even more specific information, such as that the dictionary is an English-German dictionary.

6. Mental Models. A number of rules and rule clusters organized together in the form of one or more default hierarchies give rise to a mental model. A mental model is a coherent but transitory set of rules that enables the organism to form predictions of the environment based on the available knowledge. It is very important to stress the *provisional, temporary* character of the mental models, since this is their essential difference from schemas and concepts. Although schemas, since their introduction in the 1930s by Bartlett (1932) and Piaget (1936), have also been used in a dynamic manner, so that they differ from rigid concepts, it is perhaps best to abandon the notion of schemas altogether and stress from the beginning the dynamic character of mental models as a basic knowledge structure (Johnson-Laird, 1989).[14]

Mental models are, thus, not ready-made recipes employed every time the individual faces a problem in his environment. *They are, moreover, flexible knowledge structures created anew every time from the ready-made material of rules.* They are to be understood as the final prediction or expectation that the organism makes about the environment before getting feedback from it.[15] Thus, according to whether the expectation formed is validated by the environmental feedback, the mental model can be revised, refined, or rejected altogether. The mental models thus secure the factual dynamism of the knowledge structures available to the organism, that is, they are compatible with the possibility that human beings can learn.

7. *Competition among Rules.* Up to now we have examined how rule clusters, default hierarchies, and mental models are shaped, and we have found that this happens according to the principles of complementation and "cooperation" between different rules. But the parallelism of rules, that is, the existence of numerous potential rules to guide thought and action, also implies the possibility of active competition among rules. Those rules whose conditions, that is, their IF-clauses, are satisfied by current messages compete to represent the current state of the environment and thus to guide thought and action (Holland et al., 1986, p. 22). In the example that we have been using, the two rules that can compete with each other are "IF the object has four legs and is moving, THEN it is an

14 We shall also not use the notion of the "script" as introduced by Schank and Abelson (1977). They define a script as a kind of schema that includes mainly social events and relationships, between them and the individual is involved in it as an actor or observer. Choi (1993, 1999) uses the term "paradigm" in the Kuhnian sense. But since the "mental model" as defined here is both more general and more flexible, we shall use this term.

15 "The most characteristic thing about mental life, over and beyond the fact that one apprehends the events of the world around one, is that one constantly goes beyond the information given." This citation of Jerome Bruner is taken from Nisbett and Ross (1980, p. 17). The authors comment on it as follows: "The perceiver, as Bruner (1957) recognized, is not simply a dutiful clerk who passively registers items of information. Rather, the perceiver is an active interpreter, one who resolves ambiguities, makes educated guesses about events that cannot be observed directly, and forms inferences about associations and causal relations" (ibid.).

animal" and "IF the object has four legs and is moving, THEN it is a crawling child." But if there is competition among numerous rules to guide thought and action, then there must be a selection criterion for which rule to employ. What is this selection criterion?

Holland et al., give four criteria that can be used to decide which rules will prevail in competition with others. "Thus, competition will favor those rules that (a) provide a description of the current situation (match), (b) have a history of past usefulness to the system (strength), (c) produce the greatest degree of completeness of description (specifity), and (d) have the greatest compatibility with other currently active information (support)" (Holland et al., 1986, p.49). It seems obvious that the issue of competition among rules and the selection of the "best" rules are interwoven with the issue of feedback from the environment.

8. Environmental Feedback and Dynamic Learning. The preceding theses, strictly speaking, constitute a theory of representation of the world rather than a theory of learning. *The learning mechanism functions, though, according to the same principle as the mechanism for representing the environment. Thus, there is a certain continuity in accounting for mental phenomena.* Learning takes place when the expectations of the organism are not successful in predicting or describing its environment and must thus be modified. The environmental input is hence the cause for the creation of new mental models that may provide a better guide for action in the environment. And since mental models are composed of rules, *learning is the complex mechanism of rule modification according to the feedback received from the environment.*

It is important to stress that the possibility of rule modification is crucial to the *dynamic character of the learning mechanism.* Learning is a dynamic process of trial and error.[16] Whenever an error takes place, the

---

[16] Popper's arguments run along these lines even if they are formulated in another way. The idea of rule parallelism and rule competition is to be found in his schema where the multiplicity of the tentative solutions is presented, i.e., the multiplicity of the trials. The final schema that he proposes is a refinement of that discussed in Section 3.2 and is the following (Popper 1972/1992, p. 243):

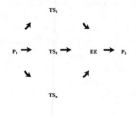

organism initiates a rule modification and forms a new expectation, a new trial, in order to solve the problem at hand. If the new trial proves successful and the problem is solved, then the learning process for this specific problem ceases. Before we turn our attention to what this rule modification is, we will discuss what happens when, after perhaps a number of unsuccessful trials, an acceptable solution to the problem is found.

9. *Storage of Problem Solutions and Unconsciousness.* When a solution to a specific problem of the organism is obtained, the rules that led to the solution will be strengthened. Success in finding a solution is translated as the success of the respective rules. Apportionment of credit to the different rules that helped the organism to solve its problem is bound to happen (Holland et al., 1986, p. 70). If the same rules often led to acceptable solutions in the past, then they will be repeatedly employed by the organism in the future.

A series of successful solutions to the same problem create what we call a *routine*. The essential characteristic of a routine is that it is employed to solve a problem without any prior reflection. In a way, the problem has ceased to be a genuine one in the eyes of the individual, since no intellectual effort and energy are required for its solution.[17]

Whenever an organism employs a problem solution from its behavioral repertoire without reflecting on it, we can say that this problem solution is used in an unconscious way. The activation of routines is thus a function of humans that does not require consciousness. Routines employed unconsciously are a kind of rule-following behavior, but the crucial fact is that since this behavior was followed often in the past, it has become standardized and thus does not need conscious effort to be revealed. In the words of Schrödinger (1958, p. 7): "The fact is only this, that new situations and new responses they prompt are kept in the light of consciousness; old and well practised ones are no longer so [kept]."

What is important for us to keep in mind is, hence, that once rules are employed successfully many times for the solution of a problem, they are successively strengthened and stored by the organism, and after a time

---

[17] Polanyi, in his discussion of the issue, refers to the case of animals (1958, p. 122): "If an animal who has solved a problem is placed once more in the original situation, it proceeds unhesitatingly to apply the solution which it had originally discovered at the cost of much effort and perhaps after many unsuccessful trials. This shows that by solving the problem the animal has acquired a new intellectual power, which prevents it from being ever again puzzled by the problem. Instead, it can now deal with the situation in a routine maner involving no heuristic tension and achieving no discovery. The problem has ceased to exist for it."

they take the form of unconscious routines. This allows the human brain to use its faculties in an "economical" way, that is, it only needs to be concerned with problems that are difficult to solve or ones that are new. Since this issue has also been discussed under the headings of "tacit knowledge," "knowing how" and "unarticulated knowledge," it seems reasonable to treat it here in some length before considering how new problems are solved by an organism.

10. "Knowing That" and "Knowing How". Up to now, we have stated that cognition and learning take place according to rules that possess the general IF . . . THEN structure. There are two categories of knowledge that can be described by this structure that we have not yet discussed. The categorical distinction is best illustrated by the terminology of Gilbert Ryle (1949) as "knowing that" and "knowing how," or, in other words, "theoretical knowledge" versus "practical knowledge." Although the rules perspective is the same for both parts of knowledge, the rules incorporating theoretical knowledge are different from the ones incorporating practical knowledge in the sense that the practical rules cannot be directly derived from the theoretical rules or vice versa.

The category of theoretical knowledge includes all the rules that generate knowledge that we express in ordinary language as "knowing that" something is such and such. Here belongs all our knowledge of singular objects and events, as well as our knowledge of causal relationships. All of our efforts to identify particular objects of our environment and classify them as "cats," "dogs," "professors," and so on are of this type of knowledge, that is, *that* such and such characteristics constitute the respective mental model of "cats," "dogs," "professors" and so on. And all of our efforts to impose causal structures on our environment and to explain that "IF such and such happens, THEN so and so will follow" belong to this broad category of theoretical knowledge. All scientific knowledge is of this type. All of this must seem familiar to everybody. Where doubts are bound to arise is obviously at the second proposed category of the type of "knowing how." Here all skills and rules of behavior are included. Swimming, cooking, and brushing one's teeth are some examples. Like Ryle, we contend that this family of knowledge is strictly different from any kind of theoretical knowledge, and that it is a common intellectualistic legend to believe that all of our acting is guided by some precedent thought operation. Theorists, who themselves are commonly involved in creating knowledge of the first type, that is, theoretical knowledge, do not seem to understand that there is also another type of knowledge, which is mostly used in everyday life.[18]

All the skills that a person possesses is of this other kind of knowledge. Riding a bicycle, for example, is an operation that can be successfully executed only where knowledge of a complex set of practical rules exists. Even if somebody reads a whole book describing accurately how to keep one's balance on a bicycle, this reading cannot replace the practical knowledge of the art.[19] Winning battles is another example. It is not the knowledge of the principles but their application that can lead to success. "A soldier does not become a shrewd general merely by endorsing the strategic principles of Clausewitz; he must also be competent to apply them. Knowing how to apply maxims cannot be reduced to, or derived from, the acceptance of those or any other maxims" (Ryle, 1949, p. 32).

The only unifying characteristic of the two categories of knowledge is that they are both rule guided. The cognitive mechanism at work is the same, and is decribed by our problem-solving framework and the employment of rules or rule clusters that solve the current problem of the organism. The distinction here is between "theoretical problems" and "practical problems." Both are solved in the same way, that is, by employing rules that if not sufficient to solve the problems, are then modified or generated anew (more on this in Section 3.4). Thus, we learn by the same principle of trial and error, to solve both our theoretical and our practical problems.

The differentia specifica of the two kinds of knowledge does not lie in the rule-guided way that we acquire our knowledge, but in the more specific level of the *communicability* of this knowledge. Theoretical knowledge can be communicated by means of language. Using a series of symbols, knowledge in the form of singular events or objects and knowledge concerning causal relationships can be transmitted from one person to other persons. It is only through language that we can communicate this sort of knowledge to others. With practical knowledge, transmission is not as easy as it is with theoretical knowledge. Skills and arts cannot be communicated by symbolic language (or languages). The most common way that "know-how" can be shared by other persons is learning by

---

[18] See Ryle (1949, p. 50): "Theorists have been so preoccupied with the task of investigating the nature, the source, and the credentials of the theories that we adopt that they have for the most part ignored the question what it is for someone to know how to perform tasks. In ordinary life, on the contrary, as well as in the special business of teaching, we are much more concerned with people's competences than with their cognitive repertoires, with the operations than with the truths that they learn."

[19] See Polanyi (1958, p. 50) and his detailed account of the difficulties of riding a bicycle.

example, that is, learning by imitation. Thus, the main characteristic of the rules of the art, or "practical rules," is "that we are usually not able to state explicitly (discursively) the manner of acting which is involved" (Hayek, 1967, p. 43).

This feature of rules incorporating know-how is of tremendous importance. It means that know-how consists of the capacity to act according to rules, which are overt enough to be discovered and followed *but which cannot always be stated in words* (Hayek, 1967, p. 44). Knowledge of how to perform certain tasks is thus not always expressible in linguistic terms and is therefore communicable mainly through imitation.[20] The process of learning how to perform certain tasks is unspecifiable in the sense that we cannot give a full account of what exactly is happening when we learn to swim, cook, play football, and so on. In the words of Polanyi (1958, p. 62): "The unspecifiability of the process by which we thus feel our way forward accounts for the possession by humanity of an immense mental domain, not only of theoretical knowledge but of manners, of laws and of many different acts which man knows how to use, comply with, enjoy or live by, without specifiably knowing their contents."

A possible objection can be raised against the assertion that all knowledge of "how" is unexpressible in words by pointing to, for example, all the cook books available in bookstores. Do they not contain recipes, that is, rules on how to prepare different types of food? Is that not sufficient to show that "knowing how" can be reduced to detailed accounts perfectly expressible in words and thus to knowledge "that"? And obviously this applies not only to cook books, but also to books on medical diagnosis, or books on economic policy or playing chess.

The answer to this objection runs as follows: However detailed an account of how a certain disease is to be diagnosed, the act of making a successful diagnosis is not guaranteed by the knowledge of this account alone. Knowing how has to do with the successful application of certain rules, and this requires skills that are not precisely communicable. What is contained in books on diagnosis or business policy are merely *ex post descriptions* of practices that have proved successful under certain circumstances, *but not explanations of how these practices can be acquired.* "We learn how by practice, schooled indeed by criticism and example, but often quite unaided by any lessons in the theory" (Ryle, 1949, p. 41).That "knowing how" is an altogether different category of knowledge from

---

[20] See Hayek (1967, p. 48): "Our capacity to imitate someone's gait, postures, or grimaces certainly does not depend on our capacity to describe these in words."

"knowing that" can also be proved in the following way. According to a familiar myth, each time before acting, we consider in which way we should perform our task. An intelligent action is, then, one in which the agent has been involved in thinking through what he is doing while undertaking the action and one in which contemplation of the appropriate actions has decisively promoted his success. In the unequaled formulation of Ryle (1949, p. 30): "To do something thinking what one is doing is, according to this legend, always to do two things; namely, to consider certain appropriate propositions, or prescriptions, and to put into practice what these propositions or prescriptions enjoin. *It is to do a bit of theory and then to do a bit of practice.*" But the consideration of the propositions themselves upon which the action is supposed to be based is itself an operation that can succeed only if this consideration has been more or less intelligent. But if any operation to be executed intelligently or successfully requires a prior theoretical operation, then we have a logical circle that nobody can evade (Ryle, 1949, p. 31). Obviously then, "knowing how" does not require any "knowledge that."[21]

11. Tacit Knowledge. The term *tacit knowledge* is used by many authors to designate all inarticulated knowledge.[22] Since confusion sometimes prevails about what exactly tacit knowledge is, and because of the inherent difficulty of comprehending such a delicate distinction, we want to make a few remarks on the subject. Tacit knowledge is not the knowledge of solutions to known problems stored by the organism and employed automatically or unconsciously anew when the same type of problem arises; thus, it is not what we have discussed in Thesis 9. Nor is tacit knowledge the practical knowledge of the know-how type – which we have extensively discussed in Thesis 10. We have seen that skills and practices, although not sufficiently expressible in language, can neverthe-

---

21 A good summary of the position on the two kinds of knowledge is given by Ryle (1949, p. 31): "Efficient practice procedes the theory of it; methodologies presuppose the application of the methods, of the critical investigation of which they are the products. It was because Aristotle found himself and others reasoning now intelligently and now stupidly and it was because Izaak Walton found himself and others angling sometimes effectively and sometimes ineffectively that both were able to give to their pupils the maxims and prescriptions of their arts. It is therefore possible for people intelligently to perform some sorts of operations when they are not yet able to consider any propositions enjoining how they should be performed. Some intelligent performances are not controlled by any interior acknowledgements of the principles applied in them."

22 On tacit knowledge, see part 1 of Polanyi (1966/1983) and part 2 of Polanyi (1958).

less be communicated by imitation. Therefore, practical knowledge is not tacit in the sense of not being transmittable.

Tacit knowledge, rather, is to be understood as the *process of acquiring* both theoretical and practical knowledge. It is the overall capacity to discover and use knowledge. It designates the potential ability to acquire all the intellectual powers that humans use in science and ordinary life. Tacit knowledge is the *dynamis* to acquire, produce, and use knowledge that is imperceptible to other persons, whether scientists or not. Accordingly, it is useful for us to retain the idea that the capacity to know is something like a miracle, inaccessible and imperceptible from any observer's perspective,[23] but obviously this need not concern us further. In the following section, we shall therefore use the distinction between communicable and noncommunicable knowledge and avoid entirely the term tacit knowledge.

3.3. OLD AND NEW PROBLEMS

In the previous section, we have discussed how the rule-based mechanism functions. The main idea is that all cognition is problem oriented and that the solutions to the problems of the individual possess a hypothetical character, even if they have often been tested in his environment. Thus, all the knowledge of the individual, regardless of the frequency of the test, remains entirely conjectural. Even when a problem has been solved in the same way many times in the past, so that the solution has been more or less standardized to become an unconscious *routine,* its conjectural character remains intact. The possibility, in other words, that even standard solutions will be proved unsuccessful in the future always exists.

Although the hypothetical character of all our solutions and thus of all our knowledge should be stressed, a distinction between old and new problems will prove very useful. Every time an individual is confronted with reality he is, literally speaking, faced with a novel situation. We have seen that, when perceiving reality, the human mind is actively interpreting and classifying it; thus, in a sense, a new cognitive achievement takes place every time. But this classification process of the mind presupposes, of course, that available classes already exist under which the current messages of the environment can be classified. When these classes do in fact

---

23 See Polanyi (1958, p. 70): "From which it follows that the inarticulate faculties – the potentialities – by which man surpasses the animals and which, by producing speech, account for the entire intellectual superiority of man, are in themselves almost imperceptible."

exist, we can speak of the relevant problem situation as an "old problem." Old problems, then, are those that can be classified under an already existing category of the mind that prescribes the appropriate solution (in the form of an IF . . . THEN rule).

If the current problem is identified as a familiar one – in the sense that it *can* be classified in an existing class – then the appropriate solution in the form of a rule will be applied automatically. In other words, whenever the human mind finds, when comparing the current problem situation with past problem situations stored and classified by it, that it is of the same type, it then automatically applies the corresponding solution designated by the respective class. In these cases we can speak of old problems.

As we have seen (Section 3.2.), if the old problems also happen to appear frequently and the respective solutions applied proved to be successful many times in the past, then these problem solutions consist of following *unconscious routines*. A large number of problems, such as choosing words while speaking, driving, and opening the refrigerator, belong to this category of unconscious routines, that is, solutions that are the learned application of rules stored in the mind and automatically invoked when needed.

But obviously, not all problems are of this kind. Whenever an old problem solution no longer works (possibly because of a change in the environment) or whenever a problem situation, when compared to past problem situations stored in the human mind, cannot be classified under any familiar type or class, we speak of a "new problem." In other words, if the mental model of the problem space currently constructed by an individual is essentially new in its characteristics, so that no ready-made solution to the problem is available, it then constitutes a new problem for the individual. Since *all* the old problems of an individual were new at some point in its history, it is important to ask what happens when an individual conceives of a situation as a new problem.

The first response by the individual to the new problem is quasi-automatic. It involves the employment of so-called inferential strategies. Processes of inference are widely discussed in psychology, and we shall only give a brief overview of them here.

Psychological research has focused mainly on how inferences concerning theoretical problems are made. There is very little literature on how inferences work when people solve practical problems. Usually, inference signifies the process of reasoning by which we draw a conclusion on the basis of available evidence or prior knowledge. Inferential problems such as the description and characterization of events, detection of covariation among events, causal inference, prediction and theory testing (Nisbett and Ross, 1980, p. 10) are normally solved by laypersons with the aid of judgmental strategies or "heuristics." Heuristics are to be understood as general strategies that provide quick solutions with little effort; they are metarules or higher-order rules that direct the employment of more specific rules in order to solve the current problem. Heuristics are to be contrasted to "algorithms," methodical procedures that guarantee success by solving problems through their lengthy, patient application. Since people in their ordinary lives usually employ rules of thumb or heuristics whenever they are confronted with a new problem, algorithms need not concern us here.

Heuristics as judgmental strategies, that is, as metarules, are employed every time the organism confronts a new theoretical problem. Two such heuristics, first discussed by Tversky and Kahneman (Kahneman and Tversky, 1972, 1982; Tversky and Kahneman, 1973, 1974), are the availability and representativeness heuristics. Nozick (1993, p. 167), gives a long list of heuristic rules that can provide the first tentative solutions to intellectual problems.[24] And Nisbett and Ross (1980) descibe how laypersons behave as intuitive scientists in many domains in which they are forced to give solutions to their problems. The common characteristic of all these heurisitcs is that they do not guarantee a solution to the problem. Furthermore, in many instances, due either to the nature of the problem or to an inappropriate use of these metarules, *heuristics may lead to errors* and thus the theoretical problem cannot be solved.

Despite their neglect in the literature, heuristics are also used to solve practical problems. We can thus also speak of inferential strategies in regard to mobilizing practical or "effector" rules. (Holland et al. 1986, p. 43) Perhaps the most powerful heuristic is reasoning and acting by *analogy* (Thagard, 1996, ch. 5). If one has found a satisfactory solution to a problem in one domain, then an analogical transfer may lead to an equally good solution in another domain.[25] If I know how to ride a bicycle and I sit for the first time on a motorcycle, I try to balance the same way as when I sit on a bicycle. Nevertheless, even in this broader perspective of con-

[24] Some of the fifteen heuristics that he enumerates are, for example: "Reduce one hard problem to a set of easier problems, and use other heuristics to solve these" (p. 170) or "With a new particular idea, formulate a little formal structure or model to embed this idea and then explore its properties and implications" (p. 171). Gigerenzer, Todd, and the ABC Group (1999) contains a large number of fast and frugal heuristics "that make us smart."

[25] As Holyoak and Thagard (1989, p. 254) emphasize, the critical step in the mobilization of analogies is the failure to solve a problem in the first place.

sidering the possibility of employing general heuristics for mobilizing all kinds of rules, that is, both theoretical and practical, nothing guarantees success. Moveover, inferential strategies, since they have the character of rules of thumb may *lead to errors*.

In our context two issues are, hence, important:

(a) The first step that a human takes to solve a new problem, either theoretical or practical, is to employ heuristics according to which the employment of more specific rules is arranged.
(b) These heuristics, which in many cases provide a quick and easy solution to the new problem, do not always guarantee success. The possibility of error, as in the case of all of our techniques and knowledge remains.

Hence, when an individual is faced with a new problem, in the first stage quasi-automatic inferential strategies are employed. This quasi-automatism implies that an inference is made in the light of consciousness, but without a long period of reflection. Therefore, the inferential strategies are to be conceived as being the first intuitive response to any problem that is interpreted as a new one.[26] There are, then, two obvious cases to be distinguished. Either the inference has been successful, and accordingly – in the terminology of rule-based systems – the inferential metarules are strengthened and applied anew in the future, or it has led to a failure. In the second case, the individual is forced to look for another solution to the new problem.

The deliberation process that the individual uses when the solution based on a quick inference has failed leads most often to the discovery of more than one solution to the new problem. In other words, the mind triggers *more than one new rule* to be applied as the solution to this new problem. In these cases we can speak, using ordinary language, of "choice

---

[26] Lane, Malerba, Maxfield, and Orsenigo (1996) model cognition involved in expert action as a "categorization-action system" operating in the same way as in our model. They contend, though, that in the case of new problems, the cognitive system still operates on a subcognitive level. "When confronted with a new situation requiring action, the system categorizes the situation according to patterns motivated by previously experienced situations. The categories are associated with particular actions: the association depends upon the valuations of the effects of the actions taken in past situations that were categorized similarly to the present situation. The categorization-action system that generates an action on the basis of this association. Roughly speaking, if previous actions in situations similar to the present situation led to good results are avoided. The comparisons and valuations that make this system work are subcognitive and essentially instantaneous" (p. 53).

problems." As Lorenz stresses, centralized nervous systems, such as the brain, can possess more than one appropriate way of behaving. The brain, as a higher Commando Center (*Kommandostelle*) informed by the senses of the current environmental situation and interpreting it as a new problem, engages in what we call in ordinary language "reflection" on which of the many behavioral patterns can be most effective. This deliberation process is nothing more than a *mental probing of alternatives*. It is the situation in which new rules are generated by the mind and are considered as candidates for providing a solution to the (new) choice problem. These new rules that are triggered are what in the theory of choice are called "alternative means."[27]

It is important that this deliberation process, during which the alternatives are created and the choice is made, occurs in the light of consciousness. Popper stresses the conscious character of choice as opposed to problems that can be solved by routines and that do not need consciousness: "But the role of consciousness is perhaps clearest where an aim or purpose (perhaps even an unconscious or instinctive aim or purpose) can be achieved by *alternative means,* and when two or more means are tried out, after deliberation. It is the case of making a new decision" (Popper and Eccles, 1977/1983, p. 126).

The conscious reflection on alternatives and the subsequent choice do not imply, though, that the alternatives are created in any predetermined manner. In the evolutionary epistemology of Campbell (1974/1987), these new alternatives (or variations in his terminology) are created following the principle of random or blind mutation. "In going beyond what is already known, one cannot but go blindly. If one can go wisely, this indicates already achieved wisdom of some general sort" (Campbell,

---

[27] See Lorenz (1976, p. 46f.): "A nervous system which is not centralized, like that of a sea urchin . . . makes it impossible for that being to completely inhibit one of a variety of potential modes of behavior and to 'choose' another one. As Erich von Holst so convincingly demonstrated with earth worms, this capability is however the most important and elementary achievement of a 'brain-like' center as is represented by the primary receptor ganglion in the case of the earthworm. This . . . 'Commando Center,' as it were, receives information from the sensory organs concerning the present environmental surroundings and is in possession of that information which determines which movement, among the many options possible, best 'fits' the situation at hand. The greater the number of potential behaviors an organism possesses, the more diversified and 'higher' capabilities it demands from the somehow managing central organ." From this citation, it is clear that what we call "choice" is a phenomenon also found in animals. The crucial difference is, of course, that humans are equipped with the faculty of imagination, which is involved in the deliberation process of choice and allows for future-oriented behavior.

1974, p. 7; 1987, p. 57). Although Campbell does not speak explicitly of any process of choice, his thesis of a practically unlimited number of possible new variations is consistent with an *unconditional notion of choice* that we will describe in more detail later (Chapter 4).[28]

When faced with a new problem, and while generating in the process of reflection the alternatives, the individual possesses in *any* case one possible alternative way to solve the new problem: to acquire ready-made solutions from the environment. This strategy is very common among human beings because they avail themselves of language as a means of communication, which greatly facilitates the transmission of messages (and problem solutions) among individuals. (As a matter of fact, language is the presupposition of a great part of cultural learning, which we will discuss in Chapter 5.)

What appears to be a new problem to an individual is obviously *not objectively* a new problem for everybody. As a matter of fact, most of the new problems that somebody faces throughout his own life, are old problems for others, for which they possess successful solutions. Therefore, many problems that are interpreted as new ones by the individual can be solved by adopting ready-made solutions from his environment instead of creating new ones. Hence, the overwhelming majority of new problems for an individual are solved by ready-made solutions (in the form of familiar rules) acquired by others. The fact that in most societies today education is the only occupation of young people until the age of fifteen, eighteen, or twenty five years suffices to prove that the ready-made solutions worked out by others are almost always employed whenever an individual faces a new theoretical or practical problem. No young man is forced to prove the theorem of Pythagoras using only his own intellectual powers, and no innovation is needed on the part of a child to brush his teeth.

Provided that the ready-made solutions acquired from the environment *always* supply one of the alternatives to choose between in order to solve the new problem, the individual mind creates all the other possible alter-

---

[28] Holland et al. (1986), who also do not handle the choice process explicitly, contend that new rules are created mainly by the recombination of old ones. Rule generation does not take place randomly. There are certain recombination techniques that use three methods to constrain rule generation and to produce plausible new rules: "1) strong rules and important messages are preferred sources of components for new rules; 2) rules and messages active at the same time are most likely to be recombined; and 3) new rules are created from existing ones by specific adaptive types of transformations" (Holland et al., 1986, p. 82).

natives ex nihilo. In an imaginative process, the individual mind devises new alternatives; *creativity* is thus a property of the human mind, which is employed when working out new alternatives in order to solve a new problem.

After creating the new alternatives, and often after acquiring ready-made alternatives from the environment, the individual decides (according to principles discussed in Chapter 4) which alternative is most appropriate to solve the problem. Like all solutions, the solution that will be applied in order to solve the problem is only *conjectural*. In other words, there is no decision that guarantees success. Failure or success is determined when the alternative solution chosen by the individual is tried out in the environment.

If the chosen alternative is tested in the environment and proves to be *unsuccessful,* that is, if it does not solve the problem, then a new problem arises that is also solved through a choice process. If, on the other hand, the chosen alternative proves to be *successful* then it will be reinforced, and the next time the same problem arises, this solution will be employed by the individual. After it has been employed successfully many times, the solution will be standardized and will become a routine. In other words, the individual will avail himself of a ready-made solution to the problem, and thus every time he is confronted with it, it will be classified as an old problem and dealt with unconsciously. The mechanism presented here, based on a distinction between old and new problems, can best be presented in Figure 1.

At this point, a very important aspect must be stressed. The distinction between old and new problems is *not* a categorial one. Instead, it designates the two ends of a continuum. Since every cognitive act includes a genuinely subjective moment, the characterization of a problem situation as either an old or a new one is always a *matter of interpretation.* This implies, then, that while forming the mental model of the problem space, *problems the individual was faced with in the past can erroneously be interpreted as new ones and vice versa.* In other words, *interpretation and classification errors* are far from impossible, and thus a subsequent puzzling behavior – from an observer's point of view – can be detected. As a matter of fact, the so-called *anomalies,* extensively discussed in the rational-choice literature, are nothing more than classification errors of individuals. The empirical evidence (see Chapter 4) that challenges the "rationality assumption" is thus thoroughly consistent with the framework discussed here. Since choice is obviously a very important aspect of human behavior, because it is related to the possibility of solving new

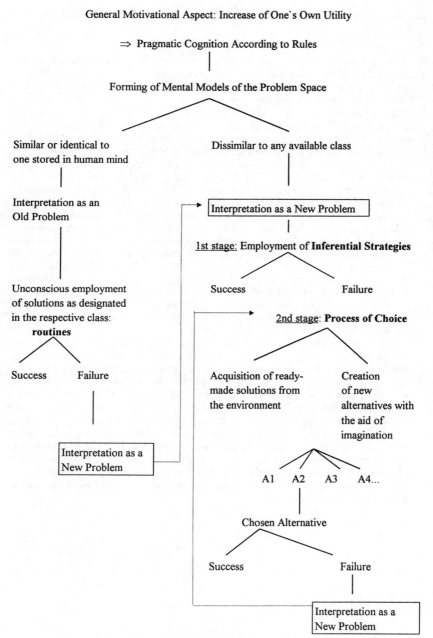

General Motivational Aspect: Increase of One`s Own Utility

⇒ Pragmatic Cognition According to Rules

Forming of Mental Models of the Problem Space

Similar or identical to
one stored in human mind

Dissimilar to any available class

Interpretation as an
Old Problem

Interpretation as a New Problem

1st stage: Employment of **Inferential Strategies**

Success   Failure

Unconscious employment
of solutions as designated
in the respective class:
routines

2nd stage: **Process of Choice**

Acquisition of ready-
made solutions from
the environment

Creation
of new
alternatives with
the aid of
imagination

Success   Failure

Interpretation as a
New Problem

A1   A2   A3   A4...

Chosen Alternative

Success   Failure

Interpretation as a
New Problem

Fig. 1 The problem-solving model.

problems by adopting a self-created alternative behavior, we shall devote a separate chapter to it.[29]

[29] As an epilogue to the theory presented here and to the distinction between old and new problems, two extended citations from two thoroughly different writters are given, which seem to suggest the same position. E. Schrödiger, in his *Mind and Matter* (1958), puts it as follows (pp. 5-6):
"On the first few repetitions a new element turns up in the mind, the 'already met with' or 'notal' as Richard Avenarius has called it. On frequent repetition the whole string of events becomes more and more of a routine, it becomes more and more uninteresting, the responses become ever more reliable according as they fade from consciousness. The boy recites his poem, the girl plays her piano sonata 'well-nigh in their sleep.' We follow the habitual path to our workshop, cross the road at the customary places, turn into side-streets etc., whilst our thoughts are occupied with entirely different things. But whenever the situation exhibits a relevant differential – let us say the road is up at the place where we used to cross it, so that we have to make a detour – this differential and our response to it intrude into consciousness, from which, however, they soon fade below the threshold, if the differential becomes a constantly repeated feature. Faced with changing alternatives, bifurcations develop and may be fixed in the same way. We branch off to the University Lecture Rooms or to the Physics Laboratory at the right point without much thinking, provided that both are frequently occuring destinations."
And one of the most prominent old institutionalists, John Commons, argues that people develop a set of "habitual assumptions," but at the same time invest energy in solving new problems (1934/1990, p. 697f.):
"When a new worker goes into a factory or on a farm, or when a beginner starts in a profession or a business, everything may be novel and unexpected because not previously met in his experience. Gradually he learns the ways of doing things that are expected from him. They become familiar. He forgets that they were novel when he began. He is unable even to explain them to outsiders. They have become routine, taken for granted. His mind is no longer called upon to think about them. . . . We speak of such minds as institutionalized. But all minds are institutionalized by whatever habitual assumptions they have acquired and they take for granted, so that they pay no attention to them except when some limiting factor emerges and goes contrary to what they were habitually expecting. . . . If the factors are continually changing, then the intellect must be lively to control the strategic ones; but if they run along as usual, then habitual assumptions are enough to take care of the complementary and routine factors."

4

The Choice Aspect

4.1. CHOICE AS A REFLECTION
OF ALTERNATIVES

From the last chapter, it should be clear that the entire issue of choice can be adequately discussed in terms of the problem-solving framework. Choice analysis is a subcase of problem solving; as we have seen, problem-solving also includes unconscious aspects such as following routines when solving old problems and quasi-automatic aspects such as inferential strategies when a new problem first arises. The incorporation of choice into this broader framework is thus theoretically valuable because no separate choice theory is needed. Nevertheless, since the phenomenon of choice has a prominent position in the theoretical social and economic sciences, a more detailed analysis of this exceptional moment of human reflection seems appropriate.[1]

Choice among alternatives always refers to the future. The reflection taking place whenever an individual discovers more than one alternative to attain an aim is always in reference to the future. We have discussed the ultimate motivation in human behavior and have summarized it in the general form of striving to increase one's own utility. In the case of choice, the motivational and cognitive aspects of behavior are strikingly interwoven. The individual seeks to order, on the basis of conjectures about future states, the different alternatives according to the effects that they

---

[1] It is characteristic that psychologists pay much less attention to choice than do economists or social scientists. The reason is, we think, that it is unproblematic to incorporate choice in a broader perspective such as problem solving or the rule-based view of cognitive systems. On the other hand, choice has been the traditional domain of economics because market prices can only be explained in terms of an evaluation of alternatives taking place before the exchange transaction.

will have in changing his utility. In other words, he tries to weigh the impact that the different alternatives will have on his utility.

This deliberation process is based on the intellectual faculty of imagination. Imagination consists of the power of the human mind to construct a future mental situation. *Phantasia* as genuine imagination "is the human faculty to combine mental images by composition and division and to create new combinations of existing things or even completely new objectives like centaurs" (Koslowski, 1990, p. 19).[2] In the cognitive terms of our framework, imagination represents the faculty for framing mental models of future situations that do not correspond to any sensual input. Imagination is thus, in a way, the capacity to *solve new problems* mentally before trying out the solution in the environment. Dreaming of traveling to China or living in the Middle Ages is thus nothing more than my imagination functioning while I am awake.

Creating new alternatives, choosing one from among them, and then trying it out in the environment is obviously a process that also takes place in higher animals. They also avail themselves of more than one alternative to solve their (new) problems, and in a way, they also "choose" the behavior they want to use. But it is a rather uncultivated instinct at work when a dog "chooses" to bark rather than to be silent. And animals evidently lack the forward-looking reflection engaged in human choice. This specific intellectual faculty is thus what we call imagination and what differentiates humans from animals.[3]

My imagination is forced to function when I face a choice problem. With the aid of this intellectual power, I can imagine what the effects of

---

[2] Koslowski (1990, pp. 18ff.), following Avicenna and Albertus Magnus, distinguishes between imaginatio, i.e., the mental faculty that imagines images that are given in the outside world, and phantasia as genuine "poetic" or "productive" imagination. We will confine the use of the term "imagination" to its meaning as a genuine phantasia. On the creative role of imagination, see also Albert (1968/1991, p. 81) and Day (1998, p. 122f.). An excellent handbook that deals with all aspects of creativity is Sternberg (1999).

[3] See Popper (1972/1992, p. 148), where he also speaks of the imagination assisting us to construct the future mentally, before we try out our new possibilities: "Seen in this light, life is problem solving and discovery – the discovery of new facts, of new possibilities, by way of trying out possibilies conceived in our imagination." See also Hume (1751/1975, p. 47): "Nothing is more free than the imagination of man; and though it cannot exceed that original stock of ideas furnished by the internal and external senses, it has unlimited power of mixing, compounding, separating, and dividing these ideas, in all the varieties of fiction and vision. It can feign a train of events, with all the appearance of reality, ascribe to them a particualr time and place, conceive them as existent, and point them out to itself with every circumstance, that belongs to any hisitorical fact, which it believes with greatest certainty."

the different alternatives open to me now are and how these effects will influence my utility. Imagination is, in this case, directly at my service to assist me in solving my choice problem and thus to increase my utility. The essential point regarding choice is, hence, that it is based on the imagination of alternatives and on the imagination of the effects of these alternatives on utility. Thus, as in all problem-solving activity, both the cognitive and the motivational elements are included. The only peculiarity is that because of the forward-looking character of choice, the imagination is involved in representing the future in the mind of the individual at the present moment.

Although imagination is always at work when the individual mind creates alternative solutions to a problem, as we have seen, one of the alternatives available for the individual to acquire knowledge consists of ready-made solutions from the environment. An aspect that should be stressed in this context is that these solutions available in the environment *are not automatically* adopted by the individual, but are always additional alternatives. In the language of a rule-based cognitive system, rules inserted from the environment compete with the rules available at that time for the right to offer a solution to the new problem.[4]

But the question arises as to whether the acquisition of ready-made alternatives from the environment does not imply a prior choice of the kind: Before choosing among the alternatives, you have to choose which ready-made alternatives from the environment are to be obtained. We contend that this prior choice situation does take place, but that the choice process does not differ qualitatively from a choice situation that includes as one of the alternatives, ready-made solutions or knowledge from the environment.

---

[4] See Holland et al. (1986, p. 96). When taken into consideration, the competition of "external" rules with the available "internal" ones can account for the explanation of a broad range of phenomena familiar in everyday life and found in empirical research. The difficulty of changing one's beliefs and expectations after a certain age is due, for example, to the fact that the rules available to the individual are strengthened to such a degree that even the most convincing rules inserted from the environment prove to be relatively weak competition. Another experimental finding, the effects of a physics course on the understanding of physical phenomena of laypeople, also shows the tendency of the people to acquire new rules in light of the old ones. The evidence of Champagne, Klopfer, and Anderson (1980) shows, for example, that although people who have attended a physics course tend to improve their "naive knowledge" of physical phenomena, no complete revision of their view of physical phenomena takes place. The notion of the "scientific paradigma" (Kuhn, 1962/1970) and the insistence of scientists on observing reality only in the light of the predominant paradigma is another case of the competition between internal and external rules.

4.2. IMAGINATION AND THE CREATIVITY OF CHOICE

For reasons of clarity and because the imagination is interwoven with both the cognitive and the motivational elements of choice, we shall distinguish between two analytical steps in the choice process: the creation of the alternatives and the evaluation of the alternatives.

1. *Imagination and the Creation of Alternatives.* Whenever an individual is faced with a new problem that allows for many alternative solutions, the problem is one of choice. The solution to this problem can be conceptualized better if it is treated in two stages, with the faculty of imagination involved in both. In the first stage, with the help of imagination, the alternative means are formulated mentally. The different courses are shaped *actively* by the individual, that is, the alternatives are *created* by the mind with the aid of imagination. This is a very important point since it implies that there are no a priori given alternatives presented to the human mind to choose from. There is no objective set of alternatives waiting to be discovered by the chooser; rather, all alternatives are the subjective mental creatures of the mind at the moment of choice. As we have seen, the mind interprets reality, classifying and constructing it actively. In the case of choice, the mind creates the alternatives, the potential ways to attain the end *ab ovo,* without interpreting any input provided by the senses. Choice is a purely speculative operation occurring entirely in the mind of the chooser. In the words of Shackle, the pioneer of the creative theory of choice, this forward-looking view of choice must be strictly distinguished from every deterministic one (1979, p. 9):

> The view of the nature of choice . . . elected as a means of adopting non-determinism, is wholly at odds with the notion of a set of choosables given ready-made to the chooser by some agency outside his own thought . . . [T]he rival choosables, namely, the courses of action and the sequels associated with them, must . . . be deemed to be originated by the chooser's self.[5]

Hesse, in an excellent article (1990), speaks of the "principle of the cognitive creation," designating the same phenomenon discussed here. During the process of the cognitive formulation of alternative pos-

---

5 See also Shackle (1979, p. 10): "My theme subverts the view of choice as a passive response of the chooser to a set of choosables each fully relevantly specified, finitely numerous and thrust upon him without his participation. . . . Choices in this view are, in their full burden and complexity of meaning, the genesis of history from moment to moment, a *ne plus ultra* of explanatory thought."

sibilities, the chooser is to a large degree unaided by experience or previous knowledge, since the essential characteristic of the choice situation is that it constitutes a new problem. This is also the reason why he is forced to be creative;[6] if the problem was classified as an old one, ready-made solutions in form of routines would be applied. Choice is, in the words of Shackle (1979, p. 54), a *beginning*, an uncaused cause and therefore a genuinely creative act.

It is important to stress that there is no reason to assume that the imagination of the agent will help him create an exhaustive set of alternatives as judged by any external standard of global optimum or by a "god-like view." There is no assurance that all agents will create the same set of alternatives in an identical situation. The creative, subjective character of human choice is also expressed in the fact that different agents will create different numbers of alternatives with different qualitative characteristics when facing a new problem. For the scientific observer, this translates into a crucial element of unpredictability concerning anyone's solution of a new problem.[7] We shall put off the issue of predictability for a moment, though, and discuss the second stage in the choice proces.

2. *Imagination and the Evaluation of Alternatives.* Since choice can be only "choice of thoughts of deeds" (Shackle, 1979, p. 2), the first stage just discussed (concerning the cognitive element of choice) is devoted to the creation of the alternatives. The second stage of the deliberation process (concerning the motivational moment of choice) involves the evaluation of the created alternatives. The agent will choose according to the general motivation of increasing his or her own utility. Naturally, then, the problem arises that from the mentally created alternatives, more than one or even all of them may contribute to the increase of the individual's utility. In order to choose, the individual must thus evaluate the alterna-

---

6 This means, in the terms of our cognitive framework, that he is forced to create *new rules.*

7 See Choi (1993, p. 51): "In a novel situation, the course of action any one individual will actually undertake is largely unpredictable. . . . The imprecision in our ability to predict the actions of others is heightened by the fact that there are many different ways to accomplish the same (broadly defined) goals. All people deprived of food for a period of time will try to overcome their hunger, but some will do so by hunting while others will proceed to gather fruit. Hunters will split off in their choice of prey, some pursuing deer, other rabbits, turkeys or whatever. Even the deer hunters will differ by their choice of weapon, be it stones, traps, guns or bows and arrows. And once the prey is caught, it can be skinned and cooked in a variety of ways. The possibilities for dealing with hunger, in brief, sum to a figure of almost unimaginable proportion. Is it any wonder that we are frequently taken by surprise by the strange customs of people in remote areas?"

tives first and then choose one of them. But according to which principle does the evaluation take place?

The imagination is also at work here. Not the imagination of future alternative states, but rather *the imagination of future alternative degrees of satisfaction.* "It is not for the sake of some formal shape of thought that the arduous business of choice would be undertaken. Emotion must be involved. In order to experience emotion, the chooser must involve himself in the state of things he contemplates, the state which his act of choice is intended to produce" (Shackle, 1979, p. 44). The individual thus assigns to the alternatives different values according to how much utility each alternative is expected to offer upon realization. The imagination, thus, also functions as a way of assigning utility values to alternatives expected to occur in a future moment of time.

Obviously, the attachment of different utilities to potential states in the light of alternative actions does not have an exact character. Instead, the chooser orders the alternative courses into more or less desired ones according to the pleasure that he imagines will occur. Only the broad effects of the individual's utility are considered and there is no exact measure, of the absolute quantity of sensation, pleasure or desire satisfaction available. Unlike the traditional utilitarianism, which assumed a cardinal utility, the actual chooser is unable to specify his utility in this absolute manner.

Modern choice theory[8] makes use of what is called an "ordinal utility function." The main idea is, of course, that the chooser orders the potential outcomes of the decision according to personal preferences. Since rational choice will be dealt with in detail later, the problems of the mathematical and probabilistic approach of expected utility theory need not concern us here. It is important, though, to stress that the idea of ordering alternatives and attaching values to them is explicitly followed here, too. For now we will emphasize only the fact that the orderings may not be complete and may not always be according to the postulated axioms of rational choice theory. This is due to the fact that the attachment of utilities to different potential outcomes is an imaginary action and thus cannot – by the nature of the thing – be exact.

After the ordering of alternatives according to the utility they are expected to bring, the choice takes place in a way that is consistent with the general motivation of the individual. The alternatives that do not contribute to an increase in individual utility are disregarded in the process of

[8] For a good overview, see Heap, Hollis, Lyons, Sugden, and Weale (1992).

choice. From the remaining ones, which to varying degrees are expected to enhance individual utility, the one is chosen that is judged to increase the utility *most*.

The weighing of alternative courses created by the imagination and the attachment of utilities to the potential outcomes – before the best alternative is chosen – is technically known as a "cost-benefit analysis." It consists of deliberating what effect each alternative will have on the individual utility. The sum of the positive effects are then the benefits of the particular alternative. Since the choice of one alternative is equivalent to the nonrealization of all the rest, the nonrealized utility of all these alternatives constitutes the "cost" of the particular alternative under consideration. Therefore, one can speak of the "net utility" of every alternative when costs are explicitly introduced into the analysis. These costs are generally psychological costs, with the exception of the case in which resources are needed in order for an alternative to be realized; in this case, the costs are monetary.[9] The alternative that most increases the net utility of the individual is then chosen.

Before closing the discussion of choice, the issue of predictability of the agent's behavior in novel problem situations must be addressed. It is clear from the preceding considerations that the scientific observer is radically limited in formulating predictions about the outcomes of an agent's choice. The only aid for an observer is the general motivational assumption of utility increase that the agent is seeking (also) in a novel problem situation. As long as an observer does not avail himself of the means to reconstruct what kinds and how many alternatives an agent's imagination is creating in the first place, genuine unpredictability of the outcome of a choice process must be admitted.[10]

---

[9] The monetary costs, of course, have an obvious importance for the explanation of economic phenomena.

[10] This is clearly stated in the following passage of Choi (1993, p. 51f.): "Although individuals can choose from countless possibilities in novel situations so that the likelihood of predicting their precise actions is unlikely in the extreme, many social scientists have led us to believe otherwise. Chief among them in this regard are economists, whose claim to being able to predict people's behavior, at least in principle, rests *inter alia* in the assumption that the choice-space is invariant. In other words, the underlying assumption (when neoclassical economists predict human behavior) is that individuals are aware of the nature of the situation, which is itself invariant. However, it is entirely possible, and even likely, that similar individuals could choose very different practices in the same situation, depending upon their perception of the event, which in turn depends on their past experiences and the way in which they sequence their experiments." See also the aphorism of Buchanan (1979, p. 40): "Choice, by its nature, cannot be predetermined and remain choice."

4.3. THE THEORY OF RATIONAL CHOICE

Reason is, and ought only to be the slave of the passions, and can never pretend to any other office than to serve and obey them. (Hume 1740/1978, p. 415).

Starting from the elementary insight that reason is only instrumental to the fulfillment of individual wishes and thus following the Humean program,[11] modern social and mathematical sciences have elaborated on a theory of rational choice. Employing the notion of utility – which comprises all pleasures and pains[12] – Neumann and Morgenstern (1944) provided the first axiomatic derivation of expected utility theory. Savage (1954) then deduced from a limited number of simple axioms all the concepts of modern decision theory: subjective probability, Bayesian learning, and the maximization of expected utility. Although there are many variants of the subjective expected utility (SEU) theory, the main idea is that the agent can order his preferences "properly," that is, according to the axioms of instrumentally rational choice under (certainty or) uncertainty and then choose in order to maximize his utility.

Although Savage himself intended to present not an empirical but rather a normative theory of choice, and although modern SEU theorists admit clearly that "as a scientific theory about human decision-making, SEU is false" (Anand, 1993, p.19), rational choice theory enjoys great resonance in the social sciences. The best-known application of rational choice theory in the economic and social sciences is the work of Becker (1976, 1986). It is not relevant here to criticize the rational choice theory as an empirical theory. An anthology of critiques refers to *rational fools* (Sen),[13] *omnis-*

---

11 Clearly, the Humean program was not the unique alternative offered by philosophy. Just to name one, Kant's theory bestows on reason a much greater role than merely being a slave to the passions. His categorical imperative designates the scope of the rational action (see Kant, 1785/1965 and 1797/1990). In the third book, chapters 1–8 of the Nicomachean Ethics, Aristotle presents the first continental rational choice theory. While examining what προαίρεσις means, he explicitly mentions that βούλευσις, i.e., thought, concerns only the means, not the ends. Cooper (1975, p. 85) interprets in the same way: "deliberation selects the action as instrumentally good only." On the first decision theory in continental history, see Guthrie (1981, pp. 345–58). The locus classicus in the German-speaking world is Kuhn (1962, pp. 275–94).

12 On utility and its use as a technical term, see Broome (1991).

13 See Sen (1977/1979, p. 102): "[T]raditional theory has *too little* structure. A person is given one preference ordering, and as and when the need arises this is supposed to reflect his interests, represent his welfare, summarize his idea of what should be done, and describe his actual choices and behaviour. Can one preference ordering do all these things? A person thus described may be 'rational' in

cient agents (Hayek),[14] and *jail birds* (Commons)[15] among the utility maximizers. Some brief comments on the issue will thus suffice.

The simplest variant of rational choice theory is obviously the choice under certainty, that is, the situation in which the agent possessing a well-defined utility function can order actions and outcomes in such a way that picking the utility-maximizing alternative seems entirely plausible. For example, in microeconomics textbooks, the individual chooser is presented as a set of indifference curves and a budget restriction, and his rational choice consists of selecting the consumption bundle that maximizes his (marginal) utility. This explanation is *not empirically wrong*. The problem is rather that this theory can be applied only in a very small number of cases and is thus of very low empirical content. In our framework, this consumer choice under certainty can be easily incorporated as a subcase of the solution to an exeptionally *well-defined problem*. The problem space is interpreted by the agent in an unambigous way (since the "objects perceived," that is, prices, quantities, qualities, etc. are easily identifiable physical objects), and therefore the agent is able to choose easily and with great exactitude the best alternative and proceed to its subsequent trial in order to solve his (new) problem.

But obviously, most real-world choice situations are not that simple. Since choice is always future-oriented, uncertainty comes into play. The rational choice theory responded to this problem by introducing into the analysis subjective probabilities. It is contended that in an uncertain environment, agents are nevertheless capable of assigning subjective probabilities to the different possible outcomes of their action and then, according to their preference ordering these outcomes to maximize their expected utility.[16]

---

the limited sense of revealing no inconsistencies in his choice behaviour, but if he has no use for these distinctions between quite different concepts, he must be a bit of fool."

14 See, e.g., Hayek (1973/1982, p. 12): "Complete rationality of action in the Cartesian sense demands complete knowledge of all the relevant facts. A designer or engineer needs all the data and full power to control or manipulate them if he is to organize the material objects to produce the intended result. But the success of action in society depends on more particular facts than anyone can possibly know."

15 See Commons (1936, p. 242f.): "But if . . . pure economic man should go along the street picking up groceries, clothing and shoes according to their marginal utility to him, he would go to jail. He must first negotiate with an owner to whom the policemen, courts and constitutions have given the right to withhold from him what he wants but does not own, until that owner willingly consents to sell his ownership."

16 For a more detailed discussion see, e.g., Wessling (1991, pp. 71–82).

The main idea of assigning subjective probabilities to outcomes is that the individuals can thus overcome the uncertainty concerning the future aided by their knowledge available at the moment of decision. Leaving formal elegance aside, the main issue is whether such models based on subjective probabilities are of empirical relevance. Accumulated evidence shows that people are – even in simple choice situations under laboratory conditions – unable to assign probabilities and choose "rationally" according to the model.[17]

The theoretical reason behind this "failure" of people to reason according to subjective probabilities is that the probabilities are unable to transform uncertainty into calculable certainty. "The assumption that probability', in some sense which can yield a numerical basis for calculation, can turn essential unknowledge into knowledge, is inherently self-contradictory" (Shackle, 1979, p. 59). "When someone says he is uncertain, what he usually means is not just that he doesnt know the chances of various outcomes, but that he doesnt know what outcomes are possible" (Loasby, 1976, p. 9). It is thus unfruitful to deal with the problem of lack of knowledge and uncertainty based on probabilistic calculations.[18]

A reaction to the empirical evidence falsifying the strict SEU theory was to acknowledge the limited computational capacity of agents and to construct a theory of bounded rationality.[19] Since the time of the seminal paper of Simon (1955), and with the accumulation of empirical evidence on the empirical invalidity of the SEU theory, the assumption of bounded

---

[17] Biases, framing effects, etc., proved in many experiments, have considerably weakened the rational choice theory. See, e.g., Goffman (1974), Kahneman and Tversky (1979, 1984), Tversky and Kahneman (1981, 1986), Gigerenzer and Todd (1999), and, for a good overview on framing and its applications, Lindenberg (1993). Economists speak of "anomalies" when economic agents do not behave as the rational-choice theory wants them to do. See, e.g., Hogarth and Reder (1987), Kahneman, Knetsch, and Thaler (1991), Thaler (1992), and Eichenberger and Frey (1993). According to the framing theory, the way individuals choose "rationally" depends on the way they interpret reality. It is obvious that our theoretical framework is consistent with the empirical evidence and with the main idea of the theory of framing. The difference consists only in the focus of the framing theory on choice; our framework is more general in stating the importance of interpretation for every kind of behavior, not only for choice problems. In addition, we do not argue (as it will become clear in the next few pages) that choice behavior or behavior in general is, or must be, rational in any way.

[18] Another way to deal with the problem of uncertainty is to build search models. Since it is not relevant here to discuss the theoretical deficits of this approach, see High (1990, ch. 3) for a detailed critical account. More specifically on the so-called Economics of Information, see Wessling (1991, pp. 83–94).

[19] For an informative review of the recent research on bounded rationality, see Conlisk (1996). See also Simon (1992a).

rationality has been used in many areas of (primarily) economic research.[20] Satisficing rather than optimizing is then propagated as the "boundedly rational" choice process.

Some other authors, such as Kirchgässner, try to defend an even weaker model of rational choice (1991, p. 47): "In this model, rationality simply means that the individual is principally in the position to act in accordance with his relative advantage, i.e. to estimate and evaluate his potential sphere of action and then to act accordingly" (translation by C. M.). Still other authors offer broader theories of rationality that do not necessarily include rational choice, but rather a reconstruction and/or explanation of human behavior in general. Boudon, for example, in a series of important articles, speaks of subjective rationality (1989) and develops a theory of synthetic (1993a, 1993b, 1994) or cognitive rationality (1998) according to which an agent is rational when he acts according to (subjectively) "good reasons." The literature on rationality and rational choice is vast, and many scientific and philosophical disciplines participate in the debate.[21] The main question usually asked is thus: what is rational choice and rational action?

We think that this is the wrong question to ask. The problem of rationality is, to a great extent, *a problem of a normative character*. Under the name of "rationality," whether perfect, bounded, or synthetic, diverse theoretical considerations on human behavior are hidden. The point of interest is, thus, not whether the label of "rational" is appropriate to the different types of behavior, but rather *how these behaviors can best be explained*.[22] The objective here must be to find the relevant empirical issue behind the diverse rational models of choice and behavior. The softer models, which consider seriously the interpretational and computational aspects, are thus easily incorporated into the cognitive, pragmatic framework used here. They are the cases in which the individual, after having interpreted the problem as a new one (and in which the inferential strategies employed have proved unsuccessful), consciously engages in reflection that leads to the creation of alternatives and the selection of the

---

[20] See, e.g., Sargent (1994) and Williamson (1975).

[21] Since the literature is vast, it would be futile to enumerate even the most important works on rationality and rational choice. For a general survey, see Sugden (1991), Wüstehübe (1991), Vriend (1996), Goldthorpe (1998), Opp (1999), and Zafirorski (1999). See also the edited volumes by Arrow et al. (1996) and Dennis (1998).

[22] A typical example of explaining behavior in the terms of rationality is found in Arthur (1994). Although he adopts, as we do, the findings of cognitive psychology, he nevertheless discusses it in the terms of "bounded rationality." For a major attack on rational choice theory from a perspective similar to ours, see Lane et al. (1996).

relatively best one. In our framework, the relevant aspect is, hence, that individuals solve problems in order to increase their utility. An external standard of judging this problem-solving behavior as "rational," "irrational," "non-rational," or "super-rational" does not exist, and even if it existed, it would not be useful.[23] And since choice is only part of the problem-solving activity, there is no need to designate the theory presented in Section 4.2. as a soft variant of rational choice theory or something equivalent. It is rather a weak theory of how people actually choose, that is, it is a theory of human choice with low empirical content.

To close these brief comments on the issue of rational choice, our main point to be stressed is once again that when people are faced with a novel situation they consciously choose what seems the best way to cope with it. But, like all solutions, the one chosen is purely conjectural and must be tested in the environment. Choice is the creative stage of the conscious mental probing of alternatives before proceeding to the trial of the one judged as the best.[24]

4.4. BEYOND *HOMO OECONOMICUS* AND *HOMO SOCIOLOGICUS*

The standard model used by economists assumes that agents are guided in their behavior by a case-by-case maximization of their utility function. The standard model used by sociologists assumes that agents' behavior is

[23] The fact that the rationality label is not useful should have been obvious since 1981, when Kagel et al. proved that even rats are capable of rational choice if "rational" is defined in the simplistic terms of textbook consumer theory.

[24] As an epilogue to rational choice theory and the rationality debate in general, an extensive citation of Kliemt (1993b, p. 43) puts the issue in the right dimensions: "Alternatively, it should be noted too that theories of perfectly rational behaviour though interesting in themselves are certainly of no relevance for explaining real world behaviour. Within the realm of real world behaviour and its explanation a concept of workable rationality must be applied. Here we face bounded rationality and real world intentions and motives. What we need then are psychological laws and theories of bounded rationality that describe and explain how real people act. Whether or not some of these acts will be called 'rational' in an imperfect sense while others that do not fulfil even these standards are called non-rational or even irrational is of minor importance. For, the explanation is not based on rationality per se but on behavioural laws. That these laws will typically link imputed beliefs and intentions to overt behaviour does not change their status within an empirical theory related to workable rationality. To find these laws rather than to define or explicate rationality as a concept is 'a crucial problem' for the social sciences. The philosophical explicatory problem of defining what we should understand by 'rationality' in a perfect sense of that term is of greatest interest for our self-understanding as rational beings. But it should be clearly distinguished from the explanatory problems of social science."

dictated by social norms. *Homo economicus* is forward-looking, intentional and responsive to incentives. *Homo sociologicus* "is *pushed* from behind by quasi-inertial forces" (Elster, 1989b, p. 99) and follows norms or rules blindly. Although not all economists follow the model of *Homo economicus* and not every sociologist uses the model of *Homo sociologicus*, it is a fact that these two antithetic models dominate the social sciences.

The preference of economists for the rational utility maximizer can be explained by their primary theoretical interest in explaining price formation in the market. The main idea of the subjective theory of value since the marginal revolution of the 1870s has been that prices are formed in an exchange process taking place after the agents have ordered their preferences and have decided which goods they want to exchange.[25] Those agents ought – according to the inherent logic of the explanation – to be modeled as choosers and, with the increasing formalization of the exchange situation, as utility maximizers.

The preference of the sociologists for modeling the agent as a norm follower can also be explained by their special theoretical interest. The Durkheim-Parsons tradition in sociology sought to find a satisfactory solution to the Hobbesian problem of social order without invoking individualistic-utilitarian considerations. Norm-guided behavior seemed to be the proper model to explain the maintenance of a workable social order. The classic statement ascribed to Duesenberry draws the boundary between economics and sociology correctly: "economics is all about how people make choices; sociology is all about why they don't have any choices to make." Hall and Taylor, in an excellent article arguing in the same vein as Duesenberry, distinguish between the calculus approach and the cultural approach (1998, pp. 17ff.). But whether people choose or not is difficult to ascertain since only behavior is observable, not choice as such. Choice is, as we have seen, a process of reflection before acting that takes place in the individual brain and thus is difficult, if not impossible, to observe. The controversy between *Homo oeconomicus* and *Homo sociologicus* is thus better to be handled in terms of overt, observable action or behavior.

Our model of problem solving incorporates both kinds of behavior. Since individuals are supposed to be able to learn by experience, it is

---

[25] Jevons, for example, views the individual agent as "exchanging from a pure regard to his own requirements or private interests. . . . [A]nyone will exchange with anyone else for the slightest apparent advantage. There must be no conspiracies" (Jevons, 1871, p. 133).

plausible that a behavioral regularity is shown whenever old problems arise or, in the terminology of Vanberg, when recurring situations take place. "Strictly speaking, every situation that one encounters is *unique* in the sense that there will always be *some* respect in which it is different from any situation one has encountered before or will encounter in the future. We can, nevertheless, meaningfully speak of *recurring situations* in the sense that any given situation is, *in certain aspects,* similar to other situations, past and future. The term behavioral regularity can then be understood as describing the fact that in recurring situations, S1 to Sn, a person is regularly exhibiting a particular behaviour A; out of a set of potential alternatives A1 to Am" (Vanberg, 1993, p. 175).

This behavioral regularity is the essential characteristic of an *enlightened Homo sociologicus,* designating continuity of behavior and distinguishing him therewith from all those sociological ideas that suggest that behavior is the effect of hidden occult forces.[26]

But this enlightened *Homo sociologicus* is only one part of the story. There are many problem situations that the individual is unable to classify as similar and, thus, is unable to employ automatically and unconsciously the appropriate solution designated in the respective class. These cases form the new problems for the individual and as a consequence, he is forced to reflect and choose before acting.[27] The individual's choice is *not always* a utility-maximizing one, as assumed by the rational choice model, but rather a human choice based on his imaginative faculties. This reflection process concerning the solution of a new problem is the essential characteristic of an *enlightened Homo oeconomicus.*

The problem-solving model thus incorporates both aspects of observed behavior, the case of problem classification and subsequent behavioral regularity and the case of reflective choice and subsequent novel behavior. The problem solver does both according to the situation and his subjective interpretation of it; he demonstrates what we may call *routine behavior*[28]

---

[26] In regard to the "strict" sociological explanations that dominated sociology for many years Boudon (1993b, p. 101) remarks: "These Molièresque explanations by 'occult qualities' bring us back to the dark side of the Middle Ages. They were considered a nec plus ultra at the time when structuralism and Marxism ruled over sociology. This time is fortunately over in most places. These explanations are so easy, however, that they remain a permanent temptation in ordinary as well as academic thinking: 'Why did he Y? Because he has internalized the norm telling him he should do Y.' We are not far from the 'virtus dormitiva'."

[27] After unsuccesfully trying out the inferential strategies that he might possess.

[28] Since we have discussed the issue of cognition and learning in terms of cognitive

whenever he classifies problems as old ones and *a choice behavior* whenever he classifies problems as new ones.[29]

From an observer's point of view, the difficulty consists in the interpretative moment that is present in every cognitive act of the agent. The prime difficulty of an external observer is thus to discern whether the actor perceives the situation as a familiar one or as a new one. When the observer can ascertain with relative certainty that the agent will interpret a problem situation as a familiar one, he can then predict that the agent will behave the same way as in the past. If the observer ascertains that the problem situation possesses a novel character in the eyes of the agent, then he can only predict that the agent will first employ some inferential strategies, and if they do not work, he will create a set of alternatives and choose the one that he will judge as most conducive to his utility. Obviously, misinterpretations may occur in the part of the agent, that is, classification errors that are bound to puzzle an observer. In these cases, the predictions regarding the behavior of the agent are bound, by an external observer, to be proved false; these cases are the "anomalies."

Before closing, a last very important point must be discussed concerning the possibility of choosing a rule. Whenever an agent is faced with a new problem, he has to choose before deciding which action to take. Depending on the situation, he might choose a single action or a stable kind of behavior, that is, a rule. When an American tourist visits Athens for the first (and perhaps for the last) time and remains for only a few hours on a hot day in August, he may choose to spend his time climbing the Acropolis or shopping in an air-conditioned shopping center; his choice in this case concerns the solution of a new problem appearing just one time. Such choices are common in social and economic life, and the choice theory employed here accounts for them. But obviously there are many situations, relevant in social and economic theory, in which agents choose rules rather than single actions. Several authors have stressed the fact that choice often concerns rules rather than single actions. Rowe (1989), for example, criticizing act individualism, that is, "the theory of rational behavior [which] has focussed on the isolated *action* as the unit of

rules of the IF . . . THEN type, it is better to avoid the term "rule-following behavior" here – although it would be the more accurate one – in order to avoid terminological confusion. We shall use instead the term "routine behavior."

29 As DiMaggio, in a discussion of recent developments in cognitive science, correctly remarks (1998, p. 701): "These developments move us beyond the polemical opposition of 'calculus' and 'culture' to ask not whether people act strategically, but rather under what conditions and how they do so."

rationality" (p. 4), guides attention to rule individualism, that is, the rational choice of rules.

In our framework, since the general motivation of every individual is to increase his own utitlity, it is obvious that he will deliberately choose to follow a rule if he *expects* that the new problem he faces will systematically appear in the same form in the future. In other words, he will reflect on the possibility of choosing to follow a rule only if he expects that the new problem situation that he perceives is representative of similar recurrent situations in the future. There are three reasons why deliberately adopting a rule seems more beneficial than choosing an alternative action as a solution to a new problem at a point in time t_0 and leaving one's options open in case the same type of problem arises in the future at time $t_1, t_2, \ldots t_n$.[30]

The first reason to adopt a rule is that to follow a rule rather than deciding each time anew involves lower decision-making costs and is apparent.[31] The second argument is central in the work of Heiner (1983, 1990). According to him, the question of whether choosing or adopting a rule is in fact superior to leaving options open for future case-by-case choices can only be answered in connection with the *competence* of the agent and the *difficulty* of the problem. As we have seen, the cognitive apparatus of an individual has been shaped in a long evolutionary process and is far from perfect in any sense. Thus, the competence of an agent to solve his problems is limited because of the restrictions of his cognitive equipment, that is, his perceptional, computational, and imaginatory capacities. Heiner argues that when the difficulty of the problem situation is great, the gap between an agent's competence and the difficulty of the decision problem (called a "C-D gap") is high. Whenever the C-D gap is high, agents are prone to adopt rules instead of acting on a case-by-case basis, since "an agent's overall performance may actually be improved by restricting flexibility to use information or to choose particular actions" (Heiner, 1983, p. 564). In other words, the agent will choose to follow a rule at time $t_0, t_1, \ldots t_n$ instead of choosing each time anew because of the expectation that due to his restricted competence and the great difficulty of the problem, the risk of making errors will be less if he follows

---

[30] See, e.g., Vanberg (1994a, pp. 17f).

[31] See, e.g., Frank (1988, p. 23): "To gather the information and do the calculation implicit in naive descriptions of the rational choice model would *consume more time and energy than anyone has.* Anyone who tried to make fully-informed, rational choices would make only a handful of decisions each week, leaving hundreds of important matters unattended. With this difficulty in mind, most of us rely on habits and rules of thumb for routine decisions."

a self-chosen rule than making constant choices, and thus his overall utility will be increased more. The third reason why an agent might choose to adopt a rule as a solution to a new problem is the case of precommitment. This is the case of binding oneself deliberately because *one expects* that by precommiting ones behavior, one will end up with a greater utility increase than otherwise.[32]

Summarizing, an agent will adopt a rule consciously when the nature of the problem is such that he can expect the same problem situation to reappear constantly in the future. This is the necessary condition for choosing to follow a rule. The sufficient conditions for this conscious choice of rule are, alternatively, high decision costs, the great difficulty of the recurrent problem, or precommitment. It should be stressed at this point that this choice need not be an optimal one in the sense of standard rational choice theory. Therefore, the common critique that the decision to adopt the rule presupposes costly information because of its complexity (Etzioni, 1987, p. 509) does not have any validity in our setting. The choice of the personal rule might prove to be an unsuccessful strategy when applied in the environment, and negative environmental feedback might lead to its improvement or rejection.

4.5. EPILOGUE: INDIVIDUAL PROBLEM SOLVING

In closing this part of our study, it seems reasonable to examine whether the problem-solving model of human behavior presented here meets the standards that we specified in Section 1.1. There we formulated three criteria that should be satisfied to provide an adequate explanation of individual behavior in the social sciences. Such an explanation should

(1) possess a nomological character,
(2) account for dynamic aspects of behavior, and
(3) allow for subjectivism.

(1) The model presented here is of nomological character, with a low empirical content. The problem-solving hypothesis suggests that the agent will choose the most promising alternative among those that he has created, whenever he is faced with a new problem (after he has applied some

---

[32] See, e.g., the discussion on Ulysses and the Sirens briefly reviewed in Section 2.3. The theory of self-management deals with the precommitment problem in an extensive way. See, e.g., Schelling (1978, 1984a, 1984b) and Thaler and Shefrin (1981). See also the interesting article by Tietzel (1988, esp. pp. 55–64). For a philosophical discussion based on the idea of more than one selves, see Elster (1986).

kind of heuristic). If the problem is a familiar one, then he will follow the routine according to the problem solution class stored in the brain. Thus, it depends on the nature of the problem as it is subjectively interpreted by the agent, whether he will choose consciously or follow a rule unconsciously. Obviously, this theory does have empirical content and, hence, is neither a prioristic nor a pure logic of choice.

To the scientific observer, the problem-solving model gives the following methodical instruction: If you want to explain the behavior of an individual X, at time t_0, in place P_0, first consider the problem that he is facing. Then consider the history of the agent and examine whether he faced the same problem in the past. If he did and if he has always responded in a standard way, then assume that he will also apply the same solution today, that is, he will follow the routine stored in the brain. If this is the first time the agent comes across this problem, then assume that he will create some alternatives and choose the one which promises the highest benefit.

There are two objections to this model that need to be discussed. The first is of a logical character and is nothing less than Hume's problem of induction. Are we justified in predicting that the agent will apply the same solution today only because he applied it in the past? The answer to this possible criticism runs as follows: The assumption here is that people learn from their experience and, thus, apply unconsciously today the problem solutions that have been successful in the past. Although they commit herewith the logical induction error, this is the only way to free their limited cognitive capacity from the need to rethink every time anew about issues that were solved in the past. The scientist-observer at the meta-level does not need to reason according to this logically fallacious way, though. At the meta-level, only the hypothesis that people learn by induction is formulated, and this hypothesis can be tested according to the epistemological standards of falsificationism.

The second objection is more fundamental. Since every problem that an agent faces is constructed subjectively (i.e., the formation of the problem space always contains an act of interpretation on the part of the agent), how is it at all possible for an external observer to know objectively what the problem is and, consequently, to predict the behavior of the agent? This objection stresses the great difficulty of accessing the "black box" of the brain. Nevertheless, the only way to formulate a theory of individual behavior with empirical content is to use all the data and methods that we have. The history of the agent and the experimental method are the unique means that we possess to obtain a nomological – though perhaps minimalist – explanation of individual behavior. Errors at the meta-level of observation are, of course, unavoidable, but these are inherent in any scientific inquiry.[33]

(2) The problem-solving model also satisfies the second criterion discussed in Section 1.1. It accounts for the dynamic aspects of behavior because it incorporates endogenous changes in behavior. Since all knowledge is conjectural and must be constantly tested in the environment, unsuccessful problem solutions are eliminated and new alternatives are created. A change of behavior is thus possible every time environmental feedback is negative in the sense that the expectations are disappointed and the problem solutions cease to be successful.

(3) The criterion that differences in behavior among individuals must be allowed is also fulfilled. There is both a subjectivism of problems and a subjectivism of problem solutions. The problem-solving framework only gives an explanation of the mechanisms of cognizing and learning and assumes self-interested behavior; it does not prescribe concretely the content of the learning process. Even though the self-interested behavior is a constant feature of human nature, diversity and heterogeneity are nevertheless secured by the different learning histories of the agents. It is this subjectivity of wants and knowledge that poses the interesting problems for social theory to which we now turn.

---

[33] There is also a stronger form of this argument that denies any possibility of intelligently explaining observed behavior from an external point of view. If one takes this argument seriously and regards its consequences, then one will necessarily reach a solipsistic position, interesting for philosophical speculation but uninteresting for scientific purposes. This radical doubt negates every possibility of explaining both individual behavior and social phenomena. To this radical skepticism, Hume's answer is still valid (1751/1975, pp. 159f.): "For here is the chief and most confounding objection to *excessive* scepticism, that no durable good can ever result from it; while it remains in its full force and vigour. We need only ask such sceptic, *What his meaning is? And what he proposes by all these curious researches?* He is immediatly at a loss, and knows not what to answer."

PART II

INSTITUTIONS

5

Shared Mental Models

Emergence and Evolution

5.1. THE ISSUE OF SOCIAL ORDER

Having given a detailed account of the problem-solving model of individual behavior in Part I of this study, we turn now to the issue of social interaction. Our main thesis is that an application of these behavioral assumptions for explanatory purposes of social sciences must proceed in two steps: First, the rise of an institutional framework must be accounted for, before, in a second stage, the social interaction *within* this institutional framework can be analyzed. The main idea, thus, is that the whole socioeconomic process is structured and directed through the institutions prevailing at a certain time and place. The set of given institutions provide the proper filter through which social and economic relationships must be viewed. Analytically, this two-stage procedure offers a twin solution to the main issue of social theory: the Hobbesian problem of social order. The problem of social order has its roots in the diagnosed self-interested behavior and the resulting potential interindividual conflict. Since the pursuit of self-interest or the striving for utility increase is an anthropological constant, a permanent source of conflict seems to exist in every society. From this social impasse, two exits seem to be possible: The first concerns the possibility of inventing and following social rules that may restrict the self-interested activity of *all or some* of the members of society. The second is the realization of mutual advantage in exchange processes. Traditionally, the first solution is addressed by political theory; the second is usually the domain of economists. As Parsons (1968) has argued, in the history of the social sciences, different authors have usually solved the problem of social order *either* by stressing the importance of (formal or informal) rules *or* by pointing to the division of labor and the gains of trade. More recently, research has focused on the possibility of solving the

Hobbesian problem of social order by stressing *both* aspects: the emergence of an order of general rules and the realization of the gains of trade within rules.

The influential Freiburg School in Germany, which is associated with the names of Walter Eucken and Franz Böhm, has stressed the interdependence of the legal order and the market order. Their main argument was that the institutional framework of an economy, understood as the entire set of legal rules, can decisively channel economic activity. Although they clearly recognized the importance of private property rights, they nevertheless failed to discuss in detail the process by which the legal rules of a society emerge. Their pioneering contribution is thus restricted to the analysis of how a competitive order – *Wettbewerbsordnung* – can be established with the aid of appropriate rules. They did not pay any attention to the issue of the emergence of rules themselves.

This theoretical gap has been filled primarily by Hayek. His theory of cultural evolution provides an explanation of how social rules emerge spontaneously, that is, as the unintended outcome of free interaction of individuals separately pursuing their own ends. The evolution of cultural rules of conduct thus plays a prominent role in Hayek's social theory, since following these rules by the individual members of society give rise to the market as a spontaneous order. Hayek's theory therefore explains both the emergence of rules and the emergence of market order within such rules. The overemphasis on evolutionary arguments in Hayek's work (especially the latest) leaves unanswered the question of the deliberate design of rules and the respective processes of collective choice, though.

North's recent work on institutional change, with its emphasis on the subjective mental models of agents, stresses the role of institutions in economic growth and provides a link between rules and outcomes. Collective choice is addressed by Constitutional Political Economy, a research program associated with James Buchanan, which deals with the issue of social order in a two-step procedure. His distinction between a constitutional and a subconstitutional level, that is, the level of rules and the level of actions within rules, provides the proper focus for the analysis of social phenomena. An elaboration of institutional problems in general is provided by different economic theories summarized under the title of "New Institutional Economics" (Furubotn and Richter, 1997) or simply "Institutional Economics" (Hodgson, 1998).

The New Institutionalism in sociology employs a choice-within-constraint framework of analysis and focuses on the social structural context that channels the interaction between individuals and groups

(Nee and Brinton, 1998, p. V). Topics such as how institutions evolve and how informal networks shape economic actions are on the research agenda of the New Institutionalism in sociology (DiMaggio, 1998; DiMaggio and Powell, 1991). Although there is more than one institutionalism in political science, they all share an interest in studying the relationship between institutions and behavior and addressing the issue of how institutions originate and change (Hall and Taylor, 1998, pp. 27ff.).

Our aim in the remaining parts of this book is to enlarge these theories and to provide an account of how institutions emerge and what their role in economic and social outcomes is. The main thrust of our argument is that the problem-solving model elaborated in Part I of this study can explain both the emergence of the institutional structure and the socioeconomic process within this structure. In other words, the problem-solving model provides analytical clarity for a consistent two-step explanation of social interaction.

This chapter will deal with the issue of shared experiences and mental models of individuals in a society, as this is a prerequisite for the analysis of the emergence of social institutions. The informal (Chapter 7) and the formal institutions (Chapter 8) of a society can emerge only when individuals share the same cognitive structure. Although the social processes described in this and the following chapters run largely parallel to each other, it is better for analytical reasons to assume now that the construction of shared mental models discussed in this chapter takes place independently of any potential conflict between individuals.

5.2. THE EMERGENCE OF SHARED MENTAL MODELS

We mentioned in Section 3.1. that the knowledge of every individual consists, regarding its origin, of three parts:

- genetic knowledge,
- cultural knowledge, and
- atomistic knowledge

After stressing the fact that genetic knowledge is irrelevant for the purposes of the social sciences (since we can safely assume that it is common among *all* individuals in a society), we then described the mechanism of individual learning and how this learning affects behavior. But we have been silent on the issue of where individual knowledge comes from and what its exact content is. Addressing this problem leads us directly to the analysis of the first social phenomenon: the emergence of social or cultural knowledge. Here we will distinguish between static and dynamic aspects. Section 5.2. focuses to the static aspect of cultural knowledge. We will consider the dynamic aspect in the discussion of the evolution of cultural knowledge in Section 5.3. In these first stages of the argument, we shall abstract from motivational issues and the possibility of conflict between individuals.

When an individual faces a new problem, he always possesses at least one possible way to solve it: to utilize ready-made solutions from the environment. This fact of direct learning instead of creating new alternatives ex nihilo each time a new problem arises means, of course, that the individual communicates with other individuals in his environment. The direct product of this communication is the "insertion of rules" in the form of problem solutions introduced into the cognitive system of the individual from the cognitive system of other individuals. In a simple model of communication, we can assume that the cognitive rules of a sender are adopted by a receiver, with the effect that after the communication act has taken place, both sender and receiver possess the same cognitive rule or rules. Acts of communication then lead to shared rules between individuals and thus give rise to correspondent default hierarchies and, in the end, to *shared mental models* (Denzau and North, 1994) (see Fig. 2).

The static aspect of these shared mental models is that they provide the framework of a common interpretation of reality. In other words, the first effect of two or more individuals sharing common cognitive structures such as mental models is that they shape the sensual input in the same way. If one generalizes this model and applies it to communication among several persons in a group or society, then it is clear that a common interpretation of reality becomes the foundation of any further social interaction. The first important (static) function of shared mental models among members of a society is the emergence of a social reality in the brains of individuals.[1]

Cognitive anthropology has recently developed a number of methods to explore empirically the content of shared mental models or, more gener-

---

[1] Koch (1995) presents a similar model, although he does not use the notion of shared mental models (p. 103): "In other words, this means that each economic subject first experiences a kind of *individual reality*. Only through *communication* will a common reality develop in certain areas. Through this, it will become possible for individuals to win partially common perceptions of facts and to pursue common goals." (Translation by C.M.). On communication see, e.g., Merten, Schmidt, and Weischenber (1994).

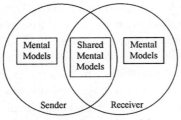

Fig. 2 Shared mental models.

ally, cognitive structures across cultures (D'Andrade, 1995). This type of theory is extremely important since it abandons both the structuralist and interpretive views of culture in favor of a more testable approach. Besides, cognitive anthropology does not view culture as a complex, integrated whole but rather as "socially inherited solutions to life problems" (ibid., p. 249) that are shared by the members of a group.[2] It seems thus that one does well to follow the advice of D'Andrade when trying to shed some light on questions associated with culture. "Of course, one can study in a scientific way the elements of culture, but to find out why cultural elements exist and how they fit together one has to step *outside* the concept of culture and look for whatever it is that creates and organizes these elements, such as the problem of biological reproduction, or the problem of getting food out of the environment, or human cognitive limitations, or personality needs, or whatever." (ibid., p. 250).

5.3. THE EVOLUTION OF SHARED MENTAL MODELS

The existence of shared mental models at a certain moment in time is important because it provides the cognitive condition for every social interaction. Still more important is the evolution of shared mental models over time because it concerns the possibility of the growth of social knowledge. According to the three types of knowledge – (a) genetic knowledge, (b) cultural knowledge, and (c) atomistic knowledge – which refer to the origin of the knowledge of every individual in a society, we can

---

[2] Prominent sociologists like DiMaggio also contend that culture is inconsistent rather than unitary and internally coherent across groups and situations. DiMaggio, in his excellent paper on "Culture and Cognition" (1997), suggests that culture works "through the interaction of shared cognitive structures" (p. 264) and draws attention to the ingenious empirical techniques that permit access to mental structures "going far toward closing the observability gap between external and subjective aspects of culture" (p. 266).

ask how this knowledge grows through time. These three categories of knowledge correspond to three levels of learning: *biological evolution, cultural evolution,* and *individual learning.*

One can roughly say that biological evolution leads to genetic knowledge, cultural evolution to cultural knowledge, and individual learning to atomistic knowledge. But this is no one-to-one correspondence. For example, we have seen in Chapter 3 that individual learning can best be modeled as a trial-and-error process. But obviously, the direct individual learning based only on the direct experience that the agent gets from his natural and social environments is an immensely slow process. Rather, it is indirect learning from other individuals that contributes most to the growth of individual knowledge. Only when agents can share their experiences and *problem solutions* with other agents can their knowledge grow in a rapid way. Some recent simulation models provide evidence that the rate of direct learning is much smaller than the corresponding rate of culturally or socially mediated learning (Hutchins and Hazlehurst, 1992.)[3] Cultural learning, for example, halves the time required to learn the relation between moon phases and tides (ibid., p. 703). Given the three levels of learning and their complex interrelationships, one is led to ask what kind of theory could provide a satisfactory explanation of the growth and transmission of knowledge.

The Gene-Culture Coevolutionary Theory (Boyd and Richerson, 1985, 1994; Durham, 1991; Laland, Kumm, and Feldman, 1995) explores how biological evolution and cultural change can influence each other. Boyd and Richerson (1985; 1994) developed a "dual inheritance model" that is important for our purposes because it provides a general hypothesis of how whole phenotypes are formed and transmitted from generation to generation. According to Boyd and Richerson, phenotypes of a population are transmitted by a process of both genetic and cultural evolution. Their main idea can be best illustrated with the aid of the diagram (Fig. 3) reproduced from Boyd and Richerson (1985, p. 6).

Starting from a population with a certain distribution of phenotypes F_{t-1}, there are two principal ways of transmitting the phenotypic traits to the next generation. The first is via mutation, recombination, and selection, which is basically a process of genetic transmission, followed by ontogeny (including ordinary learning). The second way is social or collective learning, which "causes the communication of phenotypic traits

---

[3] On social learning theories see, e.g., Boyd and Richerson (1985, pp. 38ff.) and Witt 1987a (pp. 115ff.).

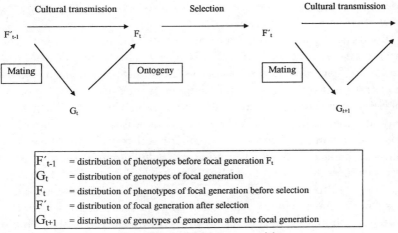

Fig. 3 The dual inheritance model.

directly from individual to individual" (Boyd and Richerson, 1985, p. 6). This second process of transmission is very important "because it ensures that culture is a population level phenomenon" (ibid.).[4]

In terms of the diagram, "to predict F_t one must know G_t, the state of the environment and the distribution of phenotypes in the previous generations, F'_{t-1}" (ibid.). As the members of the population interact with their environments in order to gather resources for purposes of reproduction, selection acts on the population, increasing the frequency of some phenotypes – the ones mostly adapted to their environment – and decreasing the frequency of others. The resulting distribution of phenotypes of the focal generation after selection is F'_t, and the process starts anew.

The main idea of Boyd and Richerson thus is that both genetic and cultural inheritance determine the phenotypic character of a population: "That is, the evolution of a cultural organism is a process that transforms the joint distribution of genotypes and phenotypes. Put another way, phenotypic characters acquired via social learning can be thought of as a pool of cultural traits that coevolves with the gene pool in a way that characters acquired through ordinary learning without culture do not.

---

4 That culture is a population-level phenomenon does not mean that it exists independently of every single individual in the population. It possesses a collective character only to the extent that it is shared by the individuals.

Social learning causes the acquisition of phenotypes to be a population level phenomenon" (1985, p. 7.)[5]

Boyd and Richerson thus reject the view of human sociobiology, which attempts to explain human behavior only on the basis of models of genetic evolution. They defend their theory as a complete treatment of the relevant transmission process in populations of humans, which necessarily includes both genetic and cultural transmission. This view is correct in a way because, as Boyd and Richerson stress, "it is not sufficient to know how the existing structures of human cultural transmission give rise to cultural change; we must also understand *why* human cultural transmission has these structures. . . . Most theorists in the social sciences do not feel any need to understand how these structures and processes that they posit might have evolved. We believe that this is a serious error. Ultimately, the human sciences must be unified with the physical and biological ones" (p. 12).

We believe that the framework of problem solving developed in Part I of this study is sufficient to prove that genetically inherited structures condition the way individuals learn. But once this step has been taken it seems to be unimportant *for the issue of social order* to inquire further into the problems of genetic inheritance.[6] The acquisition of beliefs and values by the members of a society takes place in a process of cultural evolution that is much faster than genetic transmission. In Figure 3a, our focus is on the upper part.

---

[5] Boyd and Richerson, in the following sentences of the citation given in the text, are clearly stressing the individual character of their theory: "This does not mean that cultures have mysterious lives of their own that cause them to evolve independently of the individuals of which they are composed. As in the case of genetic evolution, individuals are the primary focus of the evolutionary forces that cause cultural evolution. . . ." (1985, p. 7)

[6] For other issues this may not be true, of course. Laland, Kumm and Feldman (1995) present a case study and show how the sex ratio can change in a population as a consequence of cultural processes that result in excess female mortality. Besides, there is no need to derive any genetically hardwired preferences for reciprocity or cooperation as an outcome of human evolution, as, for example, Ben-Ner and Putterman do (1998, pp. 30ff.). Such tendencies may be hardwired in us (Mansbridge, 1998), but there is no need to formulate this ambiguous hypothesis as long as one hypothesizes a hardwired cognitive capacity to learn. The reason is that one can easily explain the observed social phenomen of cooperation based solely on the ability of humans to learn while trying to increase their own utility as will be showed in Section 7.2, without employing any further assumptions about other hardwired characteristics of human nature. In other words, for the purpose of social theory, it is methodologically appropriate to be parsimonious with the assumptions about the content of genotypes in humans.

Fig. 3a The dual inheritance model (upper part).

Summarizing, biological evolution and learning at the level of the species are important mainly in exploring the cognitive architecture of the individual. Once this step has been taken, the growth and transmission of genetic knowledge become unimportant for social science since its quantity and quality remains relatively stable for many generations. Accordingly, one should concentrate on the mechanisms of cultural evolution, which provide much more rapid growth and transmission of human knowledge than genetic evolution.

5.4. CULTURAL EVOLUTION AS COLLECTIVE LEARNING?

The process of cultural evolution concerns the growth and transmission of knowledge in time at the societal level. Cultural evolution can therefore be regarded as a process of "collective learning."

Thus, the question asked here is how the knowledge of a society, understood as its problem-solving capacity, grows and is transmitted through time.[7] In order to answer this question, it will be helpful to recall the distinction between theoretical and practical problems encountered in Section 3.3. Growth of knowledge in society means, on the one hand, the growth of theoretical problem solutions and, on the other hand, the growth of practical problem solutions acquired by the individuals of a society. Or, to put it in other terms, one can distinguish between theoretical and practical knowledge when discussing the mechanism and means of their growth and transmission.

Starting with theoretical knowledge (i.e., knowledge of the type "knowing that"), it is clear that we are dealing here with knowledge of causal relationships, that is, scientific knowledge, as well as with knowledge of singular objects and events. The growth of scientific knowledge is an evolutionary process of trial and error in which the *scientists as problem solvers*[8] are engaged in solving theoretical problems. What we call

---

[7] See the interesting remarks of Goody (1998) on the role of literacy in the diffusion of knowledge across cultures and times.

[8] Scientific work in general can be sufficiently modeled as a problem-solving activity in the Popperian tradition. Simon views even scientific discovery as a problem-solving activity: "The scientist does not think in ways that are qualitatively different from the

science is produced in an *invisible-hand process*[9] whereby individual scientists solve the problems that they perceive as important without the intention of creating a corpus of scientific knowledge as such. Scientific knowledge is in this sense objective knowledge because it exists independently of the beliefs, cognitive structures, and so on of the separate scientists. This corpus of objective knowledge is then transmitted from generation to generation with the aid of *symbols* (i.e., natural and formal languages) as the means of communication.

Thus, scientific knowledge can be interpreted as "the unplanned product of human actions" that "transcends its makers" (Popper, 1972/1992, p. 159f.) and, hence, becomes an autonomous stock of knowledge that is available in society at any moment in time and is transmittable through language. Popper, who was the most prominent exponent of the problem-solving model for the growth and transmission of scientific knowledge, placed his approach in his later writings within his framework of the "three worlds." World I consists of physical objects, World II of states of consciousness and World III of objective contents of thought that mainly include scientific and poetic thought and works of art (Popper, 1972/1992, p. 106). The three worlds interact with each other (Popper and Eccles, 1977/1983, chapter P2), that is, there are causal relations between them (Popper, 1972/1992, p. 155f.). For our present purposes, it is important to note that World III interacts with World II in a dual sense. On the one hand, scientists trying to understand their theoretical problems are undertaking "a World II attempt to grasp a World III object" (Popper and Eccles, 1977/1983, p. 39). And, on the other hand – which is relevant here – World III objects may at any moment in time become World II objects, that is, the corpus of scientific knowledge can be transmitted to the minds of the individuals in a society and become part of their mental models. The evolution of scientific knowledge has a direct counterpart in the current states of consciousness of the individuals in the society and, thus, an evolution of shared mental models concerning theoretical problem solutions takes place. Or, in other words, there is a feedback mechanism by

ways in which other professionals think, or the ways in which college students think when confronted with puzzles to solve in the psychological laboratory, or the ways in which T.C. Mits (the common man in the street) thinks" (Simon, 1992b, p. 105f.). Simon equates further the "intuition" that is supposed to lead to a scientific discovery with the common process of recognition: "if the signatures of intuition and insight are suddenness of discovery and incomplete awareness of the discovery path, then these earmarks do not distinguish these two processes from the well known and well understood process that we call 'recognition'." (Simon, 1992b, p. 116).

[9] See Chapter 6 for invisible-hand explanations.

which the objective knowledge created by scientists in an evolutionary process is absorbed by the individual minds in a society and thus gains a subjective dimension in the form of *shared mental models* of the individuals.[10]

Donald (1991), in his account of the *Origins of the Modern Mind*, stresses the importance of what he calls "External Symbolic Storage" for the transmission and accumulation of knowledge across generations. The critical innovation that has massively supported the evolution of theoretic culture was the simple habit of recording ideas, that is, "of *externalizing the process* of oral commentary on events" (p. 342), which occurred in ancient Greece from around 700 B.C. The new element was that "for the first time in history complex ideas were placed in the public arena, in an external medium, where they could undergo refinement over the longer term, that is, well beyond the life-span of single individuals" (p. 344). These External Symbolic Storage Networks have decisively driven forward theoretical knowledge, since they provided the possibility of a constant interaction between the corpus of theoretical-scientific knowledge and the theoretical problems of the individuals in a society. In other words, Donalds theory seems to formulate in scientific-cognitive terms the metaphysical theory of Popper.[11]

What about the other part of theoretical knowledge, that is, the knowledge of singular objects and events? This knowledge of singular objects and events existing at a certain time and place cannot "grow" in the sense that it extends through time, as scientific knowledge does. This kind of

---

10 Two closely associated issues are not discussed because they do not possess immediate relevance for our main problem. The first relates to the rate of growth of scientific knowledge, i.e., to whether scientific knowledge grows at a more or less steady rate or in a revolutionary way. Kuhn (1962/1970), for example, supports the view that scientific knowledge grows decisively in scientific revolutions that coincide with changes in paradigms. The second issue concerns the grade of formality of the process of scientific growth and the degree of openness of science. In different historical epochs, scientific research is organized in different ways, which obviously need not be similar to the well-organized activity taking place in modern universities and research centers. Besides, modern science is more open in the sense that scientific findings are placed in the public realm, reducing access costs (Mokyr, 1998, p. 12). In earlier historical epoches, "science was more proprietary and some parts of [it] (like alchemy and medical knowledge) actively kept secret" (Mokyr, 1998, p. 12).

11 It is interesting to compare Donald's account of the transition from mythic to theoretic culture with Bruno Snell's classic philological treatise on the same subject (1975/1986). Donald's approach schows how powerful the tools of the cognitive science can be even when applied to such complex issues as transitions in the attitudes of the mind.

knowledge exists in the brains of the members of a society, and diversity is its characteristic feature. Since every individual possesses heterogeneous knowledge of the particular forms of his environment, one cannot meaningfully talk about the growth of such knowledge. Thus, this knowledge remains to a great extent individualistic and constitutes what we have called "atomistic" knowledge.

But such knowledge can nevertheless be transmitted within groups. In small groups, such as families or firms, the transmission of such knowledge is an everyday phenomenon; but even in large groups such as societies, atomistic knowledge can be communicated. Repeated acts of communication, in which the knowledge elements concern particular objects of the physical and social environments, lead to the possession of the same cognitive rules on the part of the members of a society. Against the background of these cognitive rules, which are shared by more individuals, the interpretation of social reality tends to be homogenized, that is, the same patterns of interpretation are employed (Bandura, 1986, Chapter 2). Repeated acts of communication between members of a community lead to the diffusion of such knowledge of singular objects and events and, in the end, to *shared mental models* of the particular characteristic of the social and physical environments.[12]

The vast diversity of human culture recorded by anthropologists refers partly to mental models of this kind that are shared by members of a cultural community. What we call cultural heritage is, to a great extent, such common knowledge. When members of a society share the same experiences, that is, have the same history, acknowledge the same symbols, and so on, the divergence of their mental models tends to be reduced.[13] As Denzau and North (1994, p. 15) put it: "the cultural heritage

---

12 See Witt (1995, p. 15): "Through communication processes individuals have a tendency to develop within a social environment certain similarities in their patterns of interpretation and attitudes. Circles of communication have an 'agenda-setting' effect. This then establishes in the same, self-perpetuating manner, the frequency with which the determined pieces of information (at the expense of potential competing pieces of information) will be exchanged and be attended to by all those individuals participating." (Translation by C. M.)

13 D'Andrade (1995), in developing his "cognitive anthropology" remarks (p. 182): "Cognitive representations – properties, prototypes, schemas, models, theories – make up the stuff of culture in the mind. These representations are adaptive in simply being representations, that is, in providing maps of the world. Such a function is not trivial, since effective action requires an understanding of how the world is organized." For a more holistic view of culture as a cognitive system, see Hutchins (1995). For an illuminating discussion on the relationship between cognition and

provides a means of reducing the divergence in the mental models that people in a society have and also constitutes a means for the intergenerational transfer of unifying perceptions. We may think of culture as encapsulating the experiences of past generations of any particular group."

The fact that people with the same culture acknowledge some common symbols and share the same history facilitates the common perception and interpretation of new objects and events.[14] Thus, in a way, there is a kind of path dependency in the formation of shared mental models.[15] Hence, the more shared mental models are formed, the more homogeneous the attention, perception, and, in the end, interpretation of certain features of the environment will tend to be, and thus even more shared mental models will emerge. It can thus be safely hypothesized that some kind of self-reinforcing mechanism will occur that encourages the formation of a large number of *shared* mental models of this kind in society.[16]

Apart from theoretical knowledge, the other main type of knowledge is the practical knowledge of the know-how type. As we have discussed in Section 3.3, all the skills that a person possesses are of this kind. Swimming, cooking, walking, riding a bicycle, driving a car, typing a paper, playing games, and so on are all skills acquired by solving practical problems. The main characteristic of this knowledge of how to perform certain tasks is that it is not expressible in linguistic terms. The growth of this knowledge in society can also be understood as an evolutionary process of trial and error, but the *transmission mechanism* of this kind of knowledge is different. It consists of the direct imitation of the performance of others. Know-how is thus transmitted from one generation to another by example and imitation. Since such practical knowledge is important for the everyday life of *all individuals* in a society, one can safely hypothesize that it will both grow and be transmitted at the societal level. Better methods and techniques for performing tasks of everyday life will be tried out and selected by imitation because every single member of a society is interested

---

social context, see Knight (1997). See also Stahl (1998) and the review article of Sperber and Hirschfeld (1999).

[14] See Witt (1995, p. 15): "Moreover, for people of the same social environment, what is yielded is a general intersection, to a greater or lesser degree, in the symbolic representations of knowledge, which yields corresponding similarities in the development of their conscious states." (Translation by C. M.)

[15] Kiwit and Voigt also use the term "path dependency" – known mainly in economics – in their short discussion of the issue of perception (1995, p. 134f.)

[16] This argument, I think, finds considerable support by Holland et al. (1986, ch. 3, esp. p. 97f., and ch. 7).

in improving his own life. Thus, such knowledge will spread in society and will become part of the knowledge of every individual.

Summarizing, the growth of theoretical scientific knowledge occurs in an evolutionary process over time in societies. Theoretical knowledge of single events and objects, on the other hand, can only be communicated and diffused among individuals and therefore cannot be meaningfully assumed to grow over time. This does not mean, though, that this kind of knowledge cannot be utilized in a way that is wealth-enhancing. In fact, it can be utilized for this purpose, as we will discuss in Section 12.3. Theoretical scientific knowledge is transmitted through formal and natural languages, whereas practical knowledge can be communicated only by imitation. In this sense, one can speak of a process of *collective learning* in which the problem-solving capacity of the society grows and is transmitted through time, and which refers mainly to scientific and practical knowledge.

But obviously, when one speaks of cultural evolution as collective learning, one does not refer only to these categories of knowledge. In Hayek's theory of cultural evolution, for example, where the growth of civilization is equated with the growth of knowledge, the word "knowledge" is meant to "include all the human adaptations to environment in which past experience has been incorporated" (Hayek, 1960, p. 26). Hence, knowledge does not include "only the conscious, explicit knowledge of individuals, the knowledge which enables us to state that this or that is so and so. Still less can this knowledge be confined to scientific knowledge" (ibid., p. 25). Moreover, it includes "our habits and skills, our emotional attitudes, our tools, and our institutions – all . . . adaptations to past experience which have grown up by selective elimination of less suitable conduct" (ibid., p. 26). Hayek contends, thus, that not only our scientific and practical knowledge are growing and being transmitted through time, but also our social rules and *institutions*.

This point is of obvious importance for our discussion. So far. we have been silent on the issue of whether socially relevant knowledge, that is, knowledge concerning the solution of *social* problems, can also be meaningfully understood to grow and be transmitted over time. If this were true, then it would mean that problems of social interaction are spontaneously solved in a process of cultural evolution and that the whole framework of institutions in a society is the product of a process of collective learning. Thus, the interesting issue, formulated in general terms, becomes the following: Can a general process of cultural evolution be safely modeled and understood as a process of collective learning independently of what the cultural "memes" are?[17]

Hayek, who was one of the first to work out a general theory of cultural evolution, answers this question affirmatively.[18] He draws the analogy of social rules, used by individuals to solve the recurrent problems of social interaction, with *tools* that in the same way serve to provide standard solutions to recurrent problems.[19] His main argument is that "the various institutions and habits, tools and methods of doing things, which . . . constitute our inherited civilization" (1960, p. 62) have been submitted to "the slow test of time" (1967, p. 111) in an evolutionary process of trial and error, (1976/1982, p. 135). "Those rules which have evolved in the process of growth of society embody the experience of many more trials and errors than any individual mind could acquire" (Hayek, 1967, p. 88). According to Hayek, people, mostly in a subconscious manner, acquire and follow social rules that provide solutions to recurrent problems of social interaction in a quasi-automatic way.

There are two main arguments against this view of cultural evolution in the work of Hayek. The first concerns the notion of group selection found in many parts of Hayeks work. Hayek, in explaining the evolution of culture, stresses, on the one hand, the *innovation* of individuals experimenting with new rules, and, on the other hand, the *competition* between old and new rules and the *selection* of those that led to the success of those groups who practiced them (Hayek, 1979/1982, p. 204, n48). The criterion of selection is thus group success or, in other words, the "*transmission* of rules of conduct takes place *from individual to individual,* while what may be called the natural *selection* of rules will operate on the basis

---

[17] As Opp puts it, the interesting issue here is whether "the same hypothesis can explain the evolution of each of the items included in the term 'culture'" (Opp, 1994, p. 93)

[18] Hayek develops his argument clearly, aiming at some normative implications. His main purpose is to provide proof that individuals, when left free to interact, will give rise to a spontaneous process of cultural evolution which is in some sense beneficial or efficient. In our discussion we will deliberately neglect Hayek's controversial normative conclusions. Since our focus in this book is exclusively positive, it is only the theoretical content of Hayek's account of cultural evolution that is of interest here.

[19] "[W]e command many tools – in the widest sense of the world – which the human race has evolved and which enable us to deal with our environment. These are the results of the experience of successive generations which are handed down. And, once a more efficient tool is available, it will be used without our knowing why it is better, or even what the alternatives are" (Hayek, 1960, p. 27).

of greater or less efficiency on the resulting *order of the group*" (Hayek, 1967, p. 67).

The argument against group selection is that it is incompatible with the postulate of methodological individualism. Accordingly, one has to show a relevant feedback mechanism relating how, in the end, individuals within groups are at least indirectly benefited by following certain cultural rules. Hayek, mainly in his last book, *The Fatal Conceit* (1988, ch. 8), illustrates criteria of group success in terms of *population size* or *population growth* which clearly are not individualistic in any meaningful sense: "We may not like the fact that our rules were shaped mainly by their suitability for increasing our numbers, but we have little choice in the matter now (if we ever did). . . . In any case, our desires and wishes are largely irrelevant" (p. 134). But in order to offer a consistent explanation of cultural evolution in terms of group selection, one must explain "how individuals in a group come to follow rules that make the group successful. If there is a collective goods problem involved, the simple argument that the respective rules are group-beneficial is per se not sufficient for an explanation" (Vanberg, 1994b, p. 199, n33). In order for Hayek's theory to hold, one should therefore assume altruistic behavior on behalf of *every* member of the group. This cannot safely be hypothesized, though, because the existence of even one free rider, who enjoys the group's advantage without sharing the group costs, would suffice to falsify the assumption.[20]

As in every theoretical debate, the controversy about the role of group selection in the process of cultural evolution can only be resolved by empirical evidence. Soltis, Boyd, and Richerson (1995) present and elaborate on data on patterns of group extinction, group formation, and between-group variation in New Guinea. Their sample of ethnographic studies includes close to 100 societies, for which the percentage of groups suffering extinction each generation ranges from 1.6 percent to 31.3 per-

---

[20] Hodgson (1991) argues, contrary to Vanberg, that group selection might be relevant in a socioeconomic context, and by analogy to some biological arguments, he contends that multiple levels of selection can be distinguished in the socioeconomic world. "Given this, Hayek should be criticized, not for embracing group selection and eschewing a consistent individualism, but for failing to incorporate additional processes of selection above the group level, involving the selection of different types of institutions, including both market and non-market forms" (1991, p. 79). But Hodgson's account is unclear on how exactly these different levels of selection are supposed to work and whether there are interactions between them. Vromen (1995, pp. 171ff.) tries to provide consistency on the Hayekian notion of group selection by employing arguments of semantic nature.

cent (p. 477). From their calculations, they conclude that group selection on the basis of culture plays a greater role than the discredited mechanism of group selection in biology, where one often speaks of the "group selection fallacy." Nevertheless, their evidence suggests that group selection is unlikely to lead to the spread of a single group-beneficial trait in less than 500 to 1,000 years. Thus, group selection seems to be "too slow to account for the many cases of cultural change which occur in less than 500 to 1,000 years" (p. 482).

The second argument against Hayeks theory of cultural evolution concerns the rules-as-tools analogy.[21] Although all *personal* rules followed by individuals can easily be understood as tools to solve personal problems, social rules cannot always be viewed with the aid of the rules-as-tools analogy. This analogy "is less applicable the less the rules in question are susceptible to individual experimenting and selecting. . . . It is less plausible for rules that can only be tried out in collective experiments, in particular if the collective is a political community as opposed to, for instance, a private organization operating in a market environment" (Vanberg, 1994b, p. 187f.). One has to distinguish, thus, between levels of experimenting with rules and levels of selection of rules – for example, whether it is individual agents or collective entities such as local authorities or national governments inventing and imitating new social rules.[22] Accord-

21 See Hayek (1973/1982, p. 21): "Like all general purpose tools, rules serve because they have become adapted to the solution of recurring problem situations and thereby help to make the members of the society in which they prevail more effective in the pursuit of their aims. Like a knife or a hammer they have been shaped not with a particular purpose in view but because in this form rather than in some other form they have proved serviceable in a great variety of situations. They have not been constructed to meet foreseen particular needs but have been selected in a process of evolution. The knowledge which has given them their shape is not knowledge of particular future effects but knowledge of the recurrence of certain problem situations or tasks, of intermediate results regularly to be achieved in the service of a great variety of ultimate aims; and much of this knowledge exists not as an enumerable list of situations for which one has to be prepared, or of the importance of the kind of problems to be solved, or of the probability that they will arise, but as a propensity to act in certain types of situations in a certain manner."
22 On this issue see Vanberg (1992, p. 114f.), where he stresses: "The 'rules as tools' analogy . . . makes it appear as if the experimenting with and selecting among potential alternatives is essentially a matter of separate individual choices in both cases, for tools as well as for rules. . . . It seems obvious, however, that it is not generally applicable in the realm of rules and institutions. . . . To mention only two particular obvious examples: It is hardly possible for an individual driver to experiment with a 'left-driving rule' in a community where driving on the right side of the road is the rule; and it is simply unfeasible for an individual citizen to try out a new rule for electing a parliament – even if such individuals would firmly believe in the superiority of an alternative practice."

ingly, only those social rules individually tried out and individually imitated, if successful, can safely be hypothesized as serving as a "storage house" of experience for past generations.[23]

Concluding, Hayek's affirmative answer to the question of whether a spontaneous process of cultural evolution can lead to the full solution of the Hobbesian problem of social order does not hold. At least in modern societies, the framework of social rules does not emerge exclusively in an evolutionary process of spontaneous solutions to social problems without any deliberate collective choice. Hayek himself, in other parts of his work, seems to admit that collective or state action is necessary,[24] that is, he accepts the existence of "those rules which, because we can deliberately alter them, become the chief instrument whereby we can affect the resulting order, namely the rules of law" (Hayek 1973/1982, p. 45). Thus, a more differentiated and systematic analysis of the institutions of a society is necessary in order to account for their emergence, function, and change through time.

[23] The accumulation of experience in traditions and institutions, if true, has two important consequences. The first concerns the implications for economic growth, since a set of rules transmitted from generation to generation might be the appropriate ones to facilitate the competitive market process and thus to enable growth. This obviously important consequence will be discussed in Chapter 12. The second concerns the effects that such rules have in structuring the relations in a society. This aspect is relevant here.

[24] See, e.g., Hayek (1960, p. 62): "In some instances it would be necessary, for the smooth running of society, to secure a similar uniformity by coercion, if such conventions or rules were not observed often enough."

6

Explaining Institutions

6.1. INSTITUTIONS: INTRODUCTION

Institutions are normative social rules, that is, the rules of the game in a society, enforced either through law or through other mechanisms of social control that shape human interaction.[1]

Institutions as normative patterns of behavior serve to (partially) solve the problem of cooperation in a society by providing a more or less permanent platform of conflict resolution. They define the rules of the socioeconomic game, that is, the strategies that individuals are allowed to employ in order to follow and solve their problems. The existence of social institutions provides the first step toward overcoming the Hobbesian problem of social order, the second being the cooperation of individuals via exchange within institutional framework.

In both the economic and sociological literatures, the term "institution" is often used to designate organizations of every kind. To avoid confusion, it is useful to distinguish sharply between institutions constituting the rules of the game and organizations as corporate actors, that is, as groups of individuals bound by some rules designed to achieve a common objective (or to solve a common problem). Organizations as "corporate actors," as Coleman (1990a) calls them, are collective units characterized by a set of procedural rules that define the coordination of

---

[1] This definition follows those of both North and Parsons. According to North's definition (1990, p. 3): "Institutions are the rules of the game in a society or, more formally, are the humanly devised constraints that shape human interaction. In consequence they structure incentives in human exchange, whether political, social or economic." According to Parsons (1975, p. 97): "Institutions . . . are complexes of normative rules and principles which, either through law or other mechanism of social control, serve to regulate social action and relationships of course with varying degrees of success."

the individual members who have pooled their resources for a joint purpose.[2] They might be political organizations such as political parties, economic organizations such as firms, or educational organizations such as universities. The important point is that the rules that are constitutive for an organization as a corporate actor are relevant only for those individuals who pool their resources for a common use, not for all the members of the society. Thus, organizations when dealing with other organizations or with individuals, are submitted to those general social rules that we have called institutions, that is, they are equally constrained by the general rules of the game.

Explaining institutions is a very difficult enterprise. One of the main difficulties is that a sufficient explanation of institutions must address a series of questions that, although in a way connected, nevertheless require separate answers. An important first step toward a successful explanation is thus to ask the right questions, that is, to formulate clearly the explananda phenomena. A typical example of asking the wrong question is the case of the "functionalist fallacy" often found in sociology. This fallacy is based on the assumption that the identification of the benefits that an institution or more generally a social structure provides to a group, whether a small community or a society, also provides an answer to the question of why this institution exists and is maintained. Hence, by asking how an institution "functions," one must get, if not careful in the line of argumentation, a wrong explanation.[3]

To come to our main point: In our view a proper agenda for a study of institutions should include theoretical consideration of four issues. In other words there are four questions to be asked and answered in order to reach a coherent theory of institutions:

1. Why do institutions exist?
2. How do institutions emerge?
3. Why do institutions persist or change?
4. How are institutions adopted or enforced?

Before we proceed to the discussion of these four questions, a classification of institutions might be useful. Following the criterion of the enforcement agency of institutions, one can distinguish between formal and informal institutions. Formal institutions are enforced by law, whereas

---

[2] For the distinction between organizations and institutions see Khalil (1995).
[3] For a discussion of functionalist explanations in sociology, see Elster (1979/1984, ch. I.5) and (1983, ch. 2).

Informal Institutions	Conventions	Self-policing
	Moral Rules	First Party
	Social Norms	Third Party: Social Forces, i.e. Individuals of the Group
Formal Institutions	Law	Third Party: State

Fig. 4 The classification of institutions.

informal institutions do not need for their enforcement the state as a controller. Three kinds of informal institutions in a broad sense can be distinguished according to the enforcement agency: conventions as self-policing institutions, moral rules with the individual as a first party controller, and social norms that are enforced by the members of the social group. This classification (Fig. 4) is surely not an exhaustive one, but it offers a first orientation to what will follow. The main method of developing our argument is to attempt to provide some answers to the previously listed four questions concerning each type of institution.

But since all institutions have some common features, the most important being their character as the constitutive rules of the game, we shall first address the four issues on a more general level. Therefore, in this chapter, we shall provide some general reasons why institutions exist, how they emerge, and so on, before discussing more specifically the informal institutions (Chapter 7) and the formal ones (Chapter 8).

6.2. WHY DO INSTITUTIONS EXIST?

There are two classes of reasons that can explain the existence of institutions and both can be derived from the assumptions about individual behavior stated in Part I of this book. The first class of reasons refers to the motivational and the second class to the cognitive architecture of humans. Starting from the main motivational characteristic of human nature, which consists of individual striving to increase one's utility, it is obvious that interindividual conflicts are bound to arise. Settings where the increase of one's utility presupposes the direct or indirect cooperation of other individuals can be defined as social problems. Such settings are not "social" in the sense that the individuals involved are aware of or explicitly recognize that they are involved in such situations. But from an observer's point of view such social problems are clearly identifiable and their main characteristic is that the utility obtained by some kind of individual behavior depends in one way or another on the behavior of other individuals. Some stylized social problems are worked out in game theory, such as the well-known prisoner's dilemma, the coordination game, the game of trust, and so on.

Social rules and institutions thus exist because they provide the means of solving social problems and overcoming social conflict, and this is their most fundamental raison d'être. Life in a society without institutions would be "solitary, poor, nasty, brutish and short," as Hobbes has pessimistically described it. However, social order does not need to arise only when formal institutions enforced by a state exist; social order also exists when people share merely informal institutions. This is dependent on the relative importance of the problem situation as the individuals perceive it in each case and on whether the state as an enforcement agency is needed for social order to prevail. This, in turn, implies that formal and informal institutions sometimes complement each other and at other times act as substitutes for each other. The important fact for the moment, though, is that our first class of reasons explains the very existence of social problems and interindividual conflict as rooted in the self-interested motivations of the members of a society.

This line of argument exists in most social and political theories, and in philosophies, old and new, with the sole exception of those of the anarchists. But even the most optimistic among them usually doubt the necessity of the existence of a state, but they do not deny that at least informal institutions such as morals, social norms, and conventions are necessary for social order. Human egoism must be molded by some form of social control in order for cooperation to emerge, and institutions provide this mold.

But why do people agree on or accept institutions, that is, social normative *rules,* rather than deciding each time anew on particular norms or conventions regulating the particular conflict every time it arises? Why not solve social problems ad hoc since, in a way, every problem situation – and thus also every *social* problem – possesses a unique character? The answer to this question lies in the cognitive structure of the human mind and provides the second class of reasons explaining the existence of social institutions. The human mind is far from being a perfect organ able to perform all the difficult computations needed to solve problems arising from interaction with other minds. Because of the restriction of their cognitive capacity, all individuals mobilize their energies only when a new problem arises and follow routines when they classify the problem situation as a familiar one. This distinction is rooted in their limited computational capacity and is a means to free their minds from unnecessary operations in order to deal adequately with the problem situations arising in their environment.

When we say that the environment of the individual is *complex* we mean precisely this: His limited cognitive capacity makes his environment appear rather complicated to him and needing simplification in order to be mastered. This refers to both the natural and social environments of the individual, the latter being the focus here. Because of the perceived complexity of the social environment, people adopt – consciously or unconsciously – *rules* as solutions to social problems rather than deciding each time anew how to act and react to the settings where coordination with other individuals is needed. Rules in general, as Hayek (1976/1982, p. 8) put it, "are a device for coping with our constitutional ignorance"; they are the "device we have learned to use because our reason is insufficient to master the full detail of complex reality" (Hayek, 1960, p. 66). And social rules or institutions are our devices to deal with *recurrent* social problems arising in situations where self-interested individuals interact.[4]

The anthropologist Arnold Gehlen made the same point when he stressed the role of institutions as a means of unburdening individuals to make decisions permanently. Compared to animal behavior, human behavior, according to Gehlen, is much more plastic and adaptable to varying environments. But this plasticity and openness in behavior, although beneficial, cause uncertainty for an individual concerning the behavior of other individuals. Institutions remove this difficulty[5]: by defining general normative patterns of behavior shared by individuals, they free individuals from the need to decide each time anew. This relief provided by

---

4 Whereas the traditional sociological analysis stressed mainly the normative dimension of institutions, the new institutionalism puts a new emphasis on the cognitive dimension (Hall and Taylor [1998, p. 25], DiMaggio and Powell [1991, p. 15]). See also Lindenberg (1998, p. 718): "In NIS [New Instiutional Sociology] the full internalization argument (which implied moral guidance of behavior) has been replaced by the idea of behavior guided by cognitive processes. . . . The point is that institutionalization is linked to the establishment of cognitive habits which influence the very experience of reality (as a taken-for-granted reality) rather than just the response to reality."

5 See Gehlen (1961, p. 68): "Institutions like laws, marriage, property, etc., appear then to be supportive and formative stabilizers of those driving forces, which, thought of in isolation, appear to be plastic and lacking direction. Each culture 'stylizes' certain modes of behavior, making them obligatory and exemplary for all those who belong to it. For individuals, then, such institutions mean a release or relief from basic decisions and represent an accustomed security of important orientations, so that the behaviors themselves can occur free of reflex, consistently, and in mutual reciprocity." (Translation by C. M.)

institutions is productive, according to Gehlen, because it releases the individual's energies to concentrate on other creative enterprises.[6]

This *Entlastung* (unburdening) through institutions means that the individuals in a society classify the same set of problems as old ones and thus follow the same routines.[7] The legal rule, for example, that a firm pays salaries to its employees at the end of every month makes the problem of "salary payment" appear an old one to both managers and employees, and no decision or debate on this matter needs to take place every month. Managers and employees can concentrate their efforts on other problems and solve them creatively by mobilizing their released energies. On a more general level, the release of energies provided by institutions makes the very development of the individuality and personality of humans appear possible. Because an individual need not be concerned with the issues managed by social institutions, it is possible for him to unfold all those activities that distinguish him from others as a *unique personality*. As Gehlen (1961, p. 72) splendidly puts it: "If the institutions provide us with a schema in certain respects and if they shape our thoughts and feelings along with our behaviors and typify them, we can take advantage of these energy reserves in order to show within our particular set of circumstances the uniqueness which is bountiful, innovative, and fertile. He, who does not want to be a personality in *his own* circumstances but in *all* circumstances, can only fail" (translation by C. M.)[8]

---

6 See Gehlen (1973, p. 97): "This release is productive. This comes as a result of the beneficial degree of certainty, which comes when the individual is sustained from both inside and outside a rule structure. Once this occurs, the cognitive energies are free to flow to the top." (Translation by C. M.). See also DiMaggio (1997, p. 270f.).

7 See Hayek (1967, p. 56): "But the rules of which we are speaking generally control or circumscribe only certain aspects of concrete actions by providing a general schema which is then adapted to the particular circumstances. They will often merely determine or limit the range of possibilities within which the choice is made consciously. By eliminating certain kinds of action altogether and providing certain routine ways of achieving the object, they merely restrict the alternatives on which a conscious choice is required. The moral rules, for example, which have become part of a man's nature will mean that certain conceivable choices will not appear at all among the possibilities between which he chooses." Albert makes the same point (1978, p. 24): "The transmission of more tested and tried resolutions to problems that were generated earlier on is an 'unburdening phenomenon' (*Entlastungsphänomen*) to the extent that it saves actors from making new decisions and expending the concomitant investments in the particular problem area in question. In this way, the potential to divert said time and energies into other problem areas is gained." (Translation by C. M.)

8 Clark (1997), discussing the relationship between external institutions and the human mind, draws attention to what he calls external or environmental "scaffolding" and its role in reducing individual cognitive loads. In his view, "such scaffolding

The existence of institutions is thus also due to cognitive reasons (DiMaggio and Powell, 1991, p. 10f.); they are a means of coping with the ignorance that individuals are facing when interacting with each other. The institutions, as the rules of the game, *stabilize expectations* and thus reduce the uncertainty of the agents.[9] They provide a first structuring of their environment, a first more or less secure approximation of what will happen and what will not, and what will probably appear and what will probably not.

But although the stabilizing *function* of institutions is very important, one should be careful to avoid the functionalist fallacy and therefore distinguish clearly between cause and effect. The stabilization of expectations provided by institutions is the *effect* of their existence. The *cause* of their existence lies – along with the motivational one – rather in the more general fact of the limits of the cognitive capacities of humans.

In closing the discussion on the cognitive set of reasons for the existence of social institutions,[10] a final remark on the structural symmetry

plays a dual role: it both restricts and expands our intellectual horizons" (p. 282). See also Loasby (2000, p. 2ff): "Institutions are necessarily a mixed blessing. Cognitive maps, desicion premises, procedural rules, and the like are necessarily retrospective; they anchor the definition of problems and the repertoire of responses to past environments, and inhibit the range of experimentation. In some circumstances they may be actively misleading. . . . But in applying the logic of appropriateness they relinquish some claims on the imagination, and release it for other use. . . . As G. K. Chesterton once remarked, "A man must be orthodox on most things, or he will never have the time to practice his own heresy." The prominent anthropologist Mary Douglas (1986, p. 69) remarks: "Institutions create shadowed places in which nothing can be seen and no questions asked. They make other areas show finely discriminated detail, which is closely scrutinized and ordered." But Douglas argues mainly in a Durkheimian vein and ends her otherwise interesting book by concluding that institutions make even life and death decisions for us (ch. 9). This, clearly, is not the argument that we want to make here.

9 This is a common argument of all institutionalists, old and new. See, e.g., Commons (1924/1968, p. 138) and Hayek (1973/1982, p. 102): "The task of rules of just conduct can thus only be to tell people which expectations they can count on and which not." See also Lachmann (1963, p. 63): "What is particularly required in order to successfully coordinate the transactions of millions of people is the existence of institutions. In these institutions, an objectification is achieved for us of the million actions of our fellow men whose plans, objectives, and motives are impossible for us to know." (Translation by C. M.). See also Hall and Taylor (1998, pp. 17ff.).

10 Frey and Eichenberger (1989), although discussing the whole issue from a rational-choice perspective, reach the conclusion that one reason for the existence of institutions is individual anomalies. From our perspective, in which individual ignorance is the starting point, anomalies are the rather normal effects of the limited cognitive capacities of the individual agents. But in any case, the fact that even from a rational-choice perspective a main reason for the existence of institutions can be identified in

between cognitive rules and social rules seems in order. As we have seen in Part I of the book, the human mind can safely be modeled as an instrument of classification, with the cognitive rules as the building blocks of diverse classes. These cognitive rules of the form "IF such and such, THEN so and so" specify that if certain conditions hold, then certain changes in the environment will take place. The social rules, or rules of the game, also take the form of such hypothetical imperatives that if a certain social problem arises, one should behave in a certain manner. In other words, there is a symmetry in the formulation of *cognitive* and *social* rules, due obviously to the way the human brain functions, that facilitates the existence and emergence of the latter.

6.3. HOW DO INSTITUTIONS EMERGE?

Institutions emerge either deliberately or spontaneously, that is, either as a product of collective action or as a product of a spontaneous process of social interaction. There is a long tradition in the social sciences which can be traced back to the Scottish moral philosophers of the eighteenth century, that draws attention to social structures emerging spontaneously in evolutionary processes.[11] Hume (1740/1978, p. 529) envisioned a system of rules of justice that "is of course advantageous to the public; tho' it be not intended for that purpose by the inventors." Ferguson (1767/1966, p. 188) observes that "[n]ations stumble upon establishments which are indeed the result of human action, but not the execution of any human design." And in Smith's famous metaphor the merchant who intends only his own gain is "led by an invisible hand to promote an end which was no part of his intention" (1776/1976, p. 477.)[12]

This insight of the Scottish moral philosophers is relevant because, for the first time, the emergence of institutions is not explained exclusively by

the way people think strengthens the argument presented here.

[11] Hayek speaks of the Mandeville–Hume–Smith–Ferguson tradition in social theory (1978, p. 265).

[12] See also Smith (1790/1976, p. 184), where he speaks of the rich landlords who "in spite of their natural selfishness and rapacity, though they mean only their own conveniency, though the sole end which they propose from the labours of all the thousands whom they employ be the gratification of their own vain and insatiable desires, they divide with the poor the produce of all their improvements. They are led by an invisible hand to make nearly the same distribution of the necessaries of life which would have been made had the earth been divided into equal portions among all its inhabitants; and thus, without intending it, without making it, advance the interest of the society, and afford means to the multiplication of the species." Rothschild argues that "Smith's attitude to the invisible hand was ironical" (1994, p. 319), but her arguments are not very convincing.

conscious action aiming at their establishment. A hundred years later, Menger classified institutions into pragmatic and organic ones according to the ways in which they came into existence. The pragmatic ones "are the result of a *common will* directed toward their establishment (agreement, positive legislation etc.)," whereas the organic institutions are "the unintended result of human efforts aimed at attaining essentially *individual* goals" (1883/1985, p. 133). But even though Menger explicitly acknowledged that a large number of institutions forming the institutional framework of advanced communities is pragmatic in origin (1883/1985, p. 225), he thought that their explanation "does not challenge the sagacity of the scholar unduly" (1883/1985, p. 223). Consequently, he defined as his main objective "the theoretical understanding of those social phenomena which are not a product of agreement or of positive legislation but are the unintended results of historical developments" (1883/1985, p. 139).[13]

This bias toward the "proper" objective of the social sciences was then adopted by Hayek, who considered – in his attempt to react to what he called "rationalistic constructivism" – the main purpose of social theory "to grasp how independent action of many men can produce coherent wholes, persistent structures of relationships which serve important human purposes without having been designed for that end" (Hayek, 1952/1979, p. 141). Similarly, for Popper, the "main task of the theoretical social sciences . . . is to trace the unintended social repercussions of intentional human actions" (Popper 1963/1989, p. 342).[14]

When explaining institutions, the identification of spontaneous processes responsible for their emergence need not be the exclusive enterprise, though. Even if the intellectual energy required to explain how institutions are designed deliberately may not be great, this does not mean that they should be eliminated as *legitimate objects of explanation*. The

---

13 Menger's central question was: "How can it be that institutions which serve the common welfare and are extremely significant for its development come into being without a common will directed toward establishing them?" (1883/1985, p. 146).

14 According to Hayek (1967, p. 100n), Popper has been directly influenced by him in his view of the explananda of social sciences. Popper expresses his opinion repeatedly when he says, for example (1957, p. 65): "[O]nly a minority of social institutions are consciously designed while the vast majority have just 'grown' as the undesigned results of human actions." And further (1945/1963, vol. 2, p. 93): "It must be admitted that the structure of our social environment is man-made in a certain sense; that its institutions and traditions are neither the work of God nor of nature, but the results of human actions and decisions, and alterable by human actions and decisions. But this does not mean that they are all consciously designed, and explicable in terms of needs, hopes or motives. On the contrary, even those which arise as the result of conscious and intentional human actions are as a rule, *the indirect, the unintended and often the unwanted byproducts of such actions*."

Hayek–Popper research program[15] for the explanation of (social phenomena and thus also) social institutions might be the most important one in terms of the theoretical efforts required, but it is surely not exhaustive. In fact, some old institutionalists such as John Commons have placed emphasis on institutions arising as a product of collective action. And in the modern literature, the Public Choice theory focuses explicitly on how collective decisions lead to the emergence of the formal rules in a society.

The deliberate emergence of rules can be sufficiently illustrated if one employs the problem-solving model. On a general line of argument – irrespective of the specific kind of institution – a social rule emerges deliberately whenever many individuals *perceive* the problem situation as a new one requiring a conscious choice. A shared mental model of the problem situation is formed after repeated acts of communication between the individuals involved in the collective setting have taken place. These shared mental models are the prerequisite of the collective choice that follows the communication process. The choice of rules is a conscious act of individuals mutually recognizing the existence of a social problem requiring solution. The final outcome of the collective choice depends on the configuration of interests prevailing at the time, and on how these interests are perceived and understood as such by the agents.

The crucial difference between institutional design and the spontaneous emergence of institutions is that in the latter case the agents need not be conscious that their problem-solving activities affect other individuals.[16] Therefore, no conscious collective choice is taking place in order for an acknowledged social problem to be solved; instead, the social problem – which can be characterized as such *only* by an external observer – is solved as a side effect of the realization of individual problem-solving activities. Such explanations of social institutions are

---

15 The Hayek–Popper program although sometimes overemphasizing the relevance of spontaneous processes, is important because it views *social structures* as the explananda phenomena of social sciences. This clearly means that explaining individual behavior is not the analytical goal of the social sciences, as Simon, for example, seems to think. (For evidence, see Langlois, 1986b). In our view, an adequate explanation of individual behavior is important insofar as it provides a secure empirical basis for explaining social phenomena. Instead of *postulating* arbitrary assumptions concerning individual behavior, it is preferable to start with an empirically tested hypothesis of how people think and act that is sufficiently general for the explanatory purposes of social sciences and at the same time avoids the well-known methodological criticisms of the "realisticness of assumptions."

16 If some or all of the agents "know, suspect, or guess at the overall outcome their decentralized actions would lead to" (Langlois, 1986b, p. 242), the examined institution shall count as one that has emerged spontaneously "so long as the pursuit of that outcome is not the principal motivation for their actions" (ibid.).

clearly of the invisible hand type, that is, they identify an "aggregate mechanism which takes as 'input' the dispersed actions of the participating individuals and produces as 'output' the overall social pattern" (Ullmann-Margalit, 1978, p. 270).[17] This invisible hand process is to be understood as a filtering process "wherein some filter eliminates all entities not filling a certain pattern" (Nozick, 1994, p. 314).[18]

The spontaneous emergence of institutions can be sufficiently illustrated with the aid of the problem-solving model. An individual perceives his situation as constituating a new problem because the environment has changed, and after an act of creative choice he tries out a new solution to this problem. At this stage of the argument, this new problem is a strictly

---

17 Ullmann-Margalit (1978) distinguishes between two molds of invisible hand explanations, the aggregate and the functional-evolutionary one. The first addresses the *emergence* of an institution; the second deals with the *existence* of the social pattern or institution. In her words: "It is evident, then, that we are dealing with two quite disparate sets of questions. It follows that the molds of invisible hand explanation corresponding to them constitute two quite disparate undertakings: the first is concerned with providing *a chronicle of* (a particular mode of) *emergence*, the second with establishing *raisons d'être* ." (p. 284). Ullmann-Margalit thus identifies the functional evolutionary mold with the issue of the existence of an institution. This is perhaps reasonable in the case where the starting point of the analysis is the *function* of the examined institution for the social unit incorporating it. But it is not necessary to operate with the concepts of functionalist sociology. What function an institution has depends on the point of view that one adopts. Therefore, it is better to abandon altogether the notion of function and focus on the effects that certain institutions have for the individuals of the social group under examination. If one dispenses with functionalist sociology, then the correspondence between the aggregate mold and the emergence of an institution, on the one hand, and between the functional evolutionary mold and the existence of an institution, on the other hand, is bound to collapse. The invisible-hand explanation can then focus on the evolutionary filter, which can explain the emergence of an institution. The existence and persistence of an institution have to do with the interests of the agents as they subjectively perceive them, as we shall see in the following chapters.
18 A final remark regarding invisible-hand explanations seems in order. The notion of an institution or a social pattern arising spontaneously is a descriptive, not a normative one. "Not every pattern that arises by an invisible hand process is desirable, and something that can arise by an invisible hand process might better arise or be maintained through conscious intervention" (Nozick, 1994, p. 314). The social structure, pattern, or order under examination does not need to be judged as "efficient" or "good" in any normative way. In fact, "one could easily imagine a spontaneous order in which people were led as if by an invisible hand to promote a perverse and unpleasant end" (Vaughn, 1987/1989, p. 171). For a wonderful exposition of the normative bias of authors such as Hayek, who implicitly or explicitly judge spontaneous orders as good or efficient, see Buchanan (1977, ch. 2). For a formal statement of the invisible-hand explanation, see Heath (1992). See also Koppl (1992), who distinguishes between "type-one" and "type-two" invisible hand explanations, the second having as explanandum a new social institution.

93

personal one and the solution is employed because the agent expects that his utility will therewith increase. This novel response to a problem situation becomes an innovation at the time that other individuals decide to imitate it. In other words, innovation is a social phenomenon because it relates to new problem solutions that are also viewed as new by other individuals. (The case of an individual perceiving something as a new problem and trying out a solution that is novel to him but not to the other members of the social group, does thus not constitute an innovation.)

The reaction and imitation on the part of the other individuals gives rise to a cumulative process through which the new behavior or pattern of action becomes ever more widely adopted by those who expect therewith to better their condition (Koppl, 1992, p. 308). The diffusion of this innovative behavior among many or all members of a community brings about the solution to a problem that, from an external point of view, is a social one. In other words, a social pattern or institution arises, and the problem-solving individuals "do not have the overall pattern that is ultimately produced in mind, neither on the level of intentions nor even on the level of foresight or awareness" (Ullmann-Margalit, 1978, p. 271).

What remains is to examine how the different kinds of institutions emerge and, in the case of their spontaneous emergence, to specify the concrete invisible hand process that gives rise to them.

6.4. WHY DO INSTITUTIONS PERSIST OR CHANGE?

A complete theory of institutions should explain under what conditions institutions change, who initiates this change, and when. This is a very ambitious program, though. If one takes human creativity seriously, then an exact story of when changes in the institutional framework are to be expected and by whom they will be initiated cannot be told. Human creativity associated with an unconditional choice means that the future must remain open; thus, deterministic theories of institutional changes are impossible.[19] A full specification of the circumstances that will lead an agent (individual or corporate actor) to initiate a change in institution is thus bound to fail.

Putting the holistic theories aside, even some individualistic explanations of institutional change have been overoptimistic concerning the pos-

---

[19] We do not think that nowadays deterministic theories of social change can be seriously contended. In addition to the empirical facts, the criticism of Hayek and Popper still remain valid.

sibility of theoretical generalizations on institutional change.[20] In North and Thomas (1973), for example, the implicit model suggests that institutions derive from the optimizing decisions of individuals and respond to changes in the set of relative prices that individuals face. Thus, when relative prices change, incentives are created to construct more efficient institutions. As North pointed out later (1990, p. 7): "The persistence of inefficient institutions, illustrated by the case of Spain, was a result of fiscal needs of rulers that led to shortened time horizons and therefore a disparity between private incentives and social welfare. *Such an anomaly did not fit into the theoretical framework*" [Emphasis added]. A further problem with this model is, of course, that it implies the relative quick and frequent change of institutions. But the very existence of institutions is explained, as we have seen, by the need of individuals to have an orientation in a complex world; thus, they cannot change with the automatism and easiness that North and Thomas implied. Apart from that, this "naive theory" (Eggertsson, 1990, p. 249f.) which is also characteristic of the first neoclassical property-right theories such as that of Demsetz (1967), implies the existence of a benevolent, *omniscient* social maximizer.[21]

A change in institutions can take place in two ways. Either an institutional change is initiated by one individual and then imitated by others, so that an innovation is brought about and diffused in an evolutionary process, or an institutional change is initiated by many individuals acting collectively in order to respond to a new social problem. In both cases, the exact time and place of the institutional change obviously cannot be predicted. But even the less ambitious program of specifying the conditions that will facilitate institutional change cannot be pursued. The reason is that the solution to a personal problem perceived by an individual

---

20 For a critical review of the collectivist social theories see Dietl (1993, ch. 2.1). For informative reviews of theories on institutional change, see Gäfgen (1983), Sjöstrand (1993), Knight (1992, ch. 1), Okruch (1998, pp.106ff.), and Okruch (1999). See also the contributions in Knight and Sened (1995). On the rational choice approach to institutions, see Schotter (1981) and the review article of Calvert (1995). See also Calvert (1998).

21 See also Rutherford (1995, p. 445): "There is another problem as well. The idea of institutions responding to relative prices would seem to deny preexisting institutions any real influence over the pace and direction of change. North and Thomas do however, sometimes refer to a conservative influence exercised by existing institutions in explaining why some institutions were not challenged or why change occured in the way it did. Powerful interests may oppose change, or rapid or dramatic institutional change may undermine legitimacy and raise enforcement costs. The difficulty is that the references to this 'conservative principle' are ad hoc in nature. . . ." For a similar critique, see Field (1981).

agent or to a social problem interpreted as new by many agents includes always a creative act, that is, is fundamentally unpredictable.

An institutional change takes place whenever one or more agents think that his or their interests are better served under a new institutional arrangement than the prevailing one. This means that the agent (or agents) perceive subjectively at some time that their environmental situation constitutes a new problem. At this stage of analysis, an external observer could predict that the specific environmental situation is bound to appear as a new one to the agents by pointing to the difference that exists in comparison to the past situations faced by the agents. For example, a technological innovation might change the distribution of income in a society, causing monetary losses for some individuals and monetary gains for some others. One could predict, then (in terms of North's theory or even Marx's theory interpreted individualistically), that the problem situation in which one or more individuals find themselves will be interpreted by them as a fundamentally new one. This prediction by an external observer can be met by comparing the economic situation of the agent at time t_0 to his situation at the time t_1 and by inferring that this change has been so dramatic that even the agent must have interpreted the problem situation as a new one.[22]

Once perceived as such, the new problem will be solved in a creative way. After an individual or collective choice, new solutions will be tried out by the agents, and these solutions will be outcomes of creative deliberations. These human choices, guided by interests as they are perceived at the moment, are not predictable, and therefore the institutional changes effected by those choices are not predictable either.

In his later work, North (1981) abandoned the efficiency view of institutions, stressing the fact that the property rights of the society are devised by the rulers in their own interests and thus are typically inefficient. He also introduced "ideology" as an important factor in institutional change. He thus took a decisive step toward abandoning the neoclassical paradigm, which becomes clear in his latest publications (North, 1990, 1994, 1995a, 1995b, 1996, 1998, 2000; Denzau and North, 1994). He acknowledges that "the cognitive science offers the promise of shedding new light" (1993a, p. 162) upon the way ideologies evolve and affect

---

[22] Obviously, certain more radical subjectivist authors would not even acquiesce in this point, stressing the interpretational moment of every perceptory act that leaves the external observer helpless to make any prediction. But one need not accept this skepticism in order to prove that institutional change is difficult to predict.

institutional change, and he suggests the need to work out the theoretical link between ideology and institutional change.[23]

As soon as ideologies are introduced into the analysis as an additional determining factor of institutional change, along with the strictly economic factors, the issue becomes very complicated. For a sufficient explanation of institutional change, the exact role of ideology in affecting institutional permanence or change must be specified, as well as how ideology is linked with the prevailing economic constraints. And, of course, the questions of when ideology, when economic factors, and when both together contribute to an institutional change must be answered. Furthermore, the issue of whether both formal and informal institutions change with changes in ideologies or relative prices must be clarified.

We do not think that we can ever answer these questions completely. This pessimism is derived from the simple insight concerning the creativity of human nature. If one takes creative thought and action seriously, then the possibility of predicting institutional change is reduced dramatically. Institutions may change in one direction or another according to how the agents choose each time and depending on what form the invisible hand process or the collective action takes. The future is open, and the direction of the institutional change cannot be forecast if the social process is to remain genuinely open-ended.

The only possibility of predicting the content and direction of institutional change involves the identification of one or more invariant restrictions (Hesse, 1987) to which the social process should adapt in order for the individuals to survive. Such invariant restrictions would constitute at the same time the selective environment for a change in institutions, that is, they would constitute the criterion of selection for institutions. By pointing to the nature of such invariant restrictions, one could also predict

---

23 North suggests that one should restrict the use of the instrumental rationality assumption to cases in which "simple problems, complete information, repetitive situations, and high motivations" (1993a, p. 161) prevail. For the other, empirically more important cases, he suggests utilizing the "exciting body of theory developing in cognitive science which offers the promise of . . . providing an explanation for the way in which individuals with different experiences will derive different mental models to explain the world around them; the way by which learning will lead to a modification or alteration in the mental constructs of individuals. In short it offers the promise – as yet far from realized – of providing an explanation for the ideologies individuals and groups possess, why they evolve, what gives them durability or leads to their demise" (ibid.). Ekkehart Schlicht has also repeatedly pleaded for a richer psychological model of individual behavior that can provide a sufficient basis for explaining institutions. See Schlicht (1990, 1997, 1998). For a similar position, see Kubon-Gilke (1996).

the basic characteristics of the institutions that could exist in a global evolutionary process. The functionalist view of society assumes that such a criterion could be the *survival of the society as a whole*. A global selection process of institutions could accordingly be modeled in the way that those "appropriate" institutions are selected whose existence contributes to the survival of the social system as a whole.

From an individualistic perspective, such a criterion is obviously not valid. The only reasonable selective criterion for institutional evolution is the interests of the individuals in a society as these individuals subjectively perceive them every time to be. Hence, once an illusionary objective selection criterion disappears, only subjective interests, as the agents themselves understand them, are left as a criterion of institutional selection. This individualization, in turn, means that not even a vaguely constant or definite criterion for the selection of institutions exists and thus there is no possibility to predict the nature and quality of the institutions that will survive.

Thus, the only relatively secure theoretical proposition that can be formulated is that both economic factors and ideologies might motivate institutional change. *But this amounts to saying that in fact everything can be a cause of change, since even if redistribution of income due to some technological innovation occurred, ideologies could neutralize the tendency toward institutional change and vice versa.* Nobody can prevent, for example, a new prophet from appearing and propagating a new paradise on earth, one who will convince enough persons to follow him and to transform radically the institutional framework of the community.[24] Such attempts at great transformations periodically appear in history – socialism, religious fundamentalism, and so on – and they are not always due to the material or technological conditions prevailing in the respective society.[25]

---

[24] The fact that ideologies also induce institutional change does not mean that the bearers or propagators of those ideologies are not self-interested. We would guess that, for prophets, the utility increase comes from the success of their movement and their expected nonmonetary benefit of acquiring a position in a pantheon. And for their followers, the utility increase comes from their trust in obtaining a privileged position in the paradise on earth or in heaven. For a brilliant exposition of a similar argument in other terminology, see the first chapter of Schumpeter (1942/1950) and his analysis of Marx as a prophet.

[26] See Albert (1976, p. 51): "New ideas that could lead to new solutions to problems in all areas appear therefore to be the autonomous factors of the sociocultural development. They cannot be predicted. . . . If this is the case, then the propositional systems that were to predict the course of history . . . cannot be a rational enterprise. They belong then to the sphere of irrational prophecy, even in those instances when

Given our current state of knowledge, the only possible explanation concerns *how* institutions have changed after their change has occurred. This ex post reconstruction of either a collective action or an invisible hand process that has led to the examined social pattern or institution is in effect nothing more than answering the second postulated question of how institutions emerge. In other words, the explanandum phenomenon must be an existing social institution and the explanatory hypothesis is the story of how it has emerged.[26]

6.5. HOW ARE INSTITUTIONS ADOPTED OR ENFORCED?

The distinguishing feature of institutions as social rules, as opposed to personal rules followed by individuals, is that social rules refer to problems of interaction when many persons are involved. The most important question in settings of social interaction is thus why social rules are ever adopted and followed by individuals. This, in turn, relates to the issue of the enforcement of institutions.

As we have seen, a reasonable classification of institutions can be best provided according to the criterion of enforcement, varying from first-party enforcement characteristic of moral rules to the enforcement by the state that distinguishes legal rules. For each type of institution, we shall discuss in the following two chapters how and why it is enforced by the members of a community. At this more general level of analysis, only the general argument is to be stressed that a *learning* process underlies the enforcement of any institution, formal or informal. Social rules are adopted by the individuals and are enforced by some agency in the society only because the individuals concerned have learned sometime during their individual histories that it is in their interest to follow the rules. Persons learn in the same way, that is, by a trial-and-error process, how to behave and solve the problems which include the reactions of other indi-

they may contain ideas of some scientific interest, which, for example, is no doubt the case with Marxism. . . . Interestingly, Marxism resulted de facto in leading its very own predictions partly ad absurdum, . . . in that it made clear the independent role ideas played in historical development." (Translation by C. M.)

26 To be sure, we cannot know whether the human creativity that underlies institutional change is itself determined or not. Logically at least, one cannot exclude the possibility that creativity is deterministic and that it is only our ignorance that forces us to treat it as nondeterministic. The reason a person happens to solve a new problem in one way rather than in another may depend on some factors that we cannot identify merely from the state of our current knowledge, but that we might be able to detect sometime in the future. The question itself, whether we will ever be able to explain creativity is, in any case, unanswerable. (We are indebted to Herbert Keuth for the clarification of this point.)

viduals. In a way, the adoption of social rules is only a subcase of learning successful solutions to a specific type of a practical problem, that is, how to behave when the behavior of other individuals constitutes part of the problem.

The fact that the adoption and enforcement of social rules is modeled as a learning process is important because the conflict between *Homo oeconomicus* and *Homo sociologicus* explaining social institutions disappears. Stressing individuals as actively *learning subjects,* however, means that they calculate according to their interests (and thus are responsive to incentives) and at the same time follow adopted social rules blindly. An explanation for this is to be found in their classification of the situation. Whenever individuals interpret the social setting as a new one, they apply calculations and choices in order to adopt the solution that they expect to bring the highest benefits. But as soon as they have tried this solution a number of times and think that it works sufficiently well, and other members of the social community also seem to accept the solution to the new problem, then they blindly follow this solution constantly without rethinking the problem each time anew. They have subjectively learned that this solution works sufficiently well in this situation and therefore, to an external observer, they seem to dogmatically follow the social rule, whether social, legal, or moral norm, whenever this problem situation appears. It thus remains to classify these problem situations and to show what solutions individuals learn to apply in order to acquire a more differentiated view of how institutions are adopted or enforced.

7

Informal Institutions

7.1. CONVENTIONS

We have distinguished between three types of informal institutions according to the enforcement agency: conventions, moral rules, and social norms. Conventions are those social rules that are to a large degree self-policing in the sense that, after their emergence, no individual has an incentive to switch from the rule that everyone else is following. For a systematic discussion of conventions, we shall pose the four questions formulated in the previous chapter and we shall attempt to answer them.

1. Why Do Conventions Exist? Social conventions are solutions to social problems that are stylized in game theory as coordination games. The simplest case of a coordination game (two players, two alternatives) is presented in Fig. 5. Two Nash equilibria exist in the game, with either coordinated solution being an equilibrium. In the coordinated cases, no individual can improve his situation by deviating from playing his part in the equilibrium, given that the other individuals play their parts in the equilibrium. This means that if all individuals *expect* the others to play their parts in the Nash equilibrium, they are all better off when they play their parts in it.

The exemplification of the coordination game makes it clear that coordination problems are interaction situations of *interdependent* problem solving on the part of the individuals involved. In his classical treatise on convention, Lewis (1969) argued that conventions arise as solutions to repeated plays of coordination games played by a large number of individuals. Lewis defines *convention* as follows: "A regularity R in the behavior of members of a population P when they are agents in a recurrent situation

A

		Drive on Left	Drive on Right
	Drive on Left	(10,10)	(0,0)
B	Drive on Right	(0,0)	(10,10)

Fig. 5 The coordination game.

S is a *convention* if and only if it is true that, and it is common knowledge in P that, any instance of S among members of P,

everyone conforms to R;
everyone expects everyone else to conform to R;
everyone prefers to conform to R on condition that the others do, since S
    is a coordination problem and
uniform conformity to R is a coordination equilibrium in S" (Lewis,
    1969, p. 58).[1]

Thus, the raison d'être of conventions is that they are solutions to social problems of coordination. A typical example of such problems is traffic on a road. Another well-known example stems from Hume (1751/1975, p. 306), where "two men pull the oars of a boat by common convention for common interest, without any promise or contract." Language is another typical social phenomenon that bears the character of a convention. And there are long series of conventions that have arisen as solutions to coordination problems of economic nature such as, for example, money and credit, rules of accounting, forms of economic contracts, many industrial standards, and so on.

2. *How Do Conventions Emerge?* Conventions emerge spontaneously and therefore seem to be especially well suited for evolutionary, invisible-hand explanations. Although the game theory account is very valuable in showing why conventions exist and what their role is in solving coordination problems, it "does not give a coherent account of how people would play a game like this" [because] there is nothing in the structure of the game itself that allows the players – even purely rational players – to

---

[1] This is one of the definitions Lewis offers (1969) in his study. His final definition is relaxed "to allow for conventions that meet the present definition only for the most part or with high probability" (p. 76). Hence, the propositions are transformed into "almost-universal quantifications," so that the term "almost everyone" substitutes for the term "everyone" (p. 78).

deduce what they ought to do" (Young, 1996, p. 107). The question arises, then, of how such games are actually played.

Schelling (1960) was the first to discuss how people might behave when engaged in a setting described by the coordination game in the absence of an authority that might solve the problem externally. His explanation is clearly of the invisible-hand type[2] and stresses the importance of contextual clues available to the individuals *outside* the game that Schelling calls "focal points." Schelling experimented with coordination problems in which agents cannot communicate. He found that in an experimental setting, individuals often do very well at solving *novel* coordination problems without communication. Most often they opt for a coordination equilibrium that is somewhat *salient*. In other words, from the many possible solutions to the coordination games, the one that emerges spontaneously is the one that possesses a salience for the players, that is, that constitutes a focal point.[3]

Schelling proved that people are good at knowing what the salient focal points are, but he did not explain *how they come into being*. In his own model, Young provides such an explanation, which is based on the learning history of individuals. Their knowledge is derived "from their personal experiences and from information they pick up from others" (1996, p. 109). The important point about salience is the shared cultural context of the individuals that can give rise to particular conventions (David, 1994, p. 210; Rutherford, 1994, p. 112).

Focal points can only be understood in light of the fact that people possess shared mental models, as discussed in Chapter 5. Interacting individuals share mental models of other similar problem solutions. Thus, when they happen to face a *novel* coordination problem, they draw from this common knowledge by *analogy* to the same new solution. Since analogy is the most powerful inferential strategy that all people possess,

---

2 See Schelling (1960, p. 91): "The coordination game probably lies behind the stability of institutions and traditions and perhaps the phenomenon of leadership itself. Among the possible sets of rules that might govern a conflict, tradition points to the particular set that everyone can expect everyone else to be conscious of as conspicuous candidate for adoption; it wins by default over those that cannot readily be identified by tacit consent. The force of many rules of etiquette and social restraint, including some (like the rule against ending a sentence with a preposition) that have been divested of their relevance or authority, seems to depend on their having become 'solutions' to a coordination game: everyone expects everyone to expect observance, so that non-observance carries the pain of conspicuousness."

3 For a classical account of the emergence of money, which is clearly to be classified as a convention, see Menger (1871/1968, ch. 8). On the development of media of exchange, see also the account of Mises (1953, pp. 30–4).

the interacting persons need not have common knowledge of the concrete problem solution in the first place. It suffices if they have knowledge of similar solutions, that is, some shared mental models, and if all employ the same analogical reasoning to solve the new problem.[4] This can explain how a specific convention emerges in the first stage. Afterward, diffusion of the knowledge of the concrete solution takes place, and since the individuals are indifferent about which problem solution is established, as long as *one is* established and all participants share it, the convention becomes stabilized.

Because of common human inferential strategies, self-reinforcing mechanisms in the evolution of conventions might be at work. "If it is a matter of common knowledge that a particular convention is followed in one situation, then that convention acquires prominence for other, analogous situations" (Sugden, 1989, p. 93).[5] This implies, then, that gradually family relationships among conventions might emerge that include conventions most susceptible to analogy (ibid.). The "first come, first served" principle might be such a convention, or the "last in, first out" rule which has important economic applications when, for example, workers are laid off in recessions.

3. Why Do Conventions Persist or Change? Once established, conventions are self-policing due to the fact that no individual will considerably increase his utility if he initiates a change. *A change in conventions is thus more likely to happen by mistakes of the agents.* The possibility of error means that "there is always a chance that someone will take an unconventional action" (Young, 1996, p. 110). If enough such errors occur and accumulate, then via the learning process, they can be diffused among the persons of the group and lead to a change in the convention. Thus, the fundamental difficulty remains "that even if we know the initial state of

---

[4] We think that this is the empirical foundation of the process described by Schelling (1960, p. 57): "Finding the key, or rather finding *a* key – any key that is mutually recognized as *the* key becomes the key – may depend, on imagination more than on logic; it may depend on analogy, precedent, accidental agreement, symmetry, aesthetic or geometric configuration, casuistic reasoning, and who the parties are and what they know about each other."

[5] Sugden (1989, p. 93) gives the following example: "On my journey to work there is a narrow bridge, not wide enough for two vehicles to pass. If two drivers approach from opposite directions, which of them should give way? Coming on this problem for the first time, my prior expectation was when the drivers came into view of one another, whoever was closer to the bridge would be given the right of way. This expectation – which proved correct – was based on an analogy with the 'first come, first served' principle."

	Dove	Hawk
Dove	(2,2)	(0,8)
Hawk	(8,0)	(-3,-3)

Fig. 6 The hawk/dove game.

society, we cannot predict what the prevailing convention will be at each future date" (Young, 1996, p. 111), but the diffusion process can be modeled sufficiently.[6]

Sugden bases his argument about social convention on the well-known hawk/dove game,[7] and he shows which strategies are evolutionary stable in this game.[8] Any evolutionary stable strategy in a game with two or more evolutionary stable strategies is defined as a convention (Sugden, 1989, p. 91). As Sugden explains: "Although the initial appearance of any deviant strategy is unexplained (analogously with the role of mutation in biological theories), the extent to which it is then played depends on its degree of success" (p. 92). Nevertheless Sugden contends that "deviant play, then, is more like experiment than error" (ibid.). On this point, according to our view, Sugden is wrong. It is the distinguishing feature of conventions that people derive utility when following them only insofar as others follow them. Therefore, they will not have an incentive to *experiment* at all with another convention once they follow an established one. Experimenting might lead to failure (and in some cases, as in traffic rules, with fatal consequences), and if a person cannot expect any utility increase in the case of success, then he would rather not experiment at all. Thus, the only plausible case of the initiation of a change in conventions is the case of errors on the part of the agents.

This is also a crucial distinction between the change of conventions and the change of moral rules and social norms. Conventions change when the agents behave erroneously, possibly because they interpret the current problem situation as a new one whereas it is in reality an old one. Moral rules or social norms, on the other hand, change when somebody con-

---

6 For formal evolutionary models, see Young (1998).
7 The hawk/dove game is illustrated in Fig. 6.
8 The concept of evolutionary stability was first developed by John Maynard Smith (1982) to explain the effects of animals from a homogeneous population with different genes meeting randomly in pairwise interactions. As Sugden contends: "If we substitute utility for fitness and learning for natural selection, this approach can be adapted to explain human behavior" (1989, p. 91). Hence, "an evolutionary stable strategy (or ESS) is a pattern of behavior such that, if it is generally followed in the population, any small number of people who deviate from it will do less well than others" (ibid.).

sciously tries out a new behavior, *because he expects a utility increase from it,* and others follow him or her in the same expectation. Thus, the cause of the deviant behavior is error in the case of conventions and expectation of higher utility in the case of moral rules and social norms.

4. How Are Conventions Adopted or Enforced? We have stressed that conventions do not need an enforcement agency to ensure that people follow them. In this case, conventions are self-policing. The individuals learn either from personal experience or from others what particular convention is in force, and they adopt it because it is in their interest to do so. Since there is no genuine conflict of interests, conventions are adopted quasi-automatically, are classified by the individuals as solutions to old problems, and are followed without third-party enforcement.

7.2. MORAL RULES

In contrast to conventions, where no genuine conflict between individual and common interest is involved, moral rules are characterized primarily by the fact that they require a kind of behavior that, while socially beneficial, seems to be – at least prima facie – contrary to the interests of the individuals themselves. Typical examples of moral rules are "keep promises," "do not cheat," "respect other people's property," and "tell the truth." Such rules are to be found in every society, primitive and modern, and are typically followed by a great part of the individuals in a society, although by no means by all. Thus, the empirical phenomenon to be explained is the *existence* of moral rules in a society that are followed by *part* of the population.[9]

1. Why Do Moral Rules Exist? Moral rules are solutions to social problems best described in terms of game theory as a prisoner's dilemmas with an exit option.[10] There is much literature that attempts to explain moral behavior stylizing the underlying social problem as a prisoner's dilemma game.[11] The theoretical deficit of discussing moral behavior employing the normal prisoner's dilemma game is the counterintuitive presupposition that the agents *must* in any case play the game. Thus, moral rules in a

---

[9] The issue of whether following moral rules is rational, although of obvious importance, possesses a normative character and does not need to concern us here.

[10] Orbell and Dawes (1993) provide convincing empirical evidence from laboratory experiments that the option of refusing to participate in particular prisoner's dilemma games increases the aggregate welfare of the players.

[11] The most prominent contribution is certainly Gauthier (1986).

way possess a necessity, something that is undue for real-world settings. Regardless of the appeals that moral philosophers have made to people throughout the history to follow their "moral duties," people have not always heard them. In fact, as we shall later see, the emergence of the state and the legal order in a society can best be explained as the outcome of people's failure to pay attention to moral rules.

The crucial assumptions made in the prisoner's dilemma game with an exit option is that the expected payoffs from choosing the exit option are lower than the payoffs expected under mutual cooperation but higher than those resulting under mutual defection. This game is represented in Fig. 7.

Vanberg and Congleton discuss the game in terms of behavior or moral programs. In the tradition of Axelrod (1984), they devise simulation experiments in which different kinds of behaviors compete with each other and one can read their long-run success from the cumulative payoffs at the end of the game, when all strategies have been paired with each other. The interesting point for our setting is that the individuals are modeled as actively learning agents with memory. "In the first round of play, individuals know nothing about their counterparts. In subsequent pairings, they remember whether particular players defected in previous rounds of play or not. Of course, only the adaptive strategies make use of this information" (p. 422).

Among many strategies devised, such as the opportunistic strategy (always play and always defect), Tit for Tat (always play and use the strategy that the other player used the last time you met), and so on, a so-called prudent moral strategy is devised: Play only with those who have never previously defected, but always cooperate if one chooses to play. In other words, after the fellow player's first defection, the prudent moral exits for one round, giving then a second and final chance to the fellow player. If this player defects again, then he cease to play with him in the future.

The result of the tournaments is summarized by Vanberg and Congleton (1992) as follows (p. 427): "All in all, the simulation results suggest that a strategy of cooperating with those who have cooperated in the past and avoiding those who have defected in the past is eminently viable and is robust over a wide range of community compositions. The advantage of tolerant versions of this strategy depends on the population mix. . . . Overall, the prudent moral strategies are viable moralities." The prudent moral strategy guarantees that if it is not always the most successful – in terms of cumulative payoffs and subsequent reproductive success – it is *a*

A

B		Cooperate	Defect	Don't play
	Cooperate	(1,1)	(-2,2)	(0,0)
	Defect	(2,-2)	(-1,-1)	(0,0)
	Don't play	(0,0)	(0,0)	(0,0)

Fig. 7 The prisoner's dilemma with exit.

viable strategy in populations where even the most amoral behaviors are possible. This model can thus account sufficiently thus for the explanandum phenomenon: that moral behavior exists in the real world, although it is followed only by part of the population.[12]

2. *How Do Moral Rules Emerge?* Moral rules emerge spontaneously in an invisible-hand process. It suffices that just two individuals confronted with a problem situation make the conscious choice to cooperate in order for such a process to be introduced. If two individuals expect a higher utility from their cooperation compared to the case in which each tries to solve the problem based on his own powers, then they might opt for the innovative choice to cooperate. After the successful act of cooperation between the two, they are bound to realize that being honest was the precondition of their success and that not defecting has led to the improvement of their position. Hence, a learning process has taken place and the rule has been made familiar to them: IF I act honestly toward X and he does the same, THEN our utility will increase from our mutual cooperation."

If the cooperation is repeated and nobody defects, then the players will obviously learn that there have not been merely single acts but in fact that cooperative or honest *behavior* has led to the increase in their utility. The rule that they have learned will be transformed thus into the following one: "IF I and X *behave* honestly, THEN our utility will increase from our

[12] Witt, in an excellent paper (1986), has also stressed the role of social learning processes and the internalization of standards of conduct for the spontaneous emergence of cooperation. Although what he attempts to explain is the willingness of an individual to adhere to a non-codified commitment, his explanation is in fact what we usually label "morality" and runs along the lines of the explanation presented in the text.

mutual cooperation." Obviously then, a two-person moral network has emerged based on mutual recognition that success is founded on honest behavior between the parties.

Other individuals motivated by the same desire to increase their utility might build similar moral networks, so that in a society a large number of such networks might emerge. All of those cooperating pairs are based on some moral rules of the type prevailing in the dealings of the original pair described previously. Now, each of those moral networks might be enlarged by additional newcomers who also wish to cooperate honestly. If such enlarged cooperative networks work without anybody defecting, the learning process proceeds and the rule learned is of the following type: "IF everybody in the cooperative cluster behaves honestly, THEN our utility will increase from our mutual cooperation."

This moral rule is then transferred to individuals outside the narrow moral network, that is, it becomes generalized and applied in interaction with every other individual. This generalization obviously has a psychological background: If the individual has found that a cooperative behavior with one or more partners who also cooperate pays, he will make the inference that it is always beneficial to cooperate whenever the rest also do. Thus, the general moral rule emerges: "If everybody in society behaves honestly, then our utility will increase from our mutual cooperation."

This hypothesis stresses the fact that the emergence of moral rules is the outcome of a learning process on the part of the individuals who follow those rules. Obviously, not everybody will adopt moral rules, since whether the individual has found that behaving in a moral way is useful for him or her depends on the individual's learning history. The crucial fact about moral rules is that they are *conditional,* a characteristic due mainly to the nature of the learning process that underlies their emergence: One is willing to cooperate only on the condition that the rest also cooperate.[13]

There are three lines of argument in the vast literature on morality that support this view of the emergence of moral rules. The first line of argument is usually put forward by those philosophers who contend that

---

13 See Hume's remark on the nature of collective learning leading to the emergence of morality (1740/1978, p. 490): "It is only a general sense of common interest; which sense all the members of the society express to one another, and which induces them to regulate their conduct by certain rules. I observe, that it will be for my interest to leave another in the possession of his goods, provided he will act in the same manner with regard to me." See also Vanberg (1994a, ch. 4).

morality is best discussed in terms of moral sentiments. Mackie (1985), for example, provides an explanation of the development of morality according to the general thrust of the argument presented earlier, while stressing at the same time the emergence of moral sentiments during the process of human interaction. He poses the question (p. 215): "Why do we have an ingrained tendency to see wrong actions as calling for penalties and good actions as calling for rewards?" He answers it by suggesting that a harm inflicted by somebody is retaliated by the one who has suffered from the attack because "such retaliation will tend to benefit the retaliator since the aggressor will be discouraged from repeating the attack" (p. 216). In a second step, such retributive emotions help to characterize certain kinds of behavior as generally harmful partly *because* they are resented. This, in turn, gives rise to moral distinctions and to notions of moral disapproval with a *prescriptive* character. Hence, the essential drive of the development of moral rules come from the emotions (p. 218).[14],[15]

The explanation of the emergence of moral rules with the aid of retributive emotions based apparently on the functioning of the animal-like motivational system of humans is only one part of the story, though. In modern social sciences and especially in the so-called exchange theory in sociology,[16] *reciprocity* is presented as a general sociological mechanism that enables cooperation in society. The main argument is that in social settings with repeated interactions, mutual reinforcement of behavior

[14] This is not to say that Mackie does not consider the importance of the social interaction for the emergence of moral rules. But he contends that although the development of morality "presupposes fairly advanced intellectual powers associated with the retributive emotions" (p. 218), emotions nevertheless remain "the directing forces which sustain the resulting patterns of action" (ibid.).

[15] For a modern restatement of the theory of moral sentiments see Frank (1988), especially chapter 3, where he stresses the strategic role of emotions as reliable signaling devices to potential cooperators indicating whether or not a person can be expected to cooperate. Platteau (1994f, pp 766ff.) also stresses that moral behavior goes hand in hand with the maturation of specific emotional competencies.

[16] Reciprocity as a general mechanism for providing social order is stressed in all social sciences. In ethnology see the seminal work of Malinowski (1922/1961) and his analysis of the institution of Kula gift exchange. See also Mauss (1954/1969), Davis (1992), and Landa (1994). In sociology see the seminal contributions of Homans (1961), Blau (1964) and Emerson (1969). See also Ekeh (1974). Historically, Adam Smith was the first to speak about the "discipline of continuous dealings," and Hume remarked (1740/1978, p. 521): "Hence I learn to do a service to another, without bearing him any real kindness, because I foresee, that he will return my service, in expectation of another of the same kind, and in order to maintain the same correspondence of good offices with me or with others. And accordingly, after I have serv'd him and he is in posession of the advantage arising from my action, he is induc'd to perform his part, as foreseeing the consequences of his refusal."

takes place, that is, undesirable behavior is punished and desirable behavior is rewarded (Nee, 1998a, p. 9). Although most authors arguing in
the tradition of social exchange theory do not distinguish between social
norms and moral rules, the merit of this approach is that it stresses the
behavioral role of social rewards and punishments. Besides, the arguments
are presented mainly in terms of social exchange as a mechanism that
fosters cooperation, and therefore they are directly relevant to our
discussion.

The notion of reciprocity is obviously closely related to the conditional
form of the moral rules, since a benefit is granted to a party only upon the
(implicit) condition that it will be returned in a somehow equal form in the
future. And at least in the behavioral variant of the exchange theory
(especially in the work of G. Homans), the underlying learning mechanisms of the reciprocating process are stressed, although the psychology
used is not a cognitive one.

In laboratory experiments, Berg, Dickhaut, and McCabe (1995) have
studied trust and reciprocity in a two-stage dictator game and have found
that common history reduces "social distance" between subjects and leads
to reciprocative behavior. Hoffman, McCabe, and Smith (1998) find that
first movers trusted second movers to reciprocate even with no possibility
of punishment.

Recent empirical work of Gächter and Fehr (1999) offers additional
support for social exchange theory. In experiments, Gächter and Fehr
have managed to isolate the role of approval incentives for cooperation.
Although approval incentives alone are not sufficiently strong to cause a
reduction of freeriding, in combination with some minimal social famil-
iarity they lead to a significant rise in cooperation.[17] Approval incentives
"are the more important the greater the density of social interaction
among people" (p. 362). Thus, social exchange theory, in stressing the
role of rewards for attaining cooperation lends additional support to the
hypothesis of the emergence of moral rules presented here.

Apart from moral philosophy and exchange theory in the social sciences, a third important argument supporting the view that moral rules
are the outcome of a learning process in the course of cooperation between individuals stems from psychology. Lawrence Kohlberg (1984) has
presented a moral development theory that distinguishes between six
moral stages through which individuals in a society are predicted to pass.

---

[17] See also the conclusions of Dawes, van de Kragt, and Orbell (1988) based on a large
number of experiments on the important role of group identity in enhancing cooperation even when there are no possibilities of social rewards and reciprocity.

These six moral stages are defined in terms of (1) what is right, (2) the reason for upholding the right, and (3) the social perspective behind each stage. The six moral stages[18] are grouped into three major levels: the preconventional level (stages 1 and 2), the conventional level (stages 3 and 4), and the postconventional level (stages 5 and 6). "Level I is a preconventional person, for whom rules and social expectations are something external to the self; level II is a conventional person, in whom the self is identified with or has internalized the rules and expectations of others, especially of authorities; and level III is a postconventional person, who had differentiated his or her self from the rules and expectations of others and defines his or her values in terms of self-chosen principles" (Kohlberg, 1984, p. 173).[19]

On the basis of a huge amount of empirical material, Kohlberg argues that the moral stages are empirically true and claims "that anyone who interviewed children about moral dilemmas and who followed them longitudinally in time would come to our six stages and no others" (1984, p. 195). Kohlberg understands his theory – consistent with the hypothesis that we have offered – as a cognitive-developmental theory in which the learning process of the individuals explains the formation of moral rules *during an interacting process with other individuals.* "Basic moral norms and principles are structures arising through experiences of social interaction rather than through internalization of rules that exist as external structures; moral stages are not defined by internalized rules but by structures of interaction between the self and others" (p. 197).

---

[18] The six moral stages are the following:
  Stage 1: Heteronomous Morality
  Stage 2: Individualism, Instrumental Purpose, and Exchange
  Stage 3: Mutual Interpersonal Expectations, Relationships, and Interpersonal Conformity
  Stage 4: Social System and Conscience
  Stage 5: Social Contract or Utility and Individual Rights
  Stage 6: Universal Ethical Principles.

[19] Kohlberg (1984, p. 177) introduces the concept of "sociomoral perspective" which refers to the point of view the individual takes in defining both social facts and sociomoral values or "oughts." Corresponding to the three major levels of moral judgment, we postulate the three major levels of social perspective as follows:

	Moral Judgment	Social Perspective
I	Preconventional	Concrete individual perspective
II	Conventional	Member-of-society perspective
III	Postconventional or principled	Prior-to-society perspective

Summarizing, moral rules emerge in a process of social interaction that is of the invisible-hand type. The essential points to be stressed concerning the emergence of moral rules are three:

(1) For the process to start, it is sufficient if only two individuals start cooperating; other individuals might enter this moral network or form new ones, and through this process, moral rules will soon emerge as the spontaneous, unintended product of individuals pursuing their own interests.

(2) The moral rules that emerge are conditional *because* they appear and are maintained in a learning process; moral rules arise as individuals, while reciprocating, learn from experience that successful cooperation presupposes their existence.

(3) During the reciprocating process the motivational system of the interacting individuals is also activated, giving rise to retributive emotions; these emotions might aid considerably the reinforcement of each other's cooperative behavior and also facilitate the concurrent learning process.[20]

3. *Why Do Moral Rules Persist or Change?* A significant characteristic of the learning process that gives rise to moral rules is that it is a very long-lasting one. Trial-and-error learning is bound to work at a very slow rate

---

20 What we discuss here under the heading of morality, meaning the disposition to behave impartially, David Hume has dealt with in his treatment of the origin of the virtue of justice. All the main points stressed in the text, i.e. the learning process, the invisible-hand explanation, reciprocity, and conditional morality, are contained in the following extended citation of the *Treatise* (1740/1978, p. 498): "When therefore men have had experience enough to observe, that whatever may be the consequence of any single act of justice, perform'd by a single person, yet the whole system of actions, concurr'd in by the whole society is infinitely advantageous to the whole and to every part; it is not long before justice and property take place. Every member of society is sensible of this interest: Every one expresses this sentence to his fellows, along with the resolution he has taken of squaring his actions by it, on condition that others will do the same. No more is requisite to induce any one of them to perform an act of justice who has the first opportunity. This becomes an example to others. And thus justice establishes itself by a kind of convention or agreement; that is, by a sense of interest, suppos'd to be common to all, and where every single act is perform'd in expectation that others are to perform the like. Without such a convention, no one wou'd ever have dream'd that there was such a virtue as justice, or have been induc'd to conform his actions to it. Taking any single act, my justice may be pernicious in every aspect; and 'tis only upon the supposition, that others are to imitate my example, that I can be induc'd to embrace that virtue; since nothing but this combination can render justice advantageous, or afford me any motives to conform my self to its rules." On the moral theory of Hume, see the important survey of Kliemt (1985).

and as Kohlberg has shown, it can but does not necessarily terminate when the person becomes an adult. Thus, the interaction process must last for many years in order for the individuals to acquire a moral disposition, that is, to learn from experience the benefits of abiding by moral rules.

It is interesting to stress at this point that reciprocity, which seems to be the source of moral behavior shown by humans is also found in populations of other biological arts, such as in primates. Frans de Waal (1989, 1991) showed that chimpanzees behave according to the principle of reciprocity in food sharing when having breakfast. In the Yerkes Primate Center, nineteen chimpanzees were observed over three months to be generous toward each other in sharing food only if this generosity was consistently reciprocated. Frans de Waal has proven that the frequency with which an individual A shared food with an individual B was correlated with the frequency with which B shared its food with A. Free riding in chimpanzee populations was nearly impossible, since generosity for a second time has hardly ever been observed. Chimpanzees thus seemed to develop a horizon of expectations concerning food sharing based on the underlying reciprocity. It is thus only a small step to hypothesize that the normative dimension of human behavior is rooted in this subhuman level of expectations in primates (Voland, 1997, p. 115).

In any case, the contention that a free exchange of food (and other resources) is an original human property is falsified (Voland, 1997).[21] Ethology helps us understand the fundamental meaning of reciprocity in explaining behavior. Though, of course, it is often pernicious to draw conclusions concerning human behavior from observed regularities in animal populations, it seems that this research result supports nevertheless the argument presented here.

Since the underlying social problem to which moral rules are the solution is a general one found in every society, one can safely assume that roughly the same moral rules are bound to exist in every social community. Thus, the identical learning process will take place wherever people live together independent of the prevailing natural and cultural environments. "Major aspects of moral development are culturally universal, because all cultures have common sources of social interaction, role-taking, and social conflict which require moral integration" (Kohlberg, 1984, p. 197). To tell the truth, to keep promises, and not to

---

[21] It seems, thus, that Adam Smith was not entirely right when he stated (1776/1976, p. 17): "Nobody ever saw a dog make a fair and deliberate exchange of one bone for another with another dog. Nobody ever saw one animal by its gestures and natural cries signify to another, this is mine, that yours; I am willing to give this for that."

cheat are rules that must be followed by all individuals engaged in even the most rudimentary form of social interaction.

Because moral rules are bound to be learned by every self-conscious human being, the *content* of moral rules remains the same. What changes is only the *frequency* with which such rules are followed by the individuals in a social group. Therefore, the only critical variable that might induce change in moral rules is the size of the community within which the individuals are bound to interact.[22] *This change concerns the frequency, not the content, of moral behavior.* The dynamics associated with group size are thus, the key in reaching conclusions about the frequency of moral behavior.

Buchanan (1965/1977) has worked out the relevance of group size for the individual decision to follow a private maxim or the moral law in a Kantian sense. Although from the present perspective the acquisition of morality is not a matter of choice of a disposition, but rather a product of a continuous learning process, the main theoretical insight of Buchanan remains valid. Since the moral behavior of any individual depends on his expectation of whether the other individuals will also behave morally, and allowing for the case that everybody might stop behaving morally, the role of the group size becomes obvious.

It seems then that in small groups the frequency of moral behavior is greater than in larger groups. In other words, the well-known case of free riding in the theory of public goods (Olson, 1965) is also valid in regard to moral issues. Therefore, moral behavior must be less expected in modern societies, where the possibility of personal intercourse among the members does not exist, than in smaller communities such as primitive tribes, small villages, and neighborhoods.

This theoretical consideration can be best illustrated in relation to the exit option in the prisoner's dilemma discussed earlier. Whenever the exit costs of a certain situation are low, more available strategies will exist for anybody at any moment in time.[23] Hence, the discipline of reciprocity and

---

22 Sometimes economists and other social scientists hypothesize that market transactions can affect and even change the moral behavior of the individuals. Our argument suggests that this is a false hypothesis because moral development *occurs in childhood, before an individual engages in market activities.* For an interesting discussion of this issue see Yaffey (1998, pp. 272ff.)

23 Exit costs depend, among other things, on linguistic factors. Nettle and Dunbar (1997) argue, for example, that linguistic diversity may function as a constraint to human mobility. "The free rider, who is conceived of in many models as a ruthless exploiter of generosity who moves quickly from group to group, could not possibly survive in populations where each local group had its own language or dialect. Each

of "the shadow of the future" is relatively low when anybody can easily stop dealing with a particular person and enter a relationship with another. This is typically the case in large-number, impersonal societies in which the reciprocating mechanism functions *eclectically* and does not have the compulsory character of small communities with personal bonds. Therefore, the greater the possibility to exit due to large group size, the lower will be the frequency of moral behavior.[24] Abundant evidence offers corroboration for this theoretical contention. Crime rates are higher in big cities than in small ones. There is honor among thieves. And the extensive literature on primitive societies provided by anthropologists demonstrates that people living in tribes greatly respect the moral rules of the tribe.

4. How Are Moral Rules Adopted or Enforced? Moral rules emerge and exist only in individual brains; in this sense, one can hardly speak of moral rules as a social phenomenon without referring to the individuals who bear them. In fact, moral rules constitute an explanandum phenomenon for the social sciences only insofar as many individuals in a community follow them. From an observer's perspective, the very existence of such rules can only be indirectly inferred from the behavior that "moral individuals" show. In our problem-solving framework, the adoption of a moral rule on the part of an individual can easily be explained in terms of the distinction between old and new problems. When a person decides for the first time to cooperate, he seeks therewith to solve a new problem. After the first successful acts of cooperation have ended and the learning process has taken place, the individuals will classify this problem situation of intercourse with other individuals thereafter as an old problem and apply the moral rule automatically. According to their learning history and if individuals have had positive experiences with dealing fairly in their environment, they will employ the moral rule, often unconsciously, to solve what in their eyes appears to be an old problem.

Moral rules are from this perspective a subcategory of practical rules of the type know-how that people learn when interacting with their environment. The content of those rules refers to situations in which following the

group would be able to tell by his speech that he was an outsider and where he came from" (p. 98).

24 Obviously, mechanisms may arise in larger groups that will counterbalance this exit effect. Wofgang Kerber has suggested to us that reputation effects may diminish the importance of low exit costs in larger groups. To be known as a fair person surely enables one to find others to cooperate with more easily. This concerns only the issue of how one's own strategy will be more traceable in one's environment though (and is parallel to Frank's strategic role of emotions as signaling devices; see note 60), not the issue of the frequency of moral behavior in a large group.

interests of the individual presupposes that the interests of others can be furthered or harmed. Therefore, the moral rules that people learn always refer to other persons or to the social group as a whole.

To this theory of adoption of moral rules by trial-and-error learning, a relevant objection can be raised. One may contend that the crucial characteristic of moral rules is exactly the opposite of that presented here, that is, they are typically universal and unconditional rather than learning-specific and conditional. People act morally because they think that they are fulfilling a duty rather than just solving a problem. This argument is then strengthened by an appeal to "conscience" as the source of moral behavior and as the main driving force of people behaving in a "moral dimension."

The key in answering this question is the role of emotions in the process of acquiring the disposition of morality. During the reciprocating process and parallel to the learning process, our emotions are also molded and become "socially developed sentiments" (Mackie, 1985, p. 219), that is, our motivational system adapts to its environment. The sense of fairness and the prescriptive character of moral rules stem from the emotions formed in repeated interactions with others. Hume (1740/1978, p. 484) contended that "our sense of duty always follows the common and natural course of our passions," and Hayek explained the normative dimension of the "rules of conduct" in pointing to the feeling of fear that arises when an individual deviating from the known rules proceeds to actions with unpredictable consequences. "The knowledge of some regularities of the environment will create a preference for those kinds of conduct which produce a confident expectation of certain consequences, and an aversion to doing something unfamiliar and fear when it has been done. This establishes a sort of connection between the knowledge that rules exist in the objective world and a disinclination to deviate from the rules commonly followed in action, and therefore also between the belief that events follow rules and the feeling that one ought' to observe rules in one's conduct" (Hayek, 1967, p. 79).

Thus, the molding of our emotions happens concomitantly with the learning process and "good or bad conscience" arises as a feeling because, during the process of social interaction, not only the cognitive system but also the motivational system is responding to its environment. Once the long-lasting process of rule acquisition has taken place, both the cognitive and motivational systems are formed in such a way that respect for the moral rules is secured. Therefore, moral rules are internally enforced, and no external enforcement agency for rule compliance is needed.

7.3. SOCIAL NORMS

The issue of social norms has been traditionally a main domain of research for sociology. The Durkheim–Parsons tradition in sociology found a symmetry between norms institutionalized in social systems and values internalized in personality systems that helped provide order in social groups.[25] The reason is that "the concept of a norm at a macrosocial level, governing the behavior of individuals at a microsocial level, provides a convenient device for explaining individual behavior, taking the social system as a given" (Coleman, 1990, p. 36). But, obviously, the real issue to be explained is why norms exist and how they emerge in the first place, before one can hypothesize that they are also followed or internalized by the individuals and thus produce social order.

1. *Why Do Social Norms Exist?* Social norms exist because they provide solutions to different social problems in which conflicting individual interests prevail. Since social norms vary tremendously among different places and times, it is useless to discern stylized problems to which social norms give an answer. This variety of social settings characterized by different constellations of social interaction distinguishes social norms from moral rules. The moral rules are, to a great degree, culture-independent since they provide solutions to the more or less identical problem of cooperation that is bound to exist whenever individuals interact. Social norms, on the other hand, being also social rules, are less fundamental than moral rules in that they regulate settings appearing mainly in specific times and places. In addition, social norms are enforced by an enforcement agency external to the agent, which is usually the other individuals in the group. Thus, the definition of Axelrod (1986, p. 1097) seems appropriate: "A norm exists in a given social setting to the extent that individuals usually act in a certain way and are often punished when seen not to be acting this way."

2. *How Do Social Norms Emerge?* Social norms emerge spontaneously in an evolutionary process of the invisible-hand type. Before discussing

---

[25] See, e.g., Parsons and Shils (1951, p. 56): "[S]ystems of value standards . . . and other patterns of culture, when *institutionalized* in social systems and *internalized* in personality systems, guide the actor with respect to both the *orientation to ends* and the *normative regulation* of means and expressive activities, whenever the need-dispositions of the actor allow choices in these matters."

the mechanism of their emergence, the rational choice contribution to the issue will briefly be reviewed. The contribution of Coleman (1990b) can serve as the best example of the rational choice theory of norms. Coleman identifies two sets of conditions that give rise to norms. The first set concerns the conditions in which a demand for effective norms will arise and the second concerns the condition in which the demand will be satisfied (1990b, p. 35). According to Coleman, the genesis of a norm lies in the externalities of actions, positive or negative, that cannot be overcome by simple transactions à la Coase.[26] Thus, the main reason for a demand for norms is the external effects of actions undertaken by an individual and affecting more than one other individual, so that bargaining to internalize the externality via exchange is impossible. This demand for an effective norm can be satisfied if the sanctioning problem, or the "second-order public goods problem" can be overcome. Rational agents who are assumed to be forward-looking will sanction a deviator only when their immediate benefit outweighs their sanctioning costs. In a rational choice model this is by no means evident, however, mainly because rational agents will always have an incentive to cheat and let the other members of the group sanction the deviator. The way out of this second-order free-rider problem cannot consistently come from a rational choice perspective in the case of social norms that evidently emerge without any commitment device on the part of the agents. In fact, Coleman gives an inherently inconsistent solution to this problem when he writes: "The existence of a norm facilitates achievement of the social optimum by making use of *the social relationships* that exist in a social system to overcome the second-order free-rider problem" (1990b, p. 53).

But where do these social relationships come from? If the rational choice model is applied consistently, then even these social relationships cannot provide any certainty that the second-order public goods problem will be solved because the possibility to cheat remains intact. The second-order public goods problem is just transformed into a third-order public goods problem in which every individual in a social relationship has an incentive to cheat, and so on, ad infinitum. The only possible way to avoid such an infinite regress is obviously to *hypothesize that agents are able to learn* and thus to adopt an evolutionary perspective when accounting for the emergence of norms.

Such a perspective shares with the rational choice model the view that agents are motivated by a utility increase in their action, but it focuses on

---

[26] See Coase (1960).

their ability to learn by trial and error.[27] This model finds its straightforward application in the explanation of social norms that emerge and evolve step by step. However, in the process of their emergence, the conscious calculation of costs and benefits on the part of the agents is not the whole story.

For an invisible-hand explanation of the emergence of social norms, three stages must be distinguished. In the first stage, when agents are confronted with a situation in which they have little or no experience, that is, with a new problem situation, they "will call on the experience they have of similar situations they have faced in the past in deciding what action to take" (Binmore and Samuelson, 1994, p. 51). They will, in other words, employ some *inferential strategies* and use analogous solutions to the new problem situation. The problems that they are confronted with are practical ones, since they concern situations in which "knowledge how" is needed. But the agents do not need to be conscious of the fact that the problem they face is, from an external point of view, a social one. In fact, "people seldom have a good grasp of the strategic realities of situations which they encounter frequently in their daily lives" (ibid.). Thus, they will be aided by their experience of analogous situations to solve what appears to them to be a personal problem. If this does not work, then they will create alternative solutions and chose the one from which they expect the highest utility increase. If the trial is successful, they will apply the solution again in the future until it becomes a routine. Thus, adaptation to the new circumstances in the environment will have taken place, and a regularity in behavior will be observed.

This behavior, if successful in the sense of increasing utility for the agent who employs it, will be imitated – and this is the second stage of analysis – by other individuals who also expect a utility increase. Research in social psychology has shown that successful models of behavior tend to be imitated in a process of observational learning (Bandura, 1986). As Opp (1982, p. 64) stresses: "If, for example, a subset of members of a group performs actions which are rewarded and are observed by other members, most of the observers will expect to receive the same or similar

---

[27] See Nee and Ingram (1998, p. 29): "The evolutionary account of norms suggests that they emerge through a trial-and-error process by which members of a group negotiate and bargain over competing norms. In this view, the selection of a norm is governed by whether the members of the group are individually rewarded through their cooperation. Such rewards include the good feelings that come from membership in a group. . . . The successful attainment of rewards reinforces the norm and provides the incentives for upholding it."

rewards if they imitate the models." Learning by imitation leads to a diffusion of the behavior of the innovator and thus to the following of the same rule by many or all members of the group. This diffusion of the behavior among the members of the group also involves the diffusion of shared practical knowledge. The agents have learned that in their social environment, which they perceive as more or less given, following this behavior increases their utility. They need not necessarily realize that this behavior offers at the same time a solution to a problem that, viewed from an observer's perspective, is classified as a social one.

In the third stage of the analysis, reasons must be offered for why people who follow a certain behavior tend to sanction the deviators. The general reason, according to the general position that we defend throughout our study, must be that those who punish the deviators do so in order to increase their own utility. However, this does not mean that whenever group deviation occurs, the members of the group engage in cost–benefit analysis of whether it is beneficial or not for them to punish the deviator. The whole issue must be thought of in terms of *behavior*. Whenever people perceive that a certain behavior directly harms their interests, they will adopt a disposition to retaliate according to the reciprocity principle discussed earlier. But in the case of norms, the interesting point is obviously that the effect of deviant behavior will harm the interests of the *whole group*, not just of one individual. In those cases where people *perceive* the deviating behavior as harmful for all the members of the group, they tend to sanction a deviation every time it occurs because they generally hold that such a deviation is not a good thing. There is, in a way, always a conservative bias in society in the sense that most people expect others to adopt the behavior that most of them follow.

The obvious question arises, then, of why at all people hold such beliefs that norm deviations must be sanctioned, even if sanctioning involves costs to the sanctioner. Four arguments are relevant. First, the monitoring of social norms is often intrinsic to the social relationship; therefore, enforcement occurs as a by-product of social interaction (Nee, 1998b, p. 87; Nee and Ingram, 1998, p. 28; Nee and Strang, 1998, p. 709). Second, those who conform usually attain a higher status and power within the group, and they are therefore indirectly rewarded for their enforcing activity (Nee and Ingram, 1998, p. 30).[28] The third argument concerns the

---

[28] McAdams stresses the role of esteem in the emergence of social norms, arguing that "[t]he key feature of esteem is that individuals do not always bear a cost by granting

cognitive background of every sanctioning act. Due to the complexity of the world and the cognitive limitations of humans, they are bound to act according to the learned rule that requires punishment of deviation each time it occurs, without rethinking each time whether the *concrete act* of punishment is directly beneficial for them or not.

The fourth and most important argument has to do with the motivational system of each individual behaving as the enforcer of a regular behavior of the group. People have a preference to live in a predictable environment (Hayek, 1967, p. 79; Opp, 1982, p. 67), and whenever their expectations regarding the behavior of others are disappointed, they tend to have a feeling of uneasiness. As Schlicht in his discussion of customs has stressed, customs, that is, behavioral dispositions inherited from the past, have a "motivational force per se as brought about by history" (1993, p. 178). In other words, the mere fact that an expectation is disappointed brings about a feeling of uneasiness (Sugden, 1998, p. 85), vengefulness, or "moralistic aggression" (Trivers, 1971) in the agent. As Opp in his excellent article puts it (1982, p. 67): "Even in the case of umbrellas in the rain, people who strongly prefer to use umbrellas themselves would also prefer others to do so too. People do, in fact, generally prefer to be able to predict their environment. Thus we may assume a positive correlation between the intensity of preference for a behavior and the degree to which irregular behavior of others is costly."

This fourth argument is equivalent to the empirical hypothesis that most people increase their utility most when they live in a predictable environment. It is important to stress that this hypothesis is consistent with our main motivational assumption and is to be distinguished from any other kind of assumption regarding altruistic motivation. Empirical research might lend support to the existence of genetically hardwired other-regarding preferences in us. But as we have already stressed in Chapter 5, it is methodologically appropriate to use Ockham's razor and assume only that *most people increase their utility most when they live in a predictable environment,* which is a weaker hypothesis than the existence of hardwired feelings of love or duty *as long as both can explain the same phenomenon at issue,* that is, the sanctioniong behavior of a sufficiently large number of individuals in a group.

---

different levels of esteem to others. Because the cost is often zero, esteem sanctions are not necessarily subject to the second-order collective action problem that makes the explanation of norms difficult" (1997, p. 365). Costless esteem is therefore a by-product of social interaction.

Summarizing, due to these four reasons, every deviation from a standard behavior tends to be sanctioned. The conditions for *norm emergence* are therewith fulfilled, that is, a behavior followed by many members of a group *and* sanctioning of deviation by group members. Obviously, the degree to which members of a group will actually be prepared to proceed to sanctions will depend on how much they perceive that a deviant behavior is inflicting harm on them.

3. Why Do Social Norms Persist or Change? In his important article on the evolution of social norms, Axelrod (1986) has shown that in order for a norm to be stable in a population, an important degree of vengefulness must exist among the members of the population. His simulation results show that in fact no one has any incentives to punish a defection, except for the case that one introduces a metanorm that one must punish those who do not punish a defection. In the simulation of a "metanorms game" in which the non-punishment of a defection is itself sanctioned by the rest of the members of a group, each norm remains relatively stable once it is established. But as Elster (1989a, p. 133) points out, it is improbable that such metanorms, which sanction people who fail to sanction people who fail to sanction people, and so on, might exist in the real world. "Sanctions tend to run out of steam at two or three removes from the original violation" (Elster, 1989b, p. 10, 5 n4).

Thus, as long as at least a metanorm exists that guarantees the sanctioning of the nonsanctioneers of a primary behavior, the norm will be relatively stable. The existence of sanctions does not imply that social norms can never change, though. A change in norms presupposes, according to what we have said, *a change in the environment* that calls for a new adaptation. Such a change will either induce a subsequent change in the incentives to sanction the deviating behavior or it will alter the structure of the social problem. This, in turn, means that an innovative agent will try out different problem solutions and then adopt a routine that will be subsequently imitated by other agents; in the end, his social behavior will become a new norm. Norms are adaptive devices to environmental changes in the social setting. Thus, they are usually transformed whenever a relatively permanent shift in the social environment takes place. For example, since the percentage of females in the labor market has increased, males are expected to help with housekeeping and are sanctioned by friends when they don't.[29]

[29] Boyd and Richerson (1994), in what they call a Darwinian model of the evolution of

Nevertheless, this environmental change need not be a true or objective one, from an observer's point of view, in order for an adaptational change of norms to occur. It suffices if the pioneering individual *perceives his given environmental situation as a different one* and tries out a new behavior, and the rest follow him because they think that this new behavior will also increase their own utility. This cognitive-emotional model of norm emergence and change avoids many difficulties of the rational choice approach. The standard weakness of rational choice models that assume forward-looking agents is that they see a social norm as an equilibrium outcome without specifying a mechanism of how such an equilibrium developed (Johnson, 1997, p. 17). Besides, although equilibrium analysis does not imply determinism, and although it suggests the existence of multiple equilibria, it does not provide an adequate explanation of why a particular equilibrium will be generated from the set of possibilities shown in the analysis. These weaknesses, we contend, can be remedied by the model proposed here.[30]

4. *How Are Social Norms Adopted or Enforced?* In many sociological theories, the adoption of norms plays a central role since structure and order in society are supposed to emerge when individuals show norm-

norms, also stress the adaptational characteristics of the process of norm change. In what is basically a methodological paper, Toboso (1995, p. 72) also stresses this point: "[T]his informal institution may be gradually modified or altered if new circumstances systematically and increasingly led individuals to perceive the average results as more and more disappointing."

[30] The best modification of the rational approach is undertaken by Knight and Ensminger; see Knight (1992), Ensminger and Knight (1997), and Knight and Ensminger (1998). In the bargaining mechanism that they discuss, the question of which norm will be established is resolved by asymmetries in power. "[T]he norm most likely to be established will be the one that manifests the interests of those actors who enjoy a relative bargaining advantage" (Knight and Ensminger, 1998, p. 106). As a proxy for bargaining power they propose asymmetries in resource ownership. Since an individual behavior, to become a social norm, must be ultimately shared by all or most group members the hypothesis put forward is that it is mainly those individuals who possess bargaining power who are most able to get away with violations of established social norms and to establish a trend so that those with less power who wish to interact with them find it in their interest to comply with the new norm. But this theory does not pay due attention to the "emotions, particularly fear and outrage, that motivate sanctions" (Levi, 1997, p. 18), such as the one proposed here. Besides, it is doubtful whether it is a genuine bargaining mechanism that helps shift social norms rather than having bargaining power (Simons, 1997, p. 19). Still, the great merit of this approach is that it explicitly accounts for the benefits of social rules that generate an unequal distribution of the benefits of social interactions; but its primary application seems to be in politics and the emergence of formal rules rather than in the domain of informal rules.

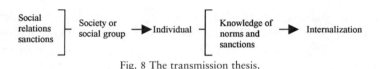

Fig. 8 The transmission thesis.

driven behavior. For example, Blau (1964, p. 253) states: "The cultural values and norms that prevail in a society are the matrix that forms the social relations among groups and individuals. These values and norms become institutionalized and perpetuated from generation to generation, although not without modification, and they shape the course of social life in the society and the social patterns that emerge in particular groups." This amounts to a common thesis in sociology, the "Thesis of the Normative Regulation of Behavior" which states that if norms are institutionalized and internalized, then the behavior that is in accordance with the norms occurs (Opp, 1979, p. 777). This thesis is closely related to a second milestone of sociological theory that Opp calls the "Transmission Thesis" and that is best illustrated by Fig. 8.[31]

Because of the existence of social relations and sanctions, social norms become well known to the individuals in a society. Once known, the social norms are internalized because of the fear of sanctions. Internalization of the norms leads to adherence to the norms, and thus individuals show norm-guided behavior.

The Thesis of the Normative Regulation of Behavior and the Transmission Thesis suffer from the obvious shortcoming that the very existence of norms is not explained in the first place. Besides, sociologists (and anthropologists) have often no explanation for why *self-interested* people should pay any attention to norms.[32] From our point of view, social norms emerge in an invisible-hand process whereby an innovative, utility-increasing solution to a social problem is initiated and becomes diffused. Deviations from it, once established, are sanctioned by group members. We have offered four arguments for why group members motivated solely by their own utility increase will bear the costs of sanctions in the first place. Once this step is taken, it is plausible to hypothesize that deviations will determine which acts are accompanied by which sanctions from the environment in the form of IF . . . THEN rules in their minds. Only in this sense will an internalization of norms (so often employed in sociology)

---

[31] Fig. 4 is reproduced from Opp (1979, p. 780) in a slightly modified form.
[32] This is not true for the sociologists who are individualistically oriented, but they are a minority in the sociological profession.

take place. Such acquisition of certain patterns of behavior on the part of individuals, once adopted, is bound to appear to an external observer as a blind, norm-driven behavior. The fact that these patterns of behavior may often change is enough to prove that what seems a lawlike behavioral pattern is only conditional on the environmental feedback and the learning histories of the individuals.

7.4. ORDER WITHOUT LAW

The existence of informal institutions in a society definitely provide some kind of order. Conventions, moral rules, and social norms that are adopted and enforced by individuals in a society help to increase the predictability of their behavior and stabilize the mutual expectations of the agents. In this sense, the informal institutions are *one* solution to the Hobbesian problem of social order, but the issue remains open as to whether this solution is partial or complete, that is, whether a society without a formal law and a state as an enforcement agency is viable.

Before we address this old question, it is useful to remember that this problem has often been discussed in a slightly different and perhaps more general way under the heading of "the tragedy of the commons." Since the time of the very influential article by Hardin (1968) and the equally challenging book by Olson (1965), the hypothesis has been put forward that "unless the number of individuals is quite small, or unless there is coercion or some other special device to make individuals act in their common interest, *rational, self-interested individuals will not act to achieve their common or group interest*" (Olson, 1965, p. 2). One could distinguish between a more economically oriented and a more sociopolitical application of this general hypothesis, which is mainly of interest here. Before proceeding to the question that concerns us here, that is, whether the informal institutions alone can solve the problem that Olson's law addresses, some empirical evidence on the economic aspect will prove useful.

In two very important books, Ostrom (1990) and Ostrom, Gardner, and Walker (1994) challenge what we have called the more "economic" validity of Olson's hypothesis. They argue that in common-pool resource problems, the pessimistic prediction of the theories of Hardin, Olson, and all those based on the prisoner's dilemma are empirically incorrect. Ostrom (1990) offers empirical evidence of case studies proving that in fact small-scale common-pool resources (CPR), where the CPR is located within one country and the number of individuals affected is between 50 and 15,000 persons (p. 26), do not always lead to "state activity" as a solution. According to the evidence, it is not necessary "that a central authority must assume continuing responsibility to make unitary decisions for a particular resource" (p. 14) or "that a central authority should parcel out ownership rights to the resource and then allow individuals to pursue their own self-interest within a set of well-defined property rights" (ibid.). Instead, Ostrom argues – in accordance with the theory presented here – that "individuals try to solve problems as effectively as they can" (p. 25), which can lead to a large variety of institutions designed to solve the CPR problem. Thus, "many successful CPR institutions are rich mixtures of 'private-like and 'public-like' institutions defying classification in a sterile dichotomy" (p. 14). A crucial factor that aids cooperation in CPR settings is the possibility of *communication* between persons in a local setting, that is, in our terms, the existence of shared mental models. "Thus, it is possible that they can learn whom to trust, what effects their actions will have on each other and on the CPR, and how to organize themselves to gain benefits and avoid harm. When individuals have lived in such institutions for a substantial time and have developed shared norms and patterns of reciprocity, they possess social capital with which they can build institutional arrangements for resolving CPR dilemmas" (p. 184).

Although those results are impressive, the condition of their validity is still the small scale, that is, small numbers of persons and the possibility of communication.[33] The alternative of Ostrom and her collaborates can best be summarized in the hypothesis that *the relatively personal relationships in small and intermediate-sized groups that remain stable for a substantial period of time guarantee the trial of different problem solutions to CPR problems that turn out to be partly successful.*[34] Obviously, in large-number settings with impersonal relationships (i.e., without com-

---

33 These are also the conditions that underlie the anthropological studies on sharing in hunting and gathering societies. People in such societies share a lot of food resources with persons outside of the nuclear family, overcoming the collective action problem by means of cooperation (Hawkes, 1993). This phenomenon, which is at the heart of a lively dispute among anthropologists (for a review see Ensminger, 1998, pp. 781ff.), appears in small-scale societies where the possibility of cooperation is given. In their laboratory experiments, Bohnet and Frey (1999) found that communication is not always required to increase cooperation in public-goods settings. In prisoner's dilemma games and dictator games, even silent identification suffices for significantly higher cooperation rates than in the case of anonymity.

34 For a more detailed exposition of the exact conditions of overcoming CPR problems and for institutional change, see Ostrom (1990, ch. 6).

munication), the tragedy of the commons remains.[35] Is an analogous reasoning valid when Olson's law is applied to the fundamental issue of the social order, which is of interest here? In a much discussed book, Ellickson (1991) answers this question in the affirmative and contends that "Order Without Law" is possible. He formulates the hypothesis that "members of a close-knit group develop and maintain norms whose content serves to maximize the aggregate welfare that members obtain in their workaday affairs with one another" (p. 167). Although this hypothesis suffers from many shortcomings, since it is more or less implied that those norms are in a way efficient (which from the evolutionary perspective adopted here need not be the case[36]), it remains at its core a defendable hypothesis, mainly in the weaker formulation that "members of tight social groups will informally encourage each other to engage in cooperative behavior" (p. 167). Ellickson provides evidence from Shasta County, California, that neighbors settle their disputes "by developing and enforcing adaptive norms of neighborliness that are not always consistent with formal legal entitlements" (p. 4). In his attempt to prove the deficits of the Coase theorem, Ellickson has found that, in Shasta County, order can prevail without law and that in fact neighbors settle their disputes according to informal social rules, not by invoking legal norms.

Ellickson's hypothesis that order can prevail without law is, as he himself recognizes, hardly novel (p. 168). In fact, it is one of the main insights of anthropology, and of exchange theory in sociology, that in relatively close-knit groups, order can prevail without the state enforcing property rights. But Ellickson provides additional empirical material from Shasta County that corroborates the general thrust of the argument; in addition, he offers a precise definition of a close-knit group. In his words, "A group is *close-knit* when informal power is broadly distributed among

---

[35] Ostrom (1990, p. 183): "When individuals who have high discount rates and little mutual trust act independently, without the capacity to communicate, to enter into binding agreements, and to arrange for monitoring and enforcing mechanisms, they are not likely to choose jointly beneficial strategies unless such strategies happen to be their dominant strategies."

[36] Up to now, we have carefully avoided providing any efficiency considerations or criteria since they are clearly of a normative character. Ellickson himself also explicitly avoids the term "efficient norms" and formulates his hypothesis so that "welfare-maximizing" norms are predicted to prevail in close-knit groups (1991, p. 172, n.18). But whether efficient or welfare-maximizing, the hypothesis predicts that the norms are in some way *collectively rational*. The famous example of vendettas prevailing mainly in such close-knit groups suffices to falsify this assumption; from an evolutionary perspective, norms such as vendettas can be explained as maladaptations to the environmment.

group members and the information pertinent to informal control circulates easily among them" (p. 177f.). In our terminology, the content of the shared mental models of the individuals in a group must be quite substantial, that is, *communication* must be frequent so that information networks can be built and, consequently, the social norms enforced. "In social life," as Ellickson mentions (p. 180), "people must worry about their reputations, because historical information can be shared."

The existence of informal institutions is undoubtedly conducive to social order. But are conventions, moral rules, and social norms *sufficient* to provide order in the absence of a state? The answer is negative. Just as the doctrine of "legal centralism,"[37] that is, the belief that most interindividual disputes are directly or indirectly settled by law[38] (Williamson, 1985, p. 165)[39] does not hold[40] the other extreme proposition – of informal institutions alone guaranteeing social order – is also invalid. In fact, Ellickson's hypothesis is based on the crucial assumption "that a close-knit group invariably has exogenous foundational rules, legal or otherwise, that endow and secure basic rights in amounts ample to support voluntary exchange" (1991, p. 174). In other words, informal institutions produce order, but obviously a stateless society is not viable, at least not in modern times.[41]

---

[37] As Galanter (1981, p. 1) puts it, the legal centralism tradition maintains that "disputes require 'access' to a forum external to the original social setting of the dispute [and that] remedies will be provided as prescribed in some body of authoritative learning and dispensed by experts who operate under the auspices of the state."

[38] Williamson (1985, p. 164): "[T]he legal centralism tradition maintains that the courts are well suited for administering justice whenever contract disputes arise. If few cases are brought to the courts for disposition, that is only becasue contracts are carefully drawn and/or because the law of contract is fully nuanced and the relevant facts are easy to display. Litigated disputes rarely arise, because the parties can anticipate their disposition and will quickly effect settlement themselves. The exceptions – that is, the cases that appear in court – merely prove the rule that court ordering is efficacious."

[39] On a critical review of the legal-centralist tradition see Ellickson (1991, pp. 138–47) and Ellickson (1998).

[40] In a seminal paper, Stewart Macaulay (1963) found that norms of fair dealing shaped and constrained the behavior of business firms in Wisconsin as much as substantive legal rules did. See also Bernstein (1996, pp. 1787ff.).

[41] Nee and Ingram present a similar argument on the necessity of third-party enforcement (1998, pp. 30ff.). In an important paper Milgrom, North, and Weingast (1990) analyze the role of Law Merchant and private judges in medieval and early modern Europe. They show that private judges can provide third-party enforcement even though they have actually no binding authority to enforce obligations (that is, they do not avail of police, jails, etc.). Such private third-party enforcement can only

Empirical evidence derived mainly from anthropology supports the view of order without law mainly for *primitive societies*. Here the classical contribution of Evans-Pritchard (1940) must be mentioned. It explains the *maintenance of order* among the Nuer, a pastoral people living in the Upper Nile region of Africa, without a formal agency enforcing the law.

Eggertsson (1990, pp. 305ff.) refers to the Icelandic Commonwealth in the period 930–1262 A.D., which survived for about 200 years, although "it lacked an executive branch of government – a principal who would monopolize the legitimate use of violence" (p. 306). But in both cases, the Nuer and the Icelandic Commonwealth, the respective societies consisted of rather homogeneous populations with kinship ties and good informational networks that helped to preserve order without formal enforcement.[42] As soon as one focuses away from primitive societies, a central enforcement agency becomes indispensable. In fact, in modern times, states as enforcing agencies of formal institutions are ubiquitous and constitute a phenomenon calling for explanation that we will address in the next chapter.

work with regard to commercial life, though – more specifically, trade – and it does not encompass the other aspects of social life. Besides, historically, the Law Merchant has been a rather rare phenomenon, and it was eventually replaced by a system of state enforcement in the late Middle Ages in Western Europe. The medieval merchant guild, on the other hand, was a more widespread phenomenon (Greif, Milgrom, and Weingast, 1994), but as in the case of the Law Merchant, it was an important institution mainly for commercial life.

[42] Bates (1983, ch. 1), in his discussion of Evans-Pritchard's evidence on the Nuer with the aid of the prisoner's dilemma, shows how compensation and arbitration function as the central mechanisms for the preservation of order in the stateless society of the Nuer. In the absence of a central enforcing agency, deterrence, cross-cutting ties, and religious beliefs act as the substitute external means of enforcement. See also the analysis of leveling and its role in producing social order in Miller and Cook (1998).

8

Formal Institutions

In the preceding chapter, we saw how informal institutions emerge, how they are adopted by the individuals, and how they are enforced. Individuals respecting conventions, following moral rules, and adopting social norms cause, as an unintended outcome of their action, the emergence of social order. In close-knit groups, informal institutions suffice to provide stability of expectations and discipline among members, mainly when group members engage in personal relationships. Thus, in primitive societies, informal institutions alone are capable of providing social order, and often such societies can dispense with an additional institution that has the explicit mission of enforcing certain social rules. Does this also hold for societies that grow bigger and in which the relations between the individuals become more and more impersonal?

De Jasay (1995) gives an affirmative answer to this question by pointing out that the so-called Large Group problem "enjoys more generous credit than its intellectual content deserves" (p. 23). De Jasay criticizes the alleged analogy "between social groups with many members and n-person indefinitely repeated prisoner's dilemmas where n is a large number, or the players are anonymous, or both" (ibid.) According to his view, society does not possess the homogeneity that the game-theoretical analogy presupposes. Moreover, society must be conceived as the sum of small groups whose individual members are in fact engaged in contracts and relations with each other. Technically speaking, individuals are engaged in many separate games rather than in one multiperson game. This, in turn, means that "there is a complex and dense web of communication in which it is both easy to send and profitable to receive information about prospective players" (p. 24). This possibility of communication is crucial since the "impersonal" relations that are supposed to be the decisive cause for the emergence of a state are transformed into personal ones. De Jasay also doubts the idea of *impersonal* exchange on empirical grounds since " a practicing business man . . . would simply see no possible occasion to deal with unknown parties otherwise than in self-enforcing contracts; least of all would he deal on credit. He would always place identified parties, banks, brokers, bondsmen, wholesalers, quality inspectors and so on, between himself and the 'nameless' credit customer" (p. 25, n9). Impersonal exchanges "are imaginary constructs, except in the world of cash-and-carry, – a world to which enforcement of any kind is irrelevant" (p. 25). De Jasay concludes that the existence of the state is to be explained by the existential risk that a stateless society runs in the case of conflict with other societies that have a protective agency, not by the alleged necessity of impartial third-party enforcement *within* a society.

De Jasay's main argument does *not* consider the necessity of enforcement in general – to our knowledge there is no author that doubts the necessity of enforcing contracts – *nor* does De Jasay deny that third-party enforcement is necessary to provide social order. In fact, his main thesis is that "enforcing coalitions will form readily, and will tend to be sufficiently powerful" (p. 22), and thus, defectors will be punished accordingly by other social group members. De Jasay, nevertheless, denies the necessity of establishing a specialized protective institution to provide third-party enforcement, his main argument being that every individual in society is simultaneously acting within different social groups whose members can sufficiently provide third-party enforcement. But this argument suffers at a crucial point: it considers individual behavior to be the same in both small groups per se and small groups that are parts of larger groups or societies. This need not be true, however.

An individual acting in a small group, as for example in a primitive society, is *bound* to behave cooperatively because he does not possess *any* alternative to exit from the group. An individual acting in one of the small groups that is part of a more inclusive society can, on the contrary, exit the group with relatively low costs. Those costs are lower if within the inclusive society the cultural background is the same, that is, language, symbols, and so on.[1] Thus, the costs of cheating in a small group of a more inclusive society are considerably lower than the defection costs in a small group per se. Cheaters will have less inhibitions to stop cheating when they are sure that they can find somebody else to cooperate with at low

---

[1] On the relationship between cultural homogeneity and exit costs see Mantzavinos (1996a).

exit costs. Because this applies to every member of a small group within a more inclusive society, and thus mobility is de facto greater, there will be, in addition, weaker individual incentives to punish the defector. If everyone knows that the defector can exit the small group at low personal exit costs, then inevitably everyone will *learn* after some time that it doesn't pay to bear the costs of punishment since the defector, to avoid discipline, might simply leave the group.

As a conclusion, one must hold that in larger groups or societies trust becomes a scarcer product since the discipline of reciprocity and the "shadow of the future" are relative low. Individuals capable of learning are bound to realize that when they act within a large group, the probability of dealing with a defector increases. Since the content of individual learning depends decisively on environmental feedback, individuals acting in large groups must be expected to learn other lessons concerning the issue of trust than individuals acting in small groups. In other words, the content of the learning process of any individual living in a primitive tribe will differ considerably from those "lessons" acquired in a modern complex society. This differentiated learning process lies at the heart of the emergence of the state as an enforcing agency.

1. Why Does the State Exist? The state exists because it provides a solution to a twin problem faced by individuals in a society: the problem of trust and protection from the aggression of individuals of the same society *and* of those of different societies.[2] The *social* problem of trust is just another facet of the issue of credible commitments (North 1993b), that is, of the social setting in which a second moving individual can exploit the trustful co-operative behavior of the first mover.[3] Güth and Kliemt (1994) present a game-theoretical stylization of this problem, which they call the "game of trust,"[4] reproduced in Fig. 9.

The two moves N, T of player 1 can be interpreted as corresponding to "no trust" and "trust" respectively. The move E refers to the "exploita-

---

2 See Albert (1978, p. 95): "The security of peace inside and outside of a society appears in fact to be only possible, to the extent that it is obtainable at all, once state authority has been established." (Translation by C. M.)

3 Güth and Kliemt (1994, p. 160) observe: "Without commitment power exchange and agreement are precarious. If one side moves first and fulfills its promise, the other one, now in the advantageous position of a second mover, does not have an incentive to comply with the terms of the agreement. . . . [This] underlying problem of trust and reward pervades social life throughout."

4 The game of trust is a variant of the stage game of Rosenthal's centipede game (1981).

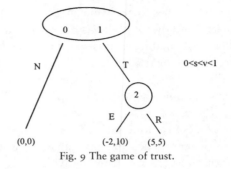

Fig. 9 The game of trust.

tion" of the trust of the first player by the second player, whereas R symbolizes "(fair) reward." At the start, player 1 must choose between the strategies N or T. If he chooses N, the interaction ends with the payoff (0,0), which in fact means that no interaction takes place because player 1 does not trust player 2. If player 1 chooses T, then player 2 has to make a further choice between strategies E (exploitation) and R (fair reward). If player 2 chooses E, then he or she gets a payoff of 10, whereas player 1 receives -2. If player 2 chooses R, then they both receive 5. The game of trust is a more illustrative representation of social settings than the much more often cited prisoner's dilemma, which is a simultaneous-move game because social interaction is typically characterized by sequential moves.

In primitive societies, the shadow of the future and the impossibility of exiting the group motivate player 2 to choose the fair reward – strategy 2. In modern societies, nothing guarantees that all players in the position of player 2 will choose R all of the time and that other players (3, 4, 5, etc.) will be always willing to punish player 2 if they choose E. A special enforcing institution arises: the state, which guarantees the punishment of individuals in the position of player 2. Its existence is also due to the benefits that the division of labor provides in the case of the production of the good "enforcement of contracts." In other words, the fact that a specialized enforcement agency arises can at first be explained by the familiar argument of classical political economy that specialization in the production of a good increases the output and is thus efficient. An additional reason for the existence of the state is the protection of the society from the aggression of other societies. Nevertheless, these two reasons might explain why states exist, but not how they emerge or how they change or why they have a *monopoly* over enforcing power. These questions will be addressed next.

2. *How Does the State Emerge?* Up to now, we have seen that the state is bound to arise once the society grows bigger and the relationships among its members become increasingly impersonal. What is the exact mechanism that leads to the emergence of the state in large societies? The key to this answer is once again the consistent application of the behavioral assumptions presented in Part I of this study. As self-interested individuals, "we are naturally partial to ourselves, and to our friends; but are capable of learning the advantage resulting from a more equitable conduct" (Hume, 1751/1975, p. 188). And since, to stay a while with Hume, "men are necessarily born in a family society . . . and are trained up by their parents to some rule of conduct and behavior" (1751/1975, p. 190), they are bound to learn the benefits of following those rules, provided that the other group members also follow them. With the enlargement of society and its advancing impersonalization, it suffices if a creative individual realizes the potential benefits of cheating and starts to free ride on the promises given by the rest. If a sufficient number of other cheaters imitate him, then an increasing group of free riders will be established after some time. This, in turn, means that the environmental input of the other individuals, that is, the honest or moral ones, will change. They will have collectively learned that *first,* cooperation is beneficial, but *second,* that free riders exist in increasing numbers, and *third,* that the punishment or protection costs have increased because of the larger numbers and the subsequently increased complexity of the relationships. This, in turn, means that they will collectively learn that protection from free riders (or trust) is a relatively scarce good.

This collective lesson will lead to a conscious demand for protection by every individual separately. Thus, everybody will face a practical problem of preventing free riding on given promises. The importance of the process of collective action becomes clear: *A demand for protection arises.* Each individual will seek to solve his problem of protection by demanding force against the free riders. The satisfaction of this demand can, in principle, occur by two alternative methods: either everybody will devote some of their time and energy to form coalitions against free riders each time they defect, or a protective agency will arise specializing in the provision of the good "protection against free riders." Considering the immense complexity of the relationships between members of a large group or society and the immense transaction costs, consisting mainly of the costs of gathering and evaluating information on the exact nature of free riding, it is reasonable to hypothesize that some creative individuals will establish and run a business providing protection. The division of labor will also take place in regard to protection, although as we will see next, the idiosyncratic nature of the provided good will cause some complications.

There is no reason to assume that, at least at the beginning, only one such protective agency is bound to exit. On the contrary, it is plausible that many protective agencies will exist within the society. Each of these "protective firms" will be characterized by the peculiarity that it will avail itself of a mechanism of violence *meant* to be exercised for the protection of its members but in fact providing an opportunity to oppress those same members it is meant to protect. No general rules of the game exist at this stage, and this fact makes this second possibility of oppression appear very appealing to the "entrepreneurs" running the protective agencies. The mere limit to such oppression will be the conventions, moral rules, and social norms that those entrepreneurs bear, since they are themselves members of a cultural community. Those informal institutions will be in a way the general rules of the game for the production of protection by the different agencies. Given the self-interested nature of humans and the impersonality of the relationships, though, those informal social rules will hardly suffice to prevent entrepreneurs from employing their mechanism of violence to oppress their customers. Nevertheless, there is no reason to assume that all protective agencies will exercise the same degree of oppression on their subjects; instead, a variety of agencies in regard to oppression will arise. In this division-of-labor stage of the argument, the situation within a society or cultural community (with shared informal institutions) will appear as depicted in Fig. 10.

Within the society or cultural community S_1, many protective agencies $P_1, P_2, P_3, \ldots P_n$ might arise. Each of them will supply protection to a group of customers depicted as $G_1, G_2, G_3, \ldots G_n$ in Fig. 10. The individuals seeking protection by P_1 belong to the group of individuals that is also protected by P_1, and they are depicted by $I_{G11}, I_{G12}, I_{G13}, \ldots I_{G1n}$ in Fig. 10. The protective agencies differ from each other in the degree of oppression that they exercise on the groups they are assumed to protect, varying from great to little or no oppression.

There will be prima facie some kind of competition among the protective agencies for customers, and individuals will avail themselves of the exit option; that is, they can, in principle, exit group 1 and enter group 2 or group *n*. This constellation necessarily reminds us of the familiar market model in which exchange between producers and consumers takes place under conditions of competition on both sides of the market. Remember, however, the previously discussed peculiarity: Each protective agency uses a violence mechanism that may be employed in a twofold

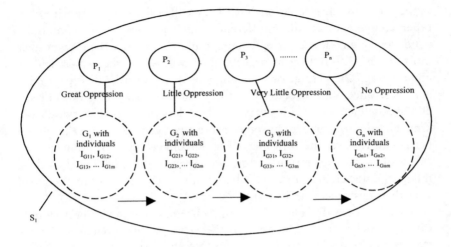

P$_1$ = Protective agency 1

G$_1$ = Group of individuals 1 supplied with protection by protective agency 1

I$_{G11}$ = Individual 1 within the Group 1 supplied with protection by protective agency 1

S$_1$ = Society or cultural community with shared informal institutions 1

Fig. 10 The protective agencies.

manner: as a means of oppression of the customers and as a means of aggression toward other protective agencies. The possibility of oppression in fact means that individuals can exit their protective agency only with prohibitive exit costs. Those exit costs might be so high that they cannot be counterbalanced by the relative facility to change to a protective agency operating in a familiar cultural environment. Therefore, we have shown in Fig. 10 the groups G$_1$, G$_2$, G$_3$, . . . G$_n$ to which the individuals seeking protection belong; this is the first crucial difference from the familiar market model.

The second difference has to do with the relationships between the protective agencies.[5] Since no rules of the game other than the informal ones exist and given the availability of the violence mechanism on the part of each protective agency, self-interested entrepreneurs will engage in one

---

5 Although Barzel (1998) offers important analytical insights on third-party enforcement and the state, he seems to neglect the dynamics of the relationships between the enforcers that complicate the issue further.

of the following three relationships: They will either cooperate with each other, compete, or remain indifferent. Which strategy will be chosen depends on which one the entrepreneurs think will increase their own utility most. In a trial-and-error process they will solve their problem by cooperating, competing, or remaining neutral toward other protective agencies. Since nothing equivalent to an antitrust law for markets exists, all the possible relationships between the rulers can appear, varying from armed battles to complete fusion of protective agencies in order to obtain better control over the customers. The outcome of this evolutionary process is obviously indeterminate, depending on the creativity of the rulers, their estimated chances to win the battles, the effectiveness of their control over their customers, and so on.

There is a considerable line of thought beginning with Hobbes, running through Locke, and culminating in Weber's view that contends that the state is a human association that can successfully claim a monopoly over the legitimate use of force in a territory.[6] In other words, these theories, although possessing different starting points and employed for diverse purposes, have in common the prediction that at some stage only one authority will arise in a society that will hold the *monopoly* of force. Nozick (1974), in developing an argument similar to the one presented here, also takes great pains to prove that in the end only one protective agency is bound to arise, which then becomes the ultraminimal state.[7]

---

[6] See the famous definition of the modern state of Max Weber (1919/1994, p. 36): "The state is that human *Gemeinschaft,* who within a certain territory (this: the territory, belongs to the distinctive feature) successfully lays claim to the *monopoly of legitimate physical force* for itself" (Translation by C. M.) See also his somehow different definition in his *Wirtschaft und Gesellschaft* (1922/1972, p. 29).

[7] See Nozick (1974, p. 26): "An ultraminimal state maintains a monopoly over all use of force except that necessary in immediate self-defense, and so excludes private (or agency) retaliation for wrong and exaction of compensation; but it provides protection and enforcement services to those who purchase its protection and enforcement policies. People who don't buy a protection contract from the monopoly don't get protected." Nozick focuses on proving that even an ultraminimal state should sharply limit self-protection without state allowance because of danger that punishment will be wrongly inflicted. Since his line of argument is mainly a normative one, Nozick stresses that individuals within the jurisdiction of the dominant protective agency *should not* use force themselves. From a positive point of view, the possibility of some individuals trying to organize their own protection is not problematic because this would mean de facto that another agency would be established. Whether this additional protective agency could survive would depend on the kinds of relations it maintained with the other agencies. (The difficulty Nozick seems to have originates from his thesis that in the end only one dominant protective agency will remain. As we shall see, if the necessity of a monopoly of force for the existence of a state proves to be false, then the problem does not occur in the first place.)

Elias (1939/1995) also suggests that the right sociological model for the emergence of the state is the dynamic theory that explains how the state comes to exist after a process of monopolization of power. In his view, the monopoly model is "a relatively precise formulation of a rather simple social mechanism which once set in motion will continue to be at work, like a clockwork" (p. 135) (translation by C. M.).

This monopoly view of the state is only partly correct, though. It is surely incorrect if the alleged monopoly of force is meant to cover the whole society or cultural community, that is, all individuals with shared mental models and informal institutions. Many historical counterexamples could be mentioned here, such as the Greek city-states of antiquity and the independent feuds in the period of feudalism in Europe in the Middle Ages. Nevertheless, the argument concerning the monopoly of force is correct in another, narrower sense: the protective agencies possess a monopoly among their own customers, that is, among the groups of individuals they protect. The reason for this monopoly does *not* have to do with efficiency considerations related to economic arguments of scale economies and the like. Protective agencies successfully claim a monopoly over the legitimate use of force in the group of individuals that they protect, not because protection is an industry that could be considered a *natural* monopoly, but because they are able to oppress their clients and compel them to accept solely *their* protection. Thus, within one society there may be many protective agencies, each one availing of a monopoly of force over its own group of clients. This does not exclude, of course, the possibility that the outcome of the competitive or cooperative evolutionary process between the different protective agencies will be a monopolistic one. In this case, only one protective agency will rule over the whole society.[8]

---

[8] Green (1990, p. 81f.) offers a similar interpretation of what could be reasonably considered as the monopoly of force claimed by a state. "The state must be a *national* monopoly, one emerging without protective regulation and purely as a consequence of certain features of the industry, namely protection, in which it operates. Such a monopoly might emerge, for example, if there were increasing returns to scale and a fairly inelastic demand (so that people continue to consume its products as the industry becomes increasingly concentrated). But if this is to be taken seriously we need to know quite a lot about the circumstances of production. Unfortunately, we cannot in fact be confident that the appropriate conditions hold. Are there really increasing returns to scale in the protection of rights? Why must a large and concentrated state be better at protecting rights than small vigilante groups? . . . But a view as popular as this is unlikely to be entirely without foundation; it does point us in the correct direction. We may instead interpret the notion of a monopoly in a simpler, static sense to mean only that the state claims supremacy for its won authority and defends its claims against those of other persons and groups in the same society."

Thus, in an evolutionary process characterized by collective learning, division of labor, and competition or cooperation between the entrepreneurs, one or more protective agencies remain in the society. Their primary function is to offer protection for a sum of money. They constitute, hence, the *protective state* or *states* taxing constituents for the supplied protection.[9] The emergence of this state or states can thus best be explained as a process of the invisible-hand type. The final configuration of the protective state is not the outcome of any conscious decision on the part of the constituents or on the part of the rulers. Each of them follows his own interests, bound only by informal institutions, and due to spontaneous group coalitions, division of labor, cooperation, or competition, one or more protective states arise that nobody consciously intended at the beginning of the process.[10]

But isn't there any difference between protective *agencies* and protective *states?* The only difference seems to be that protective agencies appear at the first stages of the invisible-hand process, whereas protective states constitute, in a way, the outcome of that process. Protective states are characterized by greater stability since both rulers and citizens have already gone through a learning process. Citizens have realized the height of the exit costs from a protective state, and rulers have learned both how other rulers react and how oppression of their constituency can be more successful. Although this stability is crucial, mainly for the evolution of law (as we will see later), the difference between protective agencies and protective states is one of degree rather than of kind. Fig. 11 depicts two alternative types of protective states that arise after the invisible-hand process of their emergence has taken place.

Comparing S_1 of Fig. 10 to S_1 of Fig. 11, we can observe two differences. In Fig. 10, the protective agencies have now become protective states and they differ in number. On the level of rulers, thus, the

[9] The term "protective state" is borrowed from Buchanan (1975), who explains the emergence of the state using a contractarian model meant to serve primarily for normative analysis. Buchanan himself explicitly acknowledges the importance of evolutionary explanations for state emergence (p. 50): "The operation of an unconstrained collectivity could scarcely emerge from national constitutional contracting among persons. Historically, an explicit stage of constitutional contracting may never have existed; the structure of rights may have emerged in an evolutionary process characterized by an absence of conscious agreement. . . . As we have noted earlier, the contractual models are not designed to be historically descriptive. They are instead, designed to assist in the development of criteria with which existing political-legal systems may be evaluated."

[10] Nozick explicitly modeled the emerge of the dominant protective agency as an invisible-hand process (1974, chs. 2 and 5).

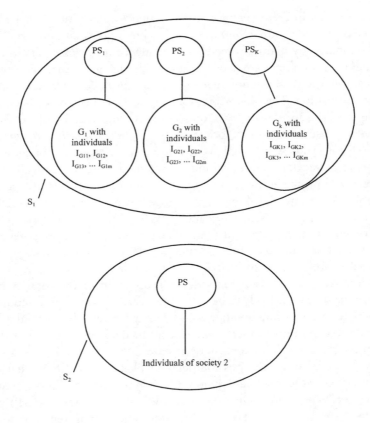

PS₁ = Protective state 1

G₁ = Group of individuals 1 supplied with protection by protective state 1

I_{G11} = Individual 1 within group 1 supplied with protection by protective state 1

S₁ = Society or cultural community with shared informal institutions 1

Fig. 11 The protective states.

difference refers to the learning process that has taken place parallel to the evolutionary restructuring of their protective agencies. The situation is now analogous to the learning process of oligopolists of microeconomic theory who have had enough time to accumulate knowledge of the behavior of their competitors in the market. The relative stability obtained among the rulers has an effect on the citizens. The individuals who are protected by one protective state can scarcely exit voluntarily. This is then the second difference between the two figures: The individual members of the protected group do *not* avail themselves of the exit option in a society dominated by many protected states. Hence no arrows exist in Fig. 11, and the group lines are depicted as continuous rather than discontinuous, signifying that the individuals are locked in once rulers have stabilized their position. The obvious reason is that once the protective states have secured their authority for a long period of time, the exit of a citizen from their jurisdiction cannot occur *unless explicitly allowed by the ruler.*[11]

Finer (1974), in a well-argued article with much historical evidence, also stresses that the exit option in the literal sense of physically exiting a territory protected by some centrally controlled force, is in fact unavailable to citizens. Speaking of the modern state, Finer (1974, p. 80) observes: "The state's borders are so well demarcated and so tightly patrolled, the government's intelligence and coercive apparatus so ubiquitous and powerful that individuals who want to leave against its wishes are reduced to hi-jacking planes or scaling Berlin Walls. Even if these restrictions were relaxed the *proportion* of the total population willing to leave is likely to be very small, partly because of the counter-pull of family, friendship and livelihood; partly because the correlate of *exit* is *entrance* and most other states restrict or deny entrance." But this phenomenon is not limited to modern states: "Even a thousand years ago, in high feudal days, the possibilities and likelihood of individual or even mass exit were much less than they might at first sight appear. The poor, however desperate their position, could not easily move unless they were 'free': the mass was not. [. . .] The feudality itself was free to come and go. [. . .] As far as individuals were concerned, the choice of exit was restricted even by the primitive political systems of the Middle Ages" (ibid.).

It seems, hence, that throughout human history, citizens have been de facto locked within the boundaries of protective states. Historical evidence seems to corroborate the complexity of the relationships between the different protective states. In fact the whole range is possible, varying from aggression and wars among them to a blend of competition and cooperation. Referring to the emergence and decline of feudalism in Western Europe in the tenth century, North analyzes how a large number of

---

[11] A ruler may in most cases not allow his citizens to leave his jurisdiction because he has an interest in taxing them. But in other cases, he will benefit from allowing citizens to exit if he feels that they are dangerous for doubting his authority. Ostracism in ancient Greek cities and the tolerance that Castro's Cuba showed to emigrants from time to time are examples of exit allowance. The crucial point is that the exit is not free, but can only be permitted (or even commanded) by the ruler.

protective states provided order within their relative small territories while engaging at the same time in complex relationships with other protective states (1981, p. 126f.): "Law and order generally existed only within the boundaries of settled areas, a condition that severely limited trade and commerce. . . . A local castle and knights were the keys to protection. The local lord was linked to overlords all the way up to the greatest lord – the king in a hierarchy of feudal obligations. Between the local lord and the king there might be several intermediate levels; but at each level the lower lord provided knight service for his immediate superior."[12]

The evolutionary view that we present here is compatible with the great diversity that is characteristic of human history. A number of regional hegemonies have lasted over prolonged historical periods: the Ottoman Empire in the Near East, the Ming and Manchu dynasties in China, the Mogul Empire in India, and the Roman Empire (Jones, 1981, p. xxii). On the other hand, in Western Europe, as we have already mentioned, there was never a hegemony after the death of Charlemagne but always a plurality of rulers engaged permanently in war. A deterministic model seems, thus, to be out of place since no definite prediction can be made about the outcome of the competition among rulers (Nye, 1997, p. 126). Either an empire or a plurality of small states engaging in competition and/or cooperation may emerge.[13]

3. Why Do (Protective) States Persist or Change? The fact that protective states stabilize after some time is significant insofar as formal law can be produced under their authority. This is impossible in the first stages of the process from small to large societies since the protective *agencies* that arise are of a more temporary character. (How formal law is produced within a protective state will be the subject of the next paragraph.) Although protective states might show greater stability than the protective agencies, changes nevertheless certainly occur. The most frequent reason for change is aggression from outside, that is, from other protective states, which lead to ever new formations. Hume went so far as to "assert the

12 See also Finer (1974, p. 92): "In the 10th century, in every place where today the map shows large states divided from their neighbours by thick black lines, there was a congeries of small or even tiny localities, over each of which rulers exercised differing ranges of authority, and which stood towards one another in varying degrees and kinds of super-ordination or subordination."
13 The evolutionary account of state emergence presented here is typically missing in the contributions of public – choice scholars and other social scientists. For a notable exception, see the illuminating article of Nye (1997). For an excellent review of theories of the state, see Levi (1988, pp. 185–204).

first rudiments of government to arise from quarrels, not among men of the same society, but among those of different societies" (1740/1978, p. 540).

History is definitely not short of wars, which in many cases have lasted for decades and that are sufficient to prove that the boundaries of protective states often change. As North mentions (1981, p. 138): "Between 1200 and 1500 the many political units of Western Europe went through numerous conflicts, alliances, and combinations as the local manor gave way to the emerging nation-state. These centuries witnessed intrigue and warfare on an ever-expanding scale." Since the reasons for warfare during human history are extremely complex, no reliable hypothesis can be formulated for their occurrence. Thus, what remains is to point, once again, at the self-interested character of human nature as the motivating cause of aggression and thus of change in the boundaries of the protective states.[14]

4. How Does the State Provide Protection? Up to now, we have focused on the emergence of the protective state and its relations to other protective states either of the same cultural community or of a different one. Now we will analyze the relations between ruler and citizens. In terms of Fig. 11, we turn now to each protective state PS in its relation to the group of individuals G that consists of its citizens. In fact, in the rest of our inquiry, we will abstract from the relations between different states, and in the remainder of the chapter we shall concentrate on what kind of protection is offered by the state to its citizens. In other words, the lower part of Fig. 11 becomes now relevant, where the society S_2 with one protective state is depicted.

Levi (1988) pleads for "bringing people back into the state" and argues that changes in relative bargaining power, transaction costs, and discount rates lead to new bargains between rulers and their constituency.

McGuire and Olson (1996) analyze alternative forms of relationships between self-interested rulers and their constituency. Provided that rulers are taxing their citizens in exchange for protection and thus prima facie have an interest to maximize tax revenues, the authors show that an invisible-hand process is at work even in the case of autocratic rulers. Even if rulers are not bound by any rules in their actions, it is in their own interest not to overtax their citizens and to provide some public goods, because only in this way can the subjects have the incentives to produce what then becomes the tax base. Thus, McGuire and Olson conclude

---

[14] On the military role in state building see Finer (1974, pp. 92ff.) Some very illuminating comments on the issue are contained in Mackaay (1997).

"that there is a hidden hand that leads encompassing and stable interests with unquestioned coercive power to act, to a significant and surprising degree, in the interests of the entire society including those who are subject to their power. The outcome from stationary banditry is not nearly as bad as might have been supposed. . . . even though most of human history is a story of rule by self-interested and often extravagant autocrats, there has been, even under such rulers, a surprising amount of progress" (p. 94).[15]

McGuire and Olson's model is based on the same idea as North's theory of the state (1981, ch. 3), that is, on conceiving the relationship between ruler and constituency as an exchange process during which protection and justice are traded for tax revenues.[16] This, in turn, implies two further complications. On the one hand, the ruler is bound to delegate some power to agents who will provide protection and collect the taxes. Since the agents of the ruler will naturally have interests different from those of the ruler, the ruler will attempt to constrain them by making rules that will be consistent with his objectives, that is, they will be designed to solve the principal–agency problem in an adequate manner.[17] This in fact

---

[15] In the German-speaking world, Hans Albert was the first to analyze clearly the relationship between rulers and constituency along these lines (1978, p. 106f.): "Conquest and oppression are those activities from which the state has fundamentally arisen. The 'pacification' of a subjected population takes place according to the interest of the conquerors. . . . The protective function of the rulers comes at a high price. Later it may become obvious that taking a considerate approach to those subjugated is more beneficial to those in power, so that they will be induced to lessen their hold. . . . In this way, the emergence of state authority can also bring with it advantages for those who are being subjugated. It is forced to attend to their welfare to a greater degree. The extension of the state apparatus requires investments which can only be financed through the population's labor revenues. The encouragement of the productivity of this labor lies also in the interest of the state authority and is only possible if the appropriate rewards can be offered. The state authority attempts then to support trade and production making in this way possible its own expansion and development." (Translation by C. M.)

[16] For an analysis of the position of the ruler, see Tullock (1987). Mackaay (1997, p. 18) summarizes the complex problem that a ruler is facing: "He or she must ward off external aggression as well as internal rebellion, all the while relying on administrators for tax collection and encouraging economic activity in as much as it is expected to increase the tax base, without eroding his or her power base. He or she might of course consider the further strategy of increasing the tax base through conquest or marriage. The administrative and military techniques known at a given time set practical limits to the viable size of the tax base. The puzzle is complex and has an element of gambling to it. One must expect different rulers be unequally handy or lucky at it." For a survey of the political economy of dictatorship see Wintrobe (1998).

[17] On the principal–agent theory see the seminal contribution of Jensen and Meckling (1976). See also Ross (1973) and the discussion in Eggertsson (1990, ch. 2.3)

means that a group of formal rules will emerge, explicitly designed to direct government affairs and emanating from a conscious will easily identifiable in the person of the ruler.[18] The further complication arising from modeling the relationship between the ruler and constituency as an exchange process concerns the *content* of the supplied protection. Up to now, we have left the term "protection" unspecified. Recalling the discussion on the emergence of the protective state in the first place, and provided that informal institutions and correspondent behavioral regularities existed prior to the emergence of the state, it is evident that protection means resolving conflicts among the constituents on the basis of existing informal social rules. Self-interested rulers, even in autocratic systems, will pay attention to the settling of disputes among their subjects since they themselves do not suffer from any utility decreases. The costs of settling disputes and of enforcement will in any case be negligible in the face of the fundamental importance of protected individual activities for productive purposes and thus of tax revenues.

These two sets of rules, which are bound to exist in every impersonal society with a central enforcement authority, correspond to what Hayek (1973/1982) calls legislation or "thesis" and law or "nomos." Legislation originates from the necessity of establishing governmental organization and appears historically later than the law in the Hayekian narrow sense of the term. As Hayek observes (1973/1982, p. 73): "Yet there can be no doubt that law existed for ages before it occurred to man that he could make or alter it. . . . What we know about pre-human and primitive human societies suggests a different origin and determination of law from that assumed by the theories which trace it to the will of a legislator." This will of a legislator was visible, at least in the first stadiums of human civilization, only in the rules pertaining to the organization of government, that is, in the commands of the ruler. With regard to the other group

---

[18] See North (1981, p. 25): "Since the utility function of the agents is not identical with that of the ruler, the ruler will specify a group of rules to attempt to enforce conduct by his agent that will be consistent with his own objectives. There will be, however, a diffusion of the powers of the ruler to the degree that the agents are not perfectly constrained by the rules." See also Barzel (2000, pp. 29ff.).

Levi (1988, p. 43) remarks: "Rulers always depend on others for some of the resources necessary to acquire and sustain rule. They depend on the generals and even the soldiers of their armies, on the owners or managers of economic wealth, on the church officials who justify their status, or on the scientists or inventors of new technologies of force. Moreover, few rulers can survive if they plunder all constituents. . . . Both to ensure stable rule and to keep their costs down, rulers must offer positive benefits to 'a minimum winning coalition' of the population in return for allegiance."

of rules, those regulating social behavior, no ruler had an interest in affecting their *content,* but only in *enforcing* them. "A ruler sending a judge to preserve the peace will normally not do so for the purpose of preserving an order he has created, or to see whether his commands have been carried out, but to restore an order the character of which he may not even know. . . . The rules which the judge enforces are of interest to the ruler who has sent him only so far as they preserve peace and assure that the flow of the efforts of the people will continue undisturbed" (Hayek, 1973/1992, p. 98).

Since law was *originally* the outcome of an evolutionary process and was derived to a large degree from the enforcement of already existing informal social rules, those same informal institutions *constrain* the will of the legislator. Although it is extremely difficult to say more on how effective this constraint is, it is nevertheless evident that the legislator cannot easily violate the sentiments of fairness, that is, the spontaneously adopted social rules of the community.[19] Hence, to slightly paraphrase Hume, at least the private law rests upon and is eventually governed by the opinion of the constituency.[20]

8.2. THE ENFORCEMENT OF PROPERTY RIGHTS

What the state protects is the property of the individuals. Legal rules enforceable by the state define the rights of individuals, and they draw at the same time the boundaries of their protected domains within which they are free to follow their own aims.[21] To say that law guarantees the protected domains of individuals equates to the guarantee of private property. "Property," understood in the broad sense of the term, includes not only the material things under the command of an individual but also "his Life, Liberty and Estate, against the injuries and Attempts of other Men" (Locke, 1690/1991, 87). The property rights assigned to individuals in a society do not refer to person–thing relationships, as is commonly as-

---

19 See also Hart (1963), who poses and answers the historical and causal question on the relationship between morals and formal law in the following way (p. 1): "Has the development of the law been influenced by morals? The answer to this question plainly is 'Yes'; though of course this does not mean that an affirmative answer may not also be given to the converse question: Has the development of morality been influenced by law?" For a discussion of this issue see Section 9.1.

20 See Hume (1777/1907, vol. I, p. 125): "Though men be much governed by interest, yet even interest itself, and all human affairs, are entirely governed by opinion."

21 See Hayek (1973/1982, p. 107): "[R]ules are required which make it possible at each moment to ascertain the boundary of the protected domain of each and thus to distinguish between the *meum* and *tuum.*"

sumed, but rather to person–person relationships.[22] The property rights are best conceived, hence, as the "rights of action" of individuals within their protected domains.[23]

The extensive property rights literature that has been produced in the last four decades[24] deals with the issue of how the structure of property rights can affect economic outcomes. Much of this economic literature nevertheless pertains, implicitly or explicitly, to efficiency considerations and possesses therefore a normative flavor. Besides, in many cases, the reference to the transactions costs goes hand in hand with automatically assuming that agents will effectively consider those transactions costs and will act so that they will be minimized. What is most important in our setting is that much of the property rights literature beginning with the classical contribution of Demsetz (1967) assumes that the state will hasten to specify property rights in such a way that efficiency will be obtained.

From the background of the model presented here, there is no reason to assume an automatism that guarantees that property rights will be specified in a way in which economic outcomes will be maximized. Rather, it must be assumed that the rulers, whether in autocratic or democratic systems, will attempt to establish property rights in such a way that their own interests will best be furthered. This does not necessarily *exclude* the possibility that they will seek to provide law *consistent* with economic growth so that they can draw tax revenues (in the case of autocratic systems) or ensure their reelection (in the case of majoritarian democracies). The main point is that the law specifying property rights is a

---

[22] See Schmid (1987, p. 5): "Property rights describe the relationships of one person to another with respect to a resource or any line of action. This person-to-person focus differs from some definitions that describe person-to-thing relationships."

See also Hayek (1973/1982, p. 108): "The classical formula that the aim of rules of just conduct is to assign to each his due (suum cuique tribuere) is often interpreted to mean that the law by itself assigns to particular individuals particular things. It does nothing of the kind, of course. It merely provides rules by which it is possible to ascertain from particular facts to whom particular things belong." See also Weimer (1997, p. 3).

[23] In one of his seminal articles, Demsetz uses the term "rights of action" as well as the term "property rights." See Demsetz (1964, p. 19): "Indeed, we can insist that a proper definition of a *right of action* include the degree to which the owner or the community is allowed to enforce the right."

[24] For an overview up to the 1970s, see Furubotn and Pejovich (1972). De Alessi (1980) provides an update stressing empirical results. For a more recent survey, see De Alessi (1990) and Eggertsson (1990, ch. 2). In the German literature see the important contribution of Meyer (1983), which contains a critical review of both the older German tradition and the contributions up to the 1980s. See also Dietl (1993, pp. 56ff.)

variable rather than a constant in the hands of the government and therefore will be employed each time to serve the interest of the government (and not the citizens) within the existing constraints.

For our present analytical purposes, it suffices to keep in mind that the legal rules specifying the property rights in a society are (a) to a large degree the outcome of a deliberate act of the legislation meant to serve the interest of the legislator within the prevailing constraints and (b) possess therefore, to a great degree, the character of a variable that can be deliberately manipulated. The setting of the property rights is an extremely important issue since it channels all the productive efforts of the individuals living in the community. In the next chapter we shall see how the informal institutions together with the legal rules of the society affect the outcomes of the market processes and are thus of decisive economic importance. But before proceeding to the analysis of the market process, we should tackle the issue of how the law is adopted by the individuals of the society and how it can provide social order.

8.3. LAW AND SOCIAL ORDER

The main effect of law is that it provides social order in societies where most relationships are impersonal. A set of legal rules is the central mechanism of conflict resolution in large societies functioning in a parallel way to the informal social institutions. The working of a legal system cannot be understood, though, without reference to the individual behavior of those who have to live under it, that is, without explaining how the legal rules channel the behavior of the members of the respective society. Since what we call social order is nothing more than a pattern of relationships identifiable at a moment in time, a full explanation of how law brings about such a pattern is bound to refer first to the mechanism of adoption of legal rules on the part of the individuals. In the case of informal institutions, we have seen in Chapter 7 how conventions, moral rules, and social norms are adopted by agents in an evolutionary, spontaneous process during which self-interested individuals learn to follow social rules in the course of solving the social problems arising in their environment. People following the same informal social rules solve at the same time, at least partly, and in an unconscious way, the problem of social order since the relative stability of their behavior makes it predictable for other agents, and in the end a global stabilization of expectations occurs, producing social coordination. The question is thus whether an analogous adoption of legal rules takes place that could explain how the legal system leads to social order.

In his classic book, Hart (1961/1994), while addressing the issue of how the legal system works, made the important distinction between *external* and *internal* points of view in the explanation of law. Hart maintains that one cannot sufficiently understand the working of legal system with the hypothesis that all individuals involved would approach it from the external point of view of an observer, who merely observes regularities in overt behavior and adapts to them in an opportunistic way. Individuals typically do *not* adapt each time to legal constraints in an optimal way, *nor* do they consider them as external data requiring attention without in fact accepting them. Legal rules, like all kinds of social rules, possess, in addition to a regularity or external aspect, a normative meaning for the actors themselves, that is, an internal aspect.[25] As Hart mentions (1961/1994, p. 90): "What the external point of view, which limits itself to the observable regularities of behavior, cannot reproduce is the way in which the rules function as rules in the lives of those who normally are the majority of society. These are the officials, lawyers, or private persons who use them, in one situation after another, as guides to the conduct of social life, as the basis for claims, demands, admissions, criticism or punishment, viz., in all the familiar transactions of life according to rules. For them the violation of a rule is not merely a basis for the prediction that a hostile reaction will follow but a *reason* for hostility." Hart, stressing the internal point of view, takes an opposite position to what Kliemt calls the "classical empiristic view" of legal theory, "which is characterized by the premise that the workings of a legal system can be understood without assuming that anybody ever adopts an internal point of view to some rule or norm and sometimes acts for nonopportunistic reasons" (1993b, p. 158).[26]

Obviously, the main explanatory issue is to build a theoretical bridge between this internal point of view and external behavior.[27] From the perspective defended here, such a bridge is not difficult to build. The

[25] See Hart (1961/1994, p. 89): "When a social group has certain rules of conduct, this fact affords an opportunity for many closely related yet different kinds of assertion; for it is possible to be concerned with the rules, either merely as an observer who does not himself accept them, or as a member of the group which accepts and uses them as guides to conduct. We may call these respectively the 'external' and the 'internal points of view'."

[26] The authors that Kliemt identifies with this "classical empiristic view" of legal theory are John Austin, Theodor Geiger in Germany, and Thomas Hobbes.

[27] See Kliemt (1993b, p. 157): "Explanations may be formed by introducing one or more bridge laws relating hypotheses about the internal point of view to external behavior."

adoption of legal rules that are a subclass of social rules requires for its explanation only an extension of the argument presented for the case of informal social rules in Chapter 7. People learn during the socialization process that deviation from certain legal norms is accompanied by sanctions imposed by the enforcement mechanism of the state. Individuals in a society, in the course of pursuing their self-interests and solving their own problems, get the environmental feedback that violation of legal rules is sanctioned, and thus they adapt their behavior to conform to the existing rules. Thus, they follow the legal rules because of the *learning process* that takes place in the process of adaptation to their environment.

Hence, what is usually called the "internalization of norms" and thus also of legal norms (which is the same thing as stressing the internal point of view in legal theory) is not an enterprise to be understood in absolute terms. It is plausible to assume instead that the adoption of legal rules by the individuals is heavily dependent on the learning process that members of a society are bound to go through when they encounter the legal system. People will not necessarily follow the legal rules blindly only because they find themselves moving in a genuinely normative dimension. Moreover, this normative standpoint is itself learned by the agents and can best be explained as the adaptation of their motivational system to their environment. The molding of the individual motivational system, which is equivalent to the adoption of an internal point of view or a genuine normativity, follows the same principles discussed in Sections 7.2 and 7.3.

Learning about the negative consequences of breaking the legal rules is greatly facilitated by the fact that people are subjected to a socialization process concerning informal rules from the very beginning of their lives. In other words, individuals are confronted with the normative dimension from childhood, and therefore it is easy for them to adopt additionally the legal norms in a later stage of their life. Besides, a large number of legal rules are also acknowledged by the individuals as moral rules, social norms, or conventions, which further facilitates their internalization. In fact, as Ellickson also stresses (1991, p. 144), "ordinary people know little of the private substantive law applicable to decisions in everyday life."[28] If this contention is correct, then people act primarily on the basis of only a scant knowledge of the *content* of legal rules; this does not affect their

---

[28] See Ellickson (1991, p. 144): "First-year law students may complain that what they are encounting is boring, but never that it is old hat. Surveys of popular knowledge of law relevant to ordinary household transactions, such as the leasing of housing or the purchase of consumer goods, invariably show that respondents have scant working knowledge of private law."

secure knowledge, though, that those legal rules will be effectively enforced. According to this line of argument it is reasonable to hypothesize that people use inferential strategies to achieve an orientation within a legal system. By using, for example, analogical reasoning, people assume that the great part of the moral and other informal rules that they have learned to follow are also part of the legal order and thus they adopt them more firmly because of the certainty that is provided by the existence of a central enforcing agency. Errors naturally occur when such inferences are used and thus agents are bound to hold falsely that some informal rules also belong to the legal system and vice versa. The main point remains intact, though: individuals adopt legal rules in a learning process that is subject to the same imperfections inherent in every learning enterprise.

That legal norms possess a motivational force of their own only insofar as individuals have learned that the respect of legal norms is beneficial can be best examplified when the behavior under different legal systems is compared. In the societies of Latin America, for example, people follow the legal rules, but their adherence is different in degree compared to other Western societies. In other words, respect for the legal system in these developing countries seems to be much less than the respect shown by citizens of developed countries. This fact can be satisfactorily explained only with the aid of the hypothesis presented here: Citizens of different polities adopt the legal rules according to the environmental feedback they get in the course of encountering the legal system. If they have learned that deviation from legal rules is not always sanctioned successfully, as is the case in many countries of Latin America, then their commitment to legal norms will be relatively weak (Pritzl, 1997; Garribaldi-Fernandez, 1998). If the state as the enforcing mechanism of law sanctions deviations effectively, as is the case in Western societies, then the respect of legal norms by citizens will be relatively great. Thus, it is evident that the internal point of view or the normative dimension is not absolute in character, but is always dependent on the content of the learning process of the individuals.

8.4. SOCIAL INSTITUTIONS: OPEN ISSUES

In Part II of this study, we have stated as an analytical goal the explanation of how, in face of the self-interested motivations of individuals, an institutional framework can possibly emerge. The rise of social institutions is the first step toward the solution of the problem of social order, since institutions constitute the rules of the game for every society. Since social rules are complexes of normative regulation that remain *relatively stable* for a certain period of time in every society, the socioeconomic process is structured and directed through the institutions prevailing at a certain time and place. How this relative stability can be best understood is the aim of the next chapter. The important fact for the moment is that the emergence of social institutions guarantees the structuring of social relationships.

There are, of course, many issues that we have not addressed in Part II of the study. The most important question that we have not posed concerns the relationship between formal and informal institutions. Although there are some contributions in the literature, one cannot speak of a coherent general theory that explains the relationship between conventions, moral rules, and social norms on the one hand and law on the other. This is due mainly to the intrinsic difficulty of the subject matter. Since this issue is as difficult as it is important, we want to offer some preliminary thoughts to stress the fields of ongoing debate and to point to some possible areas of future research.

The relationship between law and informal rules is the theme of a lively dispute in the philosophy of law (Epstein, 1996). One very influential attempt to draw a line between law and informal rules has been undertaken by H. L. A. Hart in his book *The Concept of Law* (1961). Hart, in restating in a powerful form the claims of legal positivism, tries to show that law consists in the union of what he calls "primary rules" and "secondary rules." Primary rules are those that either impose obligations or grant rights to the members of a social community and exist in all societies. In primitive societies without a state, primary rules are not only the sole social rules, they are also the only means of social control (p. 91). The secondary rules, which consist of (a) rules of recognition, (b) rules of change, and (c) rules of adjudication, are all *about* primary rules (p. 94). The law is then the union of primary rules of obligation with such secondary rules. To put it more succinctly, Hart's message is that law should be understood as the set of rules enforceable by a sovereign without regard to the substantive content of the rules in question. Hart tried to provide a criterion with which one could distinguish legal rules from other social rules.

In a powerful critique, Dworkin (1977) disputed the value of Hart's test and stressed the importance of principles in legal reasoning (1977, pp. 22ff.). While legal rules are applicable in an all-or-nothing fashion, legal principles "do not set out legal consequences that follow automatically when the conditions provided are met" (p. 25). A principle rather "states a reason that argues in one direction, but does not necessitate a particular decision" (p. 26). Since jurisprudence is unthinkable without legal principles, Dworkin maintains that no commonly accepted test exists for law and that legal rules cannot be distinguished from moral rules and principles (p. 60).

Analogous controversies, perhaps less passionate and spectacular but nonetheless about the same issue, are to be found in the sociology of law. Donald Black (1976, pp. 6–10, 105ff.) proposed the hypothesis that "Law varies inversely with other social control" (p. 107). For this contention Black offers much empirical evidence. John Griffiths (1984), rejecting what he calls the "taxonomic approach to law," argues that no fruitful distinction between "law" and "no-law" can be made (p. 43). The whole issue is discussed in the anthropology and sociology of law in terms of a theory of social control. However, as Ellickson in his competent review of the literature admitts (1991, p. 256): "Although it seems clear that law sometimes affects social mores, not much is known about when and how these feedback loops operate."

While this literature is mainly concerned with the issue of the *horizontal* distinction between the different types of social rules and the division of labor in the production of social control, psychologists have raised the equally important issue of *vertical* distinction during ontogeny. As we have seen in Section 7.2, Kohlberg has distinguished six moral stages that all individuals in a society are hypothesized to pass through. Some critics have raised the question whether these six stages are perhaps better described as stages of the development of legal beliefs.[29] Others have insisted that the hypothesis of three groups of rules, that is, personal rules, conventions, and moral rules corresponding to Kohlberg's three major levels of moral judgment, that is, preconventional, conventional, and postconventional or principled, is wrong. Instead of a vertical succession of the three types of rules, they propose that all of them exist and develop in parallel throughout an individual's life. Other evidence seems to support the thesis that in the first stages of development, moral judgments tend to be justified by pointing to law; however, in later stages (i.e., beyond stage 4), law tends to be "moralized," meaning that legal categories are justified in the arguments of the agents by pointing at moral principles (Eckensberger and Breit, 1997, p. 299). In any case, the relationship between moral judgments and the adoption of legal principles seems to be a very compex one, and ongoing research is being conducted to address this subject.[30]

---

[29] For a thoughtful discussion, see Eckensberger and Breit (1997, pp. 277ff.).

[30] Other research experiments (independent of Kohlberg's theory of moral develop-

The issue of the relationship between formal and informal social rules seems, thus, to be rather sizable. In order to construct a workable theory, one should focus on the proper analytical issues. Abstract reflections, even when supported by empirical evidence on how formal and informal rules interact, will not lead us anywhere. *One should rather specify the analysis of the relationship between formal and informal institutions with respect to a concrete phenomenon or outcome that is of interest. For our purposes, there are two questions of interest: (a) How do formal and informal rules interact to produce social order? (b) What institutional mix of formal and informal rules leads to a wealth-creating economic game?*

To our knowledge, no coherent theory exists that gives satisfactory answers to these questions. In the last chapter of this book, we try to answer the second question. Concerning the first question, the starting points are obviously the four *logical* possible relationships between formal and informal institutions in producing social order, that is, the neutral, the complementary, the substitutive, and the conflicting relationship (Kiwit and Voigt, 1995; Voigt and Kiwit, 1998). Which is *empirically* the case? One has to distinguish whether the groups or communities under discussion are small or large. As we have already seen, in the cases of small groups with intense communication, social order may be produced exclusively by informal institutions. Empirically, a number of primitive societies managed to produce social order without the aid of centrally organized sanctions; however, this is possible only where the community numbers are no more than a few thousand (Wimmer, 1997, p. 223). Thus, in small groups, there are cases in which the problem of the relationship between formal and informal rules does not arise in the first place since no formal rules exist.

The problem appears to be rather formidable in the case of large groups, though. A review of the literature proves how complex the issue is. Ellickson (1991, pp. 254ff.) discusses the different forms that the mix of the informal and legal systems may take. Both law's use of custom as a source of rules and the informal enforcement of legal rules is possible. Besides, whether the members of a society will appeal to informal rules or to courts depends on the concrete character of the dispute between them (p. 256f.).

---

ment) using the ultimatum and dictator game proved that institutions affect fairness. See Frey and Bohnet (1995), with further references to experimental results. See also the contribution of Lampe (1997) in answering the question of how law consciousness (Rechtsbewußtsein) has historically been developed.

Within a society where law prevails, many small groups following their own diverse social norms exist. Law might either undermine or reinforce the informal rules prevailing in small groups, since any member of such a group can look to the law for protection. How law affects the production of order in small groups within an inclusive society depends, among other things, on the concrete group dynamics (Posner, 1996).

In what is perhaps the most complete treatment of the problem, Nee suggests that the relationship between formal and informal norms will be closely coupled when the formal norms of an organization are perceived to be congruent with the preferences and interests of actors in subgroups. This close coupling between formal and informal rules promotes high performance in organizations and economies (Nee 1998b; Nee and Ingram, 1998, pp. 33ff.). Though this hypothesis is surely important, it suffers from a serious shortcoming: it is not correct to propose that a complementary relationship between formal and informal rules leads to beneficial outcomes (mainly because of the reduction of monitoring and enforcement costs and of uncertainty; Nee and Ingram, 1998, p. 33), *regardless of the concrete content of the rules*. In socialist systems, for example, informal rules allowing for minor efforts in state-owned enterprises existed in a political regime that forbade any kind of private property rights in regard to productive resources. The complementarity of informal and formal rules in this case did not lead to high organizational or economic performance. Nevertheless, Nee has taken the first step in elaborating on the relationship between formal and informal rules.

In summary, it seems that all four logical possible relationships between formal and informal rules have empirical counterparts.[31] A coherent the-

---

[31] See Lipford and Yandle (1997, p. 38): "Viewed as a production process, informal ordering devices, like social norms and customs, and the more fundamental governmental activities can be compatible and complementary inputs in generating order across some range of output. For example, the nation-state can provide protection of borders and offer security for property involved in extended transactions while the community provides order informally within its boundaries. But while being compatible complements at one level of production, increased use of one input at some point in the production of total order can erode the productivity of the other; the two processes can be in conflict. For example, the customs of Amishmen to provide family security by community means can conflict with a national security mandate. Lacking a constitutional constraint, political bodies seeking to extend homogenous social order by statute may not only crowd out private actions dedicated to a similar end, but also erode the community's incentives and capability to produce order by way of norms and customs."

See also the conclusion of Richard Posner on the issue (1997, p. 368): "In summary, law both complements and substitutes for norms."

For the optimistc view that what he calls "formal market order-oriented institu-

ory should specify the concrete conditions that give rise to the four possible relationships between formal and informal rules in producing social order. The starting point of such a theory must be the insight that informal rules are produced, in a way, *internally,* that is, they are endogenous to the community. By comparison, legal rules are imposed *externally* on the community as the exogenous product of the political process (Lipford and Yandle, 1997, p. 42).[32] However, there is a long way to go before we have a satisfactory theory of the interaction between formal and informal rules.[33]

The prerequisite for an explanation of the institutions of a society is an account of how subjective agents come to have shared experiences and learning histories. In Chapter 5 we introduced the term "shared mental models" in order to explain how individual members of a society obtain the same solutions to their problems and share a common stock of knowledge through communication processes. This knowledge shared by people in a society is not static but evolves over time. This, in turn, means that shared mental models evolve as well.

For the purpose of this study, it is enough to keep in mind that formal and informal institutions are both the rules of the game or, more specifically, of the market game. Once they are adopted by the members of a society, a great deal of interindividual conflict disappears. Institutions serve as devices that facilitate the conformity of individuals to the group and thus produce coordination of the agents. The coordinating property of institutions constitutes a secure insight of any institutional theory. In

---

tions" can never conflict with any informal institutions with respect to their normative content, see Mummert (1999, p. 7). Obviously, though, this argument depends on how one defines formal market-oriented institutions. If they are defined as the subclass of formal institutions that are designed to "allow for market coordination," then this claim is either only analytically true or it amounts to the proposition that all informal rules in all societies favor market coordination, which does not need to be empirically true. See, e.g., Greif (1994).

32 Ensminger (1997) presents a case study concerning land titling in Kenya and discusses the conflicts that arise when property rights changes imposed externally on a society are incompatible with social norms that have arisen internally as an outcome of spontaneous interaction.

33 Buchanan (1986) offers some intuitive thoughts *on Moral Community, Moral Order, or Moral Anarchy* and their implications for social stability and governmental action. See also Knight (1998). Uslaner (1998) discusses whether culture or (political) institutions determine political outcomes, arguing that the former is the main explanatory variable. Cooter (1996) developed a normative theory of "structural adjudication" that should help judges in common law countries in enforcing social norms in their decisions.

addition to this important feature, social institutions work as a selective environment for the exchange processes between the agents. How this occurs, what the relation is between institutions and the market, and how the market process is best theoretically conceived will be the subject of Part III of our study.

PART III

MARKETS

9

Institutions and the Market

The Aggregate Level

Es dürfte also eigentlich niemanden überraschen, daß bei geänderten sozialen Rahmenbedingungen – etwa auf Grund neuer normativer Regulierungen – aus den gleichen sozialen Gesetzen andere Prozesse und Zustände resultieren.
Hans Albert, 1976, p. 145

9.1. THE NEW INSTITUTIONALISM AND THE GERMAN *ORDNUNGSTHEORIE*

Our analytical focus in this and the following chapter will be on how the institutions, formal and informal, affect the market processes. Which role do institutions play when individuals pursue their problem-solving activities in the market? In this chapter, our primary purpose will be to show on an aggregate level that institutions can be best understood as the rules of the market game that channel the market process in a certain direction. In the next chapter, this contention will be underpinned by providing an individualistic basis of this phenomenon by employing the theory presented in Part I of the study.

Before proceeding to our main issue, a question should be mentioned that we will not address further, though it is very important. We have defined institutions as normative social rules, that is, as the rules of the game in a society, enforced either through law or by other mechanisms of social control that shape human interaction (Section 6.1). The notion of "human interaction" involves normally two aspects: (a) a process of voluntary exchange between individuals or (b) the voluntary pooling of resources by individuals for a common use. These two kinds of human interaction are commonly called "market" and "organization." The socioeconomic process that is constrained by institutions involves, therefore, both the market activities of the individuals and the actions of organizations as corporate actors (Coleman, 1990a).

Despite its obvious importance, we shall abstract from the effect of institutions on organizations and their actions during the socioeconomic process because this will lead us too far away from our theme. Such an analysis would require the elaboration of effects of institutions on different types of organizations. We shall not undertake such an examination here.

That markets always work within some rules must appear trivial to any student of social phenomena. In fact, many sociologists, following the lead of Granovetter (1985), have argued that markets are always embedded in social structures. The dominant research paradigm of economics (the social science that is supposed to focus mainly on the functioning of markets), that is, neoclassical economics, seems to neglect thoroughly the role of rules in the market process, however. This abstraction from the institutional framework within which every exchange process takes place is justified by the proponents of the neoclassical research program by their conscious attempt to provide exact economic laws that are, in turn, supposed to explain how an economy overcomes the ubiquitous phenomenon of scarcity. The market is mainly viewed as an allocating machine that solves the main problems of society, that is, what to produce, how, and for whom. The solution to these problems occurs simultaneously whenever agents, who are assumed to maximize their utility, exhaust all the exchange possibilities. This is formalized in the concept of a general economic equilibrium. In this model, no institutional analysis seems necessary mainly because the real-world societal context is eliminated and thereby gives place to a pure "universum of commodities" (Boulding, 1958 pp. 32ff.).[1]

This kind of theoretical approximation of the market phenomenon is equivalent to a narrowing of the perspective in comparison to the political economy as put forward by the classical economists. "A. Smith was engaged directly in comparing alternative institutional structures, alternative sets of constraints within which economic agents make choices" (Buchanan, 1987a, p. 585). Smith viewed political economy as "the science of the legislator" (Smith, 1776/1976, p. 490), and in his own work, he practiced comparative institutional analysis by presenting the working properties of the mercantilist regime and of the alternative regime of Natural Liberty. This type of institutional analysis has been avoided in

---

[1] Hans Albert is the leading figure in the German-speaking world in criticizing the formal decision logic of the neoclassical research program and in pleading for a market sociology. Albert (1967/1998) contains collected papers by the author published partly in the 1950s.

economic theory to the extent that it has essentially disappeared from the neoclassical research paradigm.

In the last three decades, theoretical interest in the influence of the institutional structure on the economic process has been revived in the work of a number of economists who deal with diverse themes known in the literature as the New Institutional Economics. Under this title, a set of interrelated theoretical developments is summarized: law and economics, property rights economics, the transaction costs, public choice, and constitutional political economy. The common characteristic of all such research programs is their focus on institutions and their influence on shaping economic life. We shall borrow many of the insights of this literature while developing our market theory in this part of the study.

Another program that deals with the role of institutions in the market processes is the German *Ordnungstheorie,* a theory that has mainly originated and been developed in the German-speaking world. Since the 1930s, *Ordnungstheorie,* associated mainly with the economist Walter Eucken[2] and the legal scholar Franz Böhm (1937, 1980), has tackled a number of issues currently discussed by the so-called new institutionalists primarily in the English-speaking world. Also known as the Freiburg School,[3] this research program focuses on the system of rules that define the institutional framework in which economic agents make their choices.[4] *Ordnungstheorie,* therefore, shares with the new institutional economics the rule-oriented perspective in the analysis of economic phenomena and the interest in how the institutional framework affects market outcomes.[5] Historically, the theory of economic orders, as found in W. Eucken's *The Foundations of Economics* (1939/1992), was an attempt to overcome the theoretical controversy between two approaches, those of (a) the German Historical School and (b) the Marginalist Theory and its

[2] See Eucken (1939/1992), which is available in an English translation, and Eucken (1952/1990).
[3] A recent overview of the Freiburg School is offered by Streit (1992). See also Grossekettler (1989b).
[4] The *ORDO Yearbook,* founded by Walter Eucken and Franz Böhm in 1948, serves as the main forum for contributions in the Ordnungstheorie.
[5] The scholars working in the tradition of *Ordnungstheorie* are also proponents of a liberal economic policy. So were Eucken and Böhm. The development of the "social market economy" in Germany was to a great extent based on the theoretical foundations of the *Ordnungstheorie* and *Ordnungspolitik.* Thus, this theory has been very influential in both economic theory and policy. See the contributions in Peacock and Willgerodt (1989) and Schmidtchen (1984). In our discussion, we will deliberately neglect the normative implications of the *Ordnungspolitik.*

focus on abstract analysis.[6] Eucken built a morphological apparatus of "pure forms," (i.e. alternative institutional regimes) to help him classify the great diversity of phenomena encountered in economic history so that both historical cases and abstract economic theory could be reconciled. To use the game analogy, Eucken analyzed how different types of rules give rise to different types of games. Thus, his work possesses obvious importance for the enterprise that we shall undertake in this part of our study.

9.2. MARKET EVOLUTION WITHIN INSTITUTIONAL CONSTRAINTS

There are two main ideas we shall defend: (a) markets always work within rules and (b) market competition is an evolutionary process. If one acknowledges the simple empirical fact that individuals are creative and equipped with the faculty of perceiving and solving new problems, then a shift of focus in the theoretical analysis of markets is bound to occur. Market competition does not only lead to resource allocation, as in neoclassical economics, but is also mainly a knowledge-creating and knowledge-diffusing mechanism. Economic agents, in their attempt to increase their utility while participating in markets, are forced by the pressure of competition to learn so that they may survive in the market struggle. Since individuals are capable of learning, they use this capacity not only in the other parts of their social life, but also when acting within markets. The simple fact that people learn while trying to solve their problems and are creative in doing so is enough to shift attention toward a market theory of an evolutionary type. We shall deal with such a theory in more detail in Chapter 11. However, at this stage, only a brief outline of the main ingredients of the theory seems necessary to clarify the way in which institutions channel the market process.

Motivated by the striving for increased utility, economic agents engage in exchange processes. Such processes take place because individuals expect that an exchange act will increase their utility more than if they fail to take such action. This is the Fundamental Theorem of Exchange: Voluntary trade is mutually beneficial. (That is, it increases utility for both

---

[6] This theoretical controversy also had an important methodological aspect on the "correct" way of economic theorizing. It peaked in the first *Methodenstreit*. A reading of Schmoller's review (1883) of Menger's *Untersuchungen über die Methode der Sozialwissenschaften und der politischen Ökonomie insbesondere* and of the answer in Menger (1884/1970) is enough to grasp the passion of the controversy between those two schools of economic thought. For a review, see the monumental work of Brandt (1993, pp. 235ff.).

parties involved in the exchange)" (Hirshleifer, 1984, p. 218). Economic agents can best be conceptualized as problem solvers. The specifically economic component of their behavior is simply that they are seeking to increase their utility by the consumption of goods, which they always subjectively perceive as being scarce in the face of their wants. The individuals who organize the production of those goods are the entrepreneurs. They find and transform the production factors and sell the goods in the market in accordance with their primary goal of making a profit. They have at their disposition a large range of *action parameters* that they employ in order to attain profits.

As in every other societal setting, individuals in markets do not exist on isolated islands. Moreover, they are bound to exist among other individuals who are also pursuing their own aims. In the case of markets, entrepreneurs, as the initiators of the production of goods, must reckon with competition from other entrepreneurs who are also pursuing positive profits. In markets, diverse entrepreneurs with diverse capabilities and skills struggle for profit increases and thereby create a dynamic competitive process. Under this competitive pressure, the entrepreneurs probe different problem solutions in the market environment that are intended to solve their primary problem, that is, the attainment of profits. The entrepreneurs by no means know how this primary problem can be solved. Moreover, their activities in the market are best conceptualized as an exploration of the alternative possibilities for making profits.

Market activity is, in this view, a trial-and-error process during which the entrepreneurs learn which alternatives are successful and which are not. Entrepreneurial acts are hypotheses for finding a solution to the problems of the economic agents (e.g., consumers) that is better than the other problem solutions offered currently in the market. Entrepreneurs perform tests in the market every time they offer a product of their hypothetical knowledge concerning the effectiveness of their action parameters in assuring them profits. In this profit-seeking entreprise, many action parameters are available to them: the localization of cheap resources, the location of the plant, the bribing of bureaucrats, the employment of skilled workers, the modes of financing production, the structure of the firm, the employment of different market methods, the design of different selling points, the quality of the product, the service for the customer, and so on. The entrepreneur has only hypothetical, fallible knowledge concerning the effectiveness of every single action parameter and the effectiveness of the different mixes of the action parameters in making profits. Thus, *every simple entrepreneurial* act is undertaken in conditions of uncertainty and can best be understood as a hypothetical solution waiting for environmental feedback to come from the market. Entrepreneurial activity is a trial-and-error activity, and competition is the process that arises from the rivalry of entrepreneurs learning and trying to test their hypotheses in the market environment in profitable ways.

This competitive process is driven by innovation and imitation. Innovation is the parameter mix that has never been tried out by any entrepreneur in the past in the same market environment and is successful in securing profits. Imitation is the learning from other entrepreneurs who are acting in the same market environment about the effectiveness of the innovative parameter mix and the copying activity. Innovation is, therefore, a *successful hypothesis* of the effectiveness of a certain parameter mix, and imitation is a *successful copying of this hypothesis*. Competition is, then, a dynamic process of recurrent innovations and imitations by firms struggling for profits.

Such an evolutionary model of market competition is incomplete, however, as long as the selection criterion remains unspecified.[7] The most obvious criterion of selection for the entrepreneurial hypotheses which are the units of selection in our model seems to be simply "the market." Entrepreneurs test their hypotheses and their action parameters in the market and receive from it environmental feedback. "The market" as such does not exist, however. Markets are always embedded in a framework of formal and informal institutions, that is, exchange processes always take place within a set of social rules. Once this simple truth is accepted, the notion of the market being the selection criterion of entrepreneurial acts is bound to appear misleading. On the other hand, as long as this institutional framework remains relative stable through time, it becomes increasingly plausible to consider it as the *selection environment of evolutionary market processes*.

---

[7] See Campbell (1965, p. 27), describing the three essential theoretical building blocks of sociocultural evolution as "1. The occurence of variations: heterogeneous, haphazard, 'blind', 'chance', 'random', but in any event variable. . . . 2. Consistent selection criteria: selective elimination, selective propagation, selective retention, of certain types of variations. . . . 3. A mechanism for the preservation, duplication, or propagation of the positively selected variants. . . ." See also the description in Metcalfe (1989, p. 56): "It will be as well to remind ourselves here of the essential mechanisms of evolutionary change. These are: the principle of variation, that members of the population vary with respect to at least one characteristic with selective significance; the principle of heredity, that there exist copying mechanisms to ensure continuity over time in the form of the species under investigation; and the principle of selection, that some forms are better fitted to environmental pressure and thus increase in relative significance compared to the inferior forms."

9.3. INSTITUTIONS AS THE SELECTION ENVIRONMENT OF EVOLUTIONARY MARKET PROCESSES

What will survive in the process of the competitive struggle in a market crucially depends on the social institutions that constrain this market. Institutions as the normative rules of the game divide the range of possible actions of the economic agents into those that are and are not allowed.[8] In the case of informal institutions (mainly social norms and moral rules), the economic agents must fear social control whenever they proceed to acts that are either not allowed or are disapproved of the society in which they live. The law, on the other hand, assigns property rights to economic agents, that is, the right to engage in certain types of activities and the obligation to abstain from others in a more explicit form.[9]

[8] The range of activities that is not allowed and is prescribed by the rules of the game in the society can vary enormously. A typical extreme case is the one in which no individual production activities other than for personal consumption are allowed. This is found in a centrally planned economy. (In such an economy, there is some room for markets, however, since the economic agents, once they are allowed to possess consumer goods, can exchange them in order to increase their utility.) In a centrally planned economy, the competitive struggle does not take place in the economic game itself, but rather mainly on the level of the institutions. It is the case that some individuals have persuaded the rest members of the society, most often through violent means, that all decisions concerning the scarce resources must be made collectively on the level of rules, and little or no exchange should be allowed as a mechanism of overcoming individual scarcity (Leipold, 1983). We shall abstract from this extreme case, though, which is dealt with extensively in the theory of comparative economic systems (Hensel, 1978; Leipold, 1988), and we shall concentrate on the case of the rules of the game, which generally allow for production and exchange by economic agents.

[9] There is some conceptual ambiguity in the economic literature about whether "property rights" refers only to those rights that are enforced by the state or whether those rights are also enforced by informal social control. See, e.g., Alchian (1977, p. 129): "If, in what follows, I talk as if the property rights were enforced by formal state police power, let me here emphasize that such an interpretation, regardless of what I may later say, is gross error. It seems to be fact that individuals will not stand by idly while some other person's property is stolen. It seems to be fact that *private* property rights are rights not merely because the state formally makes them so but because individuals want such rights to be enforced, at least for a vast, overwhelming majority of people. . . . The rights of individuals to the use of resources (i.e., property rights) in any society are to be construed as supported by the force of etiquette, social custom, ostracism, and formal legally enacted laws supported by the states' power of violence or punishment." In other parts of the property-rights literature, the authors seem to mean by property rights only the rights enforced by the state. To avoid confusion, we shall try to avoid this term and speak of institutions or rules of the game instead, so that the further differentiation between formal and informal institutions on which we based the discussion in Part II of our study can be retained.

When the institutions of a society allow both the organization of production by individual entrepreneurs and the exchange of resources and commodities in markets, a competitive process of innovation and imitation is set in motion. The institutions channel not only the directions of the competitive process but also the knowledge generated during this process by defining which *action parameters* may be employed by the entrepreneurs in their problem-solving activities. The rules of the game define the freedom of action for the economic agents by imposing the constraints under which they pursue their competitive activities within markets. This "competitive, or property, aspect of exchange" focuses on "the kinds of offers, forms of competition and behavior that the members of society can employ in an endeavor to get more of the goods that would otherwise go to other people" (Alchian, 1977, p. 128). Depending upon which action parameters are selected by the institutional framework, different types of entrepreneurs are bound to survive, since the means of the competitive exchange are different. "More directly, the forms and kinds of property rights sanctioned in a society define or identify the kinds of competition, discrimination, or behavior characteristic of that society" (ibid.). The insight that the quality and quantity of economic outcomes are crucially dependent on institutions is a recurrent theme in constitutional economics.[10] The very useful distinction between rules of the game and plays within the game stressed in the research program of constitutional political economy can serve as the starting point. In an excellent paper, Kerber (1996) draws a further distinction between two kinds of effects that institutions have on the competitive process.[11] The first effect is the impact that the institutions have on the content of the competitive process, and the second effect is the impact on the dynamics of competi-

---

[10] See, e.g., Brennan and Buchanan (1985, p. 1): "The same individuals, with the same motivations and capacities, will interact to generate quite different aggregate outcomes under differing sets of rules, with quite different implications for the well-being of every participant." See also Buchanan and Tullock (1962), and Buchanan (1977, 1986, 1987, 1989a and 1991).

[11] Kerber concentrates on the formal institutions, i.e., the law and its channeling function. In our approach, the informal institutions are explicitly part of the selection environment for evolutionary market processes. Hodgson (1988) also makes a plea for taking informal institutions seriously and after interpreting the classical work of Durkheim, *De la Division du Travail Social* (1893/1996), individualsitically, he concludes (p. 167): "To recapitulate: the point established here is that non-contractual elements are essential, whatever their degree of prominence, in any developed system of exchange. A 'pure' market or exchange system, on purely contractarian lines, could not work in practice and is unacceptable in theory."

tion. Stated in the game analogy, the rules define both *what* the game will look like and *how fast* it will be played.

The content of the game is determined in the following manner. Institutions divide all the actions into the categories "allowed" and "not allowed." At the same time, sanctions that agents must take into account in case they proceed into forbidden actions are prescribed. Those restrictions of the activities of individuals are included, for example, in penal, civil, patent, and antitrust laws, as well as in the existing informal societal institutions. In other words, the entrepreneurs may only use those action parameters in their competitive efforts that are not forbidden by either the legal order or the informal social forces. This, in turn, means that entrepreneurs will try out in the market only the permitted action parameters, since *the incentive structure embedded in the institutional framework* discourages the employment of those action parameters that are not allowed decisively. Economic agents are driven by the incentives rooted in the institutions to shift their capabilities toward allowed activities. But we have already sketched competition as a knowledge-creating process (for a detailed analysis, see Chapter 11). Economic agents learn in the market arena first by formulating hypotheses on the effectiveness of their action parameters, then by trying them out in the market, and finally by getting feedback in the form of economic rents. In this process of trial and error, some put forward innovative hypotheses in the expectation of greater rents and some imitate them. An accumulation and, thereby, growth of knowledge takes place in connection with the employment of certain action parameters in the competitive process. Obviously, only those hypotheses and resultant knowledge actually tried in the market can be tested and accumulated, respectively. Hence, by allowing the employment of only a limited action parameters by the economic agents, the institutions determine at the same time which type of knowledge will be tested and obtained by them.[12] *In this way, the institutions select which hypoth-*

---

12 In formulating an essentially normative argument, Demsetz stresses the same point (1989, p. 229f.): "The basic dynamic problem that challenges public policy can be stated simply: *The design of institutional arrangements that provide incentives to encourage experimentation without overly insulating these experiments from the ultimate test of survival.* The framework provided by the model of perfect competition simply is poorly designed for solving this problem. Its use diverts our attention from a correct view of the problem. The important problem is not so much a question of whether competitive behavior should be indiscriminately fostered or constrained. The question is not whether to compete, it is what *kind* of competition to sanction.

"The private property system, for example, is a broad institutional arrangement

eses will survive and which will disappear in the market process; at the same time, they channel the innovative potential of the individuals in a certain direction.[13]

Take the example of piracy. If piracy is allowed by the institutions of a society, then pirate entrepreneurs will employ guns and knives as action parameters in their effort to attain rents and will consequently acquire all the skills and knowledge necessary for their activities. As North puts it (1990, p. 77): "To be a successful pirate one needs to know a great deal about naval warfare; the trade routes of commercial shipping; the armament, rigging, and crew size of potential victims; and the market for booty. Successful pirates will acquire the requisite knowledge and skills. Such activities may well give rise to a thriving demand for improved naval warfare technology by both the pirates and the victims." Or take the example of the institutional framework in some countries of Latin America. Bribing politicians and bureaucrats is de facto allowed in many societies there. Thus, entrepreneurs must be expected to acquire knowledge about the persons working in the civil service, that is, the prices that they require for different services, the health officers responsible for product controls and their preferences, and the officers of the police department in their community. Another example concerns the regulation of utilities or other markets. Entrepreneurs acting in heavily regulated markets will try to augment their knowledge of regulation practices, past judicial cases concerning the market, the staff working in the regulation agency, and so on (Kerber, 1996, p. 316).

In determining the dynamics of the competitive process in the market, the institutional framework plays an equally crucial role. We have outlined competition as a process of innovation and imitation, of "moves and responses" (J. M. Clark, 1954, p. 326). The innovative implementation of

that encourages competition of certain types and dissuades others. It offers protection from many types of rivalry by penalizing competitors who resort to violence in carrying on their rivalry, by protecting patents and copyrights, and by penalizing impersonation. But it gives little protection from most forms of price and product competition. The importance of the private property system is not in furthering or reducing rivalry generally but in the *direction* it gives rivalry [emphasis added]. The harm to one individual in allowing competition may be as great as that resulting from theft, but we approve of the incentive effects of the former and disapprove of those of the latter."

[13] See Kerber (1996, p. 315): "Through the differentiation of the disposable action parameters at hand between allowed and not allowed, a concentration of the innovative efforts of economic subjects occurs in the area of the allowed action parameters; at the same time, the knowledge creating process taking place during [the] competitive processes is led in a certain direction." (Translation by C. M.)

action parameters on the part of the innovative entrepreneur imposes negative "pecuniary external effects" on the other entrepreneurs acting in the market.[14] These negative pecuniary external effects take the form of depreciation of the specific real and human capital that has been invested by the other entrepreneurs for production up to the point in time that the innovation took place (Kerber, 1996, p. 317, n40). "Hence, where the innovators and the adopters have strong incentives to change future transaction or contract relations so as to exploit mutually favorable innovations, the competitors driven out of the relation are forced with deteriorating future prospects. They must incur possibly quite heavy losses from depreciated (human) capital. Innovations deprive them of their 'quasi-rents' in Marshall's sense." (Witt, 1987b, p. 183). But the depreciation of the capital of the competitors is not a natural fact. Moreover, it is the institutions (in this case, mainly the legal rules) that allow innovations in the market whatever the external effects on the competitors. It is institutions that make those investment costs irreversible costs. An alternative institutional framework, say one that would force innovators to compensate competitors for their losses, would have, consequently, a thoroughly different impact on the innovative activity and thus on the competitive process.

The dynamics of the competitive process depend on the rate at which innovations occur and are adopted. This, in turn, depends on the payoffs, that is, on the utility increase expected from innovations and, thus, on the incentives to innovate. We argue here that incentives are crucially dependent on the institutional framework, since this defines whether and to what degree the fruits of the innovative activity are attributed to the innovator and whether innovations are permitted at all. By regulating the distribution of the effects of innovative activity, that is, by allocating gains and losses, the institutions determine simultaneously the dynamics of the competitive process in the market.[15]

---

14 See Witt (1987a, p. 184f.): "Further, in connection with the innovations, the role of the so-called pecuniary external effects are to be considered. The introduction of either a new product or a new technique is successful for the innovator, under the conditions of freedom of contracts when and if the demand side honors them. Conversely, the fact that the assets of competitors or factory owners can be drastically de-valued in this way plays no role. Only a veto right and/or a right of compensation could therefore ensure that no one is disadvantaged by the individual innovations and at least one individual improves his position." (Translation by C. M.). See also Witt (1993a, pp. 24ff).

15 See Kerber (1996, p. 317): "The ongoing moves, responses, and outstripping of economic subjects in competition leads to permanent redistributions between the

Although in many societies the prevailing institutional framework allowed market activities, historically the restrictions were so tight that little or no innovation occurred (Kaufer, 1986). As Witt explained (1987b, p. 187): "The far-reaching restrictions on the freedom to interact that can be observed in historical societies are instructive examples: caste, class, or status-oriented trading rules and prohibitions, entry regulations with respect to certain economic activities and professions based on descent and inheritance, customary restrictions on exchange by age grading, trading bonds, bazaar regulations, and, similarly, the guild organization of manufacturing and merchandising in early medieval Europe. From the aspects of competition by innovation, all these institutions have the same effect: They discourage or even prevent competitors who might come up with an innovation form outside current trading relations. Consequently, they protect insiders at the price of curbing the supply of new techniques and products and with it the pace of economic evolution."

9.4. THE METAPHOR OF "ARTIFICIAL SELECTION"

In our discussion of the theory of social institutions, we have stated that the identification of a relatively stable selection criterion for institutional evolution is an impossible task. The only reasonable selection criterion of institutions is the interests of the individuals in a society as these individuals subjectively perceive them every time to be. Since these interests (or preferences) are continuously changing over time, it is very difficult to predict the nature and quality of the institutions that will survive. From the previous discussion in this chapter, it should be obvious that this theoretically rather unfortunate situation in regard to institutional evolution is not present in the case of market evolution. Moreover, once the institutional framework of a society is formed, it remains, in relation to markets, relatively stable. It therefore suggests itself as a selection criterion of market evolution.

competitors. In other words, previous knowledge is devalued by new, better knowledge. It is precisely these continuously occurring or impending redistributions that provide the so important immanent incentive- and sanction-mechanism for the dynamic competitive process" (Translation by C. M.) See also Witt (1987b, p. 182): "The connection between transaction rights and innovations results from the fact that *innovations must find their way into the economic system via transactions*. The occurrence and mode of adoption of innovations, it will be argued here, is influenced by the particular institutional specification of transaction rights. At the same time, if innovations do occur, transaction rights affect the appropriation of possible gains as well as the allocation of possible losses and these, in turn, have repercussions on both the inclination to innovate further and the possible loser's incentive to take action against other agents' innovations."

This fundamental asymmetry between institutional evolution and market evolution helps to illuminate the old debate concerning the roles of economic history and economic theory in the discipline of political economy. *History matters* for crystallization of the institutional structure. The role of economic history is to describe how the evolutionary process of institutions in a certain time and place occurred. This historical element embedded in the informal and formal institutions of a society, that is, conventions, morals, social norms, and legal rules, aids decisively in explaining and predicting the direction and intensity of the competitive process within those given social rules.[16,17] The historical aspect of analysis is contained within institutions, that is, institutions are the "carriers of history" (David, 1994). This historicity means nothing more than the *learning* history of the individual members of the society, which plays a crucial rule in their economic behavior and thus in producing aggregate economic outcomes. We shall discuss this important issue in more detail in Chapter 10.

The fact that it is institutions that act as the selective environment in market evolution implies a clear abandonment of any notion of natural selection in favor of the idea of artificial selection. With the term "artificial selection," the more or less conscious, purposeful selective act is designated in contrast to the term "natural selection." Inspired by animal breeders (Mayr, 1982, p. 486) Darwin conceived of artificial selection as the conscious act of choice of the selective environment in order to achieve some desired results: "Although man does not cause variability and cannot even prevent it, he can select, preserve and accumulate the variation given to him by the hand of nature almost in any way in which he

---

[16] Bunge stresses the methodological aspect of the problem and pleads for the complementarity of the two fields of research (1996, p. 5): "An early example of a destructive philosophical controversy in social science was the *Methodenstreit* in the German-speaking world, which started in the 1880s and, to all intents and purposes, is still going on worldwide, albeit in [a] muted way. This controversy was destructive in opposing two perfectly legitimate, complementary fields of research: namely economics and economic history. As a result, each of these disciplines was retarded, instead of being enriched by its complement. . . . Paradoxically, economics won the political battle but lost the intellectual one, because, by gaining independence, it became increasingly remote from economic realities, both past and present."

[17] North acknowledges the fact that "institutions structure economic exchange in an enormous variety of forms" (1990, p. 34) and works out a typology of exchange based on the transaction cost model. He distinguishes between (a) personalized exchange, (b) impersonal exchange without a state, and (c) impersonal exchange with a state. This categorization offers the first clear picture of the relationship between institutions and markets or, more generally, between economic history and economic theory.

chooses. . . . Man may select and preserve each successive variation, with the distinct intention of improving and altering a breed, in accordance with a preconceived idea" (Darwin, 1875/1972, p. 3f.). This idea of artificial selection has been introduced explicitly into economics by John Commons. With regard to Darwin's conception, Commons stresses (1934, p. 636): "It is 'artificial' simply because it is Purpose, Futurity, Planning injected into and greatly controlling the struggle for life. Darwin admitted that his own term 'natural selection' was a misnomer, and regretted his resort to metaphor. It is more properly called blind selection, while the artificial kind is purposeful selection. Natural selection which is the natural survival of the 'fit' produces wolves, snakes, poisons, destructive microbes; but artificial selection converts wolves into dogs, nature's poisons to medicine, eliminates the wicked microbes. A Holstein cow could not survive if left to natural selection – she is a monstrosity created by artificial selection for the good she can do for man in the future."

Commons contended that political economy must be constructed as an evolutionist theory of artificial selection (Ramstad, 1994). The thesis that institutions channel the competitive process and give it a certain direction, as well as regulating its dynamics, can be also expressed in terms of the metaphor of artificial selection.[18] By selecting the parameters of competition, institutions select at the same time, artificially, which entrepreneurial hypotheses will survive. The selection of knowledge that will be tested and accumulated in the market occurs while entrepreneurs try to adapt to the institutional environment. The crucial factor is the existence of formal and informal institutions, which, being outcomes of human interaction themselves and partly of human design, impose a systematic influence on the market activities of the economic agents and force them to adapt. The artificial character of this process consists in the fact that institutions are themselves human products.

The explanatory power of the notion of artificial selection is best illustrated when combined with the idea of "population thinking," whose importance has been primarily established by the leading biologist, Ernst Mayr.[19] Population thinking is contrasted by Mayr to "typological thinking," the main difference being the emphasis on the importance of the

---

[18] See Ramstad (1994, p. 110) who comments on the notion of artificial selection in the work of Commons as follows: "[I]n his view, it-is purposeful human action – 'artificial selection' – that has transformed the 'stuggle for existence' into the wealth-producing 'machine' we refer to as the 'market system'."

[19] See Mayr (1976, pp. 26–9; 1982, pp. 45–7 and 487f.; 1985a, p. 56; 1985b, pp. 766ff.)

individual as opposed to the importance of the type. In typological think-ing or "typological essentialism" (Mayr, 1982, p. 45), species are regarded as plausibly identifiable in terms of a few basic characteristics that are representative of their type or "essence." Based on mean values, one may, accordingly, reconstruct the representative type of the species. In popula-tion thinking, species are instead described in terms of a distribution of characteristics, and it is the individuality that counts. This stress upon the individual character of every member of a species implies the crucial im-portance of variety in the evolutionary process, since it is on this variety that selection operates.[20]

Darwin (1859) borrowed the recognition of variety and diversity from the work of Malthus (1798/1926). Thus, population thinking, although it currently plays a major role in biology, was originally borrowed from economics and social science (Mayr, 1964; Hodgson, 1993, pp. 62ff.). The modern development in evolutionary economics, with its stress on variety, is thus bringing back to economic theory a view that political economy lent to biology over 100 years ago. German economists such as Arndt, Heuß, Hoppmann, Fehl, and Röpke never closed their eyes to the meaning of variety for the economic process and pioneered the German theory of competition (*Wettbewerbstheorie*), which we shall discuss in more detail in Chapter 11. However, in the mainstream economic theory of the English-speaking countries, typological thinking gained a foothold in the form of the Marshallian "representative firm" of the industry (i.e., the hypothetical firm with production costs that in long-run equilibrium are the average for the whole industry[21]). It is only since the recent revival

[20] See Mayr (1982, p. 46): "Western thinking for more than two thousand years after Plato was dominated by essentialism. It was not until the nineteenth century that a new and different way of thinking about nature began to spread, so-called popula-tion thinking. What is population thinking and how does it differ from essentialism? Population thinkers stress the uniqueness of everything in the organic world. What is important for them is the individual, not the type. They emphasize that every individual in sexually reproducing species is uniquely different from all others, with much individuality even existing in uniparentally reproducing ones. There is no 'typical' individual, and mean values are abstractions. Much of what in the past has been designated in biology as 'classes' are populations consisting of unique individuals."

[21] See Marshall (1920, p. 264f) which is characteristic of the way he eliminates variety in favor of an average or representative firm: "[A]nd for this purpose we shall have to study the *expenses of a representative producer* for that aggregate volume. On the one hand we shall not want to select some new producer just struggling into busi-ness, who works under many disadvantages, and has to be content for a time with little or no profits, but who is satisfied with the fact that he is establishing a connec-tion and taking the first steps towards building up a successful business; nor on the

of evolutionary theorizing in those countries that diversity in economics has been reemphasized.[22]

How are artificial selection and population thinking correlated? Let's start with a population in which all individuals differ in the traits or problem solutions that they employ, and this difference plays a crucial role in their relative success in securing rewards from the environment. This differential success is translated into different probabilities for the respective traits or problem solutions to be represented in future populations. It is predicted that only those traits or problem solutions will survive whose "individual carriers" are relatively more successful in adapting to their environment. Now this environment can either be naturally or artificially constructed. If it is an artificial environment, it can be predicted that the frequency of those traits or problem solutions will be higher in the popula-

other hand shall we want to take a firm which by exceptionally long-sustained ability and good fortune has got together a vast business, and huge well-ordered workshops that give it a superiority over almost all its rivals. But our representative firm must be one which has had a fairly long life, and fair success, which is managed with normal ability, and which has normal access to the economies, external and internal, which belong to that aggregate volume of production; account being taken of the class of goods produced, the conditions of marketing them and the economic environment generally."

Langlois (1997) stresses the fact that Marshall's representative firm referred to the *average* firm of the industry and admitted at the same time the underlying variation. In contrast, Pigou eliminated any notion of variety within the industry. See Langlois (1997, p. 8f.) "Marshall's notion of representativeness was quite different from later variants. In the case of the firm, Marshall understood the representative firm to reflect the typical properties not of any particular actual firms but of the population of firms as a whole. This 'composite' firm was a way of accommodating some measure of population thinking into the non-evolutionary framework of comparative statics. Marshall's successor – notably A.C. Pigou, who most often gets the blame – took a different track, building the industry up from identical atomistic firms rather than compressing a diverse industry down into a representative firm. . . . There is a third alternative: to retain an explicit population framework in which, although they are abstract constructions and may share many typical features, agents are allowed to vary along some dimensions. Such an approach would be essential for any explicit evolutionary account."

[22] See, e.g., Metcalfe (1989, p. 55f.): "The fundamental point here is that the evolutionary framework is concerned with frequencies of events and phenomena rather than with ideal, representative types and there is a considerable shift in intellectual orientation in this change of emphasis. . . . The shift from analyzing ideal cases to examining frequencies and their distribution is central to the elaboration of an evolutionary perspective of the sort we are proposing. The shift from classical to distributional modes of explanation has occurred in biology in terms of the shift from typological to population thinking about species." See also Hirshleifer (1982) and Sober (1984, sect. 5.3), as well as the earlier work of Steindl (1952) and Downie (1955). More recently, see Chiaromonte and Dosi (1992), Eliasson (1984, 1991) and Saviotti (1991).

tions that help their individual carriers to be more adaptive to the artificial environment. Hence, artificial selection of individual traits or problem solutions has taken place.

The notion of population thinking is important because it implies the continuous generation of variation within the population and the inducement of change in the distribution of traits or problem solutions in the population. This, in turn, means that the artificial selection of traits or problem solutions does not impede the openness of the process; moreover, the evolutionary process driven by constant variation remains radically open-ended due to the endogenously produced novelty. The artificial environment predetermines only the boundaries within which the whole evolutionary process can be unfolded; however, the adaptations to this environment are not themselves predefined. Artificial selection leads, therefore, to a regular and in a way directed change of the frequency of the traits or problem solutions created in the population, since the frequency of certain traits or problem solutions grows systematically, while that of certain other traits decreases.

The combination of artificial selection and population thinking is important for our discussion because it expresses in a straightforward manner how market competition within institutions can best be understood in evolutionary terms.[23] From the population of problem solutions that are tried out in the market by the economic agents, those that help their employers to succeed in adapting to their institutional environment will occur most frequently. The systematic growth of the frequency of certain problem solutions due to the prevailing social institutions means at the same time that the knowledge of the economic agents grows in a certain direction; this has profound implications for economic development. We shall turn to this issue in Chapter 12.

---

[23] See also Röpke (1977, p. 374f.): " Competition is a process that can neither be positively defined nor described. It is only meaningful to consider competition in relation to a specific rule system. Competitive ascendant and descent processes, and with them also the qualities of the ascension and the descendence, are always related to certain norms constraining behavior. In opposition to biological evolution, in a market system the 'most competent' and the 'most capable' are not entirely opportunistically chosen. In a market system, there is a much greater possibility to indirectly determine which tests of survival the system will keep at the ready for its elements through the conscious influence of the behavioral rules of the market" (Translation by C. M.).

10

Institutions and the Market

The Microeconomic Level

10.1. HOW STABLE IS THE SELECTION ENVIRONMENT?

It is clear that the ultimate selection criteria of evolutionary market activities are the preferences or interests of the economic subjects themselves and, more specifically, those of the consumers. These decide in the end which market activities will fail and which will succeed (see Section 11.3). At a first level, though, it is institutions that act as a primary selection criterion of the evolutionary market processes.

To be considered a selection criterion at all, a factor must demonstrate relative stability. The variables that ultimately affect the probability of survival of different problem solutions must remain relatively invariant so that the selection forces can operate.[1] If social institutions are to play the

---

[1] See, e.g., Dosi and Nelson (1994, p. 156f.): "Selection in the social arena and its relationship with some notion of 'fitness' immediately confronts the question of the endogeneity of the selection criteria themselves. . . . [A]lso in natural sciences it is the general case that what is selected – in favor or against – might be determined in some complicated and nonlinear ways by the distribution of actual populations present at a point in time and by their history. However, one might still hold that the selection criteria – that is, the variables ultimately affecting probabilities of survival – remain relatively invariant: for example, the rates of reproduction, or the efficiency in accessing food. In the contrary, this might not be so in many economic and social circumstances."

Metcalfe (1989, p. 57) also stresses the importance of stability in economic evolution: "Whenever there are economic differences between competing technologies there is scope for selection. But variety itself is not sufficient; the differences must be stable relative to the speed with which selection operates. In a world of perfect adaptation there would be no scope for selection. Selection is quite consistent with random technological variation but what it does require are elements of inertia to hold competing varieties in a form long enough for selection to operate."

role of those variables, they must remain relatively stable. Following our basic distinction between rules of the game and activities within the rules, our main purpose has been to prove that both levels are subject to evolutionary change.

Since both institutions and markets change, the function of social institutions as a selection environment for the evolutionary change taking place in markets is not self-evident. Moreover, this proposition must itself be proved so that the whole theory can retain its validity. In concrete terms, what must be proved is that the pace of change in institutions is slower than the pace of change in markets. Only in this case might institutions possess the relatively invariant character with regard to market changes and allow for the formulation of satisfactory empirical propositions on economic evolution.

This problem lies at the heart of the age-old debate between Alchian (1950, 1953) and Penrose (1952) on evolutionary theorizing in economics. Alchian's main argument was that even if human behavior were not purposeful or "irrational," the economist could, by looking only at the environment of the economic subjects or the firm, "state what types of firms or behavior relative to other possible types will be more viable" (p. 216).[2] Alchian proposed positive profits as a clear, straightforward criterion "according to which successful and surviving firms are selected" (1950, p. 213); Penrose opposed to the "viability analysis," the possibility of firms to change their environment. She contended that a record of the 'external environment of the firm' *in general* is not available to the analyst. Nevertheless, some characteristics of the external environment are discernible for the economist. Penrose herself named "government policies" as a possible example (p. 814). Except for the identifiability of such environmental factors, the most important issue is their relative stability. This, in turn, we cannot simply "safely assume," as Penrose suggested (ibid.), but must itself be proved. In the case where such a proof is provided, Alchian's basic idea can be retained, although at the same time partly relativized. The economist's "awareness of the survival conditions and criteria of the economic system" (Alchian, 1950, p. 217) extends only to the clearly identifiable and relatively invariant parts of it. Since it is impossible for an observer to know all details of the extended environment of a firm, atten-

---

2 See Alchian (1950, p. 215): "As circumstances (economic environment) change, the analyst (economist) can select the types of participants (firms) that will now become successful; he may also be able to diagnose the conditions most conducive to a greater probability of survival."

tion must be focused on only the relatively invariable parts because knowledge of them can be helpful in forming economic predictions.[3]

The problem that social institutions change with a tempo that is slower than the tempo of change in markets could be solved with the aid of a methodological argument. Such an argument is provided in the important contribution of Hesse (1987) on economic development and his discussion of the role of "innovative adaptation to invariant restrictions" (p. 215) for long-run economic development. In a social world of open possibilities where creative individuals act, only an evolutionary theory can offer some orientation in regard to the direction of the process of evolutionary change. An explanation of such a process is contingent, according to Hesse's main argument, on the identification of some invariant restrictions to which innovative individuals can adapt. Only in such a case can an evolutionary theory produce theoretical propositions of some empirical content; otherwise, all that can be offered is a rather nihilistic alternative of the type "everything is open."[4] Depending on the theoretical problem and the time horizon at hand, the economist may identify different invariant restrictions that, playing the role of a selection environment, will aid the formulation propositions with empirical content.[5]

An argument quite similar to Hesse's, although not placed in an evolutionary setting, is provided by Buchanan's idea of "relatively absolute absolutes" (1989b). Buchanan applies this methodological concept in different areas, such as Marshallian time and its long- and short-term facets the political constitutions, epistemology, and the rules for games. The intuitive idea expressed by the term relatively absolute absolutes is that for certain issues, a set of circumstances are to be considered given, so that fruitful conclusions may be reached. In our case, this would mean

---

[3] To be sure, this kind of theoretical proposition will have low empirical content, but adopting an evolutionary perspective abolishes the dream of accurate predictions anyway. See Hayek (1967), Faber and Proops (1991), Witt (1992a), and Nelson (1995).

[4] See Hesse (1987, p. 215): "'Innovative adaptation' appears to be a *contradictio in adiecto*, given the fact that innovations obviously eliminate restrictions. . . . in a discussion of the possibilities to explain the *direction* of economic change, one must bear in mind that the introduction of a kind of 'innovation' which finally makes possible the abolishment of *every* restriction, makes a meaningful theory of scientific development impossible. It is then not only the future 'completely open,' but this is also the case for all present periods in the past that 'everything was open'; and a theory with propositions of empirical content (that exclude possible outcomes) is not possible. What remains then is merely the (selectively) recording history" (Translation by C. M.).

[5] For a discussion of Hesse's methodological argument see Kerber (1996, pp. 305ff.).

that one declares social institutions to be the relatively absolute absolutes with regard to the evolutionary market process taking place within them.[6]

Both ideas, the innovative adaptation to invariant restrictions and the relatively absolute absolutes, are only methodological devices for coping with the issue of interest here. But if true theoretical reasons can be found in support of the proposition that institutional change is slower than change in markets, a more satisfactory link will have been provided between institutions and the market process, however. The conjecture put forward here is that such a link is in fact available in the theory of problem solving as presented in Part I of this study.

10.2. LEARNING AND THE RELATIVE STABILITY OF INSTITUTIONS

The importance of the problem of the relative stability of the rules of the game has been neglected in the literature. From a neoclassical perspective this is not strange, as the main focus of analysis is the allocation of resources in market settings; when institutions are introduced into the analysis, the focus is on how they affect resource allocation rather than how they channel knowledge creation in markets. Thus, the problem of stability of the market environment for the knowledge-creating process does not arise here at all. In the New Institutional Economics, the issue is of vital importance mainly because all policy implications depend on the relative stability of the rules of the game.[7]

The questions of whether and why institutions remain relative stable with regard to the market process unfolding within them can be answered only if one explicitly includes in the analysis the learning process of the individual agents. Until now, the whole argument has been developed on

---

6 Riker (1980) in a classical paper, after reviewing the results of social choice theory regarding the disequilibrium of tastes and the instability of political outcomes, proposes the identification of "unstable constants" (p. 445) in order to achieve some predictability of political outcomes in the short run. Although his argument is far from being in an evolutionary vein, it is methodologically similar to that of Hesse and Buchanan, suggesting that political institutions can play the role of "unstable constants" in the political process. His argument is, like that of Hesse and Buchanan, only a methodological argument, since it does not offer substantial theoretical reasons why political institutions remain relatively constant.

7 Matthews (1986) in his presidential address to the Royal Economic Society has also raised the following point: "Institutional inertia is not *necessarily* to be regarded as pathology. Institutions provide the framework for economic life. A completely flexible framework is a contradiction in terms. It is a matter for study what determines the strength of the inertia and how it varies in different contexts" (p. 914).

the aggregate level, which states the impact of institutions on the content and dynamics of the market process. In a way, we have been tacitly adopting an *external* point of view in discussing the causal relationship between institutions and the characteristics or problem solutions that survive in the market process. The relative stability of institutions can be justified only if we tackle the issue from an *internal* point of view stressing the significance of the cognitive apparatus and the learning processes on the part of the individual agents.

The crucial factor is that, at the precise moment that an individual starts exchanging in the market, he is already a socialized individual sharing the same social rules with the other market participants. He is not an ahistorical creature equipped solely with preferences that maximize utility under the constraints of, for example, given prices and available income. Although he also learns while participating in the market, a fact that has been recognized by many neoclassical models in the recent literature, the important point is that he possessed knowledge concerning the rules of the economic game even before starting to play it. This knowledge is therefore different from the knowledge he acquires *during* the market process because it is *shared* among all or almost all economic agents. (It is this shared knowledge that, in the end, channels the process of market interaction in a certain direction.)

During the socialization process, the individuals who later become the entrepreneurs of economic theory have learned the conventions, the moral rules and the social norms of the society in which they are living. When they start their business, the entrepreneurs have learned which legal rules they have to respect and up to which point their private property rights are protected or violated by the state. They are already the "legal persons" of the legal theory. The entrepreneurs share the formal and informal institutions, and thus the rules of the economic game, by sharing the same learning history that makes them the specific agents of the specific economic game.

Employing the problem-solving model presented in Part I of this study will illuminate the issue further. Since the mind is an instrument of classification that operates to solve the problems of the individual (Section 3.2), whenever some problem solutions have been tried out successfully in the environment for some time, the mind builds classes that prescribe the appropriate solution to the respective problem in the form of an IF . . . THEN rule. Every time the same problem appears, the appropriate solution in the form of a rule will be applied automatically and unconsciously by the agent. This is the case of old problems allowing for tested solutions stored in the repertoire of the mind and invoked automatically whenever needed. The argument to be made here, which is perhaps the main application of the problem-solving model, is that *when economic agents participate in markets, they have already classified all institutions as solutions to old problems in their minds.* In other words, the internal aspect of the prevailing institutions takes the form of IF . . . THEN classes in the minds of the agents, that is, of already tested problem solutions on which they do not need to reflect consciously. The rules of the economic game have their counterpart in the available classes in the minds of economic agents and are, therefore, subjectively interpreted by them as solutions to old problems.

That which, from an external point of view, seems to be the crucial characteristic of social institutions (i.e., that they are shared social rules followed by the participants of the economic game) is of an equally crucial importance when one takes the internal point of view; institutions are nothing but classes of the IF . . . THEN type, already stored in the minds of the economic agents participating in the market game. In this internal fashion, institutions are solutions to what the agents perceive as old problems that they have learned during the socialization process. What institutions are doing is to define which problems are old ones for the individual agents. They determine the range of problem-solving activities that economic agents do not need to attend to consciously while participating in the market.

This subjective counterpart of institutions, that is, old problem solutions shared by the economic agents, explains why institutions change in a lower tempo than markets. Institutional evolution presupposes that problem solutions to social conflict are tried out often by one innovative individual, who is followed by others, and become in the end *shared* by the population. Changes in institutions can take place only if all or almost all agents participate in those changes, either actively as initiators and imitators of novel problem solutions or passively by simply *learning* what the new solutions to the problem of social interaction consists of. A process of institutional change is completed only when *all* interacting individuals have formed the same classes in their minds or the same mental models. Change in institutions is equivalent to the process of building shared classes or mental models (Denzau and North, 1994) in the minds of *all* individuals; only if this learning step has taken place can one seriously talk of a change in the rules of the game. The notion of institutions as the rules of the game presupposes that all players have learned the rules before starting to play the game. This, in turn, means that changes in those rules are followed by a concomitant learning process of all players. However, since *all* players are involved in such a change, it is plausible to hypothesize that the tempo of the change in rules will be slower than that of a change in strictly individual behaviors.[8]

This is exactly the case with the market process, during which economic agents are also learning. The main characteristic of the market process is that agents do not need to have shared knowledge. In fact, the contrary is true: They are forced to acquire specific knowledge or, in our terminology, atomistic knowledge.[9] Adam Smith's main argument concerning the working of markets has been that the division of labor induces specialization, promotes different talents, and increases the productive potential of an economy. Division of labor goes hand in hand with division of knowledge among the market participants.

In order to survive under conditions of market competition, economic subjects are forced to specialize in different tasks and acquire different kinds of knowledge. This means that market participants run through different learning histories, because they are forced by market competition to confront *different* problems. *The main characteristic of markets is the division of labor and, thus, the division of knowledge among economic agents, which is directly opposite to the case of institutions, which presuppose shared knowledge of the agents.* Different agents face different problems. They then try out new problem solutions to those different (and usually quite specific) problems and build in their minds, after some time, the respective classes of appropriate problem solutions to their own problems. The very essence of markets consists in the possession of different knowledge on the part of each market participant. This, in turn, means that knowledge creation, learning, and evolutionary change are faster in markets than in institutions. A process whereby everybody is experimenting with new solutions to his own problems, where there is no further need to *share* the knowledge that one acquires with all the rest, is bound to unfold at a greater tempo than a process that exists only insofar as everybody possesses the same knowledge.

---

[8] To the extent that institutions are interrelated, their pace of change will be even slower. However, as long as we do not have a theory of the interaction between the different kinds of institutions, it is difficult to explore this effect more accurately. For insightful comments on this issue see David (1994, p. 214f.)

[9] For the definition of atomistic knowledge, see Section 3.1.

10.3. OLD PROBLEMS, NEW PROBLEMS, AND THE CHANNELING OF THE MARKET PROCESS

We have seen that the internal aspect of social institutions can best be conceptualized as solutions to old problems classified in the minds of the individuals who are participating in competitive exchange processes. The rules of the economic game have their cognitive counterpart in the shared classes of problem solutions in the minds of the economic agents. This fact has profound implications for channeling the market process via institutions. Since institutions define not only which problem solutions are to be followed when a stylized social problem arises but also determine the sanctions that an agent has to reckon with in the case of deviation, the institutions lead to uniform patterns of individual behavior once they are internalized by the agents. Of course, not every single agent will conform to the social rules, but this is an inherent problem of every aggregation that we will not address here. It suffices for the present analysis that the great majority of economic agents build the same classes or mental models concerning the social problems they usually confront.

The fact that people classify the recurrent stylized situations of social conflict as old problems allowing for already known solutions means that they do not consciously attend to them. The classification of institutions as old problem solutions at the *cognitive* level is concomitant with the unconscious following of routines at the *behavioral* level. Since the market is not the isolated entity described by the neoclassical theory, when people exchange under competitive pressure, they face in fact a great variety of problems. The hypothesis put forward here is that they classify automatically as old ones all those problems that are defined by the rules of the game, and they apply the problem solutions that the relevant institutions determine to be appropriate.

Hayek has stressed that in the great majority of cases, both formal and informal social rules "are negative in the sense that they normally impose no positive duties on any one, unless he has incurred such duties by his own actions" (1976/1982, p. 36). In these cases, the solutions to old problems as defined by the institutional framework are generally prohibitions, that is, the IF . . . THEN rules take the form "IF such and such a situation arises, THEN do not act in this or that way." Nevertheless, the problem-solving framework is equally applicable to the cases where social institutions might require positive action. This is definitely an additional advantage of the model. The notion of old problems is more general. It is independent of whether or not the problem solution contains a sanction or a reward. The main issue is that regardless of the content of the problem solution, it has been classified as such by all or almost all agents and has accordingly become shared knowledge.

This shared knowledge is the crucial factor that in the end channels the market process in a certain direction. Economic agents systematically avoid the behavior that is sanctioned by the institutions or systematically follow the behavior that is rewarded by them unconsciously. At the same time, they are freed from the need to decide anew about the most appropriate solution each time they face an old problem. By providing ready-made solutions to the agents, institutions, enforced with the aid of the sanction potential of the respective enforcing agencies, select at the same time which problems they do not need to care about consciously. *Market participants are thus directed to solve certain categories of problems in the market context whose solution is not prescribed by the rules of the market game.* They are free, then, to experiment within the constraints posed by the social institutions.

This means that economic agents concentrate their innovative potential only on those problems that arise in the markets and are not dealt with by the institutions. These problems are subjectively interpreted by the economic agents as novel and allow for creative solutions that lead to monetary profits. In other words, in the market setting, agents learn individually by starting to solve new problems, testing solutions in the market, and building respective classes in accordance with their environmental feedback. In their learning enterprise, they do not need attend to the behavior of other agents concerning a large number of problems, as they can safely assume that the others will also have internalized the problem solutions defined by the institutions. *The main effect of this coordination of expectations is the release of the learning potential of the economic agents, which can then be used when they participate in the market.*

Shared institutions are nothing more than the collective expression of the mechanization effect discussed in the psychological literature. When subjects are asked to solve a problem after having learned an appropriate solution, they tend to apply it mechanically to situations that they classify as analogous (Baron, 1994, ch. 4.2). In other words, they tend to apply the same solutions mechanically, without consciously reassessing their appropriateness every time. As Luchins put it, a habit may cease to be "a tool discriminately applied" and may become instead "a Procrustean bed to which the situation must conform. . . . In a word, instead of the individual mastering the habit, the habit masters the individual" (1942, p. 93). Such a mechanization effect occurs collectively when economic agents have learned solutions to social problems prescribed by the institutions.[10] At the same time, their cognitive abilities can be turned to the solution of problems appearing in the market.[11]

The main characteristic of problems emerging in the market is that they are temporary. Therefore, the mechanization effect does not arise.[12] Economic agents are conscious of this temporality, and they do not run the danger described by the mechanization effect while participating in markets. Since for an exchange to take place only two agents are needed, constant evaluation by market participants is possible. The diversity of exchange acts is immensely greater and more temporary than any recurrent social problem solved by social institutions. Accordingly, economic agents perceive in market settings a large number of problems as new ones, and therefore evaluate and consciously choose quite often. It is, thus, plausible that economic theory has dealt exhaustively with choice in exchange settings since the marginal revolution of 1870. Our main argument is that the choices and evaluations of the agents are only part of the story. Genuine learning also takes place in markets. This subject will be the topic of the next chapter.

[10] This fact seems to be consistent with the new institutionalism in sociology which contends that "[t]he constant repetitive quality of much organized life is explicable . . . by a view that locates the persistence of practices in both their taken-for-granted quality and their reproduction in structures that are to some extent self-sustaining" (DiMaggio and Powell, 1991, p. 9). Besides, it gives the idea of embeddedness of markets in social structure (Granovetter, 1985) a clear theoretical content.

[11] Hodgson (1997, p. 676) gives an evaluation of this mechanization effect: "On the positive side, mechanical habits help us to deal with the complexity and information overload, by removing several aspects of action from conscious deliberation. On the negative side, mechanical habits can remove important actions from the due exercise of deliberation and creative skill. This limitation is likely to be more serious with the more complex activities, and especially in a changing environment. While the very rigidity of habits is necessary to fix learning and fasten skills, such rigidity can often be disabling, particularly when faced with a new and complex problem."

[12] See the comment of Lachmann in Littlechild (1982, p. 101): "TO LEARN means to acquire knowledge. When we say that we have learned a language or calculus or how to drive a car, or call somebody 'a learned man', we mean that such knowledge, once acquired, will last a life-time as a rule. Business knowledge in competitive world (i.e., knowledge of markets) is of course altogether different since IT CANNOT LAST. Such knowledge is, on the contrary, continuously jeopardized by obsolescence. . . ."

11

The Theory of Evolutionary Competition

11.1. EVOLUTIONARY ECONOMICS, GERMAN *WETTBEWERBSTHEORIE,* AND AUSTRIAN MARKET PROCESS THEORY

Up to now, we have dealt with one of the two main deficits of the neoclassical theory, that is, the neglect of institutions, and we have shown how the institutional framework can best be incorporated in the analysis of the market phenomena. In this chapter, we shall try to eliminate the second deficit of the neoclassical economic theory, that is, its unsatisfactory way of dealing with novelty. Thus, we shall defend the idea that market competition is an evolutionary process. The starting point of such a theory of evolutionary competition is the fact of the division of knowledge among market participants that is concomitant with the division of labor in markets.[1] If one takes the issue of subjectivism seriously and acknowledges that economic agents differ not only in their wants but also in their knowledge,[2] then a theory of the market must not only provide an account of how this variety of knowledge is generated and transmitted, but also explain how it grows in competitive exchange settings.

---

[1] Hayek refers to the following citation from Mises when he identifies the problem of the division of knowledge. See Mises (1932, p. 96): "The distribution of the disposal authority over economic goods among many individuals in a social economy characterized by division of labor results in a kind of cognitive division of labor, without which the calculation in production and the process of economizing would not be possible." (Translation by C. M.)

[2] See Lachmann (1943/1977, p. 73): "In a properly dynamic formulation of the economic problem all elements have to be subjective, but there are two layers of subjectivism, rooted in different spheres of the mind, which must not be confused, viz. the subjectivism of want and the subjectivism of interpretation."

Since the time of Hayek's formulation of the central problem of economic theory of "how the spontaneous interaction of a number of people, each possessing only bits of knowledge, brings about a state of affairs in which prices correspond to costs etc." (1937/1948, p. 50f.), only a few systematic attempts have been made to address this issue directly. This is due to the fact that the predominant neoclassical analysis, even today, "instead of showing what bits of information the different persons must posses in order to bring about that result . . . fall[s] in effect back on the assumption that everybody knows everything and so evade[s] any real solution of the problem" (Hayek, 1937/1948, p. 51). The role of the invisible hand in Smith's system of free competition has been transformed in the modern mainstream theory into the notion of market equilibrium under conditions of perfect competition.[3]

The neoclassical reaction to the criticism of perfect information assumed in general equilibrium theory was the development of the so-called Economics of Information. The main idea of the models pioneered by Stigler (1961) is that economic agents characterize future prices with the aid of a probability distribution and continually update this distribution while observing the values of the relevant variables.[4] Search in such models is understood as a normal maximizing activity; an optimum of search is reached when the marginal improvement in the estimate of the price distribution (which translates into the marginal benefit of lower prices) equals the marginal cost of acquiring this information.[5] Besides, although neoclassical models do not directly depend upon it, the notion of Bayesian learning playes a dominant role in many of them. To put it succinctly, the neoclassical approach deals with the knowledge problem in the market by assuming that agents, even when they have imperfect knowledge, possess a perfect theory of learning that helps them to trans-

---

3 On the history of transformation of Smith's "free competition" into the neoclassical notion of perfect competition, see the classical contributions of Stigler (1957) and McNulty (1967). See also the more recent article by Stigler (1987) and the lecture by Vickers (1994). For a thorough history of the theory of (perfect) competition, see Machovec (1995).

4 Seminal search models that belong to this broad family of neoclassical models are Stigum (1969), Rothschild (1973), and Frydman (1982).

5 Even neoclassical writers have acknowledged the obvious problem of any search theory; Arrow's classical formulation seems appropriate here: "[T]here is a fundamental paradox in the determination of demand for information: its value for the purchase is not known until he has the information, but then he has in effect acquired it without cost" (Arrow, 1962/1971, p. 148). Besides, "[s]earch presumes that the agent already knows what to search for and how to search . . ." (Littlechild, 1986, p. 30).

form it into *perfect knowledge.*[6] The neoclassical agent lives in a world of Knightian risk rather than one of genuine uncertainty.[7]

As Boland (1997) stresses, most neoclassical models that assume learning agents employ the "bucket theory of knowledge."[8] This quantity-based view of knowledge implies that agents learn by accumulating observations or experience; the more observations they make, the more knowledge they obtain. This rather crude empiricist theory of knowledge is to be contrasted with the trial-and-error learning of evolutionary epistemology and cognitive psychology. To be sure, some modern game-theoretic approaches have abandoned notions of Bayesian learning or pure observational learning and employ models of adaptive learning instead.[9] Still, some of these models are trying to reconcile learning agents with the achievement of equilibrium in a consistent way, and thus, they typically forfeit realism.

There are three alternative approaches to neoclassical economics that take the issue of knowledge more seriously and treat it in a theoretically more satisfactory way. The first alternative approach is inspired by the work of Schumpeter (1911/1987, 1942/1950) and has been established in the last two decades under the name of Evolutionary Economics. These Neo-Schumpeterian approaches focus on the growth of knowledge rather than on its communication in markets and stress the role of novelty in the economic processes. The employment of biological analogies is common in this literature,[10] and many arguments are built around the fundamental scheme of variation and selection. In a recent overview, Nelson (1995) has stressed that in evolutionary theory "[t]he focus of attention is on a variable or set of them that is changing over time and the theoretical quest is

---

[6] See High (1990, p. 88): "In spirit, search models are models of ignorance and learning; in fact search models are models of near-perfect knowledge, predictable learning, and riskless circumstance."

[7] Littlechild (1986, p. 28): "The crucial feature of the NC [neoclassical theory] approach is that *the form that the future can take is known in advance.* 'Tomorrow' can be characterized as a vector of random variables, where the range the values can take is known today and, more important, so is the set of variables itself. The NC agent lives in a world of Knightian risk. He is unsure what the price of honey will be tomorrow, but he knows that honey will be traded. Conversely, he never finds honey in the shops if he had not previously expected it to be there."

[8] Popper introduced the term "bucket theory of the mind" in order to criticize the empiricist view of the tabula rasa, still prevalent in philosophy. See Popper (1972/1992, ch. 2).

[9] For a good overview of game-theoretical models employing adaptive learning, see Marimon and McGrattan (1995) and the references of formal models found there.

[10] This is not always true. See, e.g., Foster (1998) for arguments against the employment of biological analogies in evolutionary economics.

for an understanding of the dynamic process behind the observed change" (p. 54). The fundamental difference from the neoclassical approach lies in the stress on the endogenous forces that drive the economic process of change, from within rather than as a result of exogenous shocks. Permanent variation is generated in the market or the economic system due to the creativity of the economic agents; respectively, behavioral models that are alternatives to neoclassical optimization techniques are commonly employed in evolutionary economic theory.[11]

The German *Wettbewerbstheorie* (theory of competition) is the second alternative to the neoclassical theory of market competition. Since the 1950s, a theory of dynamic competition has been developed in Germany as a conscious attempt to provide an alternative to the theory of perfect competition. Inspired by Schumpeter, a group of German economists have consistently worked out a theory of market competition stressing process and dynamics rather than equilibrium and statics.[12] Since much of the discussion has been induced by the practical needs of antitrust policy, the German theory of competition has retained its contact with empirical reality. The central tenets of this approach are the endogenous change of market structure in the competitve process, the role of innovations and imitations that keep competition alive, and the entrepreneurial element, as well as the direct link of dynamic competition with economic growth. It is characteristic that as early as 1965, Heuss developed a General Theory of the Market (*Allgemeine Markttheorie*) that contains all the important

11 The seminal contribution on neo-Schumpeterian Economics is Nelson and Winter (1982). Overviews on evolutionary economics are Saviotti and Metcalfe (1991b), Langlois and Everett (1994), Dosi and Nelson (1994), and Nelson (1995). See also the papers in the volumes of Dosi, Freeman, Nelson, Silverberg, and Soete (1988), Dopfer and Raible (1990), Saviotti and Metcalfe (1991a), Witt (1992b, 1993b), Magnusson (1994), Andersen (1994), England (1994), Khalil and Boulding (1996), Nielsen and Johnson (1998), and Eliasson, Green and McCann (1998). In the German literature, see the collected papers in Witt (1990, 1992) and Wagner and Lorenz (1995).

12 J. M. Clark was one of the first critics of the neoclassical theory of perfect competition (1940, 1954, 1955). Clark's notion of active competition as a rivalry consisting "of a combination of (1) imitiatory actions by a business unit, and (2) a complex of responses by those with whom it deals, and by rivals" (1954, p. 326) was to our knowledge the first attempt to offer an alternative view to the predominant theory of perfect competition in the English-speaking world. But this attempt had a fragmentary character – since it had been developed mainly to be used for antitrust policy – until 1961, when Clark's work *Competition as a Dynamic Process* appeared. In Germany, as early as 1952, Helmut Arndt presented a complete theory of dynamic competition, distinguishing between the competitive phase of the innovations and the competitive phase of the imitators that yield the never-ending creative process of competition.

ingredients of temporary evolutionary economics: Schumpeterian entrepreneurs, historical time, variety, market phases, learning hypotheses, and so on, along with formal modeling. Heuss's theory was followed by a number of other contributions up to the 1990s in the German-speaking world.[13]

The third alternative approach was developed by modern Austrian Economics. The market process theory developed by Kirzner (1973, 1979, 1992) stresses the role of the entrepreneur in coordinating the individual plans in the market. It emphasizes the dynamic character of market activities that systematically lead to an equilibrium. The stress is more on the market process than on end states, and the analysis is not merely concerned with prices and quantities, but also with individual plans and their coordination in general. Another group of economists, also associated with the Austrian approach, deal in a more radical way with the lack of knowledge of economic agents. This "radical subjectivist approach" emphasizes the role of imagination and creativity in human action rather than the discovery of given (profit) opportunities. For Lachmann, the market is "a particular kind of process, a continuous process without beginning or end, propelled by the interaction between the forces of equilibrium and the forces of change" (1976a, p. 61). In the world of radical uncertainty, the "kaleidic" world of economics that Shackle discusses, a tight concept of market equilibrium is useless; all that is possible to imagine is what he calls a "kaleidic equilibrium" that "is an adjustment to each other of those matters (variables) which are under the control of businessmen, but above all, an adjustment of them to beliefs and expectations (not by any means likely to be mutually consistent amongst different people) about matters not under the individual or collective control of the businessmen" (1972/1992, p. 438).[14]

[13] See Arndt (1949, 1952, 1981, 1986), Heuss (1965, 1967, 1968, 1980, 1983), Hoppmann (1966, 1967, 1977, 1988), Kantzenbach (1967), Görgens (1969), Krüsselberg (1969, 1983), Oberender (1973), Oberender and Väth (1989), Willeke (1973, 1980), Lenel (1975, 1988), Röpke (1977, 1980, 1987, 1990a, 1990b), Schmidtchen (1976/1977, 1978, 1979, 1983, 1988, 1989, 1990), Fehl (1980, 1983, 1985, 1986, 1987), Kaufer (1980), Bartling (1980), Tolksdorf (1980, 1994), Neumann (1982), Zohlnhöfer (1982, 1991, 1996), Brandt (1984), Eickhof (1984, 1990, 1992), Kunz (1985), Borchert and Grossekettler (1985), Grossekettler (1989a), Windsperger (1986), Streit and Wegner (1989, 1992), Wegner (1992), Berg (1989, 1992), Bosch (1990), Kerber (1991, 1992, 1994, 1996, 1997). Aberle (1992), Mantzavinos (1992, 1994a, 1994b, 1996b), Wieandt (1994), Schreiter (1994), Schmidt (1996), and Knieps (1997). See also the collected papers in Cox, Jens and Markert (1981) and in Delhaes and Fehl (1997).

[14] On Austrian economics and market process theory see O'Driscoll and Rizzo (1996),

Building on these alternative approaches, we shall develop in this chapter a theory of competition that stresses the generation, transmission, and growth of knowledge in the market. The focus is on the endogenous change of knowledge that makes the market competition a genuine evolutionary process.

11.2. THE SUPPLY SIDE: THE PROBLEM-SOLVING ENTREPRENEURS

The standard market theory presented in microeconomics textbooks starts with the Marshallian distinction between demand and supply and proceeds to the determination of prices and quantities in different market forms. It should be clear from the previous analysis that the organization of production by entrepreneurs (supply side) and the organization of consumption (demand side) may exhibit great variety according to the institutional framework within which they take place. This variety cannot be satisfactorily treated by using the static toolbox of neoclassical economics, and the variety of the economic world cannot be captured by pointing only to some typical market forms such as a "perfect market," "oligopoly," or "monopoly" and to distinct action parameters such as prices, quantities, or advertising. Moreover full-fledged economic subjects participating in real-world markets face the constraints of law and informal social rules when they employ their action parameters. Thus, the exact kind of demand and supply are crucially dependent on the institutional framework. Entrepreneurs, while organizing production, building the structure of their firm, and marketing their products, are using many action parameters that an adequate market theory must account of.

In order to proceed in a systematic way, the activity of entrepreneurs on the supply side of the market will be analyzed first. Provided that institutions allow productive activities to be undertaken freely, the economic agents that organize production and sell their products in the market are the *entrepreneurs*. Since we have modeled all human activity as problem-

High (1990), and the contributions in Dolan (1976), Spadaro (1978), Rizzo (1979), Kirzner (1986), Caldwell and Boehm (1993), and Boettke and Prychitko (1994). The radical subjectivist approach is mostly clear in the work of Lachmann (1976a, 1976b, 1986, 1994), Shackle (1972/1992, 1979, 1983, 1990), Wiseman (1983b, 1990) and Buchanan and Vanberg (1991). See also the contributions in Wiseman (1983a) and Frowen (1990). Recent surveys of Austrian economics are Foss (1994) and Vaughn (1994). Collected papers on Austrian market process theory are contained in Littlechild (1990). In the German literature, Loy (1988) deals extensively with the notion of a tendency to equilibrium in the Austrian market process theory.

solving activity, entrepreneurs are best conceptualized as problem solvers. Their fundamental problem is the attainment of profits.[15]

As Kerber (1997, p. 52) stresses, the diversity and large number of available action parameters (he assumes them to be hundreds or even thousands) is therefore important because the extent of the knowledge problem that entrepreneurs face becomes clear. The production function of the standard theory summarizes the employment of action parameters and of many entrepreneurial decisions in an unacceptable way because it shifts attention away from the conjectural character of the whole production process (Blaug, 1997, p. 81). The supply of products is best understood as the testing of certain types of hypotheses: how effective is the bundle of parameters such as price, quality, service, and so on in solving the problem of consumers, that is, in satisfying their wants?[16]

---

[15] Strictly speaking, this is not correct. The main problem of entrepreneurs is to attain *economic rents* as well as *economic profits*. Depending on the institutional framework, entrepreneurs will either attain economic profits by trying to solve the problems of the consumers or invest resources in lobbying politicians, bureaucrats, and so on in order to attain economic rents in the form of subsidies, tax avoidance, and so on. The case of entrepreneurs engaging only in producing goods to satisfy consumers is, therefore, a special one. It depends on a *specific set of institutions* that prohibits what is known in the literature as "rent-seeking." To simplify the issue, we assume here that such rent-seeking activities are forbidden by the institutions and proceed in the analysis of the case that entrepreneurial activity is directed only toward satisfying the wants of the consumers. The rent-seeking literature possesses a normative flavor since economic rents are usually associated with welfare losses. From a more positive point of view, it is useful to define economic rents as the sum of net revenues that entrepreneurs earn without solving the problems of consumers; economic profits would then be the sum of net revenues (i.e., revenues minus costs) that entrepreneurs would earn by solving problems of consumers.

On rent-seeking, see the loci classici Tullock (1967), Krueger (1974), and the contributions in Buchanan, Tollison, and Tullock (1980), Rowley, Tollison, and Tullock (1988) and Congleton (1996). For a more subjectivistic approach to rent-seeking that tries to avoid value judgments, see Ricketts (1987), DiLorenzo (1988), and Brooks, Heijdra, and Lowenberg (1990).

[16] See Harper (1994 and 1996, ch. 5). Though Harper also stresses the conjectural character of entrepreneurial activities, he nevertheless employs learning theories borrowed from methodology. In his model "[l]earning is a *logical and scientific process,* rather than an internal psychological or sociopsychological process. There is no difference of kind between the methods of science and the methods of hypothesis-selection in everyday life. Like scientists, economic agents use deductive logic in the evaluation of their hypotheses" (1996, p. 21). It is surely correct that every learning enterprise, whether in science or in society, involves the trial of hypotheses and their evaluation in the light of environmental feedback. But there is also a fundamental difference; in science the stress is on *validity* and *truth,* whereas in social life knowledge does not need to be objectively, i.e., intersubjectively valid or true; it suffices that everyday knowledge is good enough to solve the problems of

The conjectural character of entrepreneurial activity is sometimes allowed for, even in the standard microeconomic theory, though. The price-revenue function of a supplier (mainly discussed in the theory of monopoly and oligopoly but also in the theory of perfect competition; Ott, 1986, pp. 158ff) shows the *conjectural* quantities that the producer estimates that he will sell when setting different prices. One also speaks of the "conjectural demand curve" (Hoppmann, 1976, p. 298) that the producer constructs with the aid of his imagination (Machlup, 1952, p. 34) and uses to make economic decisions in the production process.[17] In the model presented here, the entrepreneur makes conjectures not only about the quantities to be sold at different prices, but also about the sum of the parameters that he employs to solve the problems of the consumers or of a certain consumer group. In a sense, the difference from the standard neoclassical theory consists in the broadening of the perspective, which seems natural once the complexity of the whole process is admitted.

To attain profits, entrepreneurs must offer consumers products whose production costs are less than the revenues earned from their sale. The crucial fact about entrepreneurial activity, though, is that consumers' wants are not known with certainty; because of the variety of consumers' wants and their temporary character, the entrepreneur is faced with a constant flow of problem situations that are perceived subjectively as new ones. The conditions of demand cannot be known with certainty; they are an ever-changing variable for the entrepreneurs. Since entrepreneurs are bound to satisfy this demand, they are constantly facing new problems requiring their conscious attention and constant choices. *Entrepreneurs participating in the exchange process with the aim of making profits face a constant flow of new problems deriving ultimately from the volatility and peculiarity of consumers' wants.*

For this reason, every time a product is offered in the market, an entrepreneur is trying to solve what appears to him to be a new problem. Therefore, the supply of a certain product is at the same time equivalent to the trial of a new hypothesis on the part of the entrepreneur. The supply of a certain product always incorporates a conjecture on whether the bundle

---

practical life. Therefore, for the explanatory purposes of economics and social science in general, one has to draw from the theoretical reservoir of *psychology rather than that of philosophy of science.*

[17] See, e.g., Machlup (1952, p. 34): "It should hardly be necessary to mention that all the relevant magnitudes involved – cost, revenue, profit – are subjective, that is, perceived or fancied by the men whose decisions or actions are to be explained (i.e., the businessmen) rather than 'objective', that is, calculated by desinterested men who are observing these actions from the outside and are explaining them."

of characteristics that the specific product consists of, will satisfy the cosumers in terms that are profitable to the entrepreneur.

It is important to stress what it is meant when we say that an entrepreneur offers a product in the market. He normally has to borrow capital from banks or the capital market, identify the price and quality of resources, set the organizational structure of the firm, supervise the process of transforming the resources into marketable goods, control the quality of the product, advertise the product, set up a distribution network, consider consulting possibilities and service to be offered to the customers, set up the retail price, including the possibility of discounts, and so on. By the time a product is offered to a group of consumers, a large range of action parameters by the entrepreneur has already been employed. *Every time the entrepreneur offers a product in the market, therefore, he tests a hypothesis about the effectiveness of the sum of the action parameters in satisfying consumers' wants and, consequently, in assuring profits.*[18]

Entrepreneurs pursue their profit-seeking activities under the competitive pressure of other entrepreneurs.[19] In markets, diverse entrepreneurs with diverse skills and problem-solving capacities are struggling for profits. Competition is the process that arises from the rivalry of problem-solving entrepreneurs who are trying to test their hypotheses in the market environment in profitable ways. The competitive process is driven by innovation and imitation. "Innovation" can be defined as the parameter mix that has never been tried out by any entrepreneur in the past in the same market environment and is successful in providing profits. It is important to stress two aspects of innovation. First, *innovation is a social phenomenon:* It is not enough that an entrepreneur subjectively perceives a new problem and offers a solution that only he perceives as a new one. On the contrary, innovation is the successful hypothesis of the effectiveness of a certain parameter mix in solving a genuinely new problem faced

[18] See Loasby (1991, p. 75f.): "This is the essence of the marketing point of view. The customers of a chemical company do not buy chemicals, or even chemical effects; they buy solutions to problems. What the chemical company needs to know, therefore, is a set of answers to the following questions. What are the customer's problems? How much is a solution worth – or in contemporary jargon, what is its added value? Which of these problems can be solved by using the distinctive skills and resources which are available to the company? What alternative solutions might be available or in prospect through the use of other distinctive skills and resources – which might embody totally unrelated technologies – available in other organisations, and how effective and expensive are they likely to be? What, in a phrase, is the company's productive opportunity?"

[19] On the difference between profit-seeking (or profit-motivated striving) and profit maximization, see Nelson and Winter (1982, p. 30f).

by a consumer or a consumer group. A parameter mix qualifies as an innovation only relative to the opinions and evaluations of the consumers. Therefore, it always possesses a social dimension. Second, the possibility to innovate is inherent in every single entrepreneurial act. Since entrepreneurs are bound to act under uncertainty and since they constantly produce conjectures in the market, innovations occur any time. They are not restricted to some heroic moments originally analyzed by Schumpeter.

Innovations imply that taking the lead in the competitive process is based mainly on better knowledge. In order to survive, the other entrepreneurs are bound to imitate the successful trial of the leader; "imitation" is the learning from the innovative entrepreneur of the innovative parameter mix and subsequent copying activity. Imitation is, thus, the successful copying of the innovative hypothesis, that is, the successful response to the lead of the innovators. Since imitation is the dissemination of knowledge on the supply side of the market, a communication process is constitutive for its existence. In comparison to innovation, the imitation process thus possesses an additional social dimension. Not only the selection of the imitatory hypotheses by the consumers is necessary, but also an interpersonal communication between innovator and imitators (Witt, 1993c, p. 218).

Before proceeding to a more detailed analysis of competition as an evolutionary process of innovation and imitation on the supply side of the market, we turn to the demand side. What constitutes consumer activity, and what is its relationship to the entrepreneurial testing of hypotheses?

11.3. THE DEMAND SIDE: THE SELECTING CONSUMERS

We have seen in Section 9.3 that institutions serve as the primary selection environment of evolutionary market processes. They channel the market process in selecting at a first level the action parameters that entrepreneurs are allowed to employ. After this first selection has taken place, the entrepreneurs organize production and try out the parameter mix in the market among the pool allowed by the institutional framework. Provided that entrepreneurs act within these constraints, they are free to combine the different parameters in ways that only their own imagination limits. Therefore, we have modeled the supply side of the market as the origin of a constant flow of entrepreneurial hypotheses.

These hypotheses then undergo the ultimate test of the consumers. The economic power of consumers and their consumptive decisions are the final selection criteria of entrepreneurial hypotheses.[20] The consumer choices are, thus, the secondary selection environment of the evolutionary market process in the sense that it is consumers who determine which entrepreneurial hypotheses will survive. This second level of selection is the final one not because the process ends, but rather because consumer choices ultimately decide the success or failure of entrepreneurial conjenctures (Harper, 1996, p. 286). The decision to buy product A instead of product B is the final environmental feedback to the entrepreneurs on which product has succeeded in satisfying consumers' wants (Kerber, 1997, p. 53). It signals to the entrepreneurs that hypothesis A solves the problem of the consumer in a more satisfactory way than hypothesis B.[21]

But how is consumer activity best explained? Until now, we have diligently avoided introducing preferences into the discussion. The basic advantage of the problem-solving model is this: There is no need to argue in terms of preferences. This is also very important in the case of the consumer. The problem-solving consumer faces as a primary problem the production of his own consumption. Nevertheless, he does not produce his utility along a well-defined household production function, as is assumed in the neoclassical consumer theory (Lancaster, 1971; Becker, 1976; Stigler and Becker, 1977). As in the case of production, neoclassical theory assumes perfect knowledge also in the case of consumers. As Langlois and Cosgel (1998, p. 108) stress, neoclassical theory "require[s] the consumer to be endowed with all the knowledge, experience, and skills that the production of utility necessitates."[22] The problem-solving model offers an alternative that allows a more realistic view of consumer activity.

When discussing the problem-solving framework in Part I of our study, we pointed out that increasing one's own utility is the ultimate human problem. In the market setting, the basic problem that economic agents face is transformed into the increase of their utility by the consumption of goods. This, in turn, generates the next problem, that is, the consumption of *which* goods and *under what circumstances* will increase their utility. Since utility has a direct link with the motivational system of the agent, the door of subjectivism has been opened. It is only the agent himself who can

---

[20] See Harper (1996, p. 285): "Although *individual* consumers are price-takers who do not participate in the production process, entrepreneurs are ultimately subject to the aggregated economic power of consumers to refute their theories."

[21] See Albert (1987, p. 69): "The power of the consumer . . . does not consist of giving orders for the solutions of problems in the sphere of production, but in testing the solutions adopted by the entrepreneurs and in influencing the future activities in the sphere of production indirectly by accepting or refuting these solutions."

[22] For a similar critique see Loasby (1998, p. 98f.).

provide the link between goods purchased in the market and the production of his own utility. This link is of a peculiar character: the cognitive system of the agent must explore what his wants are as they are prescribed by the motivational system and how these wants can be satisfied with the aid of goods obtained in the market. The crucial factor is that the cognitive system provides a link between wants and their satisfaction via goods (Witt, 1998).[23]

The motivational system of the agent is constantly generating new wants.[24] The crucial characteristics of wants are their volatility and their change over time.[25] The peculiar situation of the consumer is that he has to provide a link between goods available in the market and ever-changing wants. Conventional consumer theory since the marginalist revolution of the 1870s has analyzed this situation as a case of *choosing* among alternative goods available in the market in order to satisfy the consumer's wants. The neoclassical extension of consumer theory that views consumption as production of utility retained the basic assumption of a maximizing

[23] See O'Driscoll and Rizzo (1996, p. 45): "Because individuals choose among directly observable goods or observable courses of action that produce these goods, there must be some link between the projected want satisfaction and these observables. This link is the individual's knowledge of a commodity's want-satisfying potential, i.e. the perceived production function."

[24] The term "wants" is used here since it is familiar to economists. In psychology, the phenomenon of motivation is discussed in terms of *needs*, biological and social, that give rise to human behavior. In order to retain the familiar terms for the economists, we shall refer to wants throughout this chapter. (This terminology has been established in microeconomic theory since the publication of Marshall's principles. Menger has used the term *Bedürfnis*, and German textbooks use the term *Bedürfnisbefriedigung*, i.e. need satisfaction. See, for example, the definition of Menger in the translation of Dingwall and Hoselitz (1871/1994, p. 52): "If a thing is to become a good, or in other words, it is to acquire goods-character, all four of the following prerequisites must be simultaneously present:

1. A human need.
2. Such properties as render the thing capable of being brought into a causal connection with the satisfaction of this need.
3. Human knowledge of this causal connection.
4. Command of the thing sufficient to direct it to the satisfaction of the need."

[25] See, e.g., Marshall (1920, p. 73): "Human wants and desires are countless in number and very various in kind: but they are generally limited and capable of being satisfied. The uncivilized man indeed has not many more than the brute animal; . . . As, however, man rises in civilization, as his mind becomes developed, and even his animal passions begin to associate themselves with mental activities, his wants become rapidly more subtle and more various; and in the minor details of life he begins to desire change for the sake of change, long before he has consciously escaped from the yoke of custom."

choice at the margin. The problem-solving framework allows for an alternative view, however.

It is certainly true that human wants are volatile and change over time. This is why the problems faced by consumers are typically new problems. In other words, due to the constant flow of wants, consumers have to provide *new* links between goods and wants. Therefore, they have to deal with new problems. Moreover, the variety of goods offered in the market by entrepreneurs under diverse marketing conditions enhances the novelty of the problems that consumers have to face. More often than not, consumers are therefore bound to *choose consciously* in order to solve what they subjectively perceive to be their new problems. The orthodox economic theory is therefore correct in stressing choice in market settings, since the constant flow of new consumer wants makes consumer choices indispensable. (Since these choices also function as the final selection criterion for entrepreneurial hypotheses, they, in turn, also stimulate entrepreneurs to be conscious and choose continually; thus, the whole market process is characterized by agents who are constantly choosing.)

Although correct, this view is incomplete, however. Consumers, like all human agents, are capable of learning. This fact complicates the issue. Every time a consumer buys a product and tries to satisfy a want, he is formulating a hypothesis about the effectiveness of the given product in producing utility. Since all human knowledge is hypothetical, the knowledge of the consumer concerning the want-satisfying potential of the products offered in the market is equally hypothetical. The same mechanism discussed in Part I of this study is applicable in the subcase of consumer activity. The consumer might interpret his "consuming situation" as a new problem situation typically in three cases: (a) in identifying the generation of a new want by his motivational system; (b) in perceiving the bundle of characteristics currently offered in the market as a new way to satisfy a certain want; and (c) when (a) and (b) occur simultaneously. When confronted with a novel consuming situation,[26] the consumer with the aid of his or her imagination, creates new cognitive rules of the familiar IF . . . THEN type designating alternative solutions to the new consumer problem. The consumer then chooses the bundle of characteristics incorporated in the product that is expected to solve his problem in the most satisfactory way. Evaluation of the alternatives by the consumer is among the imagined want satisfactions by the different product charac-

---

[26] For simplicity, we omit here the employment of inferential strategies or analogies as the first attempt of the consumer to solve a novel problem.

teristics. Remember from the discussion in Chapter 4 the role imagination plays in creative choices and consequently in consumer choices. "[C]hoices can be made only between images or projections of the outcomes of various cources of action" (O'Driscoll and Rizzo, 1996, p. 45).[27]

When the consumer chooses and buys the product, the consumer tests the hypothesis of how the properties of an external object may satisfy his wants and thus solve his consumer problem. If the consumer finds out that the product has not solved his new problem, he will *learn* that this problem solution is not the appropriate one and will buy a different product in the next period. If the product has solved the new problem, then the consumer will repeat the purchase of the product in the next period and after some time a new class will be created in his mind of the type "IF I buy the product X, THEN my want Y will be satisfied." In other words, the consumer will *have learned* how to solve the problem and will build after some time, the respective classes in his mind that designate product characteristics (e.g., quality, service, price etc.) to degrees of want satisfaction. This, in turn, means that, over time, consumers will create their own learning history concerning the production of their utility.

This fact is of great importance because it offers a genuinely subjective view of consumption. The very technology of consumption that is assumed in neoclassical theory to be constant is in fact the crucial characteristic that varies among consumers. For consumption to take place, the agent must *know* how product characteristics can be transformed into utility. This knowledge is both hypothetical and different among the agents. Every consumer has a different learning history and, therefore, possesses a different consumption technology in the form of different "IF . . . THEN" classes stored in his mind.

This view of the active, learning consumer has been recently stressed by the so-called capabilities approach (Loasby, 1999, ch. 4, 2000). Langlois and Cosgel (1998) draw an analogy between the capabilities (Richardson, 1972) or routines (Nelson and Winter, 1982) that are the building blocks of any productive knowledge and the capabilities, skills, or routines necessary for consumption. "Capabilities in consumption consist of various routines that help in solving problems. . . . The consumer acquires routines in order to utilize goods in the production of ultimate utility. We thus see consumption as a matter of learning about, choosing among, and creating routines" (Langlois and Cosgel, 1998, p. 110). This capabilities

---

[27] See also the discussion of subjective choice in Buchanan (1969).

view is consistent with our view of problem-solving consumers possessing different knowledge acquired slowly and expensively through a historical process of trial-and-error learning. The stress in the capabilities approach is the same as in the problem-solving approach; the production of consumer utility requires knowledge.

Obviously, however, consumption is also a social activity in the sense that there is communication of knowledge between consumers. A process of evolutionary competition is taking place not only on the supply side, but on the demand side of the market, too. Remember our discussion on how the agent typically solves a new problem; one of the alternatives that he or she always possesses is to utilize ready-made solutions from the environment (Section 5.2.). The agent (in our case the consumer) might learn directly from the environment instead of creating new alternatives ex nihilo each time a new problem arises. "The consumer has the option either of learning about and choosing among already existing routines or of creating new ones" (Langlois and Cosgel, 1998, p. 111).[28] From this possibility of learning to solve one's consumer problems by using solutions available in the environment, together with the ever-existent striving for utility increase, competition among consumers originates.

In the same way that competition on the supply side can best be explained as a continuous process of innovation and imitation, competition on the demand side is also best conceptualized as a process of innovative moves and imitative responses (Hoppmann, 1967, p. 90; Neumann, 1983, p. 51). Innovation in consumption can be defined as the solution to a consumer problem that was never tried out by any consumer in the past in the same market environment and that is successful in increasing his utility. Imitation is the successful copying of the innovative solution to the consumer problem, the successful response to the lead of the consumer-innovator. What keeps competition on the demand side alive is the learning potential of the consumers. Once an innovator has successfully solved a consumer problem and has developed a consumption technology, he communicates this knowledge to other consumers. The fact that the production of utility needs a respective stock of knowledge implies that con-

[28] Continuing from the text cited earlier, Langlois and Cosgel (1998, p. 11) state: "Some existing routines might be external to the consumer and available through markets. To meet clothing needs, for example, the consumer might simply hire a consultant who would then utilize his or her own existing routines to make decisions for the consumer. Alternatively, the consumer might acquire some of these routines through experience and exposure to social and cultural institutions. For example, the consumer might follow the current fashion or utilize institutionalized routines such as the meanings that colors generate about age and gender in a society."

sumers are willing to acquire this knowledge from innovators; thus, a diffusion process arises.

It is important to stress that the competitive process among consumers goes hand in hand with the evaluation of the diverse alternatives offered by the entrepreneurs in the market. According to their learning history and their momentary perception of their problems, consumers purchase products in the market at a certain price and signal at the same time whether or not the entrepreneurial hypotheses helped to solve their problems. These selecting acts are, in turn, the main environmental feedback for the entrepreneurs. They constitute the main means of communication between the two sides of the market, to which we turn next.

11.4. EXCHANGE AND COMMUNICATION BETWEEN SUPPLY AND DEMAND

We have outlined how competitive processes of innovation and imitation take place on both sides of the market. Obviously, understanding competition as an endogenous evolutionary process implies that a communication process is concomitant to the innovations and imitations occurring on either the supply or the demand side of the market. The communication between consumers, as well as the communication between entrepreneurs, are not independent of each other, though. Indeed, the uniqueness of markets lies in the fact that during the exchange process, a transmission of knowledge takes place, which, in turn, affects the competitive processes on both the supply and demand sides of the market. How exactly this happens is the issue that we shall address next.

In order for the selecting acts of the consumers to occur in the market, a communication structure between consumers and entrepreneurs is a prerequisite. Of the great variety of bundles of characteristics available at different prices in the market, a consumer perceives only a few. Of the large number of consumer problems in existence at any moment in time, the solution of only a few of them is targeted by the entrepreneurs. When an exchange act between a consumer and an entrepreneur takes place, the consumer selects a certain bundle of characteristics at a certain price from the background of his or her knowledge of the range of offers available in the market. The evaluation then undertaken is always among the alternatives *known to the consumer.* This is a crucial fact because it means that the available knowledge or consumption technology is always limited compared to a nonexistent standard of perfect knowledge. Though this must seem to be a natural phenomenon to anybody employing his com-

mon sense, neoclassical economics has traditionally assumed that consumers (and entrepreneurs) avail themselves, in one way or another, all of
the "relevant knowledge," that is, the knowledge of all market data in
order to make an informed choice. (In the weaker form of the hypothesis,
the agents avail themselves of an equally "relevant learning technology"
so that they can proceed after a search to a somehow perfect choice.)

What happens in the real world is that consumers form, according to
their learning histories, mental models of the characteristics of the products and the prices at which they are offered. Entrepreneurs, at the same
time, form mental models of the consumers and their problems when they
offer their products in the market. When exchange takes place, *shared
mental models* between the supply and demand sides of the market are
formed. In other words, during exchange, a communication process occurs that gives rise to shared mental models and, thus, to a shared cognitive structure. Entrepreneurs and consumers do not automatically share
"common knowledge" (Langlois and Cosgel, 1998, p. 112), nor is there a
fictitious auctioneer who cares that both sides of the market become
aware of each other. Moreover, the very rise of the common structure of
communication is the prerequisite of any exchange act. Since entrepreneurs do not always provide correct hypotheses concerning the consumers' problems, and since consumers cannot possibly know all available alternatives in the market, exchange acts are always "imperfect." The
intersubjective element in exchange consists exactly in the formation of a
shared communicative structure between consumers and entrepreneurs.
The notion of shared mental models best describes this *intersubjective
moment in exchange,* which must be strictly distinguished from any artificially imposed "objectivity of data" or the like.

To prevent a possible misunderstanding, it is important to stress that
the shared mental models arising in the exchange process are different
from the shared mental models or cognitive classes that constitute the
internal forms of social institutions, although they are of the same cognitive material. The distinguishing feature of the internalized social rules is
that they are shared by *all* market participants. The mental models that
become shared in the exchange process are, conversely, more temporary in
character; and, most important, they are shared only between *some* consumers and *some* entrepreneurs.

Once the shared mental models have been formed, the entrepreneurial
hypotheses are evaluated by the consumers according to the degree that
they solve their problems. The selecting acts of the consumers lead to two
interrelated phenomena. First, the prices of the diverse entrepreneurial

hypotheses are formed. The crucial fact is that the consumer choice does not only determine the subjective value of a certain product; instead *the consumer evaluates the entire bundle of action parameters that different entrepreneurs have employed.* Prices do not reflect scarcity of resources, but rather a more intricate, differential evaluation of entrepreneurial hypotheses. The structure of prices that is produced as the outcome of market exchange does not designate the relative scarcity of resources as they are subjectively valued by the market agents; instead, the structure of prices reflects the relative degree of want satisfaction that the different entrepreneurial hypotheses offer to the consumers. This, in turn, is important for the question of whether prices transmit knowledge that is sufficient for reaching a market equilibrium of the neoclassical type. We shall explore this issue in more detail when we discuss the results of the market process (Section 11.5.).

The selection of entrepreneurial hypotheses and the concomitant emergence of prices translates – and this is the second phenomenon – into profits or losses for the respective entrepreneurs. Economic profits and losses are the environmental feedback that entrepreneurs receive from the market. The Scitovscian concept of pecuniary external effects can be used here to characterize more accurately the nature of this feedback to the entrepreneurs.[29] Profits and losses synthesize a multitude of demand and supply conditions,[30] and they are unique in exhibiting a double dimension: a cognitive and a motivational one. On the one hand, they provide the basis for active interpretation or decoding of consumers' messages by the entrepreneurs. On the other hand, they contribute to the augmentation or devaluation of the capital employed by the entrepreneurs. There-

---

[29] Streit and Wegner (1992), who also use the Scitovscian concept of pecuniary external effects, enumerate its analytical virtues as follows: "The concept does not require the advance definition of who is competing with whom. It does not exclude the possibility that a discovery may lead to new markets. And it allows changes in market values of property rights or in components of such rights to be considered as information conveyed in a coded form, in the Hayekian sense . . . and not as a Marshallian message concerning substitution necessities" (p. 143).

[30] See Mises (1963, p. 293): "The ultimate source from which entrepreneurial profit and loss are derived is the uncertainty of the future constellation of demand and supply." Mises stresses the fact that profit and loss "does not tell us anything about the individual's increase or decrease in satisfaction or happiness. It merely reflects his fellow men's evaluations of his contribution to social cooperation. This evaluation is ultimately determined by the efforts of every member of society to attain the highest possible psychic profit. It is the resultant of the composite effect of all these people's subjective and personal value judgments as manifested in their conduct on the market. But it must not be confused with these value judgments as such" (ibid., p. 289f.).

fore, they provide the incentives or disincentives to produce further hypotheses.[31] The generation of profits and losses thus constitutes the knowledge-transmitting and sanctionary processes immanent in the market process (Kerber, 1994, p. 258). We will discuss the cognitive and motivational dimensions first of profits and then of entrepreneurial losses and what they mean for the agents themselves. Their function for the market process as a social phenomenon will be explained in Section 11.5.

We will start with the positive pecuniary external effects. The entrepreneur who realizes a profit is rewarded for the employment of a certain parameter mix in solving a consumer problem. The motivational effect of the profits is quite straightforward. By creating additional economic value for the entrepreneur and thus by augmenting his capital stock, profits enhance his entrepreneurial activities in the future. The realization of profits extends his command over economic resources in comparison to other entrepreneurs and thereby motivates him to continue to solve consumer problems in the future.

Profit is also a means of transmitting knowledge from the demand side to the supply side of the market. But profits do not contain any objectively perceptible market signals. In fact, they do not inform anybody of anything, as is tacitly assumed in neoclassical models. They constitute only objects or entities requiring interpretation.[32] Expressed in terms of the problem-solving framework, the realization of profits is equivalent to a new problem for the entrepreneur. He has to find out what the profits are due to, that is, what caused them to happen. This is not an easy task because, as we have repeatedly stressed, the entrepreneur has employed a multitude of action parameters and the corroboration of his entrepreneurial hypothesis is not directly attributable to one or more of them.[33]

---

31 See Mises (1980, p. 149), Rothbard (1970, p. 468f.), and Harper (1996, pp. 287–90).

32 See Wegner (1992, p. 51f.): "From a subjective standpoint, it is necessary to explicate what it means that 'market signals provide information'. It is important not to loose sight of the contained abbreviations. Market signals do not provide information about anything. Instead they provide the entities for the information-activities of the subjects. . . . What is decisive here for the informative function of pecuniary external effects is that they emerge as quasi non-compensatory achievements of the market, without the recipient discovering something about their root causes. A cause-effect relationship is not objectively accessible. The informative achievement of the pecuniary external effects is, from this perspective, minimal." (Translation by C. M.)

33 See, e.g., Loasby (1991, p. 78): "[W]hen organisations are generating and offering collections of characteristics, or what is sometimes called 'a total marketing package'. Without some helpful voices, as well as exit, it may not be easy for a firm to

In standard theory, the entrepreneurial loss is treated as the symmetrical case to the entrepreneurial profit. In light of the experimental evidence that "losses loom larger than gains, both as they are anticipated in the context of decision and as they are ultimately experienced" (Kahneman and Varey, 1991, p. 148), this symmetry cannot be retained, however. This phenomenon, called "loss aversion" (Kahneman and Tversky, 1984), is a robust experimental result (Lindenberg, 1993, p. 17), and it seems to be "a biological rule of obvious adaptive value, which is manifest in the priority accorded to signals of pain and danger in neural processing" (Kahneman and Varey, 1991, p. 148). The fact that people seem to experience losses more intensely than gains, in utility terms, acquires obvious importance for our setting when it is considered in relation to the so-called endowment effect (Kahneman, Knetsch, and Thaler, 1991). People tend to place more value on goods once they have acquired them. Once a good has become part of the endowment of a person, he values it more than before the acquisition. This effect of ownership on value, called by Thaler (1980) the "endowment effect," has profound implications for the motivational dimension of entrepreneurial losses.

When the result of consumer selection translates into monetary loss to an entrepreneur, a depreciation of his capital takes place. The endowment effect is fully at work then. The entrepreneur is bound to experience this diminution of capital value in a more dramatic way than the corresponding increase in capital in the case of a profit of equal monetary value. This, in turn, means that the sanctional potential of a falsification of an entrepreneurial hypothesis is greater than the rewarding potential of a respective corroboration. In practical terms, this means that in case of a loss, the entrepreneur is induced to react quickly and to mobilize all his energy in order to revise his offer successfully in the next period.

The loss that functions as a monetary sanction ensures that the entrepreneur will experience the situation as a new problem requiring a solution. As every time that an agent is confronted with a new problem, the entrepreneur is bound to act consciously. "[T]he agent who realizes a loss in the market value of one of his or her property rights usually does not know anything about what caused this negative pecuniary effect. Equally, he or she is not told how to adjust to the new situation. In a system that is based on the division of knowledge, this kind of information cannot automatically be communicated. It must be discovered." (Streit and

interpret the messages which it receives from the economy in response to such complex conjectures." See also Kerber (1996, p. 25).

Wegner, 1992, p. 143). An entrepreneur who suffers losses is facing a difficult problem; he has to decode the information contained in the negative pecuniary effect. He has to interpret the failure of his entrepreneurial hypothesis and attribute it to one or more specific action parameters that he has employed. In this task (and according to the method of solving new problems discussed in Chapters 4 and 5) he can either rely on his own creativity or directly imitate successful innovators. In the first case, he has to revise the use of one or more action parameters in the next period or even create new ones. In the second case, the task is equally difficult: he has to copy those action parameters of the innovator that were responsible for his success.[34] In both cases, the imitator has to revise his hypotheses in order to survive in the competitive process. He is forced by the market environment to produce better knowledge in the next period.

11.5. THE DRIVING FORCES OF THE MARKET: ARBITRAGE, INNOVATION, AND ACCUMULATION

Up to now, we have analyzed how entrepreneurs communicate with consumers in the exchange process, and we have determined what innovations and imitations consist of on both sides of the market. The next step is to discuss what these market activities mean for the market process at a more aggregate level. One of the oldest issues concerning market outcomes is whether the activities of entrepreneurs and consumers lead to a market equilibrium. This question has been vital for neoclassical economics because equilibrated markets mean the efficient allocation of resources in the economy. On the other hand, evolutionary economics since the time of Schumpeter stresses the role of innovation. This is obviously very difficult to combine with the notion of a static market equilibrium. It seems that in the real world, markets do both; they coordinate economic agents and, at the same time, they generate innovations endogenously and thus lead to economic growth. A sufficient theory of the market must provide an explanation of both phenomena.

The view of the market as an evolutionary process operating within rules can provide some insights concerning real-world market outcomes. The market can best be conceptualized as a simultaneous process of arbitrage, innovation, and accumulation in which interaction leads to out-

---

[34] See the discussions of Harper (1996, ch. 8) and of Kerber (1996, p. 28), both of which stress the difficulties of the entrepreneur in drawing the correct conclusions from the failure of his or her hypothesis in the market.

comes in the form of prices, technologies, and economic development. Fehl (1980, 1983, 1986) stresses that these driving forces of the market process produce a "selection order" whose illumination can provide a way out of the dilemma of equilibrium versus disequilibrium. Although all three driving forces work simultaneously, we will first discuss them separately for analytical reasons.

"Arbitrage" refers to the exchange activity taking place in the market. Kirzner stressed consistently that entrepreneurs motivated by profit opportunities are engaged in arbitrage activities that bring coordination in the market (1962, 1973, 1979, 1992, 1997). Starting with his controversy with Becker and ending with his defense of the Austrian middle-ground position (1992),[35] Kirzner has tried to show that economic agents and, more profoundly, entrepreneurs learn in a way that tends to bring equilibrium to the market.[36] There is a counterargument raised by some economists operating in the more radical Lachmann–Shackle tradition. It maintains that entrepreneurs are prone to error because of the uncertainty of the future and, thus, that the equilibrating tendencies *cannot* be of systematic in nature. These economists charge that Kirzner has given an unsatisfactory answer to this question. Kirzner's main argument is that entrepreneurs always have an *incentive* to try to avoid error;[37] in other

[35] Kirzner (1962) is an answer to an article by Becker (reprinted in Becker 1976) that contained the thesis that neoclassical market theory can be retained even if one assumes irrational behavior on the part of the agents. The middle-ground position that Kirzner defends goes back to Garrison (1982).

[36] See Kirzner (1962, p. 381): "The *essence* of this market process, it will be observed, *is the systematic way in which plan revisions are made as a consequence of the disappointment of earlier plans.* Such systematic revisions of plans, it is clear, depend on very definitely assumed patterns of rational action." And Kirzner (1992, p. 34): "What middle ground Austrians wish to assert . . . is that events that occur during the market process are subject to powerful constraining and shaping influences. These influences tend to reflect the relative urgencies of different consumer preferences, and the relative scarcities of different productive resources. Austrians, certainly, have never been under the illusion that the powerful constraining and shaping influence of the market is ever so complete as to ensure attainment, even fleeting attainment, of the equilibrium state. What Austrians have emphasized is the existence of important processes of equilibration."

[37] See, e.g., Kirzner (1992, p. 33): "It is true that the entrepreneur at time t_1, in assessing prospects at t_{10}, takes into account the possibility that those t_{10} prospects may turn out to be the results of erroneous entrepreneurial acts, say at time t_4. But this does not mean that the imagined t_{10} realities which operate on the entrepreneur's incentives at t_1 are *not* the 'true' t_{10} realities. . . . First, the entrepreneur at t_1 does have an incentive to take into account the possibility that mistakes between t_1 and t_{10} will *not* distort the situation at t_{10}. More important, entrepreneurial decisions at t_4 (and at *every* date) have every incentive *not* to be based on error. Thus at

words, Kirzner thinks that he may avoid the criticism by referring to the motivational effects that profits and losses release within the market system. But this does not answer the question of whether the homogeneous motivational pressure also induces a homogeneous learning process leading to an equilibrium.[38] Obviously, the cognitive systems of all entrepreneurs, all being human, possess the same structure; but the identical *method of learning* does not necessarily give rise to an identical *content of learning.*

Arbitrage, thus, is always an activity concomitant with active interpretation. We have seen that prior to any exchange acts, shared mental models between entrepreneurs and consumers must be formed. Communication precedes exchange, and since agents are confronted with new problems, they are bound to choose creatively every time from the background of their existing knowledge of alternatives. Their striving for utility increase or for profits ensures that they will try to choose the alternative that they subjectively perceive to be the best. But this choice might turn out to be wrong. The lesson that they will draw from their unsuccessful trial will always be reevaluated in the light of their own learning history.

In contrast to the case of institutions in which all agents possess the same learning history, in the case of exchange, the agents may have had different learning histories while participating in the market game. To the extent that this happens, they will evaluate the market lessons differently, that is, they will learn different lessons from their environmental feedback. This reasoning leads to an obvious result: only insofar as agents share the same learning history concerning the circumstances of the market can it be expected that arbitrage mobilizes equilibrating forces in the market. Whether this is the case in different markets is an empirical issue. In medieval markets, for example, repeated exchange acts between the same persons might have led with greater probability to the clearing of the market than in modern markets. Since a characteristic of modern markets

all times each and every entrepreneur is operating under the incentives set up by the 'true' underlying future realities, *as well as* by the possible 'mistake-induced' realities that may turn out to be relevant. Every entrepreneurial mistake creates a prospective intertemporal gap which offers the incentive correctly to anticipate the truth."

[38] See, e.g., the comment of Vaughn (1992, p. 258). "Certainly entrepreneurs *try* to choose the right means-ends framework, certainly they *try* to recognize past error, certainly they *try* to make their anticipation of the future 'the' correct one. But what guarantee do we have that they will succeed? They simply may be mistaken in their judgment about the course of future events."

is that the exchange takes place between different groups of entrepreneurs and consumers over time, the driving force of arbitrage toward a market equilibrium is bound to work more weakly.[39]

The communicative exchange *between* the two sides of the market gives rise to a competitive process of innovation and imitation *within* each side of the market. (We will concentrate in the following on the supply side.) Innovation is the second driving force of the market process that creates permanent variation and, thus, leads the system away from the coordination implicit in neoclassical equilibrium models. It is important to stress that innovation is generated *endogenously* in the market; profits and losses permanently motivate entrepreneurs to reinterpret their action parameters and reconsider their effectiveness.[40] In this process of active interpretation of environmental feedback (which we have discussed in detail in Section 11.4), a constant flow of qualitatively new entrepreneurial hypotheses is bound to arise. The new knowledge created by the innovators is diffused by the imitative activities of the other entrepreneurs. The efforts of the imitators to respond to the negative pecuniary effects might lead them to new innovations, since even the most immobile or passive entrepreneurs possess some creative potential.[41] Innovation is,

---

39 Obviously the effectiveness of arbitrage also depends on the volatility of the consumers' problems. There are good reasons to assume that in modern times consumers' wants are changing more rapidly, and thus arbitrage loses its effectiveness further. But the main argument in the text remains intact independent of this assumption.

40 This is the crucial difference between our view and that of Kirzner. Although Kirzner sometimes includes "innovation" in his concept of "alertness," (1985, p. 84f.), he does not integrate it systematically in his theory. See the discussion in Mantzavinos (1994, pp. 137ff.) and the comment of Witt (1987a, p. 75): "Therefore, Kirzner's contribution to evolutionary economics remains half-complete and for that reason has little explanatory power." (Translation C. M.)

41 Even Schumpeter, whose entrepreneurial figure appears more as a hero than as an ordinary businessman, did not deny that. See Schumpeter (1911/1987, p. 116): "Nevertheless, we maintain that a person is only an entrepreneur, if and when he has 'enforced a new combination' . . . and for that very reason, we also maintain that it is the rather rare occasion when, through his initiative, a person can remain an entrepreneur over a period of decades. At the same time, however, it would be equally rare to find a businessman who never experienced a moment of innovation, no matter how short-lived it may have been." (Translation by C. M.). See also Fehl (1986, p. 84, n. 14): "[C]ompetitors lagging behind will not always try to overcome their difficulties by means of imitation but also by means of innovation as well. In other words, it seems inadequate to treat innovation as an exogenous variable separated from the process of competition." See also Streit and Wegner (1992, p. 145): "It is also possible that they [i.e., the imitators] may discover an opportunity to innovate through their efforts to respond to the negative pecuniary effect that they realized."

thus, a knowledge-creation process and imitation is a knowledge-diffusion process. Both processes are motivated and steered by the communication with the other side of the market.

It is important to stress once again that an external observer cannot predict the exact time and nature of entrepreneurial innovations. There is an epistemological impossibility even when sketching the variations in entrepreneurial hypotheses that will be produced in the market.[42] In a famous lecture, Hayek (1967/1968) described this fact by calling competition a "discovery procedure" and by reminding economists that "wherever the use of competition can be rationally justified, it is on the ground that we do not know in advance the facts that determine the actions of competitors" (1978, p. 179).[43] It is therefore not surprising that the re-

See also Dosi (1988, p. 1140): "In general, it must be noticed that the partly tacit nature of innovative knowledge and its characteristics of partial private appropriability makes imitation, as well as innovation, a creative process, which involves search, which is not wholly distinct from the search for 'new' development, and which is economically expensive – sometimes even more expensive than the original innovation."

The fact that imitators can be innovative is, of course, a general phenomenon. In a visit to an exhibition on "Imitation and Invention: Old Master Prints and Their Sources," in February 1995 at the National Gallery of Art in Washington, D.C., we recorded the text of the board at the entrance to the exhibition, which is interesting for the present discussion:

"In the fifteenth and sixteenth centuries, when techniques were invented in the West for making woodcuts, engravings and etchings on paper, prints became the primary means of disseminating images throughout Europe. Issued in multiple impressions and relatively inexpensive, original prints as well as those that reproduced other works of art circulated widely. As a result, artists came in contact with each other's work, even that of distant masters, more easily than previously had been possible. The advent of printed media deeply affected the visual arts, creating an international vocabulary accessible to artists across Europe.

"The exhibition explores the impact of this explosion of artistic imagery on the printmakers, many of whom collected prints by other masters as sources of inspiration. In an age when copying was considered essential for an artist's education, printmakers imitated works they admired to refine their own techniques and develop their individual style. Imitation, however, was also a path to invention. In the course of copying, printmakers often reinterpreted sources according to their own aesthetic interests. They also engaged in artistic rivalry, seeking to surpass their models by altering the mood, composition, or technique. In this exhibition, selected woodcuts, engravings and etchings by Dürer, Rembrandt, and other old masters are shown with the prints that inspired them to illustrate the ways in which the practice of copying could prompt the creation of new and original works of art."

[42] See, e.g., Witt (1992a, p. 406f.).

[43] In fact, it is not always clear whether Hayek's discovery procedure concerns *already given* facts or *new* facts. His text allows for both interpretations. In any case, the whole spirit seems to be less neoclassical than his first essays on *Economics and Knowledge* and *The Meaning of Competition*. Kerber, in a detailed exegetic at-

cent neo-Schumpeterian literature elaborating the process of "creative destruction" (Schumpeter, 1942/1950, ch. VII) deals more extensively with the dissemination of novelty and less (or not at all) with the issue of the emergence of innovations (Witt, 1993c, p. 220).

The third driving force of the market process is accumulation. Entrepreneurs, when participating in the market, learn and thus accumulate knowledge. The primary source of their knowledge is the environmental feedback that they receive from the consumers; this feedback, in turn, motivates them to learn further by imitating other, more successful entrepreneurs. The accumulation of knowledge that takes place is, of course, of the same character as every learning process that any human agent undergoes. New classes are built in the mind of the entrepreneurs of the general type of IF . . . THEN rules. After testing their entrepreneurial hypotheses in the market for a period of time, entrepreneurs are bound to learn that the employment of certain action parameters brings them more profits than others and the respective classes are built: for example: "IF I employ organizational structure A, THEN I obtain more profits than by the employment of organizational structure B." Such classes thus comprise all knowledge acquired over time by market participation. Accordingly, a large number of problems are spontaneously classified by entrepreneurs as old problems. This, in turn, means that all entrepreneurs view some problem situations as old ones according to their *own* learning histories and employ standard solutions that have worked in the past. The accumulation of knowledge takes the form of problem solutions classified as such by the entrepreneurs.

The analogous accumulation process occurs on the demand side of the market. Consumers also learn whether the entrepreneurial hypotheses that they have bought produce more utility than the competitive problem solutions available in the market. They also form classes in their minds about the satisfying potential of different product hypotheses and, thus, an accumulation of knowledge relevant for consumption takes place. Every time consumers choose in the market, they do so based on their background knowledge stored in their minds analogous to that of the entrepreneurs.

If this view of accumulation of knowledge by entrepreneurs and consumers is correct, then a further hypothesis seems to be justified: the

tempt, nevertheless comes to the conclusion that Hayek saw competition as a discovery procedure enhancing mainly the equilibrating tendencies in the market (1994a, pp. 147ff.). See also Mantzavinos (1994, pp. 119ff.), Baumann (1993, pp. 198ff.), and Loy (1988, pp. 96ff.).

existence of cognitive path dependency as a prevalent phenomenon also in the economic world. This cognitive path dependency is more complex than in the case of institutions; the accumulation of knowledge in the market goes hand in hand with a complex mechanism of its dynamic division (and transmission).

The three driving forces of the market process – arbitrage, innovation, and accumulation – have been discussed separately here in order to provide an intermediary link between the analysis of the behavior of individual entrepreneurs and consumers and the analysis of more aggregate market properties. In the following two sections of this chapter, we will discuss these market properties or outcomes under the headings of coordination (11.6) and technologies (11.7).

11.6 THE MARKET AS A SELECTION ORDER I: THE ISSUE OF COORDINATION

The three driving forces of the market process – arbitrage, innovation, and accumulation – occur simultaneously within the given institutional framework and give rise to a "selection order" (Fehl, 1986, p. 76). As Fehl convincingly argues, this order is not to be understood as a specific *outcome* of the market process, but rather as its *constitutive property*. The selection order is the ongoing market process. Innovation constantly brings variety into the market on which the selection of consumers in the exchange process operates; the relatively more successful entrepreneurial variations are then accumulated in the minds of the entrepreneurs and the consumers. Such a *constant flow of activities* undertaken by agents able to learn is not equivalent to anything like an equilibrium in the neoclassical sense. The absence of perfect coordination is inherent in any kind of theorizing that stresses human creativity; subsequently, a persistent "misallocation of resources" in the neoclassical sense is ubiquitous.[44]

If one takes economic *change* seriously, then the issue of economic coordination must be discussed in a different light. It is important to stress that economic coordination must be conceptualized as a "coordination of knowledge" rather than a "coordination of actions" (Thomsen, 1992, p. 88f.). To understand what kind of coordination of knowledge among economic agents is possible, the discussion on the shared mental models is useful. Since the market process always takes place within institutions, the economic subjects avail themselves of shared mental models concerning

---

[44] See Röpke's aphoristic statement (1990a, p. 116): "Evolution requires allocation failure."

the rules of the game. These take the form of shared solutions to old problems for the agents and provide a first basic level of coordination. This level of coordination has been systematically ignored by neoclassical economics and is, therefore, all the more important to stress.[45] Institutions are not just a matter of "getting the prices right"; they coordinate the activities of economic agents instead. Therefore, they codetermine the patterns of prices.

The second level of coordination is spontaneously generated when the two sides of the market communicate during exchange. An accompanying phenomenon of such a communicative exchange is the spontaneous rise of price patterns. During the evolving market process, the evaluations of entrepreneurial hypotheses by the consumers imply the existence of an unintended *price-making process.*[46] Since prices arise in the evolutionary competitive process that we described earlier, they indicate the value that the entrepreneurial parameter mixes have for consumers. Prices are the aggregate expressions of a multitude of individual evaluations of entrepreneurial hypotheses. Remember that the entrepreneurial hypotheses are parameter mixes; this means that prices are not evaluations of simple objects such as automobile X. They are instead a measure of the value of hundreds of problem-solving activities of the entrepreneur who is offering the certain automobile X in the market. The higher price of automobile X in comparison with automobile Y indicates that the *set* of entrepreneurial acts and knowledge that produced X is evaluated more highly by the consumers than the *set* of entrepreneurial acts and knowledge that produced Y.

---

[45] Franz Böhm, one of the pioneers of the German *Ordnungstheorie,* sees the coordinating role of institutions, mainly of private law, very clearly. See, e.g., Böhm (1966/1980, p. 121).

[46] This should appear as an obvious and fundamental economic insight, but in the procrustean bed of neoclassical economics, usually only price-takers pass. The paradox then arises: "If everyone takes price as given, then who changes price during adjustment?" (High, 1990, p. 22). The typical answer to this question is the introduction of the fiction of the auctioneer. For example, Arrow and Hahn stress (1971, p. 322): "[the] fiction of an auctioneer is quite serious, since without it we should have to face the paradoxical problem that a perfect competitor changes prices that he is supposed to take as given." Obviously, the fiction of an auctioneer begs all the interesting questions relating to *how* prices emerge, what they in fact express, and how they act as feedback to real-world market participants. In this sense, Loasby's provocative remark seems quite justified (1991, p. 77): "I have to say that economists have no theory of how markets work."

For an overview of the literature on price adjustment, see Schmidtchen (1990, pp. 97ff.). A short but informative critique of the recent neoclassically inspired price theory is contained in Fehl and Schreiter (1993).

What implications does this have for the issue of coordination? Prices are *unique* in expressing in an aggregate and measurable form the problem solution potential of the diverse entrepreneurial hypotheses.[47] They represent aggregate statistics derived from free individual evaluations. The fact that prices are aggregate statistics does not imply that they are also *sufficient* statistics for the achievement of efficient resource allocation, as is sometimes discussed in the literature, however.[48] What prices do is reduce the amount of detail that the agents need to know in order to attain their aims (Thomsen, 1992, p. 50). To judge the coordinating power of prices, one should abandon the nirvana approach that often predominates the discussion in favor of a comparative approach (Demsetz, 1969). As O'Driscoll and Rizzo (1996, p. 39) accurately point out: "The issue is not, however, the accuracy of the price signal relative to some external standard of perfection. Prices, we admit, can and will be incorrect. The crucial point is that, overall, more information is conveyed through a market price system than without one."[49]

---

[47] See Fehl (1983, p. 82): "A free 'exchange' of information and goods between the economic subjects is necessary, so that the 'order of the disequilibrium' can be maintained through self-organization. The fact that prices play an important role in this *communication process* is evident. Nevertheless, what is important is that they must in fact achieve more than in the 'order of the equilibrium.' If one wants to understand their role in the *market process*, they can no longer be seen as merely a reflex of the equilibrium allocation. Prices must not be interpreted as vehicles of information through which the *equilibrium state* is finally achieved or approximated. Instead, what is required is the recognition that prices (though merely on the basis of *expectations* and therefore without relation to some *final state*) provide for the *selection* of the actual states of the system in disequilibrium. Therewith they modify the dissipative structure of the market system, holding it at the same time upright and contributing to the evolutionary process of self-organization.

"If the achievements of the price system are in this respect more comprehensive than in the 'order of the equilibrium,' they are also in another respect more modest. For more so than in equilibrium models, the remaining entrepreneurial action parameters become more important in disequilibrium oriented thinking. . . . Admittedly, this changes nothing of the fact that prices (and profits), as it were have a monopoly position in making heterogeneity 'measurable' and therefore usable." (Translation by C. M.)

[48] See the discussion in Grossman (1976, 1981), Grossman and Stiglitz (1976, 1980) and Loasby (1982). Many of the arguments deal with Hayek's classic position on the effectiveness of the price system in communicating information. See the informative review of the relevant literature in Thomsen (1992, ch. 3).

[49] See also Vaughn's comment on "Hayek's story" (1996, p. 839, n. 11): "It is perfectly consistent with Hayek's story that a manufacturer, for example, might want to know not just that prices have in fact changed, but the reason for a change in price of a resource in order to make better long run plans. However, he is still better off with the price information than without it."

Through the generation of prices during the market process, entrepreneurs and consumers avail themselves of an invaluable means of inferring knowledge. This knowledge concerns the value of alternatives expressed in monetary terms. But this knowledge cannot attain any perfection whatsoever. Prices are entities that require interpretation on the part of the agents. Therefore, coordination depends to a large extent on a common interpretation, that is, on the existence of shared mental models. *However, for coordination of knowledge to occur, the shared mental models must not only include the prices, but also the parameter mix to which those prices refer.* This, in turn, can be only attained if (a) the market is relatively narrow, so that all agents can learn the prevailing prices, and (b) the parameter mix that the prices evaluate is relatively uncomplicated, so that agents can interpret the prices in the same way. The degree of coordination depends, therefore, on whether these two conditions are fulfilled in reality. Where markets are highly organized with respect to trading places and times, for example, and the institutional framework is so tight that only a few action parameters can be employed, the probability of forming the necessary shared mental model and thus of achieving coordination is high.[50] It is no wonder, therefore, that all the pioneers in equilibrium economics have used examples in which these two conditions were more or less met. Edgeworth (1881) developed his idea of contracting and recontracting employing perfectly interconnected traders "collected at a point, or connected by telephones" (p. 18), and Walras (1874) used the example of the Paris stock-exchange (9e lecon).

An experimental examination by Vernon Smith on what he calls the "Hayek Hypothesis" (1982) seems to corroborate the ideas just presented. Smith proves that "strict privacy together with the trading rules of a market institution are sufficient to produce competitive market outcomes at or near 100% efficiency" (ibid., p. 167). In other words, Smith proves that when "each buyer in a market knows only his/her own valuation of *units* of a commodity, and each seller knows only his/her own costs of the *units* that might be sold" (ibid., p. 167), their participation in double auctions gives rise to a price-making process that ends in a neoclassical equilibrium. It is clear that the laboratory setting of the experiment perfectly satisfies the two conditions named earlier. First, the market is so narrow that all agents form shared mental models of all prevailing price bids and offers. Second, and more important, the entrepreneurial hypothesis (or parameter mix) taking the form of a *unit* is not only un-

[50] See Witt's very interesting attempt (1985) to provide a formal model of coordination as an evolving process of self-coordination.

complicated but is also, in fact, thoroughly determinate, so that all agents can interpret it in the same way.

Obviously, those conditions can be easily reproduced in laboratory experiments so perfectly that full coordination may arise. In the real world, deviations are bound to occur such that the prices forfeit their full coordinating power. Moreover, there is no reason to assume that prices will be the *only* information on which economic agents will base their problem-solving activities. Further, it is plausible that, for example, entrepreneurs in their pursuit of profits will consider a large number of parameters beyond the relative prices of products and resources. It is this very consideration of hundreds of other action parameters that gives rise to innovations in the manner described earlier. The occurrence of innovation is closely related to technologies and the accumulation of knowledge, which is the second phenomenon – besides prices and coordination – that is generated during the market process. The exact relationship between the selection order and the emergence of technologies is the topic of the final section of this chapter.

11.7. THE MARKET AS A SELECTION ORDER II: THE EMERGENCE OF TECHNOLOGIES

The endogenous generation of innovations is the key to the development of technologies that is an equally spontaneous outcome of the ongoing market process. The very notion of an ongoing process implies the heterogeneity of production techniques constantly employed by different entrepreneurs (Fehl, 1986, p. 77). The selection of entrepreneurial hypotheses that have been produced by different production technologies is thus translated into the selection of the relatively more successful technologies. The link between the selection of hypotheses or parameter mixes and the selection of technologies is a complex one and therefore requires careful theoretical consideration.

Up to now, we have stressed repeatedly that during the exchange process, entrepreneurs learn actively, and they form classes in their minds of problem solutions that have worked in the past. Thus, after a time, entrepreneurs will avail themselves of a great stock of knowledge stored as solutions to old problems of the general kind of IF . . . THEN rules. But what *kind* of knowledge is it that entrepreneurs accumulate during their market participation? Remember the distinction that we made in Section 3.2. between two kinds of knowledege: theoretical knowledge and practical knowledge or knowing that and knowing how. The differentia specifica, we stressed, is their *communicability:* theoretical knowledge can be communicated by means of language, whereas practical knowledge can be mainly transmitted by direct imitation.

The knowledge that entrepreneurs acquire when they test their hypotheses in the market is practical knowledge. The employment of a certain parameter mix in the effort to attain profits presupposes the knowledge of how to perform a certain task that is not easily expressible in linguistic terms. When the entrepreneur receives environmental feedback in the form of losses or profits, he learns whether or not the specific hypothesis of the knowing-how type has been successful. When an entrepreneur employs a mix of action parameters to satisfy consumer wants, he is performing a skill not verbally communicable in an accurate way to any other entrepreneur. His problem-solving activity consists in the execution of an operation that cannot be fully stated or explained in words. *Entrepreneurship is, thus, a skill acquired during the market process, a practical knowledge concerning successful, that is, profitable, employment of diverse mixes of action parameters.*[51]

Entrepreneurship is a function inherent in the market process since it concerns the continuous testing of hypotheses in the market environment.[52] The introduction of the view of the entrepreneur as the agent who

---

51 This notion of entrepreneurship is consistent with all entrepreneurial functions stressed by different authors in the history of economic thought. Marshall, for example, requires a businessman to have two faculties (1920, p. 248): " [he] must, in his first rôle as merchant and organizer of production, have a thorough knowledge of *things* in his own trade. He must have the power of forecasting the broad movements of production and consumption, of seeing where there is an opportunity for supplying a new commodity that will meet a real want or improving the plan of producing an old commodity. He must be able to judge cautiously and undertake risks boldly; and he must of course understand the materials and machinery used in his trade. But secondly in this rôle of employer he must be a natural leader of *men*. He must have a power of first choosing his assistants rightly and then trusting them fully; of interesting them in the business and of getting them to trust him, so as to bring out whatever enterprise and power of origination there is in them; while he himself exercises a general control over everything, and preserves order and unity in the main plan of the business." We doubt whether the Marshallian businessman could ever communicate all those skills verbally to another businessman. The same, we think, is true of Schumpeter's understanding of entrepreneurship (1911/1987, p. 111): "We call a firm the enforcement of new combinations and also their incorporation in plants etc. We call entrepreneurs the economic subjects whose function is the enforcement of new combinations" (Translation by C. M.) Although Schumpeter contrasts entrepreneurs to what he calls *Wirte schlechtweg* (ibid., p. 122) with regard to the novelty of the combination that they carry through in the market, the interesting point from our perspective is that all agents on the supply side act on the basis of practical knowledge. The correctness of this interpretation is enhanced by Schumpeter's careful distinction between innovation and invention (*Erfinden*) (ibid., p. 129).

52 The fact that entrepreneurship has a practical character is confirmed by the in-

solves the practical problems necessary for the attainment of profits is theoretically fruitful because it links the entrepreneurial activity directly with the testing and growth of (hypothetical) knowledge. This, in turn, helps us considerably to come to grips with the issue of technologies and the understanding of the way scientific knowledge is used in economic production.

Consider our discussion of the growth of scientific knowledge in Section 5.4. There we stressed that the growth of scientific knowledge is an evolutionary process of trial and error in which scientists are engaged in solving theoretical problems. The corpus of scientific knowledge is transmitted from generation to generation with the aid of *symbols* (i.e., natural and formal languages) as the means of communication. Scientific knowledge is objective knowledge in the Popperian sense, that is, it exists independently of the beliefs, cognitive structures, and so on of the scientists and other members of society. The important point in the present context is, then, that scientific knowledge is in principle public knowledge; everybody who is interested can have access to it without (considerable) cost.

It would be a fallacy, though, to assume that the scientific knowledge used *for the production of marketable goods* is equally free or that its use occurs in a quasi-automatic way. This erroneous simplification has long persisted in neoclassical economic theory following the lead of Arrow. In his "information-as-commodity" view, the peculiarity of scientific information is that "[t]he very use of the information in any productive way is bound to reveal it, at least in part" (1962/1971, p. 148). In other words, the transmission of information from science to a business firm, as well as between firms, has no costs. In the neoclassical world, scientific information is generally applicable and is easy to reproduce or reuse (Dosi, 1988, p. 1130). This theoretical consideration, in turn, plays a dominant role in the recent family of models known as New Growth Theory. Here the same mechanistic relationship between scientific knowledge, technological innovations, and economic growth is postulated.[53]

In fact, though, the economic use of scientific knowledge is much more complex (Rosenberg, 1994, ch. 8). The complexity of the relationship derives from the fact that scientific knowledge is used only to the degree that entrepreneurs expect economic profits from its use. Besides, scientific knowledge is not an input to an "economic sausage machine" (Langlois

creased relevance that case studies have acquired in graduate classes in business administration.

[53] See, e.g., Romer (1994). For a critique of the New Growth Theory see Langlois and Robertson, (1996).

and Robertson, 1996, p. 4) that produces marketable goods as output. Moreover, the practical knowledge that the entrepreneurs acquire from the communication with consumers is the second input along with scientific knowledge in the production process. The entrepreneurial know-how concerning the market environment provides the general frame on which the transformation of any scientific achievements must be based. This practical knowledge of the peculiar market circumstances is at the same time the constraint for the use of any scientific knowledge.

This sheds another kind of light on the nature of the technologies employed by firms run by entrepreneurs than the neoclassical type of light. A technology is the set of solutions to problems of a technoeconomic nature.[54] Part of the problem is scientific in the sense that technologists are asked to provide a workable solution, and part of the problem is economic in the sense that entrepreneurs must judge its possible profitability (Nelson, 1994, p. 139). The development of technologies occurs neither automatically nor without market constraints. "The relation between science and technology is symbiotic, not sequential" (Metcalfe, 1995, p. 462). The main complication refers, moreover, to the fact that the use and transformation of objectively available scientific results must *run through* the complex mechanism of the market process.

Before proceeding to the question of how technologies are generated during the market process, a remark on the nature of innovation seems appropriate. Remember our understanding of innovation as the novel employment of a set of action parameters. This is quite different from viewing innovation as a novel action parameter per se, for example, a new product or a new productive method. This means that innovation is not equivalent to technological innovation. When an entrepreneur, for example, changes the financial structure of his firm in a way that has not been done previously in the same market environment, he generates an innovation but *not* a technological innovation. The theory of evolutionary competition put forth here is, therefore, more general than the theory of technological competition that is often pursued in the neo-Schumpeterian literature. The development of technologies is, accordingly, best conceptualized as a spontaneous outcome of the entrepreneurial activity.

The crucial fact is that technologies are not developed by firms led by

---

54 See the definition of Metcalfe (1995, p. 455): "We define technology as the ability to carry out productive transformations. It is an ability to act, a competence to perform, translating materials, energy and information in one set of states into another more highly valued set of states. It clearly involves the ability to think, although technology is more than thoughts."

entrepreneurs for their own sake, but only as one parameter among many in their overall profit-seeking efforts. In this sense, the technologies actually developed are not necessarily the best reply to purely technical or scientific problems. The survival of the diverse technologies employed in parallel by different firms in the market depends crucially on the selective acts of the consumers in the market. They evaluate the whole bundle of parameters offered by the entrepreneurs in the market and thus only *indirectly* the technologies employed. The generation of technologies is, thus, partly codetermined by the consumers in the market.[55]

As the development of technologies is one among other business activities, the question arises of how should it be properly explained. A great body of literature has arisen in the last few years that offers convincing explanations of the phenomenon along evolutionary lines. The theory of Vincenti (1990; 1994) is illuminating in this context. Vincenti stresses the uncertainty of the process of technical advance whereby the community of scientists solves the set of technological problems that it faces in different ways. His example of aircraft technology shows that in the 1920s and 1930s, different patterns of hooking wheels to the fuselage or wings were tried out. The new body and wing designs and the more powerful engines that had already been available made a number of solutions possible. To address the problem of incorporating wheels into a more streamlined design, a number of rather blind trials of different alternatives were developed. The solution that dominated in the end was the retractable wheels, which seemed to be the most promising one at that time. The important issue is that this technical solution was not provided in a uniform, deterministic way by one ex ante completely definable aircraft engineering science solving all technological problems posed. As Dosi and Nelson mention (1994, p. 160), "the aircraft designers are largely employed in a number of competing aircraft companies, where profitability may be affected by the relative quality and cost of the aircraft designs they are employing, comparing with those employed by their competitors. But

---

[55] See Metcalfe (1995, p. 458): "A wealth of research has established that a detailed knowledge of customer needs is crucial to the innovation process, a fact that partly explains the poor results of major government civilian technology programmes which failed to take this into account." See also Wegner (1996, p. 123): "In market economies the use of new possibilities of action is decisive. This is why the demand side has been made the point of departure for the analysis of the processes of market evolution. For the demand side decides utilizability. Besides, the technological dimension involved in the attempt to discover new possibilities for action is, without doubt, made less relevant. Thus, high-tech is neither necessary nor sufficient for market success." (Translation by C. M.)

then what is better or worse in a problem solution is determined at least partially by the 'market,' the properties of an aircraft customers are willing to pay for, the costs associated with different design solutions, the strategies of the suppliers, the changes in the requirements of the buyers, etc."[56]

In a very important contribution, Metcalfe (1995) provides for the first time a full account of the two alternative views of technology and innovation in contemporary economics: the neoclassical view and the evolutionary view. The main shortcoming of the neoclassical perspective turns out to be "the emphasis on symmetric behaviour between identical firms" (p. 446). An evolutionary account of technology places more stress on the tentative character of technological innovation, the process being full of errors. The concept of a technological paradigm developed by Dosi (1982; 1988) captures the idea that each technology has its own specific framework of ideas and relationships within which its development takes place over time. "[A] technological paradigm can be defined as a 'pattern' of solution of selected technoeconomic problems based on highly selected principles derived from the natural sciences, jointly with specific rules aimed to acquire new knowledge and safeguard it, whenever possible, against rapid diffusion to the competitors. Examples of such technological paradigms include the internal combustion engine, oil-based synthetic chemistry, and semiconductor" (Dosi, 1988, p. 1127). A technological paradigm, by defining implicitly which problems are relevant and by providing a set of heuristics to solve them, reduces, in a way, the variety of technologies developed every time in an industry. Technologies evolve, then, through time along identifiable *trajectories*. A technological trajectory can be best understood as "the path of improvement taken by that technology, given technologists' perceptions of opportunities, and the market and other evaluation mechanisms that determined what kind of improvements would be profitable" (Dosi and Nelson, 1994, p. 161). Such technological paradigms and trajectories are generated during evolutionary competition in the ongoing market process. Technological knowledge is accumulated in firms run by entrepreneurs over time.

At this point, the importance of an evolutionary understanding of the firm becomes obvious. Throughout our inquiry, we have abstracted from the existence of firms and have always spoken about entrepreneurs. We

---

56 Of course, there are factors other than the market that influence the success of technological innovations. Mokyr(1998, pp. 21ff.) for example, discusses different sources of resistance to every major innovation in the history of technology. For the argument made, though, it is important to stress that consumer choices determine, at least partly, the success of a technological innovation.

shall abstain from any detailed discussion of how entrepreneurs organize their firms and to what extent the practical knowledge we identified as entrepreneurship is available on different organizational levels within the firm. It is important to stress, however, that what we called accumulation of problem solutions and thus knowledge on the level of a human agent is equivalent to what is discussed as "routines" or dynamic capabilities in the evolutionary theory of the firm.[57] The issue remains the same: on the entrepreneurial or on the firm level, knowledge is accumulated and stored in the entrepreneurial or firm memory and new problems are always perceived and solved against the existent knowledge background.[58] This, in turn, justifies the assumption that on both entrepreneurial and firm levels, cognitive path dependency is the spontaneous outcome of entrepreneurial activity. Technologies, in turn, are the direct fuel of economic development. There is, thus, a direct theoretical link between the institutional framework, the functioning of the market, the generation of tech-

---

[57] See Nelson and Winter (1982), Teece and Pisano (1994), Langlois and Robertson (1995), and Langlois and Foss (1999). The structural symmetry between the level of the entrepreneur and the level of the firm concerning their function is best illustrated by the following table, reproduced from Eliasson (1994, p. 192). It shows clearly that the theory of entrepreneurship discussed in this chapter has some analogies to what Eliasson calls "experimentally organized firm."

Competence Specification of the Experimentally Organized Firm:

1. Sense of direction (intuition)
2. Willing to take risks
3. Efficient identification of mistakes
4. Effective correction of mistakes
5. Efficient coordination
6. Efficient learning feedback to 1.

[58] The cognitive view presented here, as well as the dynamic capabilities view, seem to be consistent with what Pelikan (1989; 1993; 1997) calls economic competence. The difference is perhaps only the stress Pelikan places on the tacit, hardwired character of economic competence. See, e.g., Pelikan (1989, p. 281): "EC [economic competence] is a kind of information capital, inseparably tied to each economic agent, on which the very abilities of agents to communicate and use all other economic information repose, but which cannot be directly communicated itself."

  A predecessor of the competence view of the firm is Penrose (1959). See also Eliasson (1990) and Foss (1993). The competence view of the firm that is closest to our problem-solving model is found in Dosi and Marengo (1994, p. 160): "Indeed, we propose that competences cannot be reduced to either endowments or information partitions, but represent the problem solving features of particular sets of organizational interactions, norms, and – to some extent – explicit strategies. Competences present a significant degree of inertia and firm-specificity. Thus, as a first approximation, they could be considered as firm-specific assets but unlike 'endowments' are subject to learning and change through their very application to actual problem solving."

nologies, and economic development. This is one of the most important conclusions that we can draw from our analysis, and we shall summarize it in the final chapter.

To the degree that technologies are developed in modern times by firms, they constitute only one type of knowledge stored in the memories of the firms. A technological trajectory is, in this view, another epi-phenomenon of a certain cognitive path dependency, namely, one that refers to technological knowledge. The interesting point is that to the degree that technological paradigms exist, this cognitive path dependency is *shared* among all the firms operating within the specific paradigm. Moreover, since the very existence of technological paradigms and technological trajectories is closely linked to the practical knowledge acquired by entrepreneurs (or the firm) in their market participation, it is obvious that technologies are somehow linked to their producers and cannot be transmitted easily.

Since technological knowledge is a hybrid of theoretical and practical knowledge, it cannot be communicated merely by means of symbols; direct observation, imitation, or apprenticeship is also necessary. In the literature, this issue of communicability of technological knowledge is often discussed, following Polanyi (1958 and 1966/1983), under the heading of "tacit knowledge" (e.g., Nelson and Winter, 1982, pp. 77ff.). As we pointed out in Section 3.2., it is misleading to state that, because knowledge of the type know-how cannot be communicated verbally, it must therefore be tacit knowledge. Practical knowledge may be equally communicated by means other than words or mathematical symbols. If this is correct, then technological knowledge is also communicable, the difference being that the communication costs might be much higher than in the case of purely theoretical knowledge inexpensively obtainable through books and scientific journals. Furthermore, a specific "absorptive capacity" (Cohen and Levinthal, 1990) or "receiver competence" (Eliasson, 1990) might be necessary for the purchaser or imitator of a technology.

Since technological knowledge, far from being communicable only by symbols (as the neoclassical theory assumes), is somewhat "damned up," the knowledge spillovers between an intra- and an interindustry level are far from perfect. In an important contribution, Langlois and Robertson (1996) argue that knowledge is a far more private good than has been assumed in the neoclassical theory, and although it can be shared among firms, its transmission is expensive. Thus, the accumulation of technological knowledge over time goes hand in hand with a complex mechanism of its dynamic division. We shall not discuss further how the diffusion of technologies on the industry level occurs.[59] For our purposes, it is merely important to conclude that technologies are generated during the market process. The selection order of the market, apart from limited coordination of economic activities, also generates a set of technologies.

[59] A very good review of the literature is contained in Cohen (1995). See also the theoretical arguments by Loasby (1996; 1999, ch. 8).

12

An Application

Institutions, Markets, and Economic Development

12. 1. TWO TYPES OF THEORY FOR EXPLAINING DEVELOPMENT

One main argument throughout our survey has been that institutions come first; exchange processes always occur within institutions. The primacy of the institutions is founded both in the cognitive architecture of the human mind, that is, in the way people learn, and in the simple truth that institutions must be shared by all (or almost all) agents. To persuade those still unconvinced of the importance of institutions, one has to answer in a straightforward manner the question: what difference does it make to study institutions before analyzing the economic process?

The best way to answer this question is to provide applications of the institutional theory presented here and to show that one reaches a different set of conclusions when this theory is employed than when the institutions are omitted. Such a series of applications can be easily derived from the theory, the first and most important being that the wealth of a society depends crucially on how institutions channel the economic process. The theory may find another application in the transformation of socialist economies. The institutions of a society cannot be changed overnight because they require a very long time to become anchored in the minds of the people. Therefore, a successful transformation presupposes a long-lasting process of collective learning. Furthermore, the theory can be used on more specific levels, such as antitrust policy or social policy. The insight the market competition is an evolutionary process promotes to the antitrust authorities, for example, the avoidance of direct interventions in the market process and the restriction to changes on the level of rules that *all* entrepreneurs must respect. In the following, we will merely draw some conclusions with respect to the theory of economic development and discuss some issues of the transformation debate.

There are two theories of economic development: the institution-free theory and the institutional theory. Modern institution-free theory has two phases: the Neoclassical Theory of Growth (e.g., Solow, 1956) and the Endogenous Growth Theory (e.g. Romer, 1986, 1993, 1994; Lucas, 1988, 1993). In the first step, we will provide a short review of this theory and we will examine critically its structure and explanatory power. In Section 12.2., we will review the statistical and historical evidence and will show that both favor the institutional theory. In Section 12.3, we will discuss the essential characteristics of an economic game that is wealth-creating. Section 12.4 will analyze the institutions that give rise to such a wealth-creating game, and Section 12.5 will deal with the issue of credible commitment. Finally, Section 12.6 will give an account of the role of learning and informal institutions in maintaining the wealth-creating character of the economic game.

Traditional neoclassical growth theory employs the standard production function $Y = A e^{\mu t} K a L (1 - a)$, where Y is gross domestic product (GDP), K is the stock of human and physical capital, L is unskilled labor, A is a constant that reflects the starting position of technology in a society, and e^μ is the exogenous rate at which that technology evolves (Solow, 1956). In this formula, a is the percentage increase in the GDP that will result from a 1 percent increase in capital. The value of a is derived empirically from the share of capital in the national income accounts of different countries. The neoclassical theory assumes that capital is rewarded with its marginal product and that no external economies occur. The value $a < 1$ displays diminishing returns to capital and labor.

The focus of the theory is the process of capital formation. Increases in savings that are reflected in investment cause an increase in the ratio of capital to labor. This increase, in turn, is equivalent to a decline in the marginal product of capital. A continuous fall in the marginal product of capital corresponds to reduced savings since the income accruing to new capital will also fall. Eventually, the savings will only be sufficient to replace worn-out machines and provide equipment for new workers. At this point, the economy will evolve back to a steady state in which capital, labor, and output all grow at the same rate. The income per worker will grow and will equal μ, the annual rate of productivity improvement. The deficit of this model is that the determinants of μ (i.e., of the rate of income growth per capita) within the model are left unexplained. In other words, it is impossible to increase the rate of per capita growth in this model unless the rate of technological progress can be deliberately altered (Solow, 1994, p. 48). The main shortcoming of the model is that technological progress, though pervasive in modern economies, remains an exogenous variable.

The so-called New Growth Theory or Endogenous Growth Theory tries to remedy this deficit. In this second phase of institution-free theory the following production function is postulated: $Y = f(K, L, H; A)$, where Y is national domestic product, K is physical capital, L is unskilled labor, H is human capital, and A is knowledge in a broad sense, that is, all factors affecting technology. The main difference from the earlier model is that the production of technology is explicitly modeled and that there are no diminishing returns to capital. Thus, for growth of income per capita to be endogenously explained, a mechanism must be specified that offsets the propensity to diminishing returns. Two main mechanisms are discussed in the literature on endogenous growth.

The first mechanism is presented by Lucas (1988) and concerns the investment in human capital that yields considerable external economies. According to this model, when individuals or firms accumulate new human capital, they contribute to the productivity of the capital held by others. These external economies take place in a way on the interindustrial level and are expressed directly in the aggregate production function. These externalities operate on the aggregate level rather than on the individual agent level. They may lead to sustained growth and offset the classical effect of diminishing returns when the capital–labor ratio raises.

The second mechanism that may yield increasing returns concerns an increase in the variety or quality of machinery or intermediate inputs in the production process. Research and development (R&D) activities induce this variety and skilled labor is employed by firms to participate in these activities. Formulated schematically, the Endogenous Growth Theory in its most basic form postulates the following causal link:

R&D expenditure → increased knowledge → technological innovations new products and processes → economic growth

The technological change is made dependent on purposeful R&D activities by rational maximizers. Knowledge in this model is a nonrivalrous good, that is, one person's use of the knowledge does not diminish the knowledge available to others. These knowledge spillovers induce technological externalities to other firms and industries and lead to increasing returns becoming the engine of economic growth. What is essentially new in this theory is the modeling of deliberate investment in R&D activities on the part of the firms that endogenizes the innovation process. Research successes generate profits. Market power and profits are treated in the newer models within a framework of monopolistic competition (Romer, 1990). It is acknowledged, thus, that only some kind of imperfect competition can explain why increased expenditures on R&D can be financed by competing firms. Since the possibility either of technological progress replacing old knowledge or of new products replacing old ones is not acknowledged, Romer's models (1986, 1990) are not Schumpeterian ones. The models employed on the industry level, regardless of whether they assume perfect or imperfect competition, are still equilibrium models.

The Endogenous Growth Theory is intellectually more appealing than the Neoclassical Theory of the Solow type because it tries to explain technological progress, which is beyond doubt one of the main determinants of economic growth. There are nevertheless a series of critical points that must be raised in an assessment of the explanatory power of this more sophisticated institution-free theory.

(1) The problem of coordination of the agents is solved by the tacit assumption that economic decisions are perfectly coordinated. This assumption excludes a priori the role that institutions play in market coordination and leaves out per definitionem the main problem that developing countries face (Schreiter, 1997, p. 99). The assumption of perfect coordination implies at the same time that all economies are on the frontiers of their aggregate production function because all resources are employed where they are most valued. However, if the countries of the world were on the frontiers of their aggregate production functions, the marginal product of capital would be many times higher in the less developed countries than in the developed ones (Olson, 1996, p. 14). Robert Lucas (1990) calculated the marginal product of capital in the United States, a high-income country, and in India, a low-income country. He estimated that the marginal product of capital in India is about fifty-eight times as great as that in the United States. Even when Lucas took into consideration the differences in human capital per worker, estimating that it takes five Indian workers to supply as much labor as one American worker, the marginal product of capital in India was still five times as great as that in the United States. In a global world of interconnected financial markets, it is improbable that portfolio managers and entrepreneurs do not exploit such huge differences. As Olson rightly observes (1996, p. 14): "Obviously, the dramatically uneven distribution of capital around the world

contradicts the familiar assumption that all countries are on the frontiers of aggregate neoclassical production functions. A country could not be Pareto efficient and thus could not be on the frontier of its aggregate production unless it had equated the marginal product of capital in the country to the world price of capital. . . . Accordingly, the strikingly unequal allocation of the world's stock of capital across nations proves that the poor countries cannot be anywhere near the frontiers of their aggregate production functions." This, in turn, means that coordination is far from perfect in low-income countries and this can be remedied only by an institutional change.

(2) As we discussed in Section 11.7, the emergence of technologies is a complicated issue since technological knowledge, far from being communicable only by symbols, is somewhat "damned up" to its producers. Knowledge spillovers, which are supposed to be the source of scale economies and the engine of endogenous growth, are far from perfect on the intraindustry and interindustry levels. Since technological knowledge is less slippery and thus more private than has been assumed (e.g., by Lucas), its communication is costly (Langlois and Robertson, 1996) and it requires an absorptive capacity on the part of the receiver (Cohen and Levinthal, 1990). Thus, it is a question of incentives: whether technology will be communicated, and in what terms those incentives are embedded in the institutional structure of the economy.

(3) Some variants of the Endogenous Growth Theory are tentatively dynamic in their explanations of the market processes underlying the aggregate production functions (e.g., Grossman and Helpman, 1991, 1994). However, in the majority of the models, a general equilibrium approach is adopted. From an evolutionary perspective, technological progress is just one of many action parameters that are available to entrepreneurs seeking to increase their profits (Oberender, 1994, p. 70). The profitability of employing the R&D parameter is judged by the entrepreneurs who are constrained in their judgments and choices by a series of social rules. By defining the extent and the conditions under which R&D activities are allowed, institutions regulate simultaneously the pace of technological progress and the rate of economic growth.

The proponents of the Endogenous Growth Theory acknowledge this fact, but they have done nothing to incorporate institutions in their analysis. It is characteristic that Romer finished an important paper with the following questions (1994, p. 20f.): "But if we make use of all of the available evidence . . . we will be able to address the most important policy questions about growth: In a developing country like [the] Philippines, what are the best institutional arrangements for gaining access to the knowledge that already exists in the rest of the world? In a country like the United States, what are the best institutional arrangements for encouraging the production and use of new knowledge?" In summary, one cannot circumvent the study of institutions when analyzing economic development. This is true on theoretical grounds, and is clear when interpreting the evidence, to which we next turn.

12.2. INTERPRETING THE EVIDENCE

Two types of empirical evidence are available: (1) series of cross-country growth regressions that search for empirical linkages between long-run growth and a variety of economic and institutional factors and (2) The historical accounts of the development of different technologies, as well as broader accounts of the economic development that took place in different historical periods and/or different countries.

(1) Even a cursory glance at the statistical evidence leaves the interested reader with a feeling of dissatisfaction. The main controversy in the institution-free theory focused on the issue of convergence across countries. Neoclassical growth theory implies convergence across countries in income levels or growth rates. Given the diminishing marginal product of capital in rich countries and the equal rates of domestic saving, labor force growth, and technical progress, the poorer countries will converge to the capital–labor ratio and eventually to the capital–output ratio of the richer countries. The evidence clearly falsifies this theory: convergence in fact occurred only among the OECD countries in the period after World War II. Many countries in Latin America, Africa, Asia, and Eastern Europe did not converge to the output levels of richer countries (Pack, 1994, p. 64). In the literature, thus, it is broadly accepted that this first phase of institution-free theory must be abandoned because it does not account for the observed divergence of growth rates and income levels across countries.[1] Nevertheless, it seems that this is the only point where a consensus among growth theorists exists.

The falsification of the neoclassical growth theory does not automatically mean that the Endogenous Growth Theory is correct. Summarizing the evidence, Pack (1994, p. 69) concludes that "endogenous growth theory has led to little tested empirical knowledge." Besides, the more

---

[1] Mankiw, Romer, and Weil (1992) propose an extension of Solow's theory that "saves the phenomena." But see Grossman and Helpman's (1994) convincing critique of their arguments.

general methodological question concerns the credibility of cross-country growth regressions. Levine and Renelt (1992) have reviewed many studies and have examined the robustness of their results. They find that cross-country regressions of growth rates are very sensitive to the years included, the choice of countries, and the variables included in the regression. Small alterations of the "other" explanatory variables of the regressions overturn past results (Levine and Renelt, 1992, p. 943). They suggest only three robust correlations: a positive one between average growth rates and the average share of investment in GDP; a positive correlation between the share of investment in GDP and the average share of trade in GDP. Moreover, they have found support for a conditional-convergence hypothesis concerning a negative correlation between the initial level of income and growth over the 1960–89 period when the equation includes a measure of the initial level of investment in human capital.

The fact that investment affects growth is *a sine qua non of every theory of development*. Therefore, it is not surprising that one finds a robust correlation between investment and rates of growth. Obviously, the theoretically interesting question is: what is hidden behind the investment decisions of the agents in an economy? In section 12.4, we will discuss how a proper institutional mix can favor investment. The other interesting result is the conditional convergence of incomes when human capital is taken into consideration. Barro (1991, 1997) has also reported this finding; it seems to be a typical result of cross-country growth regressions that education levels affect growth.

Prima facie, this finding lends considerable support to endogenous growth models à la Lucas and Romer. It is nevertheless a matter of interpretation why and how human capital affects growth. Do the various proxies used for the stock of human capital capture the *process* of knowledge utilization in a society? The answer is no. In an illuminating article, Romer (1993) favors the study of what he calls "idea gaps" over "object gaps" as being the crucial variables for a true explanation of economic development. He rightly observes that "[a]s important as human capital theory is as an extension of the economics of objects, it does not capture the essential aspects of the economics of ideas" (p. 551). It is misleading to postulate that an accumulation of human capital mechanically causes growth in output because it neglects a series of important mechanisms: the dynamic division of knowledge among the members of the society, the different ways in which local knowledge and scientific knowledge affect growth, and the role that entrepreneurs play in converting scientific knowledge into technology. It is difficult, perhaps, to compress these mechanisms into well-behaving functions; nevertheless, simplistic mathematical models that neglect relevant aspects of reality should not be adopted if they have low empirical content.[2]

Since the evidence from regressions is compatible with other interpretations (Romer, 1993), one should always remember that statistics can never substitute theoretical models. Ideally, regressions should help us reject or retain a theoretical hypothesis concerning causalities between variables. In case the statistical evidence falsifies the theory, the correct step from a methodological point of view is to try to modify it. The evidence that does not corroborate the existence of convergence has falsified neoclassical growth theory. Since the statistical analysis shows that there is only a conditional convergence between rich and poor countries when a variable for human capital is included in the estimation, the original theory must be modified. One such modification, based on mathematical finesse, has been proposed by Endogenous Growth Theory. We propose a more radical modification based on a cognitive model of the human agent and the role of institutions in economic life.

(2) The second source of evidence concerns historical accounts of economic development in different countries and during diverse periods. In fact, the great bulk of work in economic history concerns the identification of the determinants of economic growth. Since economic historians typically have an instinct for interdisciplinary study, they do not adopt models only because of their mathematical appeal. North's work (1981, 1990, 1994, North and Thomas, 1973, Denzau and North, 1994, Knight and North, 1997) is a deliberate attempt to shift attention away from institution-free theories toward a political economy that serves as an institutional theory of economic development. His work shows the primary importance of institutions for wealth in the West, as well as the institutional pathology of the less developed countries. Rosenberg (1994) has stressed the role of technology for economic growth, and Rosenberg and Birdzell (1986) have analyzed how innovation led to the West's expansion of trade and the development of natural resources. Jones (1981) states that one of the prime conditions of development in Europe has been its

---

[2] See the remark of Pack (1994, p. 68f.): "[R]egression equations that attempt to sort out the sources of growth also generally ignore interactions in the growth process. For example, a significant coefficient on initial education levels is typically found. But if new knowledge from abroad had not been introduced, or domestic productivity based on R&D had not increased as substantially, the return to education would have been less. Indeed, the external effects of high educational levels suggested by Lucas (1988) are most likely to occur when new technology is being introduced rapidly."

competitive political arena and the recent historical studies contained in Bernholz, Streit, and Vaubel (1998) offer additional support to an institutional theory of economic development that tries to specify the links between institutional framework, innovation, and economic growth.

12.3. THE FOUR ELEMENTS OF A WEALTH-CREATING GAME

The alternative to models of the institution-free type is a theory that stresses the importance of incentives and knowledge embedded in the institutional framework of the society that ultimately brings about economic growth. According to this view, institutions are the real carriers of economic change and the proper model is an evolutionary one.[3] The aim of the analysis throughout this book has been to show that evolutionary reasoning can be successfully applied to both the change of institutions and the market processes. We have proposed as a unifying theoretical structure a problem-solving model that specified how individuals collectively create and learn from the institutions of the society and how they communicate their knowledge in exchange settings. How does the evolutionary process in institutions and markets lead to economic growth?

On a very general level, the answer is that economic growth occurs when the problem-solving capacity of the society increases (Vanberg, 1992). When the members of the society have acquired the skills and knowledge to solve the problems that arise in their environment, they are in a position to channel natural resources in order to realize their aims and goals. Increased problem-solving capacity means more physical options to exploit natural resources effectively, and this eventually leads to the creation of wealth. Hayek, for example, equates economic growth with the growth of knowledge in a society and suggests the continuous experimentation of individuals as the driving force behind it. He postulates that only the freedom to experiment and innovate can effect "an increase in knowledge which enables us not merely to consume more of the same things but to use different things, and often things we did not even know before" (1960, p. 43). Our analysis has shown that only a more *disaggregated* treatment of the different kinds of institutions, both formal and

---

3 Recently, North acknowledged the necessity of evolutionary theorizing (1996, p. 6): "From Veblen and Marshall on, there have been repeated calls for making economics an evolutionary discipline, one which draws its inspiration from evolutionary biology rather than from classical mechanics. . . . The inspiration for a dynamic model must come from some variant of evolutionary reasoning."

informal, along with a separate examination of the market process can provide a systematic account of the growth and transmission of knowledge in a society.

To see how the stock of knowledge increases in society, remember first the classification of knowledge presented in Section 5.4. Theoretical knowledge of the type "know that" can either be scientific knowledge of causal relationships or knowledge of singular objects and events. Practical knowledge is of the type "know how" and cannot be communicated by means of symbols. For economic growth to occur, people must use their knowledge in a wealth-enhancing way. In Section 5.4, we discussed and rejected Hayek's theoretical proposal that not only our scientific and practical knowledge but also our social rules and institutions grow through time. Throughout Part II of this study, we showed that there is an evolution of social institutions and the knowledge embedded in them. Nevertheless, there is also a different kind of process behind the emergence of conventions, moral rules and social norms (i.e., informal institutions), and law (i.e., formal institutions). We contended that knowledge embedded in the institutions of a society, though continuously evolving, *does not grow in any meaningful sense*. Rather, as North has consistently stressed, different institutional paths are possible. It is rather historical chance whether a set of social rules are the "appropriate" ones to facilitate wealth-enhancing competitive market processes and thus enable economic growth.

The central questions for a theory of economic development are the following:

(1) What institutional mix leads to wealth-creating market processes?
(2) Once this institutional mix of formal and informal institutions is adopted, what does such a wealth-creating market process look like?

We will start by answering the second question. There are four mechanisms that mobilize the available theoretical and/or practical knowledge of a society and either transform it or help to transform it into economic value.

1. *Technology*. There is an intricate theoretical link between market processes, development of technologies, and economic growth. As we have seen in Section 11.7, theoretical scientific knowledge can be economically utilized only after running through the complex mechanism of the market

process. Thus, technology is not directly driven by science.[4] In the channeled process of evolutionary competition, entrepreneurs develop technologies as one among many competitive parameters submitted to the evaluative choices of consumers. The kinds of technologies developed depend on two selective factors: (a) the institutions defining the allowed action parameters for the entrepreneurs and (b) the consumers who select the bundles of parameters offered by the entrepreneurs, who therefore also indirectly select the employed technologies as well. The selected technologies either reduce the quantity of output or augment the output with a quantity of employed resources that remains constant. The spread of the technologies in the same industry, across industries, and throughout the whole economy then transforms the theoretical scientific knowledge into products and services of economic value.

2. *Organizational Structures*. The choice of appropriate organizational structures is a critical means of combining different skills and capabilities to exploit natural resources more effectively. This parameter lies in the hands of entrepreneurs, and its constant differentiation allows adaptation to the competitive environment of the market. The great diversity of size, functions, and legal forms that organizations show allows the transforma-

---

[4] See Rosenberg and Birdzell (1986, p. 262): "There is a long-standing controversy. . . . Some believe that technological advance is predominately a fortuitous spin-off from that branch of scientific research which is guided only by a desire to add to knowledge. Others believe that technological advance is a systematic response to human needs, mediated through economic markets that promise large rewards for successful innovation."

Even proponents of Endogenous Growth Theory take the second position that Rosenberg and Birdzell sketch in the preceding quotation. See, e.g., Grossman and Helpman (1991, p. 26f.): "Some might argue that technology is driven by science, which may proceed at a pace and in a direction that is largely independent of economic incentives. But few scholars of industrial innovation accept this view. The commercial exploitation of scientific ideas almost always requires a substantial investment of resources. This is the conclusion of countless studies of particular industries and innovations. . . . According to these studies, firms have invested in new technologies when they have seen an opportunity to earn profits. In fact, a large proportion of the scientific research conducted in the OECD countries is financed by private industry. In such a setting, the institutional, legal, and economic environments that determine the profitability of these investments must surely affect the pace and direction of technological change. And even in the less developed countries, where technical knowledge would seem to be available 'off the shelf', learning to use that technology is far from costless . . . , and the rate of dissemination reflects the institutions, property-rights regime, and pricing structure that together determine the private profitability of acquiring knowledge."

tion of the knowledge of their members into economic products and services. Both the practical skills (know-how) of the workers and employees and their theoretical knowledge of singular objects and events can be utilized only if a suitable organizational form is adopted. Capabilities and local knowledge of the organization, along with natural resources, are the main inputs in the production on the microlevel. To the degree that technologies are developed by firms, organizational structures additionally serve to absorb and store technological knowledge and divide it among the units of the enterprise. [5]

3. *Open Markets.* In order for the market process to be wealth-creating, every individual must have the opportunity to participate in it. Evolutionary competition can prevail only if the incumbent entrepreneurs (regardless of whether they are monopolists or not) fear that they will lose market share to potential competitors. Only if markets are kept free of entry barriers can consumers evaluate the parameter mixes offered by entrepreneurs in a way that best reflects their subjective valuations. In other words, for a market process to show its coordinating and wealth-creating properties, consumers must be able to evaluate the bundle of action parameters that every potential and actual entrepreneur wants to offer.

Open markets mean the extension of trade within the same country or between different countries. We know from A. Smith that the larger the market is, the greater is the division of labor. An extension of the market and of the division of labor go hand in hand with a division of knowledge. Therefore, the larger the market, the greater the possibility of the utilization of available knowledge. An extension of exchange processes independent of their origin (spontaneous or intended, as, for example, by intergovernmental agreements on free trade) accommodates both the transformation of the knowledge and the problem-solving capacity of the involved persons into economic wealth.

The main wealth-increasing effect of big markets is the increase in the rewards of innovation, whether technological, organizational, or any other kind of novel employment of action parameters. The bigger profits that an extended market offers to innovating entrepreneurs act as the main incentive for future innovations. Rosenberg and Birdzell (1986) identified this incentive aspect of large markets as one of the main deter-

---

[5] This is a crucial difference from the formal models employed by the institution-free theory of economic development, which consider the transfer of technological knowledge in terms of the black box of the production function. Since technological knowledge is divided in an enterprise according to its internal organizational structure, it is not easily available in the form of blueprints.

minants of the economic growth of the West: "As the growth of markets increased the rewards for economic innovation, it came to be conducted on a very large scale, as an explicit or implicit goal of a great many enterprises. Its incentives were measured in money rather than honors or personal satisfaction, but they supplied the needed motivation" (p. 266). Open markets provide additional incentives for testing entrepreneurial hypotheses; at the same time, they facilitate the capture of all possible gains from trade and the growth of the problem-solving capacity of the individuals involved.

4. *Money.* Prices are *unique* in expressing the problem-solving potential of the diverse entrepreneurial hypotheses in an aggregate and measurable form (see Section 11.6). Prices arise spontaneously in the exchange process and reflect the evaluations of the entrepreneurial parameter mixes by the consumers. In nonbarter economies, prices are expressed in money terms, and thus all calculations of the individuals presuppose a certain value of the medium of exchange.[6] Only if the value of money is constant will these calculations be correct and exchange processes can unfold without friction. Smith taught us that frictionless exchange enhances the division of labor in society. Extended division of labor leads to greater utilization of knowledge in the society, as we discussed earlier. Thus, the constant value of money facilitates in an extraordinary way the unfolding of wealth-creating market processes. However, the role of money is crucial only in market economies. In centrally planned economies, for example, consumers do not choose among parameter mixes freely, and entrepreneurs do not decide on investment projects or production methods themselves. Since prices do not guide the economic process in such economies, money is neither essential for their regulation (Eucken, 1952/1990, p. 256) nor beneficial in utilizing the available knowledge.

Summarizing the answer to the question "What does a wealth-creating market process look like?" we might say the following: (a) Technological progress takes place only when the profitability of scientific results has been tested in the market. Technology is one main determinant of economic growth. (b) Flexible organizational structures allow the combination of available skills and capabilities of the members of the firm in order to exploit natural resources effectively. (c) Open markets extend the division of knowledge and provide additional incentives for innovations that increase the economic value of resources. (d) The constant value of money facilitates exchange by making the price calculations of individuals cor-

6 On the role of money in a system of exchange, see Eggertsson (1990, pp. 231ff.).

rectly reflect the values of goods and services. All four points must be understood as the general economic conditions that lead to an increase in the problem-solving capacity of an economy. They are therefore to be seen as the key economic elements for long-run economic growth.

12.4. WHICH INSTITUTIONS PERMIT A WEALTH-CREATING MARKET GAME?

We now turn our attention to the first question: What mix of formal and informal institutions will lead to wealth-enhancing exchange processes? Asked differently, under which rules does an economic game arise that is characterized by technological progress, flexible organizational structures, open markets, and a constant value of money?

When analyzing the concrete content of such an institutional mix, we should keep in mind two facts. First, the emergence and adoption of the institutions of a society is made possible and is always accompanied by a concomitant, long-lasting learning process on the part of the individuals. Second, it is by no means evident that the appropriate institutional mix will arise automatically. All institution-free models of economic growth implicitly assume this fact. Identifying the informal institutions and the organization of the polity that lead to a wealth-enhancing economic game is a rather complicated enterprise, however.

Starting with the formal institutions, first, secure property rights (private and communal) and, second, economic institutions maintaining open markets are the sine qua non for wealth-creating market processes. Secure private property rights guarantee agents that their assets can be availed upon in a definite and uncontestable way. The expectation and fear of arbitrary confiscation either by the state or by fellow citizens shortens the individual agent's horizon, increases his subjective discount rate, and provides disincentives for all main economic activities, that is, production, exchange, and investment (Alston, Eggertsson, and North, 1996). The most important effect of secure property rights is that entrepreneurs can employ their parameters in the market with confidence that they will reap all the benefits of successful problem-solving decisions. Technologies may arise and the organizational structure of firms may change freely, since entrepreneurs have the incentives to experiment with their action parameters in the secure knowledge that they will be rewarded accordingly.

Economic institutions maintaining open markets contain the withdrawal of all tariff and nontariff barriers in international trade, the guarantee of free access to product and factor markets, free entry to all occupations and trades, and the declaration of cartel agreements as null and void. Further, money-issuing authority must be granted to every private bank that wishes to issue money, provided that the market is kept open to any potential entrant.[7]

Thus, secure property rights give rise to (a) technological progress and (b) flexible organizational structures, and appropriate economic institutions maintain (c) open markets and (d) the constant value of money through competition between money-issuing authorities. In other words, clearly allocated and protected private property rights and a set of economic institutions guaranteeing open markets are the key factors for an appropriate market process leading to wealth creation.

12.5. CREDIBILITY AND COMMITMENT

Obviously, all kinds of formal institutions are concerned with the organization of polity. The state, as the strategic agent, can provide secure property rights and appropriate economic institutions; this triggers a market process that utilizes all available knowledge and transforms it into economic wealth. But this concerns only the *content* of the appropriate formal institutions. On the other hand, however, every state avails itself of a violence mechanism that may be employed for two purposes: either to protect the property of the citizens and tax the fruits of their economic efforts or to confiscate their wealth and property, manipulating the formal institutions to its advantage. This is the old Hobbesian problem that Weingast (1993) calls the fundamental political dilemma of an economic system: "a government strong enough to protect property rights is also strong enough to confiscate the wealth of the citizens" (p. 287). In other words, besides the *content* of the appropriate formal institutions, there is the problem of the *credible commitment* of the state to provide and main-

---

7 The issue of the proper monetary rules that are sufficient to guarantee the constant value of money is too big to be treated here satisfactorily. On the abolition of government monopoly, see Hayek, (1978). Hayek summarizes his proposal on proper monetary arrangements as follows (1979/1982, p. 57): "To understand what is involved here requires freeing oneself of deeply ingrained habits, and a rethinking of much monetary theory. If the abolition of the government monopoly led to the general use of several competing currencies, that would in itself be an improvement on a governmental monetary monopoly which has without exception been abused in order to defraud and deceive the citizens; but its main purpose would be to impose a very necessary discipline upon the governmental issue of currency through the threat of its being displaced by a more reliable one. In that case the ordinary citizen would still be able in his daily transactions to use the kind of money with which he is now familiar but one which he could at last trust."

tain what is needed for a wealth-creating economic game.[8] How can a government establish such a commitment?

One way is by setting a precedent of "responsible behavior," that is, by building a reputation that it will enforce persistently and without discrimination, a set of rules (North and Weingast, 1989/1996). Practically, this means that the same government must stay in power for a long period of time (Grossman, 2000, p. 7) and have a time preference that allows repeated honoring of the rules. The agents learn after some time that the government respects and enforces the rules, and this reputation will act as a credible commitment. Such responsible behavior has seldom been observed throughout history, though. Fiscal necessity has often led rulers to confiscate wealth. In medieval Europe, the financing of wars, for example, has typically been a reason for rulers to raise funds from the population, reneging on the terms to which they had agreed (North and Weingast, 1989/1996). A contemporary example is found in many post communist countries. Even if the new governments intended to make credible commitments to secure property rights by reputation-building, the learning history of the agents would seriously impede this effort. The Communist Party that ruled in each country expropriated most private wealth after assuming power (Diermeier, Ericson, Freyen and Lewis, 1997, p. 21). Thus, reputation-building alone is insufficient to provide a credible commitment.

Is there a specific type of political regime that can provide, in comparison to alternative ones, more credible commitments for appropriate institutions? Obviously, an anarchist regime cannot guarantee any security of property rights, and the gains of trade are gigantic under any type of government that provides order as compared to a stateless society with a large population. The discussion in the literature is, therefore, centered on the comparison of autocratic versus democratic regimes and how they affect economic outcomes. An autocratic regime seems to be unable to provide a credible commitment to secure property rights, since it has a short time horizon[9] and there is no one to force it to keep its commitments

---

[8] See North and Weingast (1989/1996, p. 134): "Rules the sovereign can readily revise differ significantly in their implications for performance from exactly the same rules when not subject to revision. . . . For economic growth to occur the sovereign or government must not merely establish the relevant set of rights, but must make credible commitment to them."

[9] As Olson (1993, p. 571) observes: "Many autocrats at least at times, have had short time horizons: the examples of confiscations, repudiated loans, debased coinages, and inflated currencies perpetrated by monarchs and dictators over the course of history are almost beyond counting."

(Olson, 1991, p. 153). Democracy seems prima facie to be a more credible regime. However, there is no theoretical reason to assume that a majority coalition assuming power will be ready to respect the minority's property. An unrestrained democracy cannot guarantee to the losers of the elections that their property will not be expropriated. Moreover, even if a democratic majority respected the property rights system, it would by no means be evident that it would credibly commit itself to the *appropriate* institutions of a wealth-enhancing economic game. Further, positive political theory has stressed the absence of a majority rule equilibrium, which implies that no policy is stable (e.g., Riker, 1980; Ordeshook, 1992).

Thus, on theoretical grounds, neither autocracy nor unrestrained democracy will provide favorable institutions. Empirical evidence seems to corroborate the theoretical considerations.[10] In an important article, Przeworski and Limongi (1993) reviewed eighteen studies that generated twenty-one statistical findings on the relationship between political regimes and economic growth. Eight studies were in favor of democracy, eight were in favor of authoritarianism, and five discovered no difference. The authors' conclusion is "that we do not know whether democracy fosters or hinders economic growth" (p. 64).[11] Obviously, the theorizing in terms of vague regime distinctions is not very fruitful. It does not help to explain whether and how governments credibly commit to the appropriate rules of the game, and it does not allow for adequate statistical testing.

The only way that a government can be made to honor its commitment is to be constrained in the exertion of its power by certain institutions. The constitution is the most frequent commitment device used to restrain governments. Constitutions typically specify the obligations of the state, set the limits of its power, and define the rights of the citizens. Appropriate constitutions that help create a wealth-enhancing game must respect two principles: the rule of law (Hayek, 1960) and market-preserving federalism (Weingast, 1993, 1995, 1997a; Qian and Weingast, 1997). To avoid confusion, it is important to stress that these two principles are not rules

---

10 See, e.g., Barro (1997, p. 61): "Thus, there is only the suggestion of a nonlinear relation in which more demcracy raises growth when political freedoms are weak but depress growth when a moderate amount of freedom is already established. One cannot conclude from this evidence that more or less democracy is a critical element for economic growth." See also Barro (1996).

11 Sirowy and Inkeles (1991), in their review of the empirical studies, also stress the inconclusiveness of the evidence (p. 149). Przeworski and Limongi (1997) show that, in any case, the causal relationship according to which economic development leads to democracy does not hold. After reviewing the modernization debate in political science, they conclude that according to their statistical findings, "[t]he emergence of democracy is not a by-product of economic development" (p. 177).

of the law, that is, they are not themselves legal rules; they are instead metalegal doctrines that provide the general guidelines about which legal rules must be constructed if economic development is to occur.

The rule of law means that legal rules must be general and abstract and "must apply to those who lay them down and those who apply them – that is, to the government as well as the governed" (Hayek, 1960, p. 155). The law must be known and certain, that is, it must not be subjected to sudden and unpredictable changes. Further, it must be applied equally to all. The separation of powers is clearly an integral part of the rule of law (Hayek, 1960, p. 210); an independent judicial system that impartially enforces contracts (North, 1993b, p. 21) is an essential element of the principle and has immense importance for a wealth-creating economic game.[12]

Formal rules that are constructed according to the rule of law provide solutions to a dual problem of credible commitment. The state commits itself to respect the freedoms and rights of the citizens independent of any change of persons having governmental power. At the same time, such formal rules provide a credible limit to the exertion of political power by governmental authorities in favor of a group or groups of citizens. By limiting private power, formal rules shield the society from the influence of organized private interests and distributional coalitions.

Olson (1982) introduced the trade-off between the economic gains of stable rules and the waste that distributional coalitions cause mainly to stable societies where their pernicious activities have the time to unfold.[13] The German economist Walter Eucken (1952/1990) proposed a "strong" state as the medicine for the rent-seeking disease. The strength of the state can be captured neither by the number of decrees issued by the government nor by the size of the governmental expenses, however. A strong state is instead an *impartial* state, one that does not grant special privileges

---

[12] On some specific issues concerning the creation of a legal infrastructure in order to improve economic performance see Posner (1998).

[13] See Olson (1982, p. 165): "The dense network of distributional coalitions that eventually emerges in stable societies is harmful to economic efficiency and growth, but so is instability. There is no inconsistency in this; just as special-interest groups lead to misallocations of resources and divert attention from production to distributional struggle, so instability diverts resources that would otherwise have gone into productive long-term investments into forms of wealth that are more easily protected, or even into capital flights to more stable environments. On the whole, stable countries are more prosperous than unstable ones and this is no surprise. But, other things being equal, the most rapid growth will occur in societies that have lately experienced upheaval but are expected nonetheless to be stable for the foreseeable future."

to powerful private interests but instead enforces the rules of the economic game effectively and without discrimination.

The second constitutional principle that helps the appropriate rules for a wealth-enhancing economic game arise is what Weingast calls "market-preserving federalism" (1993, 1995, 1997a; Qian and Weingast, 1997). Such federalism is a system of political decentralization with four characteristics[14]: (1) a hierarchy of governments with a delineated scope of authority so that each government is autonomous in its own sphere of authority; (2) local governments with primary economic regulatory authority within their jurisdictions; (3) a federal government with the authority to sustain a common market and to ensure the mobility of goods, services, and factors of production across subgovernmental jurisdictions; and (4) no possibility of borrowing by governments and no revenue sharing among them so that they face hard budget constraints.

Such political decentralization founded on a federalist structure guarantees interjurisdictional competition (Mantzavinos and Vanberg, 1996). Local jurisdictions offer diverse economic institutions and public goods and raise taxes to finance them. Given the federal guarantee of mobility, resources will exit the jurisdictions with a relatively inferior institutional structure and enter ones with institutions that meet local demands. Since factor mobility is less than perfect due to high exit costs (at least for unskilled labor), some of the economic restrictions that citizens are *not* willing to pay for will survive. Nevertheless, since capital and skilled labor are mobile, interjurisdictional competition will provide incentives for political leaders to provide the appropriate rules of the game.

To summarize, in order to establish a wealth-enhancing economic game, a government must provide the appropriate formal institutions and *credibly commit to them*. Secure property rights and economic institutions maintaining open markets are the appropriate set of formal rules for a wealth-creating game. Governments can credibly commit to such a set of rules if they are constrained by constitutions that are structured according to the principle of the rule of law and of market-preserving federalism. Such constitutions can serve as commitment devices for governments that wish to provide secure property rights and economic institutions maintaining open markets. These, in turn, encourage the generation of tech-

---

[14] For the four characteristics, we draw from Riker (1964) and Weingast (1995; 1997a).

nologies and flexible organizational structures while at the same time abolishing the barriers to entry into markets and securing the constant value of money. All these constellations together lead to long-run economic growth.[15]

In explaining different rates of long-run growth in different historical periods and regimes (North and Thomas, 1973; Jones, 1981; North, 1981, 1990, Rosenberg and Birdzell, 1986), economic history has shown the immense importance of credible government commitments, especially in terms of freedom from arbitrary wealth confiscation and seizure of private property by governments. Market-preserving federalism fosters long-run economic growth, as the examples of the United States, Switzerland, and China after the reforms of 1978 show (Weingast, 1995, Lewis, 1997, Qian and Weingast, 1997). It is not a necessary condition, though, as the examples of economic growth in Japan, Hong Kong, Taiwan, and France demonstrate (Bernholz, 1993).

The statistical evidence seems to provide additional support for the hypothesis just formulated. Knack and Keefer (1995) have constructed indexes of the security of property rights using data provided by private firms that assess country risk for interested investors. These data include several dimensions of the security of property and contract rights such as the rule of law, repudiation of contracts by government, expropriation risk, quality of the bureaucracy, and corruption in government. Their result is that these indexes are strong predictors of economic growth. Keefer and Knack (1997), using data from the same sources, conclude that the institutional environment is one main obstacle to convergence

---

[15] In an excellent article, Demsetz (1998) doubts that institutions always influence market size and determine technical change. He reverses the chain of causation, arguing that often technical change, by affecting transport costs, increasing per capita wealth, and helping to sustain a larger population, itself leads to larger markets. The general thrust of Demsetz's argument is that institutions do not always play the primary role in generating economic development, and this is most importantly so at the earliest stage of economic progress. Initial endowments including weather, terrain, plants, animals, and minerals are the main determinants of economic development at the beginning of human history. It is the distribution of these initial endowments among different groups that creates different opportunities to profit from institutional and technical changes. Demsetz argues that in some cases, noninstitutional considerations may be the more important source of technical change or economic progress. The main shortcoming of Demsetz's analysis is that he only considers formal institutions. As we have tried to argue in this book, however, informal institutions at least, must come first, because they are anchored in the minds of the people.

between poor and rich countries. Barro (1997, p. 28) also finds that among other variables, "greater maintenance of the rule of law is favorable to growth." Borner, Brunetti, and Weder (1995) and Brunetti (1997) find that political credibility is an important determinant of growth.

In order to measure economic liberty, Scully and Slottje (1991) constructed rankings using fifteen attributes of economic liberty. They find that countries that rank low with respect to their relative degree of economic freedom have correspondingly low levels of economic growth. Torstensson (1994), in a study of sixty-eight developed and developing countries, finds a strong negative statistical relationship between the rates of growth of per capita GDP and the index of risk of arbitrary government seizure of private property as proposed by Scully and Slottje (1991). Leblang (1996), using the governmental exchange controls and the total credit allocated to private enterprises as a percentage of GDP as proxies to measure property rights also finds a statistically significant impact on economic growth. Alesina (1998) also finds support for the hypothesis that institutional quality, as measured by protection of property rights, the rule of law, bureaucratic efficiency, and absence of corruption, is important for economic growth. Hall and Jones (1997, 1999) argue that the enormous variation in output per worker across countries can be only partially explained by differences in physical and human capital. They offer convincing statistical evidence that differences in what they call "social infrastructure," that is, the institutions and government that determine the economic environment, cause large differences in capital accumulation and educational attainment, which, in turn, lead to large differences in income across countries. Olson, Sarna, and Swamy (2000) show also that productivity growth is higher in better-governed countries using a number of variables, such as risk of expropriation, risk of repudiation, rule of law, and so on, in order to measure the quality of the country's institutions.

It is characteristic that all these studies avoid the dichotomy between autocracy and democracy and do not search for any relationship between political regime and economic growth. They try instead to make the causal link between individual freedom within institutional constraints and production of economic value more operational by searching for a statistical relationship between individual rights and economic growth.[16] The most comprehensive study in this vein is that of Gwartney, Lawson, and Block

---

[16] These studies thus avoid the critique of Przeworski and Limongi (1993). See the interesting remarks in Pies (1997, pp. 44ff.) and Voigt (1998, p. 218f.). See also the discussion in Paraskewopoulos (1997) and the important study of Görgens (1983).

(1996), which encompasses 103 countries in the period between 1975 and 1995. Two of their results are of interest in our context: (a) there is a robust positive correlation between rights securing economic freedom and per capita income and (b) there is a robust positive correlation between rights securing economic freedom and growth rates.[17] Wu and Davis (1999), in their statistical exploration of the relationships between economic freedom, the level of income, and the rate of economic growth, also conclude that "it is economic freedom that really matters in economic growth. Political freedom is rather the fruit of economic development."[18]

12.6. WHAT INFORMAL INSTITUTIONS FOSTER ECONOMIC GROWTH?

We have discussed which formal institutions are more likely to bring about economic growth and what type of government can credibly commit to those institutions. What remains is an analysis of the other part of the institutional framework, that is, the informal rules that are most conducive to a wealth-creating economic game. It is clear that informal institutions alone cannot explain the differences in the pattern of economic growth across societies. The natural experiments that history has performed offer decisive support to this thesis. Germany, China, and Korea were divided by the accidents of history and came as a result to live under different formal rules during most of the post–World War II period. The economic performances of West Germany, South Korea, Hong Kong, and Taiwan have been incomparably greater than those of East Germany,

---

[17] See also Gwartney and Lawson (1997; 1998) and Easton and Walker (1997).

[18] This is also consistent with the finding of Gwartney, Lawson, and Halcombe (1999). An interesting result has been reported by Lian and Oneal (1997). They find that political fragmentation is unrelated to the rate of economic development in a cross-national study of ninety-eight countries in the period 1960–85. This finding is consistent with our hypothesis that formal rules constructed according to the rule of law at a more general level suffice for the creation of a wealth-creating game. More specific variables such as the number of political parties do not seem to be empirically relevant, however. For evidence about a number of specific political variables and their impact on economic growth, see also Fedderke and Klitgaard (1998).

Haber and Razo (1998), in a highly original empirical study, explore the impact of the Mexican revolution on economic performance. Their results suggest that there is no necessary connection between political instability and the security of property rights. This finding can be explained, though, if one keeps in mind that political *stability* is not identical with political *credibility* and that according to the theory presented here, credibility depends considerably on informal institutions (see Section 12.6).

North Korea, and mainland China (Olson, 1996, p. 19). The informal rules that the populations in the divided nations shared did not reverse the different trajectories of growth. *Societies with the same cultural heritage but different formal rules will have different patterns of economic growth.*

Societies that have the same formal institutional structure but different informal rules are also bound to follow different economic paths. In other words, formal institutions alone are not sufficient to lead to economic growth. The experience with the transformation process of the ex-communist countries in Eastern Europe seems to corroborate this thesis. The dogmatic transplantation of a set of formal institutions that prevailed for decades or centuries in the countries of the West to these countries of the East did not automatically allow a good economic performance.[19] Formal rules remain a piece of paper as long as they are not followed by the citizens.

Putnam (1993), in an excellent book, argues that the different paths of northern and southern Italy are due mainly to differences in the prevailing civic traditions. Networks of civic engagement like neighborhood associations, choral societies, cooperatives, sport clubs, and so on that prevail in northern Italy encourage the participation of citizens in the social and political life in a "horizontal" way. Southern Italy, in contrast, is characterized by vertical bonds that often lead to dependency and "clientelistic" attitudes in social and political life. Putnam traces these differences in civic engagement observable in modern Italy to distinctive cultural traditions that have endured for nearly a thousand years. One main finding of Putnam's study is that "[s]ocial context and history profoundly condition the effectiveness of [formal] institutions" (p. 182).[20]

Recent statistical evidence illuminates the role of informal rules in enhancing economic performance. La Porta, Lopez-De-Silanes, Shleifer,

---

19 And North (1991) pointed out that the adoption of the U.S. Constitution by South American countries did not lead to democracy and economic growth.

20 Partly related to Putnam's work and partly independent of it, a body of literature has appeared in the last few years that explores the role of informal rules under the heading of "social capital." (For a competent review and references to all relevant literature see Woolcock [1998]). See also Putnam (1995). Though part of the literature, mainly the empirical one, is of immediate importance for our work, it is better to avoid theorizing using the term "social capital." The reason is that the term "capital" always possesses a positive meaning since it is assumed that capital produces wealth. However, social capital may obviously have negative effects on economic development if its content is not the appropriate one. Thus, it is the quality of social capital rather than its quantity that matters for economic development, a fact that strongly differentiates it from physical or human capital. Besides, the term "social capital" might conceal the crucial fact that it is not an aggregate, but instead is alway shared by members of a group.

249

and Vishey (1997), using data from the World Values Survey, offer evidence that support Putnam's hypothesis. More generally, they find that "trust" is weakly associated with a higher per capita GNP growth in a sample of forty countries. Knack and Keefer (1997) provide strong evidence that "trust" and "civic cooperation" have a significant impact on aggregate economic activity, though they find that dense horizontal networks – as measured by group memberships – are unrelated to trust and "civic norms" and to economic performance.[21] Besides, their evidence suggests that "formal institutional rules that constrain the government from acting arbitrarily are associated with the development of cooperative norms and trust" (p. 1284).

It seems, thus, that the sufficient condition for economic growth exists only when both formal and informal institutions build an appropriate framework for a wealth-creating game. With respect to the production of social order, we have seen in Section 8.4 that all four logical relationships between formal and informal institutions are possible. Formal and informal rules can be neutral, complementary, substitutive, or conflicting in producing social order; and since we lack a coherent theory, it is very difficult to specify the concrete conditions that give rise to these four possible relationships. With regard to economic growth, though, the relationship between formal and informal rules is clearly complementary. What kinds of informal rules used by the individual agents enhance the security of property rights and help support open markets?

This issue is seldom addressed in the literature.[22] Avner Greif (1994, 1997b) provides an important theoretical structure for the explanation of

---

[21] Temple and Johnson (1998), based on an updating of the Adelman–Morris Index, find that a number of social variables are strong predictors of economic growth. Thus, they provide complementary evidence to La Porta et al. (1997) and Knack and Keefer (1997).

[22] Cooter (1997) argues in a Hayekian vein that social norms are always efficient and that law must be transformed only to make it consistent with them in order for economic development to occur. This view is simplistic because it postulates that formal and informal rules need only be complementary in order for development to result. However, the fact that formal and informal rules are or can be made complementary is independent of the relevant fact of the appropriate *content* of the rules. As Gray (1997) remarks, the social norm of female circumcision, if complemented by a corresponding legal rule, will hardly lead to development. The social norms that emerged in socialist countries and were in many respects collectivist were complemented by corresponding legal rules without leading to economic development. In sum, stating that the appropriate *relationship* between formal and informal rules with regard to economic growth is a comlementary one does not give any information concerning the appropriate *content* of the rules.

differential growth in societies that includes a discussion of the role of informal social rules. He has compared Genoese traders with a group of eleventh-century traders from the Muslim world known as the Maghribi traders. The Genoese traders, being part of the Latin world, had individualistic cultural beliefs, in contrast to the Maghribis, who adopted the more collectivist cultural beliefs of Islamic society. The cultural beliefs of these two groups gave rise to systematic differences in their organizational structures. The Maghribis developed in-group communication networks to enforce collective action (i.e., an enforcement mechanism typical of relatively small, homogeneous groups). The individualistic beliefs of the Genoese traders, by comparison, encouraged bilateral enforcement mechanisms and induced a low level of communication, which "led to a societal organization based on legal, political, and (second-party) economic organizations for enforcement and coordination" (p. 942). Greif draws the conclusion that the Maghribis' societal organization resembles that of contemporary developing countries, whereas that of the Genoese has the same structure as those institutions prevalent in the West. This suggests that the individualistic culture may provide incentives to capture the gains of trade more efficiently in the long-run.[23]

This is confirmed by Lal (1998), who contends that what he calls "cosmological beliefs," that is, beliefs "related to understanding the world around us and humankind's place in it which determine how people view their lives" (p. 7f) are crucial for explaining economic development. Without negating the importance of material interests, he analyzes how different cosmological beliefs give rise to divergent paths of economic development. Lal finds that individualism is the cosmological belief to be found only in the West and the crucial element for its material success. The birth of this unique cosmological belief, individualism, is traced back to

---

[23] Platteau (1994a, 1994b) stresses the role of generalized morality in the successful development story of the Western world. He argues (1994b, p. 770): "[I]f limited group morality is understood as morality restricted to *concrete* people with whom one has close identification while generalized morality is morals applicable to abstract people (to whom one is not necessarily tied through personal, family or ethnic links), there is good sense in arguing that *the Western world has a somewhat unique history rooted in a culture of individualism pervaded by norms of generalized morality.*" Jones (1995) analyzes in an explorative paper the literature on culture and its relationship to economic change but fails to provide a theory that captures the relationship between culture and the economy. King (1999) demonstrates the substantial economic value of Humanism when it turned out that its norms and customs helped the Dutch long-distance trader to find more, and more willing, trade partners in the East Indies.

two papal revolutions in the sixth and eleventh centuries. According to Lal, it was a "package" of the cosmological beliefs of individualism, political decentralization, and the application of the "inquisitive Greek spirit" that led to the success of the West (p. 173).

Weingast (1993, 1997b) addresses the relationship between formal and informal rules in terms of a *self-enforcing constitution*.[24] The institutional limits to state action laid down in the constitution require a sufficient number of citizens who are willing to support it. Weingast suggests that there is a great range of opinions among citizens about the appropriate role of the state and what actions constitute a transgression of citizens' rights. The essence of the problem is the *coordination* of diverse opinions and the construction of a consensus about a set of state actions that trigger citizens' reactions. "[L]imits become self-enforcing when citizens hold these limits in high enough esteem that they are willing to defend them by withdrawing support from the sovereign when he attempts to violate these limits. To survive, a constitution must have more than philosophical or logical appeal; citizens must be willing to defend it" (Weingast, 1997b, p. 251).

Weingast argues, accordingly, in a Humean vein that holds that "though men be much more governed by interest yet even interest itself and all human affairs, are entirely governed by opinion" (Hume, 1777/1907, p. 125). To survive, each constitution must be based on a respective constitutional culture. What is of interest here is that those constitutions that are constructed according to the principle of the rule of law need to be supported by the appropriate civic culture, one that both opposes government transgressions and polices the state in a coordinated manner.[25] Simple or even trivial as this truth might sound, it is of tremen-

---

[24] See also Ordeshook (1992). For a thoroough survey on the emergence, maintenance and change of constitutions see Voigt (1999).

[25] See Hayek (1960, p. 206): "[The rule of law] will be effective only in so far as the legislator feels bound by it. In a democracy this means that it will not prevail unless it forms part of the moral tradition of the community, a common ideal shared and unquestioningly accepted by the majority." See also the interesting remarks of Eggertsson concerning constitutional stability (1999, p. 15f).

See Weingast (1993, p. 305): "[A] society [that] is characterized by the rule of law has two interrelated characteristics. First, it possesses institutions that limit and define the legitimate boundaries of the state action. Second, these institutions are themselves maintained in part by a set of shared beliefs among citizens who react against the state when the latter attempts to transgress the boundaries defined by those institutions."

dous importance for the maintenance of the institutional stability that guarantees a wealth-creating economic game.

The formal institutional framework most supportive of a wealth-creating economic game, as described in Sections 12.4 and 12.5, must be *complemented* by the appropriate informal rules. In terms of our theory, individuals must share the same solution to the problem of government transgression of citizens' rights – a solution that can be implemented every time that the state actors do not respect the limits laid down in the constitution. The fact that formal and informal rules are complementary in creating a wealth-increasing economic game has three important implications.

(1) We have consistently argued throughout this book that the mechanisms behind the emergence of formal and informal rules are distinct. *If this is true, then it would seem to be a rather seldom case that the spontaneous evolutionary process of the emergence of informal institutions and the conscious design of a polity coincide in an institutional mix that is appropriate for a wealth-creating economic game.* In a way, two distinct processes following very different logics and directions must coincidentally result in a framework suitable for economic growth to happen. The chances that this will happen do not seem to be high, however.

(2) The fact that formal and informal rules are complementary in producing economic growth has a further implication. Since all social rules must be anchored in the agents' minds in order to coordinate social behavior, the effects of the learning processes must be analyzed. *Because formal rules must be learned by the participants of the economic game so that they can produce their results, the rate of the change of formal rules must be lower than the rate at which they are learned by all agents involved.* Institutional stability is possible only if the social rules have had the time to be adopted by the persons involved; enough time must elapse to allow the fruits or gifts of the institutional framework to be assessed adequately.

The transition that is taking place in the countries of Eastern Europe and the former Soviet Union exemplifies the ineffectiveness of formal rules alone in producing economic results. As long as these formal rules are not "lived" by the agents (even if they are of the appropriate type to enhance a wealth-creating game), they cannot possibly yield any favorable economic effects. For example, the more than three hundred constitutional amendments that the Russian Congress of Peoples' Deputies enacted between June 1990 and October 1992 (Kiernan and Bell, 1997, p.

118) presumably had no effect on the economic game other than completely confusing the agents.[26] Thus, taking the learning processes seriously offers a decisive argument against any form of "shock therapy" in the postcommunist economies. Since the economic and political transformations underway in Eastern Europe and the former Soviet Union are wide-ranging, the agents are constantly confronted with new problems to be solved for which no previously tested solutions, already stored in their minds, exist. The solutions to all these new problems require even more cognitive capacities on the part of the agents. Therefore, only after a sufficient period of time has elapsed for the learning processes to take place can one hope for the creation of adequate problem solutions.

(3) The complementary relationship between formal and informal institutions, plus the presence of learning, creates path dependence. Institutional path dependence captures the idea that once an institutional framework is established, increasing returns are induced (North, 1990, p.95). The main mechanism effecting institutional path dependence is a cognitive one.[27] Setting up institutions requires social learning on the part of the players. The agents must form cognitive classes in their minds in the form of solutions to old problems. By the time this learning process has been completed, a considerable period of time has already elapsed and therefore the initial setup costs are very high. Once all players have formed the same classes in their minds, the institutional mix starts solving a variety of social problems in a certain way. One can speak of the "increasing returns of an institutional framework" in the sense that once the problem solutions are learned by the agents, they are applied unconsciously each time similar problems arise. Thereby, the problem-solving capacities of the

---

[26] Przeworski (1997, p. 82) has put it succinctly: "The world is full of governments that issue innumerable decrees with little effect on the behavior of economic agents."

[27] See, e.g., Tamborini (1997, p. 59): "Complexity, selective perception and pattern recognition entail another crucial aspect of the constructive cognitive process: *path dependence.* . . . First, individual perceptual experience is always conditional on the place where, and the time when, signals emanate from an object. Second, and consequently, two different individuals may well select different subsets of signals, or focus on different levels of perception, thus drawing different experiences from the 'same' reality." As Tamborini stresses, cognitive path dependence is founded on the recent results of the cognitive science, which "show that differences in individual experiences are the rule, not an extravagant exception; more specifically this approach can shed light on the reasons why individuals can apparently be 'locked in' different interpretations of their common environment" (ibid.). On cognitive path dependence, see also Choi (1993, p. 52). For a view similar to the one proposed here see Greif (1997a, p. 89).

agents are economized. Once a population shares the same problem solutions, self-reinforcing mechanisms such as coordination effects or self-reinforcing expectations (Arthur, 1994b, p. 112, Arthur, 1997) ensure that these solutions will be reapplied in the future. Societies may follow, then, divergent paths that no one wishes.

Technological path dependence is also founded in cognitive path dependence.[28] The way in which a novel technological problem is solved when it first arises determines, to a great extent, how the following group of problems will be solved. Since the solution to a novel technological problem must be tested in the market, it is the consumer's choice that finally determines which technology will prevail. The "small events and chance circumstances" (Arthur, 1994b, p. 113) that determine the success of a technology have to do with the conditions of selection in the market. Active consumers will learn after some time that buying the VHS video technology will enable them to use more films than by buying Sony Betamax. They will, thus, learn which technology increases their utility more, and this knowledge will give rise to a self-reinforcing mechanism. Analogous learning effects on the production side of the market will provide another self-reinforcing mechanism that could generally lead to the dominance of a certain technology. In any case, it is the underlying learning process that at least partly determines which technological path will prevail.

Institutions channel the market process and codetermine the rise of technologies. *Path dependence in economic outcomes is a cumulative phenomenon due to both institutional and technological path dependence. These, in turn, are anchored in cognitive path dependence which determines the overall direction that the process of collective learning in the society takes.*

Looking ahead, a theory of economic development should take the issue of learning into account much more seriously in order to explain why societies throughout history have taken such divergent paths. In other words, a valid explanation of the economic development of different societies must pay simultaneous attention to the evolution of institutions and the economic evolution in each society. This implies that any future development in the theory of economic growth must unite two

---

[28] Path dependence was originally discussed as technological path dependence. See, e.g., David (1985) and Arthur (1994b). For clarification of the meaning of the term, see David (1997, pp. 13ff.)

strands of theories that have developed largely independently of one another: New Institutionalism and Evolutionary Economics.[29]

[29] Pelikan remarks (1992, p. 43f.) that there are "two strands of evolutionary economics which have virtually ignored each other. These are, on the one hand, the neo-schumpeterian studies of the evolution of industrial structures under capitalism, such as Nelson and Winter (1982), and, on the other hand, the studies of the evolution of institutional rules, such as Hayek (1967) and North (1990)." In an accompanying footnote, he adds (p. 44, fn.5) that North takes an important step towards linking the two and that his own work is a step in a similar direction. In fact, Pelikan's work on economic systems is an excellent example of a unified evolutionary approach; see Pelikan (1987, 1988, 1992, 1997). Coriat and Dosi (1998) also plead for a unified evolutionary approach.

Literature that seems to take a more unifying approach includes Pejovich's (1996) work on how different property rights are linked to technological innovation. He compares three alternative types of property rights, i.e., (a) private property rights, (b) property rights in a labor-managed economy, and (c) collectively owned property, and shows that with respect to the generation of innovations, (a) does better than (b) and (b) does better than (c). Moreover, the contributions concerning *National Innovation Systems* edited by Nelson (1993) provide empirical evidence of how innovation systems and consequently technological development are shaped by national institutions and laws in a series of countries. See also the more recent volume edited by Edquist (1997).

See also Hesse's important attempt to provide a consistent explanation of long-term economic development along evolutionary lines (Hesse, 1992a, 1992b, 1996).

Concluding Observations: Unified Social Science as Political Economy?

We conclude this book with a general remark. The main idea put forth in this inquiry referred to a specific perspective of the social world, its main ingredients being methodological individualism, the assumption of self-interested behavior, and the idea of channeling human behavior through social institutions. This set of principles characterized the theoretical program of political economy before its gradual transformation into neoclassical economics. These powerful core ideas are not a priori restricted to any particular social sphere or historical period, though. They can, therefore, serve as a general research program for the social sciences.

A genuine political economy that would fill the "cognitive, motivational, and institutional vacuum" of neoclassical economics (Albert, 1979, p. 11) would at the same time provide a platform for the unification and further development of the social sciences. Such a political economy would not be vulnerable to the familiar criticism of "economic imperialism" for two reasons. First, it would integrate the different disciplines of the social sciences in the general project of the study of institutions. The unique vantage point and specialized knowledge of every discipline could be united in the common institutional perspective that seems to be of equal importance in political science, sociology, and economics. Second, it would not adopt neoclassical microeconomics as its microfoundation. The behavioral model of problem solving inspired by cognitive psychology and evolutionary epistemology retains the virtues of the rational-choice model without neglecting the rule-guided dimension of human behavior. In the proposed synthesis, *Homo oeconomicus* and *Homo sociologicus* are transformed into the individual as a problem solver.

With the use of such a behavioral model, the issue of social order can be addressed as a whole. The complex of social relationships includes both interindividual conflict and the possibility of realizing mutual benefits.

The principal conclusion of this book is that institutions provide the filter through which diverse settings of social coordination and social conflict are transformed into a workable social order. Exchange acts constitute the basic means for attaining mutual benefit. However, a main thesis of this study is that this kind of human interaction is decisively shaped by the prevailing institutions. In this sense, there are neither exchange activities per se nor purely economic relationships that are not embedded in an institutional framework.

References

Aberle, Gerd (1992): *Wettbewerbstheorie und Wettbewerbspolitik*, 2nd ed. Stuttgart: Kohlhammer.

Akerlof, George A. and William T. Dickens (1982): "The Economic Consequences of Cognitive Dissonance," in *The American Economic Review*: 72, 307–19.

Albert, Hans (1967/1998): *Marktsoziologie und Entscheidungslogik*, 2nd rev. ed. Tübingen: J. C. B. Mohr (Paul Siebeck).

Albert, Hans (1968/1991): *Traktat über kritische Vernunft*, 5th rev. ed. Tübingen J. C. B. Mohr (Paul Siebeck).

Albert, Hans (1976): *Aufklärung und Steuerung*. Hamburg: Hoffmann und Campe Verlag.

Albert, Hans (1978): *Traktat über rationale Praxis*. Tübingen: J. C. B. Mohr (Paul Siebeck).

Albert, Hans (1979): "The Economic Tradition – Economics as a Research Programme for Theoretical Social Science," in Karl Brunner (ed.), *Economics and Social Institutions – Insights from the Conferences on Analysis and Ideology*, pp. 1–27. Boston: Nijhoff.

Albert, Hans (1987): "Is Socialism Inevitable? Historical Prophecy and the Possibilities of Reason," in Svetozar Pejovich (ed.), *Socialism: Institutional, Philosophical, and Economic Issues*, pp. 55–88. Dordrecht, Boston, and Lancaster: Kluwer.

Alchian, Armen (1950): "Uncertainty, Evolution and Economic Theory," in *Journal of Political Economy*: 58, 211–21.

Alchian, Armen (1953): "Comment," in *American Economic Review*: 43, 600–3.

Alchian, Armen (1977): *Economic Forces at Work*, Indianapolis: Liberty Press.

Alesina, Alberto (1998): "The Political Economy of High and Low Growth," in *Annual World Bank Conference on Development Economics 1997*, pp. 217–37. Washington, D.C.: World Bank.

Alston, Lee J., Thráinn Eggertsson, and Douglass C. North (1996): "The Evolution of Modern Institutions of Growth," in Lee J. Alston, Thráinn Eggertsson, and Douglass C. North (eds.): *Empirical Studies in Institutional Change*, pp. 129–33. Cambridge: Cambridge University Press.

Anand, Paul (1993): *Foundations of Rational Choice under Risk*. Oxford: Clarendon Press.

References

Andersen, Esben S. (ed.) (1994): *Evolutionary Economics. Post-Schumpeterian Contributions*. London and New York: Pinter.

Anderson, John R. (1983): *The Architecture of Cognition*. Cambridge, Mass.: Harvard University Press.

Anderson, John R. (1990): *Cognitive Psychology and Its Implications*, 3rd ed. New York: Freeman.

Aristotle: *Nicomachean Ethics* (1967): German translation of Olof Gigon. Zürich and München: Deutscher Taschenbuch Verlag.

Arndt, Helmut (1949): "Konkurrenz und Monopol in Wirklichkeit" in *Jahrbücher für Nationalökonomie und Statistik*: 161, 222–96.

Arndt, Helmut (1952): *Schöpferischer Wettbewerb und klassenlose Gesellschaft*. Berlin Duncker & Humblot.

Arndt, Hemut (1981): "Macht und Wettbewerb" in Helmut, Cox, Jens, Uwe, and Markert Kurt (eds.) (1981), pp. 49–78.

Arndt, Helmut (1986): *Leistungswettbewerb und ruinöse Konkurrenz in ihrem Einfluß auf Wohlfahrt und Beschäftigung*. Berlin Duncker & Humblot.

Arrow, Kenneth J. (1962/1971): "Economc Welfare and the Allocation of Resources for Invention" in *The Rate and Direction of Inventive Activity: Economic and Social Factors*, pp. 609–26. Princeton: Princeton University Press, reprinted in D. M. Lamberton (ed.): *Economics of Information and Knowledge*, pp. 141–59. Harmondsworth: Penguin Books.

Arrow, Kenneth J. (1994): "Methodological Individualism and Social Knowledge," in *American Economic Review (Papers and Proceedings)*: 84, 1–9.

Arrow Kenneth J., Enrico Colombatto, Mark Perlman and Christian Schmidt (eds.) (1996): *The Rational Foundations of Economic Behavior*. New York: St. Martin's Press.

Arrow, Kenneth J. and Frank H. Hahn (1971): *General Competitive Analysis*. San Francisco: Holden-Day.

Arthur, Brian (1994a): "Inductive Reasoning and Bounded Rationality," in *American Economic Review (Papers and Proceedings)*: 84, 406–11.

Arthur, Brian (1994b): *Increasing Returns and Path Dependence in the Economy*. Ann Arbor: University of Michigan Press.

Arthur, Brian (1997): "Beyond Rational Expectations: Indeterminacy in Economic and Financial Markets," in John N. Drovak and John V. C. Nye (eds.): *The Frontiers of the New Institutional Economics*, pp. 291–304. San Diego: Academic Press.

Axelrod, Robert (1984): *The Evolution of Cooperation*. New York: Basic Books.

Axelrod, Robert (1986): "An Evolutionary Approach to Norms," in *American Political Science Review*: 80, 1095–111.

Bandura, Albert (1986): *Social Foundations of Thought and Action: A Social Cognitive Theory*. Englewood Cliffs, N.J.: Prentice-Hall.

Baron, Jonathan (1994): *Thinking and Deciding*, 2nd ed. Cambridge: Cambridge University Press.

Barro, Robert J. (1991): "Economic Growth in a Cross Section of Countries," in *Quarterly Journl of Economics*: 106, 407–43.

Barro, Robert J. (1996): "Democracy and Growth," in *Journal of Economic Growth*: 1, 1–27.

References

Barro, Robert J. (1997): *Determinants of Economic Growth*. Cambridge, Mass. and London: MIT Press.

Bartlett, Frederic (1932): *Remembering*. Cambridge: Cambridge University Press.

Bartling, Hartwig (1980): *Leitbilder der Wettbewerbspolitik*. München: Vahlen.

Barzel, Yoram (1998): "The State and the Diversity of Third Party Enforcers," unpublished paper presented at the Second Annual Conference of the International Society for the New Institutional Economics, Paris, September 1998.

Barzel, Yoram (2000): "Property Rights and the Evolution of the State," in *Economics of Governance*: 1, 25–51.

Bates, Robert H. (1983): *Essays on the Political Economy of Rural Africa*. Cambridge: Cambridge University Press.

Baumann, Bernd (1993): *Offene Gesellschaft, Marktprozeß, und Staatsaufgaben*. Baden-Baden: Nomos.

Becker, Gary (1976): *The Economic Approach to Human Behavior*. Chicago and London: University of Chicago Press.

Becker, Gary (1996): *Accounting for Tastes*. Cambridge, Mass.: Harvard University Press.

Ben-Ner, Avner and Louis Putterman (1998): "Values and Institutions in Economic Analysis," in Avner Ben-Ner and Louis Putterman (eds.): *Economics, Values, and Organization*, pp. 3–69. Cambridge: Cambridge University Press.

Berg, Hartmut (1989): "Wettbewerb als dynamischer Prozeß. Idealtypus und Realität," in Andreae, Clemens-August, Jochen Kirchhof and Gert Pfeiffer (eds.): *Wettbewerb als Herausforderung und Chance, Festschrift für Werner Benisch*, Köln etc: Karl Heymanns, pp. 27–48.

Berg, Hartmut (1992): "Wettbewerbspolitik," in *Vahlens Kompendium der Wirtschaftstheorie und Wirtschaftspolitik*, vol. 2, 5th ed., München: Vahlen, pp. 239–300.

Berg, Joyce, John Dickhaut, and Kevin McCabe (1995): "Trust, Reciprocity and Social History," in *Games and Economic Behavior*: 10, 122–42.

Bernard, Luther L. (1924): *Instinct*, New York: Holt, Rinehart & Winston.

Bernholz, Peter (1993): "Constitutions as Governance Structures: The Political Foundations of Secure Markets. Comment," in *Journal of Institutional and Theoretical Economics*: 149, 312–20.

Bernholz, Peter, Manfred E. Streit, and Roland Vaubel (1998): *Political Competition, Innovation and Growth*. Berlin: Springer.

Bernstein, Lisa (1996): "Merchant Law in a Merchant Court: Rethinking the Code's Search for Immanent Business Norms," in *University of Pennsylvania Law Review*. vol. 144, pp. 1765–821.

Binmore, Ken and Larry Samuelson (1994): "An Economist's Perspective on the Evolution of Norms," in *Journal of Institutional and Theoretical Economics*: 150/1, 45–63.

Black, Donald (1976): *The Behavior of Law*. New York and London: Academic Press.

Black, Donald (1984): "Social Control as a Dependent Variable," in Donald Black (ed.), *Toward a General Theory of Social Control*, vol. 1, pp. 1–36. Orlando etc: Academic Press.

Blau, Peter (1964): *Exchange and Power in Social Life*. New York: Wiley.

References

Blaug, Marc (1997): *Not Only an Economist.* Cheltenham: Edward Elgar.

Boettke, Peter and David L. Prychitko (eds.) (1994): *The Market Process: Essays in Contemporary Austrian Economics.* Aldershot: Edward Elgar.

Böhm, Franz (1937): *Die Ordnung der Wirtschaft als geschichtliche Aufgabe und rechtsschöpferische Leistung.* Stuttgart and Berlin: Kohlhammer.

Böhm, Franz (1966/1980): "Privatrechtsgesellschaft und Marktwirtschaft," in *Ordo:* 17, 75–151 and reprinted in Böhm (1980), pp. 105–68.

Böhm, Franz (1980): *Freiheit und Ordnung in der Marktwirtschaft.* Ernst-Joachim Mestmäcker (ed.). Baden-Baden: Nomos.

Bohnet, Iris and Bruno S. Frey (1999): "The Sound of Silence in Prisoner's Dilemma and Dictator Games," in *Journal of Economic Behavior & Organization:* 38, 43–57.

Boland, Lawrence A. (1997): "Knowedge in Economic Models," unpublished paper presented at the conference on "Abandoning the Hypothesis of Omniscience in Economics: What Are the Implications?", January 1997, Fribourg, Switzerland.

Borchert, Manfred and Heinz Grossekettler (1985): *Preis- und Wettbewerbstheorie.* Stuttgart, Berlin, Köln, and Mainz: Kohlhammer.

Borner, Silvio, Aymo Brunetti and Beatrice Weder (1995): *Political Credibility and Economic Development.* New York: St. Martin's Press.

Bosch, Alfred (1990): "Market Process as an Evolutionary Process," in Alfred Bosch, Peter Koslowski and Reinhold Veit (eds.): *General Equilibrium or Market Process,* pp. 77–98. Tübingen: J. C. B. Mohr (Paul Siebeck).

Boudon, Raymond (1989): "Subjective Rationality and the Explanation of Social Behavior," in *Rationality and Society:* 1, 173–96.

Boudon, Raymond (1993a): "Toward a Synthetic Theory of Rationality," in *International Studies in the Philosophy of Science:* 7, 5–19.

Boudon, Raymond (1993b): "More on 'Good Reasons': Reply to Critics," in *International Studies in the Philosophy of Science:* 7, 87–102.

Boudon, Raymond (1994): "Reconstructing Complex Systems Needs a Complex Theory of Rationality," in Hans-Ulrich Derlien, Uta, Gerhardt, and Fritz W. Scharpf (eds.): *Systemrationalität und Partialinteresse. Festschrift für Renate Mayntz,* pp. 167–88. Baden-Baden: Nomos Verlagsgesellschaft.

Boudon, Raymond (1998): "Limitations of Rational Choice Theory," in *American Journal of Sociology:* 104, 817–28.

Boulding, Kenneth (1958): *The Skills of the Economist.* Cleveland: Howard Allen.

Bowles, Samuel (1998): "Endogenous Preferences: The Cultural Consequences of Markets and other Institutions," in *Journal of Economic Literature:* 36, 75–111.

Boyd, Robert and Peter J. Richerson (1985): *Culture and the Evolutionary Process.* Chicago and London: Chicago University Press.

Boyd, Robert and Peter J. Richerson (1994): "The Evolution of Norms: An Anthropological View," in *Journal of Institutional and Theoretical Economics:* 150, 1, 72–87.

Brandt, Karl (1984): "Das neoklassische Marktmodell und die Wettbewerbstheorie," in *Jahrbücher für Nationalökonomie und Statistik:* 199, 17–122.

References

Brandt, Karl (1993): *Geschichte der deutschen Volkswirtschaftslehre, vol. 2: Vom Historismus bis zur Neoklassik*. Freiburg: Haufe Verlag.

Brennan, Geoffrey and James M. Buchanan (1985): *The Reason of Rules – Constitutional Political Economy*. Cambridge: Cambridge University Press.

Brooks, Michael A., Ben J. Heijdra, and Anton D. Lowenberg (1990): "Productive versus Unproductive Labor and Rent Seeking: Lessons from History," in *Journal of Institutional and Theoretical Economics*: 146, 419–38.

Broome, John (1991): "Utility," in *Economics and Philosophy*. 7, 1–12.

Bruner, Jerome S. (1957): "On Going Beyond the Information Given," in Jerome S. Bruner: *Contemporary Approaches to Cognition*, pp. 41–69. Cambridge, Mass.: Harvard University Press.

Brunetti, Aymo (1997): *Politics and Economic Growth*. Paris: OECD.

Buchanan, James M. (1965/1977): "Ethical Rules, Expected Values, and Large Numbers," in *Ethics*: 76, 7–13 and reprinted in James M. Buchanan: *Freedom in Constitutional Contract. Perspective of a Political Economist*, pp. 151–68. College Station: Texas A&M University Press.

Buchanan, James M. (1979): *What Should Economists Do?* Indianapolis: Liberty Fund.

Buchanan, James M. (1969): *Cost and Choice*. Chicago: Markham.

Buchanan, James M. (1975): *The Limits of Liberty. Between Anarchy and Leviathan*. Chicago: University of Chicago Press.

Buchanan, James M. (1977): *Freedom in Constitutional Contract. Perspective of a Political Economist*. College Station: Texas A&M University Press.

Buchanan, James M. (1986): *Liberty, Markets, and State: Political Economy in the 1980's*. New York: New York University Press.

Buchanan, James M. (1987a): "Constitutional Economics," in *The New Palgrave – A Dictionary of Economics*: 1, 585–8.

Buchanan, James M. (1987b): *Economics – Between Predictive Science and Moral Philosophy*. College Station: Texas A&M University Press.

Buchanan, James M. (1989a): *Explorations into Constitutional Economics*. College Station: Texas A&M University Press.

Buchanan, James M. (1989b): "The Relatively Absolute Absolutes," in James Buchanan: *Essays on Political Economy*, pp. 32–46. Honolulu: University of Hawaii Press.

Buchanan, James M. (1991): *The Economics and the Ethics of Constitutional Order*. Ann Arbor: University of Michigan Press.

Buchanan, James M., Robert D. Tollison, and Gordon Tullock (eds.) (1980): *Toward a Theory of the Rent – Seeking Society*. College Station: Texas A&M University Press.

Buchanan, James M. and Gordon Tullock (1962): *The Calculus of Consent – Logical Foundations of Constitutional Democracy*. Ann Arbor: University of Michigan Press.

Buchanan, James M. and Viktor Vanberg (1991): "The Market as a Creative Process," in *Economics and Philosophy*: 7, 167–86.

Bunge, Mario (1996): *Finding Philosophy in Social Science*. New Haven and London: Yale University Press.

References

Caldwell, Bruce J. and Stephan Boehm (eds.) (1993): *Austrian Economics: Tensions and New Directions*. Norwell, Mass: Kluwer.

Calvert, Randall L. (1995): "The Rational Choice Theory of Institutions: Cooperation, Coordination, and Communication," in Jeffrey S. Banks and Eric A. Hanushek (eds.): *Modern Political Economy*, pp. 216–67. Cambridge: Cambridge University Press.

Calvert, Randall L. (1998): "Explaining Social Order: Internalization, External Enforcement, or Equilibrium," in Karol Soltan, Eric, M. Uslaner, and Virginia Haufler (eds.): *Institutions and Social Order*, pp. 131–62. Ann Arbor: The University of Michigan Press.

Campbell, Donald T. (1974/1987): "Evolutionary Epistemology," originally published in Schilpp, Paul A. (ed.), *The Philosophy of Karl Popper*, pp. 413–63, La Salle, Ill.: Open Court, 1974, and reprinted in Gerard Radnitzsky and W. W. Bartley III (eds.), *Evolutionary Epistemology, Rationality and the Sociology of Knowledge*, pp. 48–114, La Salle, Ill.: Open Court, 1987.

Campbell, Donald T. (1965): "Variation and Selective Retention in Socio-Cultural Evolution," in Herbert R. Barringer, George I. Blanksten, and Raymond W. Mack (eds.): *Social Change in Developing Areas*, pp. 19–49. Cambridge, Mass.: Schenkman.

Champagne, A. B., L. E. Klopfer, and J. H. Anderson (1980): "Factors Influencing the Learning of Classical Mechanics," in *American Journal of Physics*. 48, 1074–107.

Chiaromonte, Giovanni F. and Giovanni Dosi (1992): "The Microfoundations of Competitiveness and Their Macroeconomic Implications," in Dominique Foray and Christopher Freeman (eds.): *Technology and Competitiveness*, pp. 107–134. London: Pinter.

Choi, Young Back (1993): *Paradigms and Conventions*. Ann Arbor: University of Michigan Press.

Choi, Young Back (1999): "Conventions and Economic Change: A Contribution Toward a Theory of Political Economy," in *Constitutional Political Economy*: 10, 245–64.

Clark, Andy (1997): "Economic Reason: The Interplay of Individual Learning and External Structure," in John Drovak and John V. C. Nye (eds.): *The Frontiers of the New Institutional Economics*, pp. 269–90. San Diego: Academic Press.

Clark, John M. (1940): "Toward a Concept of Workable Competition," in *American Economic Review*: 30, 241–56.

Clark, John M. (1954): "Competition and the Objectives of Government Policy," in Edward H. Chamberlin (ed.), *Monopoly and Competition and Their Regulation*, pp. 317–37. London: MacMillan.

Clark, John M. (1955): "Competition: Static Models and Dynamic Aspects," in: *The American Economic Review*: 45, 450–62.

Clark, John M. (1961): *Competition as a Dynamic Process*. Washington, D.C.: The Brookings Institution.

Coase, Ronald H. (1960): "The Problem of Social Cost," in *Journal of Law and Economics*: 3, 1–44.

Cohen, Wesley M. (1995): "Empirical Studies of Innovative Activity," in Paul Stoneman (ed.), *Handbook of the Economics of Innovation and Technological Change*, pp. 182–264. Oxford and Cambridge, Mass.: Blackwell.

Cohen, Wesley M. and Daniel. A. Levinthal (1990): "Absorptive Capacity: A New Perspective on Learning and Innovation," in *Administrative Science Quarterly:* 35, 128–52.

Coleman, James S. (1990a): *Foundations of Social Theory*. Cambridge, Mass.: Harvard University Press.

Coleman, James S. (1990b): "The Emergence of Norms," in Michael Hechter, Karl-Dieter Opp, and Reinhard Wippler (eds.): *Social Institutions*, pp. 35–59. Berlin and New York: Walter de Gruyter.

Commons, John R. (1924/1968): *Legal Foundations of Capitalism*. Madison, Milwaukee, and London: University of Wisconsin Press.

Commons, John R. (1936): "Institutional Economics," in *American Economic Review:* 26, 237–49.

Commons, John R. (1934/1990): *Institutional Economics. Its Place in Political Economy*. New Brunswick and London: Transaction.

Congleton, Roger (ed.) (1996): *Rent-Seeking*. Aldershot: Edward Elgar.

Conlisk, John (1996): "Why Bounded Rationality?" in *Journal of Economic Literature:* 34, 669–700.

Cooper, John M. (1975): *Reason and Human Good in Aristotle*. Cambridge, Mass.: Harvard University Press.

Cooter, Robert D. (1996): "Decentralized Law for a Complex Economy: The Structural Approach to Adjudicating the New Law Merchant," in *University of Pennsylvania Law Review:* 144, 1643–96.

Cooter, Robert D. (1997): "The Rule of State Law and the Rule-of-Law State: Economic Analysis of the Legal Foundations of Development," in *Annual World Bank Conference on Development Economics 1996*, pp. 191–217. Washington D.C.: The World Bank.

Coriat, Benjamin and Giovanni Dosi (1998): "The Institutional Embeddedness of Economic Change: An Appraisal of the 'Evolutionary' and 'Regulationist' Research Programmes," in Klaus Nielsen and Björn, Johnson (eds.): *Institutions and Economic Change*, pp. 3–32. Cheltenham: Edward Elgar.

Cosmides, Leda and John Tooby (1992): "Cognitive Adaptations for Social Change," in J. Barkow, L. Cosmides, and J. Tooby (eds.): *The Adapted Mind: Evolutionary Psychology and the Generation of Culture*, pp. 163–228. New York: Oxford University Press.

Cosmides, Leda and John Tooby (1994): "Better Than Rational: Evolutionary Psychology and the Invisible Hand," in *American Economic Review (Papers and Proceedings):* 84, 327–32.

Cox, Helmut, Uwe Jens and Kurt Markert (eds.) (1981): *Handbuch des Wettbewerbs*. München: Vahlen.

D'Andrade, Roy (1995): *The Development of Cognitive Anthropology*. Cambridge: Cambridge University Press.

Darwin, Charles (1859): *The Origin of Species by Means of Natural Selection*. London: Watts.

Darwin, Charles (1875/1972): *The Variation of Animals and Plants Under Domestication*. 2nd ed. New York: AMS Press.

David, Paul (1985): "Clio and the Economics of QWERTY," in *American Economic Review:* 75, 332–7.

David, Paul (1994): "Why Are Institutions the 'Carriers of History'?: Path Dependence and the Evolution of Conventions, Organizations and Institutions," in *Structural Change and Economic Dynamics:* 5, 205–20.

David, Paul (1997). "Path Dependence and the Quest for Historical Economics: One More Chorus of the Ballad of QWERTY," in *University of Oxford, Discussion Papers in Economic and Social History:* 20.

Davis, John (1992): *Exchange*. Buckingham: Open University Press.

Dawes, Robyn M., Alphons, J. C. van de Kragt, and John M. Orbell (1988): "Not Me or Thee, But We: The Importance of Group Identity in Eliciting Cooperation in Dilemma Situations – Experimental Manipulations," in *Acta Psychologica:* 68, 83–97.

Day, Richard H. (1998): "Bounded Rationality and Firm Performance in the Experimental Economy," in Gunnar Eliasson, Christopher Green and Charles McCann, Jr. (eds.): *Microfoundations of Economic Growth*, pp. 119–30. Ann Arbor: The University of Michigan Press.

De Alessi, Louis (1980): "The Economics of Property Rights: A Review of the Evidence," in *Research in Law and Economics:* 2, 1–47.

De Alessi, Louis (1990): "Development of the Property Rights Approach," in *Journal of Institutional and Theoretical Economics:* 146, 6–11, 19–23.

Delhaes, Karl von and Ulrich Fehl (1997): *Dimensionen des Wettbewerbs*. Stuttgart: Lucius & Lucius.

Demsetz, Harold (1964): "The Exchange and Enforcement of Property Rights," in *Journal of Law and Economics:* 7, 11–26.

Demsetz, Harold (1967): "Towards a Theory of Property Rights," in *American Economic Review:* 57, 347–59.

Demsetz, Harold (1969): "Information and Efficiency: Another Viewpoint," in *Journal of Law and Economics:* 12, 1–22.

Demsetz, Harold (1989): *Efficiency, Competition, and Policy. The Organization of Economic Activity*, vol. II. Oxford: Basil Blackwell.

Demsetz, Harold (1998): "Dogs and Tails in the Economic Development Story," paper presented at the Second Annual Conference of the International Society for the New Institutional Economics, Paris, September 1998.

Dennis, Ken (ed.) (1998): *Rationality in Economics: Alternative Perspectives*. Boston,Dordrecht,London: Kluwer.

Denzau, Arthur and Douglass C. North (1994): "Shared Mental Models: Ideologies and Institutions," in *Kyklos:* 47, 3–31.

Diermeier, Daniel, Joel M. Ericson, Timothy Freye, and Steven Lewis (1997): "Credible Commitment and Property Rights: The Role of Strategic Interaction Between Political and Economic Actors," in Weimer, David L. (ed.), *The Political Economy of Property Rights*, pp. 20–42. Cambridge: Cambridge University Press.

Dietl, Helmut (1993): *Institutionen und Zeit*. Tübingen: J. C. B. Mohr (Paul Siebeck).

References

DiLorenzo, Thomas (1988): "Property Rights, Information Costs and the Economics of Rent Seeking," in *Journal of Institutional and Theoretical Economics:* 144, 318–32.

DiMaggio, Paul (1997): "Culture and Cognition," in *Annual Review of Sociology:* 23, 263–87.

DiMaggio, Paul (1998): "The New Institutionalisms: Avenues of Collaboration," in *Journal of Institutional and Theoretical Economics:* 154, 696–705.

DiMaggio, Paul and Walter Powell (1991): "Introduction," in Walter Powell and Paul DiMaggio (eds.): *The New Institutionalism in Organizational Analysis,* pp. 1–38. Chicago and London: University of Chicago Press.

Dolan, Edwin (ed.) (1976): *The Foundations of Modern Austrian Economics.* Kansas City: Sheed and Ward.

Donald, Merlin (1991): *Origins of the Modern Mind. Three Stages in the Evolution of Culture and Cognition.* Cambridge, Mass.: Harvard University Press.

Dopfer, Kurt and Karl- F. Raible (eds.) (1990): *The Evolution of Economic Systems. Essays in Honour of Ota Sik.* London: MacMillan.

Dosi, Giovanni (1982): "Technological Paradigms and Technological Trajectories: A Suggested Interpretation of the Determinants and Directives of Technological Change," in *Researcch Policy:* 11, 147–62.

Dosi, Giovanni (1988): "Sources, Procedures and Microeconomic Effects of Innovation," in *Journal of Economic Literature:* 26, 1120–71.

Dosi, Giovanni, Christopher Freeman, Richard Nelson, Gerald Silverberg, and Luc Soete (eds.) (1988): *Technical Change and Economic Theory.* London: Pinter.

Dosi, Giovanni and Richard R. Nelson (1994): "An Introduction to Evolutionary Theories in Economics," in *Journal of Evolutionary Economics:* 4, 153–72.

Dosi, Giovanni and Luigi Marengo (1994): "Some Elements of an Evolutionary Theory of Organizational Competences," in Richard W. England (ed.), *Evolutionary Concepts in Contemporary Economics,* pp. 157–78. Ann Arbor: University of Michigan Press.

Douglas, Mary (1986): *How Institutions Think.* Syracuse, New York: Syracuse University Press.

Downie, Jack (1955): *The Competitive Process.* London: Duckworth.

Drobak, John N. (1998): "A Cognitive Science Perspective on Legal Incentives," paper presented at the Second Annual Conference of the International Society for the New Institutional Economics, Paris, September 1998.

Durham, W. H. (1991). *Coevolution: Genes, Culture, and Human Diversity.* Stanford: Stanford University Press.

Durkheim, Emile (1893/1996): *De la Division du Travail Social.* 4th ed. Paris: Quadrige/Presses Universitaires de France.

Dworkin, Ronald (1977): *Taking Rights Seriously.* Cambridge, Mass.: Harvard University Press.

Easton, Stephen T. and Michael A. Walker (1997): "Income, Growth, and Economic Freedom," in *American Economic Review (Papers and Proceedings):* 87, 328–32.

Eckensberger, Lutz H. and Heiko, Breit (1997): "Recht und Moral im Kontext von Kohlbergs Theorie der Entwicklung moralischer Urteile und ihrer handlungstheoretischern Rekonstruktion," in Ernst-Joachim Lampe (ed.), *Zur Entwicklung von Rechtsbewußtsein*, pp. 253–340. Frankfurt am Main: Suhrkamp.

Edgeworth, Francis Y. (1881): *Mathematical Psychics*. London: Kegan Paul.

Edquist, Charles (ed.) (1997): *Systems of Innovaton. Technologies, Institutions and Organizations*. London and Washington, D.C.: Pinter.

Eggertsson, Thráinn (1990): *Economic Behavior and Institutions*. Cambridge: Cambridge University Press.

Eggertsson, Thráinn (1999): "Norms in Economics – With Special Reference to Economic Development," unpublished paper, Max-Planck-Institute for Research into Economic Systems, Jena.

Eichenberger, Reiner and Bruno Frey (1993): " 'Superrationalität' oder: Vom rationalen Umgang mit dem Irrationalen," in *Jahrbuch für Neue Politische Ökonomie:* 12, 50–84.

Eickhof, Norbert (1984): "Zur Erhaltung und Förderung des Wetbewerbs," in Albert Hans (ed.), *Ökonomisches Denken und soziale Ordnung*, pp. 225–44. Tübingen: J. C. B. Mohr (Paul Siebeck).

Eickhof, Norbert (1990): "Wettbewrb, Wettbewerbsfreiheit und Wettbewerbsbeschränkungen," in *Hamburger Jahrbuch für Wirtschafts- und Gesellschaftspolitik:* 35, 225–38.

Eickhof, Norbert (1992): "Marktstruktur und Wettbewerbsprozeß," in *Ordo:* 43, 173–92.

Ekeh, Peter P. (1974): *Social Exchange Theory: The Two Traditions*. London: Heinemann.

Elias, Norbert (1939/1995): *Über den Prozeß der Zivilisation*, vol. 2. 19th ed. Frankfurt am Main: Suhrkamp.

Eliasson, Gunnar (1984): "Microheterogeneity of Firms and the Stability of Industrial Growth," in *Journal of Economic Behavior and Organization:* 5, 249–74.

Eliasson, Gunnar (1990): "The Firm as a Competent Team," in *Journal of Economic Behavior and Organization:* 13, 275–98.

Eliasson, Gunnar (1991): "Deregulation, Innovative Entry and Structural Diversity as a Source of Stable and Rapid Economic Growth," in *Journal of Evolutionary Economics:* 1, 49–63.

Eliasson, Gunnar (1994): "The Theory of the Firm and the Theory of Economic Growth," in Lars Magnusson (ed.) (1994), pp.173–201.

Eliasson, Gunnar, Christopher Green, and Charles R. McCann, Jr. (eds.) (1998): *Microfoundations of Economic Growth*. Ann Arbor: University of Michigan Press.

Ellickson, Robert C. (1991): *Order Without Law*. Cambridge, Mass: Harvard University Press.

Ellickson, Robert C. (1998): "Law and Economics Discovers Social Norms," in *Journal of Legal Studies*, 27, 537–52.

Elster, Jon (1979/1984): *Ulysses and the Sirens. Studies in Rationality and Irrationality.* rev. ed., Cambridge: Cambridge University Press.

Elster, Jon (1983): *Explaining Technical Change*. Cambridge: Cambridge University Press.

Elster, Jon (ed.) (1986): *The Multiple Self*. Cambridge: Cambridge University Press.

Elster, Jon (1989a): *The Cement of Society. A Study of Social Order.* Cambridge: Cambridge University Press.

Elster, Jon (1989b): "Social Norms and Economic Theory," in *Journal of Economic Perspectives:* 3, 99–117.

Emerson, Richard M. (1969): "Operant Psychology and Exchange Theory," in R. L. Burgess and D. Bushell, (eds.): *Behavioral Sociology,* pp. 379–405. New York: Columbia University Press.

England, Richard W. (ed.) (1994): *Evolutionary Concepts in Contemporary Economics.* Ann Arbor: University of Michigan Press.

Ensminger, Jean (1997): "Changing Property Rights: Reconciling Formal and Informal Rights to Land in Africa," in John N. Drobak and John V. C. Nye (eds.): *The Frontiers of the New Institutional Economics,* pp. 165–96. San Diego. Academic Press.

Ensminger, Jean (1998): "Anthropology and the New Institutionalism," in *Journal of Institutional and Theoretical Economics:* 154, 774–89.

Ensminger, Jean and Jack, Knight (1997): "Changing Social Norms," in *Current Anthropology:* 38, 1–24.

Epstein, Richard A. (1996): "Norms: Social and Legal," in *The Good Society:* 6, 1–7.

Etzioni, Amitai (1987): "On Thoughtless Rationality (Rules-of-Thumb)," in *Kyklos:* 40, 496–514.

Eucken, Walter (1939/1992): *The Foundations of Economics.* Berlin, Heidelberg, New York, Tokyo: Springer.

Eucken, Walter (1952/1990): *Grundsätze der Wirtschaftspolitik.* 6th ed. Tübingen: J. C. B. Mohr (Paul Siebeck).

Evans-Pritchard, E. E. (1940): *The Nuer: A Description of the Modes of Livelihood and Political Iinstitutions of a Nilotic People.* Oxford: Clarendon Press.

Faber, Malte and John L. R. Proops (1991): "Evolution in Biology, Physics and Economics: A Conceptual Analysis," in Paolo Saviotti and Stanley Metcalfe (eds*.*). *Evolutionary Theories of Economic and Technological Change,* pp. 58–87. Reading: Harwood Academic Publishers.

Fedderke, Johannes and Robert Klitgaard (1998): "Economic Growth and Social Indicators: An Exploratory Analysis," in *Economic Development and Cultural Change.* vol. 46, 455–89.

Fehl, Ulrich (1980): "Wettbewerbsprozesse in walrasianischer Perspektive," unpublished manuscript of a Habilitation – Thesis, University of Marburg.

Fehl, Ulrich (1983): "Die Theorie dissipativer Strukturen als Ansatzpunkt für die Analyse von Innovationsproblemen in alternativen Wirtschaftsordnungen," in Alfred Schüler, Helmut Leipold, and Hannelore Hamel (eds.): *Innovationsprobleme in Ost und West,* pp. 65–89. Stuttgart: Gustav Fischer.

Fehl, Ulrich (1985): "Das Konzept der Contestable Markets und der Marktprozeß," in Gottfried Bombach, Bernhard Gahlen and Alfted E. Ott (eds.): *Industrieökonomik: Theorie und Empirie,* pp. 29–52. Tübingen: J. C. B. Mohr (Paul Siebeck).

Fehl, Ulrich (1986): "Spontaneous Order and the Subjectivity of Expectations: A Contribution to the Lachmann–O' Driscoll Problem," in Israel Kirzner (ed.), *Subjectivity, Intelligibility and Economic Understanding, Essays in Honor of*

Ludwig M. Lachmann on his Eightieth Birthday, pp. 72–86. London: Macmillan.

Fehl, Ulrich (1987): "Unternehmertheorie, Unternehmertypen und Marktanalyse," in Manfred Borchert, Ulrich Fehl and Peter Oberender (eds.): *Markt und Wettbewerb, Festschrift für Ernst Heuß zum 65. Geburtstag*, pp. 17–37. Bern und Stuttgart: Haupt.

Fehl, Ulrich and Carsten Schreiter (1993): "Neuere Entwicklungen in der Preistheorie," in *Wirtschaftswissenschaftliches Studium: 22*, 276–85.

Fehl, Ulrich and Peter Oberender (1994): *Grundlagen der Mikroökonomie*. 6th ed. München: Vahlen.

Ferguson, Adam (1767/1966): *An Essay on the History of Civil Society*. Edinburgh: Edinburgh University Press.

Festinger, Leon (1957): *A Theory of Cognitive Dissonance*. Stanford: Stanford University Press.

Field, Alexander James (1981): "The Problem with Neoclassical Institutional Economics: A Critique with Special Reference to the North/Thomas Model of Pre-1500 Europe," in *Explorations in Economic History: 18*, 174–98.

Finer, Samuel E. (1974): "State-Building, State Boundaries and Border Control," in *Social Science Information: 13*, 79–126.

Foss, Nicolai J. (1993): "Theories of the Firm: Contractual and Competence Perspectives," in *Journal of Evolutionary Economics: 3*, 127–44.

Foss, Nicolai J. (1994): *The Austrian School and Modern Economics: Essays in Reassessment*. Copenhagen: Handelshojskolens Forhag.

Foster, John (1998): "Competition, Competitive Selection and Economic Evolution," *Papers on Economics and Evolution #9801*, Max-Planck-Institute for Research into Economic Systems.

Frank, Robert (1988): *Passions within Reason. The Strategic Role of the Emotions*. New York and London: W. W. Norton.

Frankfurt, Harry G. (1971): "Freedom of the Will and the Concept of a Person," in *Journal of Philosophy: 68*, 5–20.

Frey, Bruno and Iris Bohnet (1995): "Institutions Affect Fairness: Experimental Investigations," in *Journal of Institutional and Theoretical Economics: 151*, 286–303.

Frey, Bruno S. and Reiner Eichenberger (1989): "Anomalies and Institutions," in *Journal of Institutional and Theoretical Economics: 145*, 423–37.

Frowen, Stephen F. (1990): *Unknowledge and Choice in Economics. Proceedings of a Conference in Honour of G. L. S. Shackle*. London: Macmillan.

Frydman, Roman (1982): "Towards an Understanding of Market Process: Individual Expectations, Learning and Convergence to Rational Expectations Equilibrium," in *American Economic Review: 72*, 652–68.

Furubotn, Eirik G. and Svetozar Pejovich (1972): "Property Rights and Economic Theory: A Survey of Recent Literature," in *Journal of Economic Literature: 10*, 1137–62.

Furubotn, Eirik G. and Rudolf Richter (1997): *Institutions and Economic Theory: An Introduction to and Assessment of the New Institutional Economics*. Ann Arbor: University of Michigan Press.

References

Gächter, Simon and Ernst Fehr (1999): "Collective Action as a Social Exchange," in *Journal of Economic Behavior and Organization*: 39, 341–69.

Gäfgen, Gerhard (1983): "Institutioneller Wandel und ökonomische Erklärung," in *Jahrbuch für Neue Politische Ökonomie*: 2, 19–49.

Galanter, Marc (1981): "Justice in Many Rooms: Courts, Private Ordering, and Indigenenous Law," in *Journal of Legal Pluralism*: 19, 1–47.

Gardner, H. (1985): *The Mind's New Sciences*. New York: W. W. Norton.

Garibaldi-Fernandez, Jose Alberto (1998): "Legal Traditions, Formal Enforcement and Rationality," paper presented at the Second Annual Conference of the International Society for the New Institutional Economics, Paris, September 1998.

Garrison, Roger W. (1982): "Austrian Economics as the Middle Ground: Comment on Loasby," in Israel Kirzner (ed.), 1982, pp. 131–8.

Gauthier, David (1986): *Morals by Agreement*. Oxford: Clarendon Press.

Gehlen, Arnold (1961): *Anthropologische Forschung*. Reinbek bei Hamburg: Rowohlt.

Gehlen, Arnold (1962): *Der Mensch*. 7th ed., Frankfurt a.M.: Athenäum Verlag.

Gehlen, Arnold (1973): *Moral und Hypermoral – Eine pluralistische Ethik*. Frankfurt a.M.: Athenäum Verlag.

Gigerenzer, Gerd and Peter M. Todd (1999): "Fast and Frugal Heuristics: The Adaptive Toolbox," in Gerd Gigerenzer, Peter M. Todd, and the ABC Research Group (1999), pp. 3–34.

Gigerenzer, Gerd, Peter M. Todd, and the ABC Research Group (1999): *Simple Heuristics that Make Us Smart*. Oxford: Oxford University Press.

Goffman, Erwing (1974): *Frame Analysis. An Essay on the Organization of Experience*. Cambridge, Mass.: Harvard University Press.

Goldthorpe, John H. (1998): "Rational Action Theory for Sociology," in *British Journal of Sociology*, 49, 167–92.

Goody, Jack (1998): "Literacy and the Diffusion of Knowledge Across Cultures and Times," in Borba Navaretti, Giorgio, Partha Dasgupta, Karl-Göran Mäler, and Domenico Siniscalo (eds.): *Creation and Transfer of Knowledge*, pp. 167–77. Berlin, Heidelberg, New York, Tokyo: Springer.

Görgens, Egon (1969): *Wettbewerb und Wirtschaftswachstum*. Freiburg: Rombach.

Görgens, Egon (1983): *Entwicklungshilfe und Ordnungspolitik*. Bern und Stuttgart: Haupt.

Granovetter, Marc (1985): "Economic Action and Social Structure: The Problem of Embeddedness," in *American Journal of Sociology*: 91, 481–500.

Gray, Cheryl W. (1997): "Comment on 'The Rule of State Law and the Rule-of-Law State: Economic Analysis of the Legal Foundations of Development,' by Robert D. Cooter," in *Annual World Bank Conference on Development Economics 1996*, pp. 218–21. Washington D. C.: World Bank.

Green, Leslie (1990): *The Authority of the State*. Oxford: Clarendon Press.

Greif, Avner (1994): "Cultural Beliefs and the Organization of Society: A Historical and Theoretical Reflection on Collectivist and Individualist Societies," in *Journal of Political Economy*: 102, 912–50.

Greif, Avner (1997a): "On the Interrelations and Economic Implications of Economic, Social, Political, and Normative Factors: Reflections from Two Late Medieval Societies," in John N. Drobak and John V. C. Nye (eds.): *The Frontiers of the New Institutional Economics*, pp. 57–94. San Diego: Academic Press.

Greif, Avner (1997b): "Contracting, Enforcement, and Efficiency: Economics beyond the Law," in *Annual World Bank Conference on Development Economics 1996*, pp. 239–65. Washington, D.C.: World Bank.

Greif, Avner, Paul Milgrom and Barry Weingast (1994): "Coordination, Commitment and Enforcement: The Case of the Merchant Guild," in *Journal of Political Economy*, 102, 745–76.

Griffiths, John (1984): "The Division of Labor in Social Control," in Donald Black (ed.), *Toward a General Theory of Social Control*, vol. 1, pp. 37–70. Orlando and New York: Academic Press.

Grossekettler, Heinz (1989a): "Marktprozesse als Gegenstand theoriegeleiteter empirischer Analysen: Ein Forschungsbericht," in Bernhard Gahlen, Bernd Meyer, and John Schumann (eds.): *Wirtschaftswachstum, Strukturwandel und dynamischer Wettbewerb. Ernst Helmstädter zum 65. Geburtstag*, pp. 321–57. Berlin: Springer.

Grossekettler, Heinz (1989b): "On Designing an Economic Order. The Contributions of the Freiburg School," in Donald A. Walker (ed.), *Twentieth-Century Economic Thought*, vol. 2, pp. 38–84. Aldershot: Edward Elgar.

Grossman, Gene M. and Elhanan Helpman (1991): *Innovation and Growth in the Global Economy*. Cambridge, Mass.: MIT Press.

Grossman, Gene M. and Elhanan, Helpman (1994): "Endogenous Innovation in the Theory of Growth," in *Journal of Economic Perspectives*: 8, 23–44.

Grossman, Herschel I. (2000): "The State: Agent or Proprietor?" in *Economics of Governance*: 1, 3–11.

Grossman, Sanford J. (1976): "On the Efficiency of Competitive Stock Markets Where Traders Have Diverse Information," in *Journal of Finance*: 31, 573–85.

Grossman, Sanford J. (1981): "An Introduction to the Theory of Rational Expectations Under Asymmetric Information," in *Review of Economic Studies*: 48, 541–59.

Grossman, Sanford J. and Joseph E. Stiglitz (1976): "Information and Competitive Price Systems," in *American Economic Review*: 66, 246–53.

Grossman, Sanford J. and Joseph E. Stiglitz (1980): "On the Impossibility of Informationally Efficient Markets," in *American Economic Review*: 70, 393–408.

Güth, Werner and Hartmut Kliemt (1994): "Competition or Co-operation: On the Evolutionary Economics of Trust, Exploitation and Moral Attitudes," in *Metroeconomica*: 45, 155–87.

Guthrie, William K. C. (1981): *A History of Greek Philosophy, vol. VI: Aristotle: an Encounter*. Cambridge: Cambridge University Press.

Gwartney, James, and Robert Lawson (1997): *Economic Freedom of the World. 1997 Annual Report*. Vancouver: The Fraser Institute.

Gwartney, James, and Robert Lawson (1998): *Economic Freedom of the World. 1998/1999 Interim Report*. Vancouver: The Fraser Institute.

References

Gwartney, James, Robert Lawson, and Walter Block (1996): *Economic Freedom of the World: 1975–1995*. Vancouver: The Fraser Institute.

Gwartney, James, Robert Lawson, and Randall Holcombe (1999): "Economic Freedom and the Environment for Economic Growth," in *Journal of Institutional and Theoretical Economics*: 155, 643–63.

Haber, Stefan and Armando Razo (1998): "Political Instability and Economic Performance. Evidence from Revolutionary Mexico," in *World Politics*: 51, 99–143.

Hall, Peter A. and Rosemary C. R. Taylor (1998): "Political Science and the Three New Institutionalisms," in Karol Soltan, Eric M. Uslaner, and Virginia Haufler (eds.): *Institutions and Social Order*, pp. 15–43. Ann Arbor: University of Michigan Press.

Hall, Robert E. and Charles I. Jones (1997): "Levels of Economic Activity Across Countries," in *American Economic Review (Papers and Proceedings)*: 87, 173–77.

Hall, Robert E. and Charles I. Jones (1999): "Why Do Some Countries Produce So Much More Output Per Worker Than Others?" in *Quarterly Journal of Economics*: 114, 83–116.

Hardin, Garrett (1968): "The Tragedy of the Commons," in *Science*: 162, 1243–8.

Harper, David (1994): "A New Approach to Modeling Endogenous Learning Processes in Economic Theory," in *Advances in Austrian Economics*: 1, 49–79.

Harper, David (1996): *Entrepreneurship and the Market Process*. London and New York: Routledge.

Hart, H. L. A. (1961/1994): *The Concept of Law*. 2nd ed. Oxford: Clarendon Press.

Hart, H. L. A. (1963): *Law, Liberty and Morality*. Stanford: Stanford University Press.

Hawkes, Kristen (1993): "Why Hunter-Gatherers Work: An Ancient Version of the Problem of Public Goods," in *Current Anthropology*: 34, 341–61.

Hayek, Friedrich A. (1937/1948): "Economics and Knowledge," in *Economica*: IV, 33–54, reprinted in Hayek (1948), pp. 33–56.

Hayek, Friedrich A. von (1948): *Individualism and Economic Order*. Chicago: Chicago University Press.

Hayek, Friedrich A. von (1952): *The Sensory Order. An Inquiry into the Foundations of Theoretical Psychology*. London: Routledge & Kegan Paul.

Hayek, Friedrich A. von (1952/1979): *The Counter-Revolution of Science. Studies on the Abuse of Reason*. 2nd ed. Indianapolis: Liberty Press.

Hayek, Friedrich A. von (1960): *The Constitution of Liberty*. London: Routledge & Kegan Paul.

Hayek, Friedrich A. von (1967): *Studies in Philosophy, Politics and Economics*. London: Routledge & Kegan Paul.

Hayek, Friedrich A. von (1973/1982): *Rules and Order*, vol. I of *Law, Legislation and Liberty*. London: Routledge & Kegan Paul.

Hayek, Friedrich A. von (1976/1982): *The Mirage of Social Justice*, vol. II of *Law, Legislation and Liberty*. London: Routledge & Kegan Paul.

Hayek, Friedrich A. von (1978): *Denationalization of Money.* 2nd ed., London: Institute of Economic Affairs.

Hayek, Friedrich A. von (1979/1982): *The Political Order of a Free People,* vol. 3 of *Law, Legislation and Liberty.* London: Routledge & Kegan Paul.

Hayek, Friedrich A. von (1988): *The Fatal Conceit. The Errors of Socialism.* London: Routledge & Kegan Paul.

Heap, Shaun Hargreaves, Martin Hollis, Bruce Lyons, Robert Sugden, and Albert Weale (1992): *The Theory of Choice. A Critical Guide.* Oxford and Cambridge, Mass.: Basil Blackwell.

Heath, Eugene (1992): "Rules, Function and the Invisible Hand: An Interpretation of Hayek's Social Theory," in *Philosophy of the Social Sciences:* 22, 28–45.

Heiner, Ronald A. (1983): "The Origin of Predictable Behavior," in *American Economic Review.* 73, 560–95.

Heiner, Ronald A. (1990): "Imperfect Choice and the Origin of Institutional Rules," in *Journal of Institutional and Theoretical Economics:* 146, 720–6.

Helmstädter, Ernst (1989): "Was ist dynamischer Wettbewerb?" in Clemens-August Andreae, Jochen Kirchhof, and Gert Pfeiffer (eds.): *Wettbewerb als Herausforderung und Chance. Festschrift für Werner Benisch,* pp. 17–26. Köln, Berlin, Bonn, München: Carl Heymanns.

Helmstädter, Ernst (1990): "Marktstruktur und dynamischer Wettbewerb. Theoretische Grundlagen der Schumpeter – Hypothesen," in Bernhard Gahlen (ed.), *Marktstruktur und gesamtwirtschaftliche Entwicklung,* pp. 159–74. Berlin, Heidelberg, New York, Tokyo: Springer.

Hensel, Paul (1978): *Grundformen der Wirtschaftsordnung. Marktwirtschaft – Zentralverwaltungswirtschaft.* 3rd ed. München: Beck.

Herdzina, Klaus (1985): "Marktentwicklung und Wettbewerbsverhalten," in Gottfried Bombach, Bernhard Gahlen, and Alfred E. Ott (eds.): *Industrieökonomik. Theorie und Empirie,* pp. 105–20. Tübingen: J. C. B. Mohr (Paul Siebeck).

Herdzina, Klaus (1988): *Möglichkeiten und Grenzen einer wirtschaftstheoretischen Fundierung der Wettbewerbspoltik.* Tübingen: J. C. B. Mohr (Paul Siebeck).

Herdzina, Klaus (1990): "Marktstruktur und dynamischer Wettbewerb – Theoretische Grundlagen der Schumpeter – Hypothesen," in Bernhard Gahlen (ed.): *Marktstruktur und gesamtwirtschaftliche Entwicklung,* pp. 175–80. Berlin, Heidelberg, New York, Tokyo: Springer.

Herdzina, Klaus (1993): *Wettbewerbspolitik.* 4th ed. Stuttgart: Gustav Fischer.

Hesse, Günter (1987): "Innovationen und Restriktionen. Zum Ansatz der Theorie der langfristigen wirtschaftlichen Entwicklung," in Manfred Borchert, Ulrich Fehl, and Peter Oberender (eds.): *Markt und Wettbewerb. Festschrift für Ernst Heuß zum 65. Geburtstag,* pp. 195–226. Bern and Stuttgart: Paul Haupt.

Hesse, Günter (1990): "Evolutorische Ökonomik oder Kreativität in der Theorie," in Ulrich Witt (ed.): *Studien zur Evolutorischen Ökonomik I,* pp. 49–73. Berlin Duncker & Humblot.

Hesse, Günter (1992a): "A New Theory of Modern Economic Growth," in Witt (ed.) (1992b), pp. 81–103.

Hesse, Günter (1992b): "Land Use Systems and Property Rights," in *Journal of Evolutionary Economics:* 2, 195–210.

Hesse, Günter (1996): *Von der Geschichtsphilosophie zur evolutorischen Ökonomik.* Baden-Baden: Nomos Verlagsgesellschaft.

Heuss, Ernst (1965): *Allgemeine Markttheorie.* Tübingen and Zürrich: J. C. B. Mohr (Paul Siebeck).

Heuss, Ernst (1967): "Zum heutigen Stand der Wettbewerbstheorie in Deutschland," in *Ordo:* 18, 411–16.

Heuss, Ernst (1968): "Die Wettbewerbs- und Wachstumsproblematik des Oligopols," in H. K. Schneider (ed.): *Grundlagen der Wettbewerbspolitik,* pp. 50–70. Berlin: Duncker & Humblot.

Heuss, Ernst (1980): "Wettbewerb," in *Handwörterbuch der Wirtschaftswissenschaften:* 8, 679–97.

Heuss, Ernst (1983): "Methodische Bemerkungen zur Preis- und Wettbewerbstheorie," in Harald Enke, Walter Köhler, and Wilfried Schulz (eds.): *Struktur und Dynamik der Wirtschaft–Beiträge zum 60. Geburtstag von Karl Brandt,* pp. 61–74. Freiburg i. Br.: Rombach.

High, Jack (1990): *Maximizing, Action, and Market Adjustment.* München, Hamden, and Wien: Philosophia Verlag.

Hirshleifer, Jack (1982): "Evolutionary Models in Economics and Law," in R. O. Zerbe, Jr. (ed.): *Research in Law and Economics:* 4, pp. 1–60. Greenwich CT: JAI Press.

Hirshleifer, Jack (1984): *Price Theory and Application,* 3rd ed. Englwood Cliffs, N.J.: Prentice-Hall.

Hobbes, Thomas (1651/1991): *Leviathan.* Richard Tuck (ed.). Cambridge: Cambridge University Press.

Hodgson, Geoffrey M. (1988): *Economics and Institutions. A Manifesto for a Modern Institutional Economics.* Cambridge: Polity Press.

Hodgson, Geoffrey M. (1991): "Hayek's Theory of Cultural Evolution: An Evaluation in the Light of Vanberg's Critique," in *Economics and Philosophy:* 7, 67–82.

Hodgson, Geoffrey M. (1993): *Economics and Evolution. Bringing Life Back into Economics.* Cambridge: Polity Press.

Hodgson, Geoffrey M. (1997): "The Ubiquity of Habits and Rules," in *Cambridge Journal of Economics:* 21, 663–84.

Hodgson, Geoffrey M. (1998): "The Approach of Institutional Economics," in *Journal of Economic Literature:* 36, 166–92.

Hoffman, Elisabeth, Kevin A. McCabe, and Vernon L. Smith (1998): "Behavioral Foundation of Reciprocity: Experimental Economics and Evolutionary Psychology," in *Economic Inquiry:* 36, 335–52.

Hogarth, Robin M. and Melvin W. Reder (eds.) (1987): *Rational Choice.* Chicago: University of Chicago Press.

Holland, John H. (1986): "Escaping Brittleness: The Possibilities of General Purpose Machine Learning Algorithms Applied to Parallel Rule-Based Systems," in R. S. Michalski, J. G. Carbonell, and T. M. Mitchell (eds.): *Machine Learning: An Artificial Intelligence Approach,* vol. 2, pp. 593–623. Los Altos, Calif.: Morgan Kaufmann.

Holland, John H., Keith J. Holyoak, Richard Nisbett, and Paul R. Thagard, (1986): *Induction: Processes of Inference, Learning and Discovery.* Cambridge, Mass.: MIT Press.

Holyoak, Keith J. and Paul R. Thagard (1989): "A Computational Model of Analogical Problem Solving," in Stella Vosniadou and Andrew, Ortony (eds.): *Similarity and Analogical Reasoning,* pp. 242–66. Cambridge: Cambridge University Press.

Homans, George C. (1961): *Social Behavior: Its Elementary Forms.* New York: Harcourt Brace Jovanovic.

Hoppmann, Erich (1966): "Von der Preistheorie zur Wettbewerbstheorie," in *Ordo:* 17, pp. 369–81.

Hoppmann, Erich (1967): "Wettbewerb als Norm der Wettbewerbspolitik," in *Ordo:* 18, pp. 77–94.

Hoppman, Erich (1976): "Preisunelastizität der Nachfrage als Quelle von Marktbeherrschung," in Helmut Gutzler, Wolfgang Herion, and Joseph H. Kaiser (eds.): *Wettbewerb im Wandel. Festschrift für Eberhard Günther,* pp. 283–306. Baden-Baden: Nomos Verlagsgesellschaft.

Hoppmann, Erich (1977): *Marktmacht und Wettbewerb – Beurteilungskriterien und Lösungsmöglichkeiten.* Tübingen: J. C. B. Mohr (Paul Siebeck).

Hoppmann, Erich (1988): *Wirtschaftsordnung und Wettbewerb.* Baden-Baden: Nomos Verlagsgesellschaft.

Hume, David (1740/1978): *A Treatise of Human Nature.* Oxford: Oxford University Press.

Hume, David (1748/1975): *An Enquiry Concerning Human Understanding.* Oxford: Oxford University Press.

Hume, David (1751/1975): *An Enquiry Concerning the Principles of Morals.* Oxford: Oxford University Press.

Hume, David (1777/1907): *Essays. Moral, Political, and Literary,* vol. I, T. H. Green and T. H. Grose (eds.). London: Longmans, Green.

Hutchins, Edwin (1995): *Cognition in the Wild.* Cambridge, Mass.: MIT Press.

Hutchins, Edwin and Brian Hazlehurt (1992): "Learning in the Culture Process," in Chrisopher G. Langdon, Charles Taylor, J. Doyne Farmer and Steen Rasmussen (eds.): *Artificial Life II,* pp. 689–706. Redwood City, Calif.: Addison-Wesley.

Irrgang, Bernhard (1993): *Lehrbuch der Evolutionären Erkenntnistheorie.* München and Basel: E. Reinhardt.

Jasay de, Anthony (1995): "Conventions: Some Thoughts on the Economics of Ordered Anarchy," in *Lectiones Jenenses, Max-Planck-Institute for Research into Economic Systems,* vol. 3, Jena.

Jensen, Michael C. and William H. Meckling (1976): "Theory of the Firm: Managerial Behavior, Agency Costs and Ownership Structure," in *Journal of Financial Economics:* 3, 305–60.

Jevons, William Stanley (1871): *Theory of Political Economy.* London: Macmillan.

Johnson, James (1997): "Comment," in *Current Anthropology:* 38, 16–17.

Johnson-Laird, Philip N. (1989): "Mental Models," in Michael Posner (ed.), *Foundations of Cognitive Science,* pp. 469–99. Cambridge, Mass.: MIT Press.

References

Jones, Eric L. (1981): *The European Miracle*. Cambridge: Cambridge University Press.

Jones, Eric L. (1995): "Culture and its Relationship to Economic Change," in *Journal of Institutional and Theoretical Economics:* 151/2, 269–85.

Kagel, J. H., R. C. Battalio, H., Rachlin, and L. Green (1981): "Demand Curves for Animal Consumers," in *Quarterly Journal of Economics:* 96, 1–15.

Kahneman, Daniel and Amos Tversky (1972): "Subjective Probability: A Judgment of Representativeness," in *Cognitive Psychology:* 3, 430–54.

Kahneman, Daniel and Amos, Tversky, (1979): "Prospect Theory: An Analysis of Decision Under Risk," in *Econometrica:* 47, 263–91.

Kahneman, Daniel and Amos, Tversky (1982): "Judgment of and by Representativeness," in Daniel Kahneman, Paul Slovic, and Amos Tversky (eds.): *Judgement Under Uncertainty: Heuristics and Biases,* pp. 84–98. Cambridge: Cambridge University Press.

Kahneman, Daniel and Amos Tversky (1984): "Choices, Values and Frames," in *American Psychologist:* 39, pp. 341–50.

Kahneman, Daniel, Jack L. Knetsch, and Richard H. Thaler (1991): "The Endowment Effect, Loss Aversion and Status Quo Bias," in *Journal of Economic Perspectives:* 5, 193–206.

Kahneman, Daniel and Carol Varey (1991): "Notes on the Psychology of Utility," in Jon Elster and John E. Roemer (eds.): *Interpersonal Comparisons of Well-Being,* pp. 127–63. Cambridge: Cambridge University Press.

Kant, Immanuel (1785/1965): *Grundlegung zur Metaphysik der Sitten.* Hamburg: Felix Meiner Verlag.

Kant, Immanuel (1797/1990): *Kritik der praktischen Vernunft.* Hamburg: Felix Meiner Verlag.

Kantzenbach, Erhard (1967): *Die Funktionsfähigkeit des Wettbewerbs.* 2nd rev. ed. Göttingen: Vandenhoeck & Ruprecht.

Kaufer, Erich (1980): *Industrieökonomik. Eine Einführung in die Wettbewerbstheorie.* München: Vahlen.

Kaufer, Erich (1986): "The Incentives to Innovate under Alternative Property Rights Assignments with Special Reference to the Patent System," in *Journal of Institutional and Theoretical Economics:* 142, 210–26.

Kaufman, Bruce E. (1999): "Emotional Arousal as a Source of Bounded Rationality," in *Journal of Economic Behavior and Organization:* 38, 135–44.

Keefer, Philip and Stefan Knack (1997): "Why Don't Poor Countries Catch Up? A Cross-National Test of an Institutional Exploration," in *Economic Inquiry:* 35, 590–602.

Kerber, Wolfgang (1991): "Evolutionäre Wettbewerbsprozesse über mehrere Wirtschaftsstufen: Das Beispiel 'Industrie-Handel–Konsumenten,'" in *Ordo:* 42, 325–49.

Kerber, Wolfgang (1992): "Innovation, Handlungsrechte und evolutionärer Marktprozeß," in Ulrich Witt (ed.) (1992c), pp. 171–95.

Kerber, Wolfgang (1994): "Evolutorischer Wettbewerb. Zu den theoretischen und institutionellen Grundlagen der Wettbewerbsordnung," unpublished manuscript of Habilitation-Thesis, University of Marburg.

Kerber, Wolfgang (1996): "Recht als Selektionsumgebung für evolutorische Wettbewerbsprozesse," in Birger P. Priddat and Gerhard Wegner (eds.): *Zwischen Evolution und Institution – neue Ansätze in der ökonomischen Theorie*, pp. 301–30. Marburg: Metropolis-Verlag.

Kerber, Wolfgang (1997): "Wettbewerb als Hypothesentest: Eine Evolutorische Konzeption wissenschaffenden Wettbewerbs," in Karl von Delhaes and Ulrich Fehl (1997), pp. 29–78.

Khalil, Elias (1995): "Organizations versus Institutions," in *Journal of Institutional and Theoretical Economics: 151*, 445–66.

Khalil, Elias L. and Kenneth E. Boulding (eds.) (1996): *Evolution, Order and Complexity*. London and New York: Routledge.

Kiernan, Brendan and Francis X. Bell (1997): "Legislative Politics and the Political Economy of Property Rights in Post-Communist Russia," in David L. Weimer (ed.), *The Political Economy of Property Rights*, pp. 113–38. Cambridge: Cambridge University Press.

Kirchgässner, Gebhard (1991): *Homo Oeconomicus*. Tübingen: J. C. B. Mohr (Paul Siebeck).

Kirzner, Israel (1962): "Rational Action and Economic Theory," in *Journal of Political Economy: 70*, 1962, 380–85.

Kirzner, Israel (1973): *Competition and Entrepreneurship*. Chicago and London: University of Chicago Press.

Kirzner, Israel (1979): *Perception, Opportunity and Profit*. Chicago and London: University of Chicago Press.

Kirzner, Israel (1992): *The Meaning of Market Process*. London and New York: Routledge.

Kirzner, Israel (1997): "Entrepreneurial Discovery and the Competitive Market Process: An Austrian Approach," in *Journal of Economic Literature: 35*, 60–85.

Kirzner, Israel (ed.) (1986): *Subjectivism, Intelligibility and Economic Understanding*. London: Macmillan.

Kiwit, Daniel and Stefan Voigt (1995): "Überlegungen zum institutionellen Wandel unter Berücksichtigung des Verhältnisses interner und externer Institutionen," in *Ordo: 46*, 117–48.

Kliemt, Hartmut (1985): *Moralische Institutionen*. Freiburg and München: Verlag Karl Alber.

Kliemt, Hartmut (1993a): "Constitutional Commitments. On the Economic and Legal Philosophy of Rules," in *Jahrbuch für Neue Politische Ökonomie: 12*, 145–73.

Kliemt, Hartmut (1993b): "Perfect and Workable Rationality: A Comment on Raymond Boudon's Paper," in *International Studies in the Philosophy of Science: 7*, 41–3.

Knack, Stephen and Philip Keefer (1995): "Institutions and Economic Performance: Cross-Country Tests Using Alternative Institutional Measures," in *Economics and Politics: 77*, 207–27.

Knack, Stephen and Philip Keefer (1997): "Does Social Capital Have An Economic Payoff? A Cross-Country Investigation," in *Quarterly Journal of Economics: 112*, 1251–88.

References

Knieps, Günter (1997): "Wettbewerbspolitik," in *Springer's Handbuch der Volkswirtschaftslehre* 2, pp. 40–79. Berlin, Heidelberg, New York, Tokyo: Springer.

Knight, Jack (1992): *Institutions and Social Conflict.* Cambridge: Cambridge University Press.

Knight, Jack (1997): "Social Institutions and Human Cognition: Thinking About Old Questions in New Ways," in *Journal of Institutional and Theoretical Economics:* 153, 692–9.

Knight, Jack (1998). "The Bases of Cooperation: Social Norms and the Rule of Law," in *Journal of Institutional and Theoretical Economics:* 154, 754–63.

Knight, Jack and Douglass North (1997): "Explaining Economic Change: The Interplay Between Cognition and Institutions," in *Legal Theory:* 3, 211–26.

Knight, Jack and Itai Sened (1995): *Explaining Social Institutions.* Ann Arbor: University of Michigan Press.

Knight, Jack and Jean Ensminger (1998): "Conflict Over Changing Social Norms: Bargaining, Ideology and Enforcement," in Mary Brinton and Victor Nee (eds.): *The New Institutionalism in Sociology,* pp. 105–26. New York: Russell Sage Foundation.

Koch, Lambert (1995): "Evolutorische Wirtschaftspolitik. Der prozessual-kommunikative Charakter wirtschaftspolitischer Steuerung," in *Ordo:* 46, 101–15.

Kohlberg, Lawrence (1984): *Essays on Moral Development.* Vol. II: *The Psychology of Moral Development. The Nature and Validity of Moral Stages.* New York: Harper & Row.

Koppl, Roger (1992): "Invisible-Hand Explanations and Neoclassical Economics: Toward a Post Marginalist Economics," in *Journal of Institutional and Theoretical Economics:* 148, 292–313.

Korobkin, B. Russell and Thomas S. Ulen (1999): "Law and Behavioral Science: Removing the Rationality Assumptions from Law and Economics," *Discussion Paper, Max Planck Institute for Research into Economic Systems,* Jena.

Koslowski, Peter (1984/1989): *Evolution und Gesellschaft. Eine Auseinandersetzung mit der Soziobiologie.* 2nd ed., Tübingen: J. C. B. Mohr (Paul Siebeck).

Koslowski, Peter (1990): "The Categorial and Ontological Presuppositions of Austrian and Neoclassical Economics," in Alfred Bosch, Peter Koslowski, and Reinhold Veit (eds.): *General Equilibrium or Market Process,* pp. 1–20. Tübingen: J. C. B. Mohr (Paul Siebeck).

Krueger, Anne O. (1974): "The Political Economy of the Rent-Seeking Society," in *American Economic Review:* 64, 291–303.

Krug, Barbara (1999): "On Custom in Economics: The Case of Humanism and Trade Regimes," in *Journal of Institutional and Theoretical Economics:* 155, 405–28.

Krüsselberg, Hans-Günther (1969): *Marktwirtschaft und ökonomische Theorie.* Freiburg: Rombach.

Krüsselberg, Hans-Günther (1983): "Paradigmenwechsel in der Wettbewerbstheorie?," in Harald Enke, Walter Köhler, and Wilfried Schulz (eds.): *Struktur und Dynamik der Wirtschaft – Beiträge zum 60. Geburtstag von Karl Brandt,* pp. 75–97. Freiburg i. Br.: Rombach.

Kubon-Gilke, Gisela (1996): "Institutional Economics and the Evolutionary Metaphor," in *Journal of Institutional and Theoretical Economics:* 152, 723–38.

Kuhn, Helmut (1962): "Der Mensch in der Entscheidung: Prohairesis in der Nikomachischen Ethik," in: *Das Sein und das Gute,* pp. 275–95. München: Kösel-Verl., first published in Dieter Heinrich, Walter Schulz, and Karl-Heinz Volkmann-Schluck (eds.) (1960): *Die Gegenwart der Griechen im neueren Denken. Festschrift für Hans-Georg Gadamer zum 60. Geburtstag* with the title "Der Begriff der Prohairesis in der Nikomachischen Ethik," pp. 123–40, Tübingen: J.C.B. Mohr (Paul Siebeck).

Kuhn, Thomas (1962/1970): *The Structure of Scientific Revolutions.* 2nd enlarged ed. Chicago: University of Chicago Press.

Kunz, Harald (1985): *Marktsystem und Information.* Tübingen: J. C. B. Mohr (Paul Siebeck).

Lachmann, Ludwig (1943/1977): "The Role of Expectations in Economics as a Social Science," in *Economica:* 10, 13–23, reprinted in Lachmann (1977), pp. 65–80.

Lachmann, Ludwig (1963): "Wirtschaftsordnung und wirtschaftliche Institutionen," in *Ordo:* 14, 63–77.

Lachmann, Ludwig (1976a): "From Mises to Shackle: An Essay on Austrian Economics and the Kaleidic Society," in *Journal of Economic Literature:* 14, 54–62.

Lachmann, Ludwig (1976b): "On the Central Concept of Austrian Economics: Market Process," in Edwin Dolan (ed.) (1976), pp. 126–32.

Lachmann, Ludwig (1977): *Capital, Expectations and the Market Process.* Kansas City: Sheed, Andrews and McMeel.

Lachmann, Ludwig (1986): *The Market as an Economic Process.* Oxford: Blackwell.

Lachmann, Ludwig (1994): *Expectations and the Meaning of Institutions.* Don Lavoie (ed.) London and New York: Routledge.

Lal, Deepak (1998): *Unintended Consequences.* Cambridge, Mass., and London: MIT Press.

Laland, Kevin N., Jochen Kumm, and Marcus W. Feldman (1995): "Gene-Culture Coevolutionary Theory," in *Current Anthropology:* 36, 131–56.

Lampe, Ernst-Joachim (1997): "Zur Entwicklung des Rechtsbewußtseins in der altrömischen Gemeinde," in Ernst-Joachim Lampe (ed.), *Zur Entwicklung von Rechtsbewußtsein,* pp. 182–213. Frankfurt am Main Suhrkamp.

Lancaster, Kelvin (1971): *Consumer Demand. A New Approach.* New York and London: Columbia University Press.

Landa, Janet Tai (1994): *Trust, Ethnicity and Identity.* Ann Arbor: Michigan University Press.

Lane, David, Franco Malerba, Robert Maxfield, and Luigi Orsenigo (1996): "Choice and Action," in *Journal of Evolutionary Economics,* 6, 43–76.

Langlois, Richard N. (1986a): *Economics as a Process. Essays in the New Institutional Economics.* Cambridge: Cambridge University Press.

Langlois, Richard N. (1986b): "Rationality, Institutions, and Explanation," in Langlois (ed.) (1986a), pp. 225–55.

Langlois, Richard N. (1998): "Rule-Following, Expertise, and Rationality: a New Behavioral Economics?" Kenneth Dennis (ed.): *Rationality in Economics: Alternative Perspectives,* Dordrecht, Boston, Lancaster: Kluwer.

Langlois, Richard N. and Metin M. Cosgel (1998): "The Organisation of Consumption," in Marina Bianchi (ed.), *The Active Consumer,* pp. 107–21. London and New York: Routledge.

Langlois, Richard N. and Michael J. Everett (1994): "What is Evolutionary Economics?" in Lars Magnusson (ed.): pp. 11–47.

Langlois, Richard N. and Nicolai J. Foss (1999): "Capabilities and Governance: The Rebirth of Production in the Theory of Economic Organization," in *Kyklos:* 52, 201–18.

Langlois, Richard N. and Paul L. Robertson (1995): *Firms, Markets and Economic Change: A Dynamic Theory of Business Institutions.* London and New York: Routledge.

Langlois, Richard N. and Paul L. Robertson (1996): "Stop Crying Over Spilt Knowledge: A Critical Look at the Theory of Spillovers and Technical Change," paper presented at the MERIT Conference on Innovation, Evolution and Technology, August 25–7, Maastricht, the Netherlands.

La Porta, Rafael, Florencio Lopez-De-Silanes, Andrei Shleifer, and Robert W. Vishny (1997): "Trust in Large Organizations," in *American Economic Review (Papers and Proceedings):* 87, 333–8.

Leblang, David A. (1996): "Property Rights, Democracy and Economic Growth," in *Political Research Quarterly.* 49, 5–26.

Leipold, Helmut (1983): "Der Einfluß der Property Rights auf hierarchische und marktliche Transaktionen in sozialistischen Wirtschaftssystemen," in Alfred Schüller (ed.), *Property Rights und ökonomische Theorie,* pp. 185–217. München: Vahlen.

Leipold, Helmut (1988): *Wirtschafts- und Gesellschaftssysteme im Vergleich.* 5th rev. ed. Stuttgart: Gustav Fischer Verlag.

Lenel, Hans Otto (1975): "Walter Euckens ordnungspolitische Konzeption, die wirtschaftspolitische Lehre in der Bundesrepublik und die Wettbewerbstheorie von heute," in *Ordo:* 26, 22–78.

Lenel, Hans Otto (1988): "Konzentration und Wettbewerb," in *Ordo:* 39, 137–62.

Levi, Margaret (1988): *Of Rule and Revenue.* Berkeley: University of California Press.

Levi, Margaret (1997): "Comment," in *Current Anthropology:* 38, 17–18.

Levine, Ross and David Renelt (1992): "A Sensitivity Analysis of Cross-Country Growth Regressions," in *American Economic Review:* 82, 942–63.

Lewin, Kurt (1936): *Principles of Topological Psychology.* New York: McGraw Hill.

Lewis, David (1969): *Convention. A Philosophical Study.* Oxford: Basil Blackwell.

Lewis, Steven (1997): "Marketization and Government Credibility in Shangai: Federalist and Local Corporatist Explanations," in David L. Weimer (ed.), *The Political Economy of Property Rights,* pp. 259–87. Cambridge: Cambridge University Press.

Lian, Brad and John R. Oneal (1997): "Cultural Diversity and Economic Development: A Cross-National Study of 98 Countries," in *Economic Development and Cultural Change*: 46, 61–77.

Lindenberg, Siegwart (1993): "Framing, Empirical Evidence, and Applications," in *Jahrbuch für Neue Politische Ökonomie*: 12, 11–38.

Lindenberg, Siegwart (1998): "The Cognitive Turn in Institutional Analysis? Beyond NIE and NIS?," in *Journal of Insitutional and Theoretical Economics*: 154, 716–27.

Lipford, Jody and Bruce Yandle (1997): "Exploring the Production of Social Order," in *Constitutional Political Economy*: 8, 37–55.

Littlechild, Stephen C. (1982): "Equilibrium and the Market Process," in Israel Kirzner (ed.), pp. 85–102.

Littlechild, Stephen C. (1986): "Three Types of Market Process," in Richard N. Langlois (ed.) (1986a), pp. 27–39.

Littlechild, Stephen C. (ed.) (1990): *Austrian Economics*, Vol. III. Aldershot: Edward Elgar.

Loasby, Brian J. (1976): *Choice, Complexity, and Ignorance*. Cambridge, Cambridge University Press.

Loasby, Brian J. (1982): "Economics of Dispersed and Incomplete Information," in Kirzner, Israel (ed.) (1982), pp. 111–30.

Loasby, Brian J. (1991): *Equilibrium and Evolution*. Manchester and New York: Manchester University Press.

Loasby, Brian J. (1996): "The Organisation of Industry and the Growth of Knowledge," *Lectiones Jenenses: Max-Plank-Institute for Research into Economic Systems*, Vol. 7, Jena.

Loasby, Brian J. (1998): "Cognition and Innovation," in Marina Bianchi (ed.), *The Active Consumer*, pp. 89–106. London and New York: Routledge.

Loasby, Brian J. (1999): *Knowledge, Institutions and Evolution in Economics*. London and New York: Routledge.

Loasby, Brian J. (2000): "Market, Institutions and Economic Evolution," in *Journal of Evolutionary Economics*: 10, 297–309.

Locke, John (1690/1991): *Two Treatises of Government*. reprint of 2nd ed. Peter Laslett (ed.). Cambridge: Cambridge University Press.

Lorenz, Konrad (1941): "Kants Lehre vom Apriorischen im Lichte gegenwärtiger Biologie," in *Blätter für deutsche Philosophie*: 15.1, 95–124.

Lorenz, Konrad (1943): "Die angeborenen Formen möglicher Erfahrung," in *Zeitschrift für Tierpsychologie*: 5, 235–409.

Lorenz, Konrad (1959): "Gestaltwahrnehmung als Quelle wissenschaftlicher Erkenntnis," in *Zeitschrift für experimentelle und angewandte Psychologie*: 6, 118–65.

Lorenz, Konrad (1965): *Evolution and Modification of Behavior*. Chicago: Chicago University Press.

Lorenz, Konrad (1973): *Die Rückseite des Spiegels. Versuch einer Naturgeschichte menschlichen Erkennens*. München and Zürich: Piper.

Lorenz, Konrad (1976): "Die Vorstellung einer zweckgerichteten Weltordnung," in *Anzeiger der österreichischen Akademie der Wissenschaften, Philosophisch-Historische Klasse*. 113 Jg., pp. 39–51.

References

Loy, Claudia (1988): *Marktsystem und Gleichgewichtstendenz*. Tübingen: J. C. B. Mohr (Paul Siebeck).

Lucas, Robert E. (1990): "Why Doesn't Capital Flow from Rich to Poor Countries?" in *American Economic Review (Papers and Proceedings)*: 80, 92–6.

Lucas, Robert E. (1993): "Making a Miracle," in *Econometrica*: 61, 251–72.

Lucas, Robert E. (1988): "On the Mechanics of Economic Development," in *Journal of Monetary Economics*: 22, 3–42.

Luchins, Abraham (1942): "Mechanization in Problem Solving: The Effect of *Einstellung*," in *Psychological Monographs* 54 (6, Whole No. 248).

Macaulay, Stewart (1963): "Non-Contractual Relations in Business: A Preliminary Study," in *American Sociological Review*: 28, 55–70.

Machlup, Fritz (1952): *The Economics of Seller's Competition*. Baltimore: John Hopkins University Press.

Machovec, Frank M. (1995): *Perfect Competition and the Transformation of Economics*. London and New York: Routledge.

Mackaay, Ejan (1997): "The Emergence of Constitutional Rights," in *Constitutional Political Economy*: 8, 15–36.

Mackie, John (1985): *Persons and Values*. Oxford: Oxford University Press.

Magnusson, Lars (ed.) (1994): *Evolutionary and Neo-Schumpeterian Approaches to Economics*. Boston, Dordrecht, London: Kluwer.

Malinowski, Branislaw (1922/1961): *Argonauts of the Western Pacific*. New York: E. P. Dutton.

Malthus, Thomas (1798/1926): *An Essay on the Principle of Population, as it Affects the Future Improvement of Society, with Remarks on the Speculations of Mr. Godwin, M. Condorcet, and other Writers*. reprinted with notes by James Bonar, London: Macmillan.

Mankiw, N. Gregory, David Romer and David N. Weil (1992): "A Contribution to the Empirics of Economic Growth," in *Quarterly Journal of Economics*: 107, 407–38.

Mansbridge, Jane (1998): "Starting with Nothing: On the Impossibility of Grounding Norms Solely in Self-Interest," in Avner Ben-Ner and Louis Putterman (eds.): *Economics, Values and Organization*, pp. 151–68. Cambridge: Cambridge University Press.

Mantzavinos, Chrysostomos (1992): "Contestable Markets, das neoklassische Marktmodell und die Wettbewerbstheorie," in *Jahrbücher für Nationalökonomie und Statistik*: 209, 60–6.

Mantzavinos, Chrysostomos (1994a): *Wettbewerbstheorie. Eine kritische Auseinandersetzung*. Berlin: Duncker & Humblot.

Mantzavinos, Chrysostomos (1994b): "Positive und normative Wettbewerbstheorie: der Versuch einer Systematisierung," in Alfred E. Ott (ed.), *Probleme der unvollkommenen Konkurrenz*, pp. 65–73. Tübingen and Basel: Francke Verlag.

Mantzavinos, Chrysostomos (1996a): "Federalism and Individual Liberty," unpublished paper, University of Freiburg.

Mantzavinos, Chrysostomos (1996b): "Markt und Wettbewerb: Eine unvermeindliche Dualität," unpublished paper, University of Freiburg.

Mantzavinos, Chrysostomos and Viktor Vanberg (1996): "Sozialpolitik und Standortwettbewerb. Die ordnungspolitische Perspektive," in Bernhard Külp (ed.), *Arbeitsmarkt und Arbeitslosigkeit,* pp. 315–43. Freiburg i. Br.: Rudolf Haufe Verlag.

Marimon, Ramon and Ellen, Mc Grattan (1995): "On Adaptive Learning in Strategic Games," in Alan Kirman and Mark Salmon (eds.): *Learning and Rationality in Economics,* pp. 63–101. Oxford and Cambridge, Mass.: Blackwell.

Marshall, Alfred (1920): *Principles of Economics.* 8th ed. London: Macmillan Press.

Maslow, Abraham (1970): *Motivation and Personality.* rev. ed. New York: Harper & Row.

Matthews, R. C. O. (1986): "The Economics of Institutions and the Sources of Growth," in *The Economic Journal,* 96, 903–18.

Mauss, Marcel (1954/1969): *The Gift: Forms and Functions of Exchange in Archaic Societies.* London: Routledge and Kegan Paul.

Maynard Smith, John (1982): *Evolution and the Theory of Games.* Cambridge: Cambridge University Press.

Mayr, Ernst (1964): "Introduction," in Charles Darwin. *On the Origin of Species.* facsimile of the 1st ed., pp. vii–xxvii. Cambridge, Mass.: Harvard University Press.

Mayr, Ernst (1976): *Evolution and the Diversity of Life: Selected Essays.* Cambridge, Mass.: Harvard University Press.

Mayr, Ernst (1982): *The Growth of Biological Thought.* Cambridge, Mass.: Harvard University Press.

Mayr, Ernst (1985a): "How Biology Differs from the Physical Sciences," in David J. Depew and Bruce H. Weber (eds.): *Evolution at the Crossroads: The New Biology and the New Philosophy of Science,* pp. 43–63. Cambridge, Mass.: MIT Press.

Mayr, Ernst (1985b): "Darwin's Five Theories of Evolution," in David Kohn (ed.), *The Darwinian Heritage,* pp. 755–72. Princeton: Princeton University Press.

McAdams, Richard H. (1997): "The Origin, Development, and Regulation of Norms," in *Michigan Law Review:* 96, 338–433.

McClelland, David, J. W. Atkinson, R. A. Clark, and E. L., Lowell, (1976): *The Achievement Motive,* 2nd ed., New York: Irvington.

McClelland, David (1961): *The Achieving Society.* Princeton, N.J.: Van Nostrand.

McGuire, Martin C. and Mancur Olson (1996): "The Economics of Autocracy and Majority Rule: The Invisible Hand and the Use of Force," in *Journal of Economic Literature:* 34, 1996, 72–96.

McNulty, Paul J. (1967): "A Note on the History of Perfect Competition," in *Journal of Political Economy:* 75, 359–99.

Menger, Carl (1871/1968): *Grundsätze der Volkswirtschaftslehre,* 2nd ed. Friedrich A. von Hayek (ed.), Tübingen: J. C. B. Mohr (Paul Siebeck).

Menger, Carl (1871/1994) *Principles of Economics.* translated by James Dingwall and Bert F. Hoselitz. Grove City, Pa.: Libertarian Press.

Menger, Carl (1883/1985): *Investigations into the Method of the Social Sciences with Special Reference to Economics.* New York and London: New York University Press.

Menger, Carl (1884/1970): "Die Irrtümer des Historismus in der deutschen Nationalökonomie," in *Kleinere Schriften zur Methode und Geschichte der Volkswirtschaftslehre,* 2nd ed. Friedrich A. von Hayek (ed.), Tübingen: J. C. B. Mohr (Paul Siebeck).

Merten, Klaus, Siegfried J. Schmidt, and Siegfried Weischenber (eds.) (1994): *Die Wirklichkeit der Medien: Eine Einführung in die Kommunikationswissenschaften.* Opladen: Westdeutscher Verlag.

Metcalfe, Stanley (1989): "Evolution and Economic Change," in Aubrey Silberston (ed.), *Technology and Economic Progress,* pp. 54–85. Basingstoke, Hampshire: Macmillan.

Metcalfe, Stanley (1995): "The Economic Foundations of Technology Policy: Equilibrium and Evolutionary Perspectives," in Paul Stoneman (ed.), *Handbook of the Economics if Innovation and Technological Change,* pp. 409–512. Oxford and Cambridge, Mass.: Blackwell.

Metcalfe, Stanley (1998): *Evolutionary Economics and Creative Destruction.* London and New York: Routledge.

Meyer, Willi (1983): "Entwicklung und Bedeutung des Property Rights-Ansatzes in der Nationalökonomie," in Alfred Schüller (ed.), *Property Rights und ökonomische Theorie,* pp. 1–44. München: Verlag Franz Vahlen.

Milgrom, Paul M., Douglass C. North, and Barry R. Weingast (1990): "The Role of Institutions in the Revival of Trade: The Law Merchant, Private Judges, and the Champagne Fairs," in *Economics and Politics:* 2, 1–23.

Miller, Gary and Kathleen Cook (1998): "Leveling and Leadership: Hierarchy and Social Order," in Karol Soltan, Eric, M. Uslaner, and Virginia Haufler (eds.), *Institutions and Social Order,* pp. 67–100. Ann Arbor: University of Michigan Press.

Mises, Ludwig von (1932): *Die Gemeinwirtschaft.* 2nd ed. Jena: Verlag von Gustav Fisher.

Mises, Ludwig von (1940): *Nationalökonmie. Theorie des Handelns und Wirtschaftens.* Genf: Edition Union.

Mises, Ludwig von (1953): *The Theory of Money and Credit.* 2nd ed. New Haven, Conn.: Yale University Press.

Mises, Ludwig von (1963): *Human Action.* 3rd ed., Chicago: Henry Regnery.

Mises, Ludwig von (1980): *Planing for Freedom and Sixteen Other Essays and Addresses.* 4th ed., South Holland, Ill.: Libertarian Press.

Mokyr, Joel (1998): "Science, Technology and Knowledge: What Historians Can Learn from an Evolutionary Approach," *Papers on Economics and Evolution* #9803, Max-Planck-Institute for Research into Economic Systems.

Mummert, Uwe (1999): "Informal Institutions and Institutional Policy – Shedding Light on the Myth of Institutional Conflict," *Discussion Paper 02–99, Max-Planck-Institute for Research into Economic Systems.*

Murray, Henry A. (1938): *Explorations in Personality.* New York: Oxford University Press.

Nee, Victor (1998a): "Sources of the New Institutionalism," in Victor Nee and Mary C. Brinton (eds.): *The New Institutionalism in Sociology,* pp. 1–16. New York: Russell Sage Foundation.

References

Nee, Victor (1998b): "Norms and Networks in Economic and Organizational Performance," in *American Economic Review (Papers and Procedings)*: 88, 85–9.

Nee, Victor and Paul Ingram (1998): "Embeddedness and Beyond: Institutions, Exchange, and Social Structure," in Victor Nee and Mary C. Brinton (eds.): *The New Institutionalism in Sociology*, pp. 19–45. New York: Russell Sage Foundation.

Nee, Victor and David Strang (1998): "The Emergence and Diffusion of Institutional Forms," in *Journal of Institutional and Theoretical Economics*: 154, 706–15.

Nee, Victor and Mary C. Brinton (1998): "Introduction," in Victor Nee and Mary C. Brinton (eds.): *The New Institutionalism in Sociology*, pp. XIV–XIX. New York: Russell Sage Foundation.

Nelson, Richard R. (ed.) (1993): *National Innovation Systems. A Comparative Analysis*. New York and Oxford: Oxford University Press.

Nelson, Richard R. (1994): "The Coevolution of Technologies and Institutions," in Richard W. England (ed.) (1994), pp. 139–56.

Nelson, Richard R. (1995): "Recent Evolutionary Theorizing About Economic Change," in *Journal of Economic Literature*: 33, 48–90.

Nelson, Richard R. and Sidney G. Winter (1982): *An Evolutionary Theory of Economic Change*. Cambridge, Mass.: Belknap Press of Harvard University Press.

Nettle, Daniel and Robin I. M. Dunbar (1997): "Social Markets and the Evolution of Reciprocal Exchange," in *Current Anthropology*: 38, 93–9.

Neumann, Carl W. (1982): *Historische Entwicklung und heutiger Stand der Wettbewebstheorie*. Königstein/Ts.: Athenäum.

Neumann, Carl W. (1983): *Allgemeine Wettbewerbstheorie und Preismißbrauchsaufsicht*. Neuwied and Darmstadt: Luchterhand.

Neumann, John von and Oskar Morgenstern (1944): *Theory of Games and Economic Behavior*. Princeton: Princeton University Press.

Newell, Allen and Herbert Simon (1972): *Human Problem Solving*. Englewood Cliffs, N.J.: Prentice-Hall.

Nielsen, Klaus and Björn Johnson (eds.) (1998): *Institutions and Economic Change*. Cheltenham: Edward Elgar.

Nisbett, Richard and Lee Ross (1980): *Human Inference: Strategies and Shortcomings of Social Judgment*. Englewood Cliffs, N.J.: Prentice-Hall.

North, Douglass C. (1981): *Structure and Change in Economic History*. New York: W. W. Norton.

North, Douglass C. (1990): *Institutions, Institutional Change and Economic Performance*. Cambridge: Cambridge University Press.

North, Douglass C. (1991): "Institutions," in *Journal of Economic Perspectives*: 5, 97–112.

North, Douglass C. (1993a): "What Do We Mean by Rationality?" in *Public Choice*: 77, 159–62.

North, Douglass C. (1993b): "Institutions and Credible Commitments," in *Journal of Institutional and Theoretical Economics*: 149, 11–23.

North, Douglass C. (1994): "Economic Performance Through Time," in *American Economic Review*: 84, 359–68.

North, Douglass C. (1995a): "Five Propositions about Institutional Change," in Jack Knight and Itai Sened (eds.): *Explaining Social Institutions*, pp. 15–26. Ann Arbor: University of Michigan Press.

North, Douglass C. (1995b): "The New Institutional Economics and Third World Development," in John Harriss, Janet Hunter, and Colin M. Lewis (eds.): *The New Institutional Economics and Third World Development*, pp. 17–26. London: Routledge.

North, Douglass C. (1996): "Economic Performance Through Time: The Limits to Knowledge," unpublished paper presented at the Conference on Fundamental Limits to Knowledge in Economics at the Santa Fe Institute, Santa Fe, New Mexico, July 31–August 3.

North, Douglass C. (1998): "Where Have We Been and Where Are We Going?," in Avner Ben-Ner and Louis Putterman (eds.): *Economics, Values, and Organization*, pp. 491–508. Cambridge: Cambridge University Press.

North, Douglass C. (2000): "Big-Bang Transformations of Economic Systems: An Introductory Note," in *Journal of Institutional and Theoretical Economics*: 156, 3–8.

North, Douglass C. and Barry R. Weingast (1989/1996): "Constitutions and Commitment: The Evolution of Institutions Governing Public Choice in Seventeenth-Century England," in *The Journal of Economic History*: 149, 803–32 and reprinted in Lee J. Alston, Thráinn Eggertsson, and Douglass C. North (eds.): *Empirical Studies in Institutional Change*, pp. 134–65. Cambridge: Cambridge University Press.

North, Douglass C. and Thomas Robert (1973): *The Rise of the Western World: A New Economic History*. Cambridge: Cambridge University Press.

Nozick, Robert (1974): *Anarchy, State, and Utopia*. Oxford: Blackwell.

Nozick, Robert (1993): *The Nature of Rationality*. Princeton: Princeton University Press.

Nozick, Robert (1994): "Invisible-Hand Explanations," in *American Economic Review (Papers and proceedings)*: 84, 314–18.

Nye, John V. C. (1997): "Thinking about the State: Property Rights, Trade, and Changing Contractual Arrangements in a World with Coercion," in John N. Drobak and John V. C. Nye (eds.): *The Frontiers of the New Institutional Economics*, pp. 121–42. San Diego: Academic Press.

Oberender, Peter (1973): *Industrielle Forschung und Entwicklung. Eine theoretische und empirische Analyse bei oligopolistischen Marktprozessen*. Bern and Stuttgart: Haupt.

Oberender, Peter (1994): "Industrieökonomik," in *Wirtschaftswissenschaftliches Studium*: 23, 65–73.

Oberender, Peter and Andreas Väth (1989): "Von der Industrieökonomie zur Marktökonomie," in Peter Oberender (ed.), *Marktökonomie, Marktstruktur und Wettbewerb in ausgewählten Branchen der Bundesrepublik*, pp. 1–27. München: Verlag Franz Vahlen.

O'Driscoll, Gerald and Mario Rizzo (1996): *The Economics of Time and Ignorance*. 2nd ed., London and New York: Routledge.

Okruch, Stefan (1998): "Der Wandel von Rechtsnormen in evolutorischer Perspektive," in Gerhard Wegner and Josef Wieland (eds.): *Formelle und Informelle Institutionen: Genese, Interaktionen und Wandel,* pp. 101–51. Marburg: Metropolis-Verl.

Okruch, Stefan (1999): *Innovation und Diffusion von Normen.* Berlin: Duncker & Humblot.

Olson, Mancur (1965): *The Logic of Collective Action.* Cambridge, Mass.: Harvard University Press.

Olson, Mancur (1982): *The Rise and Decline of Nations.* New Haven and London: Yale University Press.

Olson, Mancur (1991): "Autocracy, Democracy and Prosperity," in Richard J. Zeckhauser (ed.), *Strategy and Choice,* pp. 131–57. Cambridge, Mass.: MIT Press.

Olson, Mancur (1993): "Dictatorship, Democracy and Development," in *American Political Science Review:* 87, 567–76.

Olson, Mancur (1996): "Big Bills Left on the Sidewalk: Why Some Nations Are Rich, and Others Poor," in: *Journal of Economic Perspectives:* 10, 3–24.

Olson, Mancur, Naveen Sarna, and Anand Swamy (2000): "Governance and Growth: A Simple Hypothesis Explaining Cross-Country Differences in Productivity Growth," in *Public Choice:* 102, 341–64.

Opp, Karl-Dieter (1979): "The Emergence and Effects of Social Norms. A Confrontation of Some Hypotheses of Sociology and Economics," in *Kyklos:* 32, 775–801.

Opp, Karl-Dieter (1982): "The Evolutionary Emergence of Norms," in *British Journal of Social Psychology:* 21, 139–49.

Opp, Karl-Dieter (1994): "Evolution of Norms: An Anthropological View. Comment," in *Journal of Institutional and Theoretical Economics:* 150, 1, 93–6.

Opp, Karl-Dieter (1999): "Contending Conceptions of the Theory of Rational Action," in *Journal of Theoretical Politics:* 11, 171–202.

Orbell, John M. and Robyn M. Dawes (1993): "Social Welfare, Cooperator's Advantage, and the Option of Not Playing the Game," in *American Sociological Review:* 58, 787–800.

Ordeshook, Peter C. (1992): "Constitutional Stability," in *Constitutional Political Economy:* 3, 137–75.

Ortman, Andreas and Gerd Gigerenzer (1997): "Reasoning in Economics and Psychology: Why Social Context Matters," in *Journal of Institutional and Theoretical Economics:* 153/4, 700–10.

Ostrom, Elinor (1990): *Governing the Commons.* Cambridge: Cambridge University Press.

Ostrom, Elinor (1998): "A Behavioral Approach to the Rational Choice Theory of Collective Action," in *American Political Science Review:* 92, 1–22.

Ostrom, Elinor, Roy Gardner, and James Walker (1994): *Rules, Games, and Common-Pool Resources.* Ann Arbor: University of Michigan Press.

Ott, Alfred E. (1986): *Grundzüge der Preistheorie.* 3rd ed. Göttingen: Vandenhoeck & Ruprecht.

Pack, Howard (1994): "Endogenous Growth Theory: Intellectual Appeal and Empirical Shortcomings," in *Journal of Economic Pespectives:* 8, 55–72.

Paraskewopoulos, Spiridon (1997): "Das Problem der wirtschaftlichen Unterentwicklung," in Spiridon Paraskewopoulos (ed.), *Wirtschaftsordnung und wirtschaftliche Entwicklung*, pp. 3–20. Stuttgart: Lucius & Lucius.

Parsons, Talcott (1968): "Utilitarianism. Sociological Thought," in *International Encyclopedia of the Social Sciences*, vol. 16, pp. 229–36. New York and London: Macmillan.

Parsons, Talcott (1975): "Social Structure and the Symbolic Media of Exchange," in Peter M. Blau (ed): *Approaches to the Study of Social Structure*, pp. 94–120. New York and London: Free Press.

Parsons, Talcott and E. A. Shils (1951): "Values, Motives, and Systems of Action," in Parsons, Talcott and E.A. Shils: *Toward a General Theory of Action*, pp. 47–275. Cambridge, Mass.: Harvard University Press.

Peacock, Alan and Hans Willgerodt (1989): *German Neo-Liberals and the Social Market Economy.* London: Macmillan.

Pejovich, Svetozar (1996): "Property Rights and Technological Innovation," in *Social Philosophy and Policy:* 13, 168–80.

Pelikan, Pavel (1987): "The Formation of Incentive Mechanisms in Different Economic Systems," in Stefan Hedlund (ed.), *Incentives and Economic Systems*, pp. 27–56. London and Sydney: Croom Helm.

Pelikan, Pavel (1988): "Can the Imperfect Innovation System of Capitalism Be Outperformed?" in Giovanni Dosi, Christopher Freeman, Richard Nelson, Gerald Silverberg, and Luc Soete (eds.): *Technical Change and Economic Theory*, pp. 370–98. London and New York: Pinter Publishers.

Pelikan, Pavel (1989): "Evolution, Economic Competence and the Market for Corporate Control," in *Journal of Economic Behavior and Organization:* 12, 279–303.

Pelikan, Pavel (1992): "The Dynamics of Economic Systems, or How to Transform a Failed Socialist Economy," in *Journal of Evolutionary Economics:* 2, 39–63.

Pelikan, Pavel (1993): "Ownership and Efficiency: The Competence Argument," in *Constitutional Political Economy:* 4, 349–92.

Pelikan, Pavel (1997): "Allocation of Economic Competence in Teams: A Comparative Institutional Analysis," unpublished manuscript, the Industrial Institute for Economic and Social Research.

Penrose, Edith (1952): "Biological Analogies in the Theory of the Firm," in *American Economic Review:* 42, 804–19.

Penrose, Edith (1959): *The Theory of the Growth of the Firm.* Oxford: Oxford University Press.

Piaget, Jean (1936): *La naissance de l'intelligence chez l'enfant.* Neuchatel and Paris: Delachau et Niestle.

Pies, Ingo (1997): "Autokratie versus Demokratie: Die politischen Voraussetzungen wirtschaftliche Entwicklung," in Spiridon Paraskewopoulos (ed.), *Wirtschaftsordnung und wirtschaftliche Entwicklung*, pp. 43–69. Stuttgart: Lucius & Lucius.

Platteau, Jean-Philippe (1994a): "Beyond the Market Stage Where Real Societies Exist – Part I: The Role of Public and Private Order Institutions," in *The Journal of Development Studies:* 30, 533–77.

Platteau, Jean-Philippe (1994b): "Beyond the Market Stage Where Real Societies Exist – Part II: The Role of Moral Norms," in *The Journal of Development Studies*. vol. 30, pp. 753–817.

Polanyi, Michael (1958): *Personal Knowledge*. London: Routledge.

Polanyi, Michael (1966/1983): *The Tacit Dimension*. Gloucester, Mass.: Peter Smith.

Popper, Karl R. (1934/1971): *Die Logik der Forschung*. 4th ed., Tübingen: J. C. B. Mohr (Paul Siebeck).

Popper, Karl R. (1945/1963): *The Open Society and Its Enemies. Vol.II: The High Tide of Prophecy: Hegel, Marx, and the Aftermath*. 4th ed. Princeton, N.J.: Princeton University Press.

Popper, Karl R. (1956/1982): *The Open Universe: An Argument for Indeterminism*, Vol. II. *of the Postscript to The Logic of Scientific Inquiry*. W.W. Bartley III (ed.). London: Hutchinson.

Popper, Karl R. (1957): *The Poverty of Historicism*. London: Routledge.

Popper, Karl R. (1963/1989): *Conjectures and Refutations. The Growth of Scientific Knowledge*. 5th rev. ed. London and New York: Routledge.

Popper, Karl R. (1972/1992): *Objective Knowledge. An Evolutionary Approach*. Oxford: Clarendon Press.

Popper, Karl R. (1978/1987): "Natural Selection and the Emergence of Mind," in *Dialectica*: 22,3, 339–55 and reprinted as chapter VI in Gerard Radnitzky and W.W. Bartley III (eds.), pp. 139–55.

Popper, Karl R. (1979): *Die beiden Grundprobleme der Erkenntnistheorie*. Eggers T. Hansen (ed.) Tübingen: J. C. B. Mohr (Paul Siebeck).

Popper, Karl R. (1987): "Die erkenntnistheoretische Position der evolutionären Erkenntnistheorie," in Rupert Riedl and Franz Wuketits (eds.) (1987), pp. 29–37.

Popper, Karl R. and John C. Eccles (1977/1983): *The Self and Its Brain. An Argument for Interactionism*. London: Routledge.

Popper, Karl R. and Konrad Lorenz (1988): *Die Zukunft ist offen*, 3rd ed. München and Zürich: Piper.

Posner, Eric (1996): "The Regulation of Groups: The Influence of Legal and Nonlegal Sanctions on Collective Action," in *The University of Chicago Law Review*: 63, 133–97.

Posner, Richard A. (1980): "A Theory of Primitive Society, with Special Reference to Law," in *Journal of Law and Economics*: 23, 1–53.

Posner, Richard A. (1997): "Social Norms and Law: An Economic Approach," in *American Economic Review (Papers and Proceedings)*: 87, 365–9.

Posner, Richard A. (1998): "Creating a Legal Framework for Economic Development," in *The World Bank Research Observer*: 13, 1–11.

Pritzl, Ruppert (1997): *Korruption und Rent-Seeking in Lateinamerika – Zur politischen Ökonomie autoritärer politischer Systeme*. Baden-Baden: Nomos Verlagsgesellschaft.

Przeworski, Adam (1997): "Comment," in David L. Weimer (ed.): *The Political Economy of Property Rights*, pp. 80–3. Cambridge: Cambridge University Press.

References

Przeworski, Adam and Fernando Limongi (1993): "Political Regimes and Economic Growth," in *Journal of Economic Perspectives:* 7, 51–69.

Przeworski, Adam and Fernardo Limongi (1997): "Modernization. Theories and Facts," in *World Politics:* 49, 155–83.

Putnam, Robert (1993): *Making Democracy Work.* Princeton: Princeton University Press.

Putnam, Robert D. (1995): "Bowling Alone: America's Declining Social Capital," in *Journal of Democracy:* 6, 65–78.

Qian, Yingyi and Barry R. Weingast (1997): "Federalism as a Commitment to Preserving Market Incentives," in *Journal of Economic Perspectives:* 11, 83–92.

Quine, Willard V. O. (1969): *Ontological Relativity and Other Essays.* New York: Columbia University Press.

Rabin, Matthew (1998): "Psychology and Economics," in *Journal of Economic Literature:* 36, 11–46.

Radnitzky, Gerhard and W.W. Bartley III (1987): *Evolutionary Epistemology, Rationality, and the Sociology of Knowledge.* La Salle, Ill.: Open Court Press.

Ramstad, Yngve (1994): "On the Nature of Economic Evolution: John R. Commons and the Metaphor of Artificial Selection," in Lars Magnusson (ed.) (1994), pp. 65–121.

Richardson, G. B. (1972): "The Organisation of Industry," in *Economic Journal:* 82, 883–96.

Ricketts, Martin (1987): "Rent-Seeking, Entrepreneurship, Subjectivism and Property Rights," in *Journal of Institutional and Theoretical Economics:* 143, 457–66.

Riedl, Rupert and Franz M. Wuketits (eds.) (1987): *Die Evolutionäre Erkenntnistheorie. Bedingungen. Lösungen. Kontroversen.* Berlin: Parcy.

Riker, William H. (1964): *Federalism.* Boston: Little, Brown.

Riker, William (1980): "Implications from the Disequilibrium Majority Rule for the Study of Institutions," in *American Political Science Review:* 74, 432–46.

Rizzo, Mario (ed.) (1979): *Time, Uncertainty, and Disequilibrium: Exploration of Austrian Themes.* Lexington, Mass: Lexington Books, D. C. Heath.

Robbins, Lionel (1935): *On the Nature and Significance of Economic Science.* London: Macmillan.

Romer, Paul M. (1986): "Increasing Returns and Long-Run Growth," in *Journal of Political Economy:* 94, 1002–37.

Romer, Paul M. (1990): "Endogenous Technological Change," in *Journal of Political Economy:* 98, 71–102.

Romer, Paul M. (1993): "Idea Gaps and Object Gaps in Economic Development," in *Journal of Monetary Economics:* 32, 534–73.

Romer, Paul M. (1994): "The Origins of Endogenous Growth," in *Journal of Economic Perspectives:* 8, 3–22.

Röpke, Jochen (1977): *Die Strategie der Innovation.* Tübingen: J. C. B. Mohr (Paul Siebeck).

Röpke, Jochen (1980): "Zur Stabilität und Evolution marktwirtschaftlicher Systeme aus klassischer Sicht," in Erich Streissler and Christian Watrin (eds.): *Zur*

Theorie marktwirtschaftlicher Ordnungen, pp. 124–62. Tübingen: J. C. B. Mohr (Paul Siebeck).

Röpke, Jochen (1987): "Möglichkeiten und Grenzen der Steuerung wirtschaftlicher Entwicklung in komplexen Systemen," in Manfred Borchert, Ulrich Fehl, and Peter Oberender (eds.): *Markt und Wettbewerb. Festschrift für Ernst Heuss.* Bern and Stuttgart: Haupt, pp. 17–37.

Röpke, Jochen (1990a): "Evolution and Innovation," in Kurt Dopfer and Karl F. Raible (eds.) (1990), pp. 111–20.

Röpke, Jochen (1990b): "Extremes Unternehmenswachstum im ökonomischen Evolutionsprozeß," in *Ordo:* 41, 151–72.

Rosenberg, Nathan (1994): *Exploring the Black Box.* New York: Cambridge University Press.

Rosenberg, Nathan and L. E. Birdzell, Jr. (1986): *How the West Grew Rich.* New York: Basic Books.

Rosenthal, R. W. (1981): "Games of Perfect Information, Predatory Pricing and the Chain Store Paradox," in *Journal of Economic Theory:* 25, 92–100.

Ross, Stephen A. (1973): "The Economic Theory of Agency: The Principal's Problem," in *American Economic Review:* 62, 134–9.

Rothbard, Murray N. (1970): *Man, Economy, and State. A Treatise on Economic Principles.* Los Angeles: Nash.

Rothschild, Emma (1994): "Adam Smith and the Invisible Hand," in *American Economic Review (Papers and Proceedings):* 84, 319–22.

Rothschild, Michael (1973): "Models of Market Organization with Imperfect Information," in *Journal of Political Economy:* 81, 1283–308.

Rowe, Nicholas (1989): *Rules and Institutions.* Ann Arbor: University of Michigan Press.

Rowley, Charles K., Robert D. Tollison, and Gordon Tullock (eds.) (1988): *The Political Economy of Rent-Seeking.* Boston: Kluwer.

Rutherford, Malcolm (1994): *Institutions in Economics. The Old and the New Institutionalism.* Cambridge: Cambridge University Press.

Rutherford, Malcolm (1995): "The Old and the New Institutionalism: Can Bridges Be Built?" in *Journal of Economic Issues:* 24, 443–51.

Ryle, Gilbert (1949): *The Concept of Mind.* London: Penguin Books.

Sargent, Thomas J. (1994): *Bounded Rationality in Macroeconomics.* Oxford: Clarendon Press.

Savage, Leonard J. (1954): *The Foundations of Statistics.* New York: Wiley.

Saviotti, Paolo P. (1991): "The Role of Variety in Economic and Technological Development," in P. Paolo Saviotti and Stan Metcalfe (eds.) (1991a), pp. 172–208.

Saviotti, Paolo P. and Stan J. Metcalfe (eds.) (1991a): *Evolutionary Theories of Economic and Technical Change.* Reading: Harwood Academic.

Saviotti, Paolo P. and Stan J. Metcalfe (1991b): "Present Developement and Trends in Evolutionary Economics," in Paolo P. Saviotti and Stan J. Metcalfe (1991a), pp. 1–30.

Schank, Roger and Robert Abelson (1977): *Scripts, Plans, Goals and Understanding.* Hillsdale, N.J.: Erlbaum.

References

Schelling, Thomas C. (1960): *The Strategy of Conflict*. Cambridge, Mass.: Harvard University Press.

Schelling, Thomas C. (1978): "Egonomics, or the Art of Self-Managment," in *American Economic Review, (Papers and Proceedings)*: 68, 290–4.

Schelling, Thomas C. (1980): "The Intimate Contest for Self-Command," in *Public Interest*: 60, 94–118.

Schelling, Thomas C. (1984a): *Choice and Consequence*. Cambridge, Mass.: Harvard University Press.

Schelling, Thomas C. (1984b): "Self-Command in Practice, in Policy and in a Theory of Rational Choice," in *American Economic Review (Papers and Proceedings)*: 74, 1–11.

Schlicht, Ekkehart (1990): "Rationality, Bounded or Not, and Institutional Analysis," in *Journal of Institutional and Theoretical Economics*: 146, 703–19.

Schlicht, Ekkehart (1993): "On Custom," in *Journal of Institutional and Theoretical Economics*: 149, 179–203.

Schlicht, Ekkehart (1997): "Patterned Variation: The Role of Psychological Dispositions in Social and Institutional Evolution," in *Journal of Institutional and Theoretical Economics*: 153/4, 722–36.

Schlicht, Ekkehart (1998): *On Custom in the Economy*. Oxford: Clarendon Press.

Schmid, Allan (1987): *Property, Power, and Public Choice. An Inquiry into Law and Economics*. New York: Praeger.

Schmidt, Ingo (1996): *Wettbewerbspolitik und Kartellrecht*. 5th rev. ed. Stuttgart: Lucius & Lucius.

Schmidtchen, Dieter (1976/1977): "Wider den Vorwurf, das neoklassische Wettbewerbskonzept sei tautologisch: Eine Antikritik aus wissenschaftslogischer und markttheoretischer Sicht," in *Jahrbücher für Nationalökonomie und Statistik*: 191, 428–54.

Schmidtchen, Dieter (1978): *Wettbewerbspolitik als Aufgabe. Methodologische und systematische Grundlagen für eine Neuorientierung*. Baden-Baden: Nomos Verlagsgesellschaft.

Schmidtchen, Dieter (1979): "Ausbeutung aufgrund einer Wettbewerbsbeschränkung durch Zustand? Kritische Analyse der theoretischen Grundlagen einer freiheitsgefährdenden Wettbewerbspolitik," in *Ordo*: 30, 273–94.

Schmidtchen, Dieter (1983): *Property Rights, Freiheit und Wettbewerbspolitik*. Tübingen: J. C. B. Mohr (Paul Siebeck).

Schmidtchen, Dieter (1984): "German 'Ordnungspolitik' as Institutional Choice," in *Journal of Institutional and Theoretical Economics*:140, pp. 54–70.

Schmidtchen, Dieter (1988): "Fehlurteile über das Konzept der Wettbewerbsfreiheit," in *Ordo*: 39, pp. 111–35.

Schmidtchen, Dieter (1989): "Evolutorische Ordnungstheorie oder: Die Transaktionskosten und das Unternehmertum," in *Ordo*: 40, pp. 161–82.

Schmidtchen, Dieter (1990): "Preise und spontane Ordnungs – Prinzipien einer Theorie ökonomischer Evolution," in Witt, Ulrich (ed.) (1990), pp. 75–113.

Schmoller, Gustav (1883): "Zur Methodologie der Staats- und Socialwissenschaften," in *Jahrbuch für Gesetzgebung, Verwaltung und Volkswirtschaft im deutschen Reiche (Schmollers Jahrbuch)*: 7, 239–58.

Schotter, Andrew (1981): *The Economic Theory of Social Institutions.* Cambridge: Cambridge University Press.

Schreiter, Carsten (1994*): Evolution und Wettbewerb von Organisationsstrukturen.* Göttingen: Vandenhoeck & Ruprecht.

Schreiter, Carsten (1997): "Humanvermögen und Wirtschaftsordnung: Konsequenzen der neuen Wachstumstheorie für die Entwicklungsländer?" in Spyridon Paraskewopoulos (ed.): *Wirtschaftsordnung und wirtschaftliche Entwicklung,* pp. 72–119. Stuttgart: Lucius & Lucius.

Schrödinger, Erwin (1958): *Mind and Matter.* Cambridge: Cambridge University Press.

Schumpeter, Joseph A. (1908): *Das Wesen und der Hauptinhalt der theoretischen Nationalökonomie.* Berlin Duncker & Humblot.

Schumpeter, Joseph A. (1911/1987): *Theorie der wirtschaftlichen Entwicklung.* 7th ed. Berlin Duncker & Humblot.

Schumpeter, Joseph A. (1942/1950): *Capitalism, Socialism and Democracy.* 3rd ed. New York: Harper.

Schütz, Alfred (1967): *The Phenomenology of the Social World.* trans. George Walsch and Frederick Lehnert. Evanston, Ill.: Northwestern University Press.

Schütz, Alfred and Thomas Luckman (1973): *The Structures of the Life-World,* trans. R. M. Zaner and H. T. Engelhardt, Jr. Evaston, Ill.: Northwestern University Press.

Scully, Gerald W. and Dan J. Slottje (1991): "Ranking Economic Liberty Across Countries," in *Public Choice:* 69, 121–52.

Selten, Reinhard (1990): "Bounded Rationality," in *Journal of Institutional and Theoretical Economics:* 146, 649–58.

Sen, Armartya (1977/1979): "Rational Fools: A Critique of the Behavioural Foundations of Economic Theory," in Frank Hahn and Martin Hollis (eds.): *Philosophy and Economic Theory,* pp. 87–109. Oxford: Oxford University Press.

Sen, Amartya (1987): *On Ethics and Economics.* Oxford and Cambridge, Mass.: Blackwell.

Shackle, G. L. S. (1972/1992): *Epistemics and Economics.* New Brunswick, N.J., and London: Transaction.

Shackle, G. L. S. (1979): *Imagination and the Nature of Choice.* Edinburgh: Edinburgh University Press.

Shackle, G. L. S. (1983): "The Bounds of Unknowledge," in Jack Wiseman (ed.) (1983a), pp. 28–37.

Shackle, G. L. S. (1990): *Time, Expectations and Uncertainity in Economics.* J. L. Ford (ed.) Aldershot: Edward Elgar.

Simon, Herbert (1955): "A Behavioral Model of Rational Choice," in *Quarterly Journal of Economics:* 69, 99–118.

Simon, Herbert (1973): "The Structure of Ill-Structured Problems," in *Artificial Intelligence:* 4, 181–202.

Simon, Herbert (1992a): "Bounded Rationality," in *The New Palgrave Dictionary of Money and Finance,* pp. 226–7. London and Basingstoke: Macmillan.

Simon, Herbert (1992b): "Scientific Discovery as Problem Solving," in Massimo Egidi and Robin Marris (eds.): *Economics, Bounded Rationality and the Cognitive Revolution,* pp. 102–19. Hants: Edward Elgar.

References

Simons, Anna (1997): "Comment," in *Current Anthropology*: 38, 19–20.

Sirowy, Larry and Alex Inkeles (1991): "The Effects of Democracy on Economic Growth and Inequality: A Review," in Alex Inkeles (ed.): *On Measuring Democracy*, pp. 125–56. New Brunswick and London: Transaction.

Sjöstrand, Sven-Erik (1993): "On Institutional Thought in the Social and Economic Sciences," in Sven-Erik Sjöstrand (ed.): *Institutional Change: Theory and Empirical Findings*, pp. 3–31. New York: M. E. Sharpe.

Smith, Adam (1776/1976): *An Inquiry Into the Nature and Causes of the Wealth of Nations*. Edwin Cannan (ed.). Chicago: University of Chicago Press.

Smith, Adam (1790/1976): *The Theory of Moral Sentiments*. Oxford: Oxford University Press.

Smith, John M. (1982): *Evolution and the Theory of Games*. Cambridge: Cambridge University Press.

Smith, Vernon L. (1982): "Markets as Economizers of Information: Experimental Examination of the 'Hayek Hypothesis'," in *Economic Inpuiry*: 20, 165–79.

Snell, Bruno (1975/1986): *Die Entdeckung des Geistes*. 6th rev. ed. Göttingen: Vandenhoeck & Ruprecht.

Sober, Elliott. (1984): *The Nature of Selection – Evolutionary Theory in Philosophical Focus*. Cambridge, Mass.: MIT Press.

Solow, Robert (1956): "A Contribution to the Theory of Economic Growth," in *Quarterly Journal of Economics*: 70, 65–94.

Solow, Robert (1994): "Perspectives on Growth Theory," in *Journal of Economic Perspectives*: 8, 45–54.

Soltan, Karol, Eric M. Uslaner, and Virginia Haufler (1998): "New Institutionalism: Institutions and Social Order," in Karol Soltan, Eric M. Uslaner, and Virginia Haufler (eds.): *Institutions and Social Order*, pp. 3–14. Ann Arbor: University of Michigan Press.

Soltis, Joseph, Robert Boyd, and Peter J. Richerson (1995): "Can Group-Functional Behaviors Evolve by Cultural Group Selection?" in *Current Anthropology*: 36, 473–94.

Spadaro, Louis (ed.) (1978): *New Directions in Austrian Economics*. Kansas City: Sheed, Andrews and McMeel.

Sperber, Dan and Lawrence Hirschfeld (1999): "Culture, Cognition, and Evolution," in Robert A. Wilson and Frank C. Kehl (eds.): *The MIT Encyclopedia of the Cognitive Sciences*, pp. cxi–cxxxii. Cambridge, Mass.: MIT Press.

Stahl, Silke R. (1998): "Persistence and Change of Economic Institutions – A Social-Cognitive Approach," *Papers on Economics and Evolution #9808, Max-Planck-Institute for Research into Economic Systems*.

Steindl, Joseph (1952): *Maturity and Stagnation in American Capitalism*. Oxford: Blackwell.

Sternberg, Robert J. (ed.) (1999): *Handbook of Creativity*. Cambridge: Cambridge University Press.

Stigler, George (1957): "Perfect Competition, Historically Contemplated," in *Journal of Political Economy*: 65, 1–17.

Stigler, George (1961): "The Economics of Information," in *Journal of Political Economy*: 69, 213–25.

Stigler, George (1987): "Competition," in *The New Palgrave. A Dictionary of Economics:* 1, 531–36.

Stigler, George and Gary Becker (1977): "De Gustibus Non Est Disputandum," in *American Economic Review:* 67, 76–90.

Stigum, B. (1969): "Competitive Equilibrium under Uncertainty," in *Quarterly Journal of Economics:* 83, 553–61.

Streit, Manfred E. (1992): "Economic Order, Private Law and Public Policy. The Freiburg School of Law and Economics in Perspective," in *Journal of Institutional and Theoretical Economics:* 148, 675–704.

Streit, Manfred E. and Gerhard Wegner (1989): "Wissensmangel, Wissenserwerb und Wettbewerb. Transaktionskosten aus evolutorischer Sicht," in *Ordo:* 40, 183–200.

Streit, Manfred E. and Gerhard Wegner (1992): "Information, Transaction and Catallaxy. Refections on Some Key Concepts of Evolutionary Market Theory," in Ulrich Witt (ed.) (1992b), pp. 125–49.

Sugden, Robert (1989): "Spontaneous Order," in *Journal of Economic Perspectives:* 3, 85–97.

Sugden, Robert (1991): "Rational Choice: A Survey of Contributions from Economics and Philosophy," in *Economic Journal:* 101, 751–85.

Sugden, Robert (1998): "Normative Expectations: The Simultaneous Evolution of Institutions and Norms," in Avner Ben-Ner and Louis Putterman (eds.): *Economics, Values, and Organization,* pp. 73–100. Cambridge: Cambridge University Press.

Tamborini, Roberto (1997): "Knowledge and Economic Behaviour. A Constructivist Approach," in *Journal of Evolutionary Economics:* 7, 49–72.

Teece, David J. and Gary Pisano (1994): "The Dynamic Capabilities of Firms: An Introduction," in *Industrial and Corporate Change:* 3,3, 537–56.

Temple, Jonathan and Paul A. Johnson (1998): "Social Capability and Economic Growth," in *Quarterly Journal of Economics:* 113, 965–90.

Thagard, Paul (1996): *Mind. Introduction to Cognitive Science.* Cambridge, Mass.: MIT Press.

Thaler, Richard (1980): "Toward a Positive Theory of Consumer Choice," in *Journal of Economic Behavior and Organization:* 1, 39–60.

Thaler, Richard (1992): *The Winner's Curse. Paradoxes and Anomalies of Economic Life.* New York: Free Press.

Thaler, Richard (2000): "From Homo Economicus to Homo Sapiens," in *Journal of Economic Perspectives:* 14, 133–41.

Thaler, Richard and H. M. Shefrin (1981): "An Economic Theory of Self-Control," in *Journal of Political Economy:* 89, 392–406.

Thomsen, Esteban F. (1992): *Prices and Knowledge. A Market-Process Perspective.* London and New York: Routledge.

Tietzel, Manfred (1988): "Zur Theorie der Präferenzen," in *Jahrbuch für Neue Politische Ökonomie:* 7, 38–71.

Toboso, Fernando (1995): "Explaining the Process of Change Taking Place in Legal Rules and Social Norms: The Case of Institutional Economics and New Institutional Economics," in *European Journal of Law and Economics:* 2, 63–84.

References

Tolksdorf, Michael (1980): "Stand und Entwicklungstendenzen der Wettbewerbstheorie," in *Wirtschaft und Wettbewerb:* 30, 785–803.

Tolksdorf, Michael (1994): *Dynamischer Wettbewerb.* Wiesbaden: Gabler.

Torstensson, Johan (1994): "Propery Rights and Economic Growth: An Empirical Study," in *Kyklos:* 47, 231–47.

Trivers, R. (1971) "The Evolution of Reciprocal Altruism," in *Quarterly Review of Biology:* 46, 45–57.

Tullock, Gordon (1967): "The Welfare Costs of Tariffs, Monopolies and Theft," in *Western Economic Journal:* 5, 224–32.

Tullock, Gordon (1987): "Autocracy," in Gerhard Radnitzky and Peter Bernholz (eds.): *Economic Imperialism – The Economic Method Applied Outside the Field of Economics,* pp. 365–81. New York: Paragon House.

Tversky, Amos and Daniel Kahneman (1973): "Availability: A Heuristic for Judging Frequency and Probability," in *Cognitive Psychology:* 5, 207–32.

Tversky, Amos and Daniel Kahneman,(1974): "Judgment Under Uncertainty: Heuristics and Biases," in *Science:* 185, 1124–31.

Tversky, Amos and Daniel Kahneman (1981): "The Framing of Decisions and the Psychology of Choice," in *Science:* 211, 453–58.

Tversky, Amos and Daniel Kahneman (1986): "Rational Choice and the Framing of Decisions," in *Journal of Business:* 59, 251–78.

Ullmann-Margalit, Edna (1978): "Invisible-Hand Explanations," in *Synthese:* 39, 263–91.

Uslaner, Eric M. (1998): "Field of Dreams: The Weak Reeds of Institutional Design," in Karol Soltan, Eric M. Uslaner, and Virginia Haufler (eds.): *Institutions and Social Order,* pp. 101–27. Ann Arbor: University of Michigan Press.

Vanberg, Viktor J. (1982): *Markt und Organisation.* Tübingen: J. C. B. Mohr (Paul Siebeck).

Vanberg, Viktor J. (1992): "Innovation, Cultural Evolution and Economic Growth," in Ulrich Witt (ed.): *Explaining Process and Change. Approaches to Evolutionary Economics,* pp. 105–21. Ann Arbor: University of Michigan Press.

Vanberg, Viktor J. (1993): "Rational Choice, Rule-Following and Institutions. An Evolutionary Perspective," in Uskali Mäki, Bo Gustafsson, and Christian Knudsen (eds.): *Rationality, Institutions and Economic Methodology,* pp. 171–200. London and New York: Routledge.

Vanberg, Viktor J. (1994a): *Rules and Choice in Economics.* London and New York: Routledge.

Vanberg, Viktor J. (1994b): "Cultural Evolution, Collective Learning and Constitutional Design," in David Reisman (ed.): *Economic Thought and Political Theory,* pp. 171–204. Boston, Dordrecht, and London: Kluwer.

Vanberg, Viktor J. and Roger D. Congleton (1992): "Rationality, Morality and Exit," in *American Political Science Review:* 86, 418–31.

Vaughn, Karen (1987/1989): "Invisible Hand," in *The New Palgrave: The Invisible Hand,* pp.168–72. London: Macmillan Press.

Vaughn, Karen (1992): "The Problem of Order in Austrian Economics: Kirzner vs. Lachmann," in *Review of Political Economy,* 4, 251–74.

Vaughn, Karen (1994): *Austrian Economics in America: The Migration of a Tradition.* Cambridge: Cambridge Universtiy Press.

Vaughn, Karen (1996): "Economic Policy for an Imperfect World," in *Southern Economic Journal:* 62, 833–44.

Vickers, John (1994): *Concepts of Competition.* Oxford: Clarendon Press.

Vincenti, Walter (1990): *What Engineers Know and How They Know It?* Baltimore and London: Johns Hopkins University Press.

Vincenti, Walter (1994): "The Retractable Airplane Landing Gear and the Northrup Anomaly: Variation – Selection and the Shaping of Technology," in *Technology and Culture:* 35, 1–33.

Voigt, Stefan (1997): "Positive Constitutional Economics: A Survey," in *Public Choice:* 90, 11–53.

Voigt, Stefan (1998): "Das Forschungsprogramm der Positiven Konstitutionenökonomik," in Gerd Grözinger and Stephan Panter (eds.): *Konstitutionelle Politische Ökonomie,* pp. 279–319. Marburg: Metropolis Verlag.

Voigt, Stefan (1999): *Explaining Constitutional Change.* Cheltenham and Northampton: Edward Elgar.

Voigt, Stefan and Daniel Kiwit (1998): "The Role and Evolution of Beliefs, Habits, Moral Norms, and Institutions," in Herbert Giersch (ed.): *Merits and Limits of Markets,* pp. 83–108. Berlin, Heidelberg, New York, Tokyo: Springer.

Voland, Eckart (1997): "Von der Ordnung ohne Recht zum Recht durch Ordnung. Die Entstehung von Rechtsnormen aus evolutionsbiologischer Sicht," in Ernst-Joachim Lampe (ed.): *Zur Entwicklung von Rechtsbewußtsein,* pp. 111–33. Frankfurt am Main: Suhrkamp.

Volckart, Oliver (2000): "The Open Constitution and Its Enemies: Competition, Rent-Seeking, and the Rise of the Modern State," in *Journal of Economic Behavior and Organization:* 42, 1–17.

Vollmer, Gerhard (1975/1994): *Evolutionäre Erkenntnistheorie.* 6th ed. Stuttgart: Hirzel.

Vriend, Nicolaas J. (1996): "Rational Behavior and Economic Theory," in *Journal of Economic Behavior and Organization:* 29, 263–85.

Vromen, Jack J. (1995): *Economic Evolution. An Enquiry into the Foundations of New Institutional Economics.* London and New York: Routledge.

Waal, Frans de (1989): "Food Sharing and Reciprocal Obligations Among Chimpanzees," in *Journal of Human Evolution:* 18, 433–59.

Waal, Frans de (1991): "The Chimpanzee's Sense of Social Regularity and Its Relation to the Human Sense of Justice," in *American Behavioral Scientist:* 34, 335–49.

Wagner, Adolf and Hans-Walter Lorenz (eds.) (1995): *Studien zur Evolutorischen Ökonomik III.* Berlin: Duncker & Humblot.

Walras, Léon (1874): *Éléments d'Économie Politique Pure.* Lausanne: Imprimerie L. Cobaz & Cie .

Walsh, Vivian (1994): "Rationality as Self-Interest versus Rationality as Present Aims," in *American Economic Review (Papers and Proceedings):* 84, 401–5.

Weber, Max (1919/1994): *Politik als Beruf.* Tübingen: J. C. B. Mohr (Paul Siebeck).

Weber, Max (1922/1972): *Wirtschaft und Gesellschaft.* 5th ed. Tübingen: J. C. B. Mohr (Paul Siebeck).

Wegner, Gerhard (1992): "Wissensnutzung in Märkten," in *Jahrbuch für Sozial-wissenschaft:* 43, 44–64.

Wegner, Gerhard (1996): *Wirtschaftspolitik zwischen Selbst-und Fremdsteuerung – ein neuer Ansatz.* Baden-Baden: Nomos Verlagsgesellschaft.

Weimer, David L. (1997): "The Political Economy of Property Rights," in David L. Weimer (ed.): *The Political Economy of Property Rights,* pp. 1–19. Cambridge: Cambridge University Press.

Weingast, Barry R. (1993): "Constitutions as Governance Structures: The Political Foundations of Secure Markets," in *Journal of Institutional and Theoretical Economics:* 149, 286–311.

Weingast, Barry R. (1995): "The Economic Role of Political Institutions: Market-Preserving Federalism and Economic Growth," in *Journal of Law, Economics, and Organization:* 11, 1–31.

Weingast, Barry R. (1997a): "The Political Commitment to Markets and Mar-ketization," in David L. Weimer (ed.), *The Political Economy of Property Rights,* pp. 43–9. Cambridge: Cambridge University Press.

Weingast, Barry R. (1997b): "The Political Foundations of Democracy and the Rule of Law," in *American Political Science Review:* 91, 245–63.

Wessling, Ewald (1991): *Individuum and Information.* Tübingen: J. C. B. Mohr (Paul Siebeck).

Wieandt, Axel (1994): *Die Entstehung, Entwicklung und Zerstörung von Märk-ten durch Innovationen.* Stuttgart: Schäffer – Poeschel.

Willeke, Franz-Ulrich (1973): *Grundsätze wettbewerbspolitischer Konzeptionen.* Tübingen, J. C. B. Mohr (Paul Siebeck).

Willeke, Franz-Ulrich (1980): *Wettbewerbspolitik.* Tübingen, J. C. B. Mohr (Paul Siebeck).

Williams, Bernard (1973): *Problems of the Self.* Cambridge: Cambridge University Press.

Williamson, Oliver (1975): *Markets and Hierarchies: Analysis and Antitrust Im-plications.* New York: Free Press.

Williamson, Oliver (1985): *The Economic Institutions of Capitalism* , New York: Free Press.

Wilson, Robert A. and Frank C. Kehl (eds.) (1999): *The MIT Encyclopedia of the Cognitive Sciences.* Cambridge, Mass.: MIT Press.

Wimmer, Hannes (1997): "Theorien zur Entstehung des Staates," in Ernst-Joachim Lampe (ed.), *Zur Entstehung von Rechtsbewußtsein,* pp. 214–52. Frankfurt am Main: Suhrkamp.

Windsperger, Josef (1986): "Wettbewerb als dynamischer Prozeß," in *Ordo:* 37, 125–40.

Wintrobe, Ronald (1998): *The Political Economy of Dictatorship.* Cambridge: Cambridge University Press.

Wiseman, Jack (ed.) (1983a): *Beyond Positive Economics?* New York: St. Martin's Press.

Wiseman, Jack (1983b): "Beyond Positive Economics – Dream and Reality," in Jack Wiseman (ed.) (1983a), pp. 13–27.

Wiseman, Jack (1990): "General Equilibrium or Market Process: An Evaluation," in Alfred Bosch, Peter Koslowski, and Reinhold Veit (eds.): *General Equilibrium or Market Process*, pp. 145–63. Tübingen: J. C. B. Mohr (Paul Siebeck).

Witt, Ulrich (1985): "Coordination of Individual Economic Activities as an Evolving Process of Self-Organisation," in *Economie appliquée*: 37, 569–95.

Witt, Ulrich (1986): "Evolution and Stability of Cooperation without Enforceable Contracts," in *Kyklos*: 39, 1986, 245–66.

Witt, Ulrich (1987a): *Individualistische Grundlagen der Evolutorischen Ökonomik*. Tübingen: J. C. B. Mohr (Paul Siebeck).

Witt, Ulrich (1987b): "How Transaction Rights Are Shaped to Channel Innovativeness," in *Journal of Institutional and Theoretical Economics*: 143, 180–95.

Witt, Ulrich (ed.) (1990): *Studien zur Evolutorischen Ökonomik I*. Berlin: Duncker & Humblot.

Witt, Ulrich (1992a): "Evolutionary Concepts in Economics," in *Eastern Economic Journal*: 18, 405–19.

Witt, Ullrich (ed.) (1992b): *Explaining Process and Change: Approaches to Evolutionary Economics*. Ann Arbor: University of Michigan Press.

Witt, Ulrich (ed.) (1992c): *Studien zur Evolutorischen Ökonomik II*. Berlin: Duncker & Humblot.

Witt, Ulrich (1993a): "Wann kommt es eigentlich zu wirtschaftlichem Fortschritt?" in Adolf Wagner (ed.): *Dezentrale Entscheidungsfindung bei externen Effekten*, pp.19–35. Tübingen: Francke Verlag.

Witt, Ulrich (ed.) (1993b): *Evolutionary Economics*. Aldershot: Edward Elgar.

Witt, Ulrich (1993c): "Turning Austrian Economics into an Evolutionary Theory," in Bruce J. Caldwell and Stephan Boehm (eds.) (1993), pp. 215–36.

Witt, Ulrich (1995): "Moralität vs. Rationalität – Über die Rolle von Innovation und Imitation in einem alten Dilemma," in Adolf Wagner and Lorenz Hans-Walter (eds.): *Studien zur Evolutorischen Ökonomik III*, pp.11–33. Berlin: Duncker & Humblot.

Witt, Ulrich (1998): "Learning to Consume – A Theory of Wants and the Growth of Demand," *Papers on Economics and Evolution #9806, Max-Planck-Institute for Research into Economic Systems*.

Woolcock, Michael (1998): "Social Capital and Economic Development: Toward a Theoretical Synthesis and Policy Framework," in *Theory and Society*: 27, 151–208.

Wu, Wenbo and Otto A. Davis (1999): "The Two Freedoms, Economic Growth and Development: An Empirical Study," in *Public Choice*: 100, 39–64.

Wuketis, Franz M. (ed.) (1984): *Concepts and Approaches in Evolutionary Epistemology. Towards an Evolutionary Theory of Knowledge*. Dordrecht: Reidel.

Wüstehübe, Axel (1991): "Vollständige oder unvollständige Rationalität? – Zur aktuellen Diskussion um einen pragmatischen Rationalitätsbegriff," in *Philosophische Rundschau*. 38. Jg., 257–74.

Yaffey, Michael (1998): "Moral Standards and Transaction Costs: Long-Term Effests," in Klaus Nielsen and Björn Johnson (eds.): *Institutions and Economic Change*, pp. 258–90. Cheltenham: Edward Elgar.

Yerkes, R. M. and J. D. Dodson (1908): "The Relation of Strength of Stimulus to Rapidity of Habit-Formation," in *Journal of Comparative Neurology and Psychology*: 18, 459–82.

Young, H. Peyton (1996): "The Economics of Convention," in *Journal of Economic Perspectives*: 10, pp. 105–122.

Young, H. Peyton (1998): *Individual Strategy and Social Structure*. Princeton. Princeton University Press.

Zafirovski, Milan (1999): "What Is Really Rational Choice? Beyond the Utilitarian Concept of Rationality," in *Current Sociology*: 47, 47–113.

Zohlnhöfer, Werner (1982): "Wettbewerb – Modell und Wirklichkeit," in Clemens-August Andraea and Werner Benisch (eds.): *Wettbewerbsordnung und Wettbewerbsrealität. Festschrift für Arno Sölter zum 70. Geburtstag*, pp. 15–25. Köln, Berlin, Bonn, München: Heymanns.

Zohlnhöfer, Werner (1991): "Marktstruktur und funktionsfähiger Wettbewerb. Versuch einer Erweiterung des Konzepts von Kantzenbach," in *Hamburger Jahrbuch für Wirtschafts- und Gesellschaftspolitik*: 36, 71–85.

Zohlnhöfer, Werner (1996): "Das normative Element in der wettbewerbstheoretischen Doktrinbildung," in Jörn Kruse and Otto G. Mayer (eds.): *Aktuelle Probleme der Wettbewerbs- und Wirtschaftspolitik. Erhard Kantzenbach zum 65. Geburtstag*, pp. 101–17. Baden-Baden: Nomos Verlagsgesellschaft.

Author Index

Abelson, Robert, 27n14
Aberle, Gerd, 192n13
Akerlof, George A., 11n1
Albert, Hans, 5n3, 6, 8n8, 44n2,
    88n7, 98, 145n15, 161–2,
    198n21, 257
Albertus Magnus, 44n2
Alchian, Armen, 167n9, 179
Alesina, Alberto, 247
Alston, Lee J., 240
Anand, Paul, 50
Andersen, Esben S., 191n11
Anderson, J.H., 45n4
Aristotle, 50
Arndt, Helmut, 175, 191n12
Arrow, Kenneth J., 53n21, 189n5,
    215n46, 220
Arthur, Brian, 53n22, 255
Avenarius, Richard, 42n29
Avicenna, 44n2
Axelrod, Robert, 107, 118

Bandura, Albert, 76, 120
Baron, Jonathan, 186
Barro, Robert J., 233, 243n10, 247
Bartlett, Frederic, 27
Bartley, William W. III, 18n3
Bartling, Hartwig, 192n13
Barzel, Yoram, 137n5, 146n18
Bates, Robert H., 130n42
Baumann, Bernd, 213n43
Becker, Gary, 50, 197, 209

Bell, Francis, 253
Ben-Ner, Avner, 72n6
Berg, Hartmut, 192n13
Berg, Joyce, 111
Bernholz, Peter, 235, 246
Bernstein, Lisa, 129n40
Binmore, Ken, 120
Birdzell, L.E. Jr., 234, 238, 246
Black, Donald, 154
Blau, Peter, 110n16, 124
Block, Walter, 247
Boehm, Stefan, 193n14
Böhm, Franz, 66, 163, 215
Boettke, Peter, 193n14
Bohnet, Iris, 127n33, 155n30
Boland Lawrence A., 190
Borchert, Manfred, 192n13
Borner, Silvio, 247
Bosch, Alfred, 192n13
Boudon, Raymond, 53, 56n26
Boulding, Kenneth, 162, 191n11
Bowles, Samuel, 11n4
Boyd, Robert, 70–2, 80, 123n29
Brandt, Karl, 164, 192n13
Breit, Heiko, 154
Brennan, Geoffrey, 168n10
Brinton, Mary, 67
Brooks, Michael A., 194n15
Broome, John, 50n12
Bruner, Jerome S., 27n15
Brunetti, Aymo, 247
Buchanan, James M., 49n10, 66,

Buchanan, James M. (*cont.*)
    93n18, 115, 140n9, 157n33,
    162, 168n10, 180, 193–4, 201
Bunge, Mario, 173n16

Caldwell, Bruce J., 193n14
Calvert, Randall L., 95n20
Campbell, Donald, 16n2, 17, 38,
    166n7
Champagne, A.B., 45n4
Chiaromonte, Giovanni F., 176n22
Choi, Young Back, 27n14, 47n7,
    49n10, 254n27
Clark, Andy, 88n8
Clark, John M., 170, 191n12
Coase, Ronald, 119
Cohen, Wesley, 225–6, 231
Coleman, James S., 83, 118–9, 161
Commons, John R., 42n29, 51, 89,
    n9, 92, 174
Congleton, Roger, 107, 194n15
Conlisk, John, 52n19
Cook, Kathleen, 130
Cooper, John M., 50
Cooter, Robert D., 157n33, 250n22
Coriat, Benjamin, 256n29
Cosgel, Metin, 198, 201, 204
Cosmides, Leda, 20–1
Cox, Helmut, 192n13

D'Andrade, Roy, 69, 76n13
Darwin, Cahrles, 173–5
David, Paul, 103, 173, 184n9, 255
Davis, John, 110n16
Davis, Otto, 248
Dawes, Robyn M., 106n10, 111n17
Day, Richard H., 44n2
De Alessi, Louis, 148n24
Delhaes, Karl von, 192n13
Demsetz, Harold, 95, 148, 169n12,
    216, 246
Dennis, Ken 53n21
Denzau, Arthur, 68, 76, 96, 183, 234
Dickens, William T., 11n1
Dickhaut, John, 111
Diermeier, Daniel, 242
Dietl, Helmut, 95n20, 148n24

DiLorenzo, Thomas, 194n15
DiMaggio, Paul, 5n3, 57n29, 67,
    69n2, 88–9, 187n10
Dodson, J.D., 11n3
Dolan, Edwin, 193n14
Donald, Merlin, 75
Dopfer, Kurt, 191n11
Dosi, Giovanni, 176n22, 178n1,
    191n11, 212n41, 220–4,
    256n29
Douglas, Mary, 89n8
Downie, Jack, 176n22
Drobak, John N., 5n3
Dunbar, Robin I.M., 115
Durkheim, Emile, 55, 168n11
Durham, W.H., 70
Dworkin, Ronald, 152

Easton, Stephen T., 248n17
Eccles, John, 38, 74
Eichenberger, Reiner, 52n17, 89n10
Eckensberger, Lutz, 154
Edgeworth, Francis Y., 217
Edquist, Charles, 256n29
Eggertsson, Thráinn, 95, 130,
    145n17, 148n24, 239n6, 240
Eickhof, Norbert, 192n13
Einstein, Albert, 18
Ekeh, Peter P., 110n16
Elias, Norbert, 139
Eliasson, Gunnar, 176n22, 191n11,
    224n57, 225
Ellickson, Robert C., 128, 129, 151,
    154–5
Elster, Jon, 14, 55, 59n32, 84n3, 123
Emerson, Richard M., 110n16
England, Richard W., 191n11
Ensminger, Jean, 124, 127n33,
    157n32
Epstein, Richard A., 152
Ericson, Joel, 242
Etzioni, Amitai, 59
Eucken, Walter, 66, 163, 164, 239,
    244
Evans-Pritchard, E., 130
Everett, Michael, 191n11

Faber, Malte, 180n3
Fedderke, Johannes, 248
Fehl Ulrich, 175, 192n13, 209, 211n41, 214–6
Fehr, Ernst, 111
Feldman, Marcus W. 70, 72n6
Ferguson, Adam, 90
Festinger, Leon, 11
Field, Alexander James, 95n21
Finer, Samuel E., 142–4
Foss, Nicolai J., 193n14, 224n57
Foster, John, 190n10
Frank, Robert, 58n31, 110n15
Frankfurt, Harry G., 13n6
Freeman, Christopher, 191n11
Frey, Bruno, 52n17, 89n10, 155n30
Freyen, Timothy, 242
Frowen, Stephen F., 193n14
Frydman, Roman, 189n4
Furubotn, Eirik G., 66, 148n24

Gächter, Simon, 111
Gäfgen, Gerhard, 95n20
Galanter, Marc, 129n37
Gardner, H., 22
Gardner, Roy, 126
Garibaldi-Fernandez, Jose Alberto, 152
Garrison, Roger W., 209n35
Gauthier, David, 106n11
Gehlen, Arnold, 13n7, 87–8
Gigerenzer, Gerd, 21, 36n24, 52n17
Görgens, Egon, 192n13, 247n16
Goffman, Erwing, 52n17
Goldthorpe, John H. 53n21
Goody, Jack, 73n7
Granovetter, Marc, 162, 187n10
Gray, Cheryl W., 250n22
Green, Christopher, 191n11
Green, Leslie, 139n8
Greif, Avner, 130n41, 157n31, 250–1, 254n27
Griffiths, John, 154
Grossekettler, Heinz, 163, 192n13
Grossman, Gene M., 232n1
Grossmann, Herschel, 242

Grossman, Sanford J., 216n48
Güth, Werner, 133
Guthrie, William K.C., 50n11
Gwartney, James, 247–8

Haber, Stephan, 248n18
Hahn, Frank H., 215n46
Halcombe, Randall, 248n18
Hall, Peter A., 55, 67, 87n4, 89n9
Hall, Robert E., 247
Hardin, Garrett, 126
Harper, David, 194n15, 197, 206n31, 208
Hart, H. L. A., 147n19, 150, 152
Haufler, Virginia, 5n3
Hawkes, Kristen, 127n33
Hayek, Friedrich A. von, 19n6, 24, 32, 51, 66, 78–9, 81–2, 87–94, 117, 122, 146–8, 180, 185, 188–9, 212, 216n48, 235–6, 240, 243–4, 252n25, 256n29
Hazlehurst, Brian, 70
Heap, Shaun Hargreaves, 48n8
Heiner, Ronald, 58
Heath, Eugene, 93n18
Heijdra, Ben, 194n15
Helpman, Elhanan, 231, 232n1
Hensel, Paul, 167n8
Herdzina, Klaus, 192n13
Hesse, Günter, 46, 97, 180, 256n29
Heuss, Ernst, 175, 191–2
High, Jack, 52n18, 190n6, 193n14, 215
Hirschfeld, Lawrence, 77n13, 176n22
Hirshleifer, Jack, 165
Hobbes, Thomas, 138
Hodgson, Geoffrey M., 66, 80n20, 168n11, 175, 187n11
Hoffman, Elisabeth, 111
Hogarth, Robin M., 52n17
Holland, John H., 8, 22–9, 36, 39, 45n4
Hollis, Martin, 48n8
Holyoak, Keith J., 8, 22, 36n25
Homans, George C., 110–1
Homer, 14n8

Hoppman, Erich, 175, 192n13, 195, 202
Hume, David, 12, 23n10, 44n2, 50, 61n33, 90, 102, 109–10, 113n20, 117, 135, 143, 147
Hutchins, Edwin, 70, 76n13

Ingram, Paul, 120n27, 121, 129n41, 156
Inkeles, Alex, 243
Irrgang, Bernhard, 18n3

Jasay, Anthony de, 131–2
Jens, Uwe, 192n13
Jensen, Michael C., 145n17
Jevons, William Stanley, 55n25
Johnson, James, 124
Johnson, Björn, 191n11
Johnson, Paul, 250n21
Johnson-Laird, Philip N., 27
Jones, Charles, 247
Jones, Eric L., 143, 234, 246, 215n23

Kagel, J.H, 54n23
Kahneman, Daniel, 36, 52n17, 207
Kant, Immanuel, 16, 50n11
Kantzenbach, Erhard, 192n13
Kaufman, Bruce E., 11n3
Kaufer, Erich, 172, 192n13
Keefer, Philip, 246, 250
Kehl, Frank, 22
Kerber, Wolfgang, 116n24, 168, 170–1, 180n5, 192n13, 194, 197, 206–8, 212
Keuth, Herbert, 99n26
Khalil, Elias, 84n2, 191n11
Kiernan, Brendan, 253
Kirchgässner, Gebhard, 53
Kirzner, Israel, 192, 193, 209–11
Kiwit, Daniel, 77n15, 155
Klitgaard, Robert, 248
Kliemt, Hartmut, 54n24, 113, 133, 150
Klopfer, L. E., 45n4
Knack, Stephen, 246, 250
Knetsch, Jack L., 52n17, 207
Knieps, Günter, 192n13

Knight, Jack, 77n13, 95n20, 124n30, 157n33, 234
Koch, Lambert, 68n1
Kohlberg, Lawrence, 111–3, 154
Koppl, Roger, 93n18, 94
Korobkin, Russell, 5n3
Koslowski, Peter, 19n6, 44
Kragt, Alphons J.C. van, 111
Krueger, Anne O., 194n15
Krüsselberg, Hans-Günther, 192n13
Kubon-Gilke, Gisela, 97n23
Kuhn, Helmut
Kuhn, Thomas, 23n12, 45n4, 50n11, 75n10
Kumm, Jochen, 70, 72n6
Kunz, Harald, 192n13

Lachmann, Ludwig, 89n9, 187–8, 192–3, 209
Lal, Deepak, 251
Laland, Kevin N., 70, 72n6
Lampe, Ernst-Joachim, 155
Lancaster, Kelvin, 197
Landa, Janet Tai, 110n16
Lane, David, 37n26, 53n22
Langlois, Richard N., 92, 191n11, 198, 201–2, 204, 220, 224–5, 231
La Porta, Rafael, 249–50
Lattimore, Richard 14n8
Lawson, Robert, 247–8
Leblang, David A., 247
Leipold, Helmut, 167
Lenel, Hans Otto, 192n13
Levi, Margaret, 124n30, 143–4, 146n18
Levine, Ross, 233
Levinthal, Daniel, 225, 231
Lewin, Kurt, 11
Lewis, David, 101–2
Lewis, Steven, 242, 246
Lian, Brad, 248n18
Limongi, Fernando, 243, 247n16
Lindenberg, Siegwart, 5n3, 52n17, 207
Lipford, Jody, 156n31

Littlechild, Stephen C., 187n12,
  189n5, 190n7, 193n14
Loasby, Brian, 52, 89n8, 195n18,
  198n22, 201, 206n33, 215–6,
  226n59
Locke, John, 138, 147
Lopez-De Silanes, Florencio, 249
Lorenz, Konrad, 16, 17, 18n3, 38
Lorenz, Werner, 191n11
Lowenberg, Anton, 194n15
Loy, Claudia, 193n14, 213n43
Lucas, Robert E., 228–31, 233–4
Luchins, Abraham, 186
Lyons, Bruce, 48

Macaulay, Stewart, 129n40
Machlup, Fritz, 195
Machovec, Frank M., 189n3
Mackaay, Ejan, 144n14, 145
Mackie, John, 110, 117
Magnusson, Lars, 191n11
Malerba, Franco, 37n26
Malinowski, Branislaw, 110n16
Malthus, Thomas, 175
Mankiw, N. Gregory, 232n1
Mansbridge, Jane, 72n6
Mantzavinos, Chrysostomos, 132n1,
  192n13, 211n40, 213n43, 246
Marengo, Luigi, 224n58
Marimon, Ramon, 190n9
Markert, Kurt, 192n13
Marshall, Alfred, 175–6, 199n24,
  219n51
Marx, Karl, 96, 98n24
Maslow, Abraham, 10–11
Matthews, R.C.O., 181n7
Mauss, Marcel, 110n16
Maxfield, Robert, 37n26
Maynard Smith, John, 105n8
Mayr, Ernst, 20, 173–5
McAdams, Richard H., 121n28
McCabe, Kevin, 111
McCann, Charles, 191n11
McClelland, David, 11n2
McGrattan, Elen, 190n9
McGuire, Martin C., 144–5

McNulty, Paul J., 189n3
Meckling, William H., 145n17
Menger, Carl, 91, 103, 164, 199n24
Merten, Klaus, 68n1
Metcalfe, Stanley, 166n7, 176n22,
  178n1, 191n11, 220, 222–3
Meyer, Willi, 148n24
Milgrom, Paul, 129n41, 130n41
Miller, Gary, 130n42
Mises, Ludwig von, 6, 103, 205–6
Mokyr, Joel, 75, 223n56
Morgenstern, Oscar, 50
Mummert, Uwe, 157n31
Murray, Henry A., 11n2

Nee, Victor, 67, 111, 120–1, 129n41,
  156
Nelson, Richard, 178n1, 180n3, 190–
  1, 196n19, 201, 220, 222–5,
  256n29
Nettle, Daniel, 115
Neumann, Carl W., 192n13, 202
Neumann, John von, 50
Newell, Allen, 7, 8, 23
Nielsen, Klaus, 191n11
Nisbett, Richard, 8, 22, 27n15, 36
North, Douglass C., 66, 68, 76, 83n1,
  95–6, 129n41, 133, 142, 144–
  6, 170, 183, 234–6, 240, 242,
  244, 246, 249n19, 254, 256n29
Nozick, Robert, 36, 93, 138, 140n10
Nye, John V.C., 143

O'Driscoll, Gerald, 192n14, 199n23,
  201, 216
Oberender, Peter, 192n13, 231
Okruch, Stefan, 95n20, 173
Olson, Mancur, 126, 128, 144–5,
  230, 242–4, 247, 249
Oneal, John, 248n18
Opp, Karl-Dieter, 53n21, 79n17, 120,
  122, 125
Orbell, John M., 106n10, 111
Ordeshook, Peter C., 243, 252n24
Orsenigo, Luigi, 37n26
Ortman, Andreas, 21
Ostrom, Elinor, 5n3, 126, 128

Ott, Alfred E., 195

Pack, Howard, 234n2
Paraskewopoulos, Spiridon, 247n16
Parsons, Talcott, 55, 65, 83n1, 118
Peacock, Alan, 163
Pejovich, Svetozar, 148n24, 256n29
Pelikan, Pavel, 224n58, 256n29
Penrose, Edith, 179, 224n58
Piaget, Jean, 27
Pies, Ingo, 247n16
Pisano, Gary, 224n57
Platteau, Jean-Philippe, 110n15,
    251n23
Polanyi, Michael, 13n7, 29n17, 31–4,
    225
Popper, Karl R., 18–23, 28n16, 38,
    44n2, 74–5, 91–2, 94, 190n8
Posner, Eric, 156
Posner, Richard A., 156n31, 244
Powell, Walter, 67, 89, 187n10
Pritzl, Ruppert, 152
Proops, John L.R., 180n3
Prychitko, David L., 193n14
Przeworski, Adam, 243, 247n16, 254
Putnam, Robert, 249–50
Putterman, Louis, 72n6

Qian, Yingyi, 243, 246
Quine, Willard, V. O., 25

Rabin, Matthew, 41
Raible, Karl, 191n11
Radnitzky, Gerhard, 18n3
Ramstad, Yngve, 174
Razo, Armando, 248n18
Reder, Melvin W., 52n17
Renelt, David, 233
Richardson, G.B., 201
Richerson, Peter J., 70–2, 80, 123
Richter, Rudolf, 66
Ricketts, Martin, 194n15
Riedl, Rupert, 18n3
Riker, William H., 181n6, 243,
    245n14
Rizzo, Mario, 192–3, 199n23, 201,
    206

Robertson, Paul, 220, 224–5, 231
Röpke, Jochen, 11n3, 175, 177n23,
    192n13, 214n44
Romer, Paul M., 220n53, 228, 230–4
Rosenberg, Nathan, 220, 234, 238,
    246
Ross, Lee, 27n15, 36
Ross, Stephen A., 145n17
Rothbard, Murray N., 206n31
Rothschild, Emma, 90n12
Rothschild, Michael, 189n4
Rowe, Nicholas, 57
Rowley, Charles K., 194n15
Rutherford, Malcolm, 95n21, 103
Ryle, Gilbert, 30–3

Samuelson, Larry, 120
Sargent, Thomas J., 53n21
Sarna, Naveen, 247
Saviotti, Paolo P., 176n22, 191n11
Schank, Roger, 27n14
Schelling, Thomas C., 59n32, 103–4
Schleifer, Andrei, 249
Schlicht, Ekkehart, 97, 122
Schmid, Allan, 148
Schmidt, Ingo, 192n13
Schmidt, Sigfried J., 68n1
Schmidtchen, Dieter, 163, 192n13,
    215n46
Schmoller, Gustav, 164
Schotter, Andrew, 95n20
Schreiter, Carsten, 192n13, 215n46,
    230
Schrödinger, Erwin, 29, 42n29
Schumpeter, Joseph A., 3, 98n24,
    190–1, 197, 208, 211n41, 213,
    219n51
Scully, Gerald W., 247
Selten, Reinhard, 12
Sen, Amartya, 4, 50
Sened, Itai, 95n20
Shackle, G.L.S., 46–7, 52, 192, 193,
    209
Shefrin, H. M., 59n32
Shils, E. A., 118
Silverberg, Gerald, 191n11

Simon, Herbert, 7, 8, 23, 52, 73–4, 92
Simons, Anna, 124
Sirowy, Larry, 243n11
Sjöstrand, Sven-Erik, 95n20
Slick, Moritz, 23n12
Slottje, Dan, 247
Smith, Adam, 90n12, 110n16, 162, 184, 238–9
Smith, John M., 105n8
Smith, Vernon L., 111, 217
Snell, Bruno, 75n11
Sober, Elliott, 176n22
Soete, Luc, 191n11
Solow, Robert, 228–9, 232
Soltan, Karol, 5n3
Soltis, Joseph, 80
Spadaro, Louis, 193n14
Sperber, Dan, 77n13
Stahl, Silke R., 77n13
Steindl, Joseph, 176n22
Sternberg, Robert J., 44n2
Stigler, George, 189, 198
Stiglitz, Joseph, 216n48
Stigum, B., 189n4
Strang, David, 121
Streit, Manfred, 163n3, 192n13, 205n29, 207, 211n41, 235
Sugden, Robert, 48n8, 53n21, 104–5, 122
Swamy, Anand, 247

Tamborini, Roberto, 23n11, 254n27
Taylor, Rosemary, 55, 67, 87n4, 89n9
Teece, David J., 224
Temple, Jonathan, 250n21
Thagard, Paul, 8, 22, 36
Thaler, Richard, 5n3, 52n17, 59n32, 207
Thomas, Robert, 95, 234, 246
Thomsen, Esteban F., 216
Tietzel, Manfred, 59n32
Toboso, Fernando, 124
Todd, Peter M., 36n24, 52n17
Tolksdorf, Michael, 192n13
Tollison, Robert, 194n15

Tooby, John, 20, 21
Torstensson, Johan, 247
Trivers, R., 122
Tullock, Gordon, 145n16, 168n10, 194n15
Tversky, Amos, 36, 52n17, 207

Ulen, Thomas, 5n3
Ullmann-Margalit, Edna, 93–4
Uslaner, Eric M., 5n3, 157n33

Väth, Andreas, 193n13
Vanberg, Viktor J., 56, 58n30, 80–1, 107, 109n13, 193n14, 235, 246
Varey, Carol, 207
Vaubel, Roland, 235
Vaughn, Karen, 93n18, 193n14, 210n38, 216n49
Vickers, John, 189n3
Vincenti, Walter, 222
Vishny, Robert, 250
Voigt, Stefan, 77n15, 155, 247n16, 252n24
Voland, Eckart, 114
Vollmer, Gerhard, 18n3
Vriend, Nicolaas J., 53n21
Vromen, Jack J., 80n20

Waal, Frans de, 114
Wagner, Adolf, 191n11
Walker, James, 126
Walker, Michael, 248
Walras, Léon, 217
Walsh, Vivian, 4
Weale, Albert 48n8
Weber, Max, 138
Weder, Beatrice, 247
Wegner, Gerhard, 192n13, 204n29, 206n32, 208, 211n41, 222n55
Weil, David, 232n1
Weimer, David L., 148n22
Weingast, Barry R., 129–30, 24–6, 252
Weischenber, Sigfried 68n1
Wessling, Ewald 51n16, 52n18
Wieandt, Axel, 192n13
Willeke, Franz-Ulrich , 192n13
Williams, Bernard, 14n7

Williamson, Oliver, 53n20, 129
Willgerodt, Hans, 163n5
Wilson, Robert A., 22
Wimmer, Hannes, 155
Windsperger, Josef, 192n13
Winter, Sidney G., 191n11, 201, 224–
  5, 256n29
Wintrobe, Ronald, 145n16
Wiseman, Jack, 193n14
Witt, Ulrich, 19n6, 70n3, 76–7,
  108n12, 171, 180n3, 191n11,
  197, 199, 211–13, 217n50

Woolcock, Michael, 249n20
Wu, Wenbo, 248
Wuketis, Franz M., 18n3
Wüstehübe, Axel, 53n21

Yaffey, Michael, 115
Yandle, Bruce, 156n31
Yerkes, R.M., 11n3
Young, H. Peyton, 103–5

Zafirofski, Milan, 53n21
Zohlnhöfer, Werner, 192n13

Subject Index

accumulation, 208, 213–14, 218, 247
action parameters, 165, 168–9, 193–4, 196, 208, 217–19, 221, 237–8, 240
adaptive problems, 20
analogy, 36, 103–4, 152, 200n26
anomalies, 40, 89n10
a priorism, 5–6, 60
arbitrage, 208–11, 214
auctioneer, 204, 215n46
autocratic systems, 144, 148, 242–3, 247

blind-variation-and-selective-retention process, 17
bounded rationality, 52
behavioral programs
    closed, 20
    open, 20

capabilities approach, 201–2, 224, 238–9
collective action, 90, 92, 97, 99, 135
collective choice, 82, 92, 96, 167n8
collective learning, 70, 73, 78, 140, 227, 255
common-pool resource problems, 126–7
communicability of knowledge, 31, 218, 225
competitive order, 66

competitive process
    content, 168–9

dynamics, 168, 170–1
constitution, 243–5, 252–3
consumer, 201–2, 237
consumption
    subjective view, 201
    technology of, 201–3
cooperative network, 109
coordination game, 86, 101–3
creativity, 40, 94, 192
credible commitments, 133, 228, 241–8
cultural memes, 79

default hierarchy, 26, 68
deliberation process, 38, 44, 47, 50n11, 96
democracy, 243, 247, 248n19, 252n25
deterministic theories of institutional change, 94
dictator game, 111, 127
division of knowledge, 184, 188, 207, 214, 226, 233, 238–9
division of labor, 65, 134–6, 140, 154, 184, 188, 238–9
dual inheritance model, 70

economic development
    institution-free theory of, 228–30, 238n5, 240
economics of information, 189–90
endowment effect, 207

entrepreneur, 165–6, 170–4, 182, 192–3, 196, 203–9, 211, 213, 218–20, 223, 227, 230–3, 237, 240
entrepreneurial activity, 165–6, 191, 195, 197, 224
entrepreneurship, 219, 224
equilibrium, 124, 191, 209–11, 214, 216n47, 217, 230
  equilibrating tendencies, 209, 210, 213n43
  general economic equilibrium, 162, 189
  kaleidic equilibrium, 192
  market equilibrium, 189, 205, 208
  multiple equilibria, 124
evolutionary psychology, 20–2
evolutionary stability, 105
exchange theory in sociology, 110, 128
external point of view
  and explanation of law, 150

focal point, 103
free riding, 115, 135
Freiburg School, 66, 163
functionalist fallacy, 84

game of trust, 86, 133–4
group selection falllacy, 81

hawk/dove game, 105
heuristics, 36–7, 60, 223
homo oeconomicus, 54, 56, 100, 257
homo sociologicus, 54, 56, 100, 257
horizontal distinction between social rules, 154
humanistic theory of growth motivation, 10

ideology, 96–8
imagination, faculty of, 44, 46, 56, 192
imitation, 77, 121, 166, 168, 170, 196–7, 202–3, 208, 211–12, 218, 225
induction, 22–3, 60

inferential strategies, 35–6, 43, 56n27, 57, 103–4, 120, 152, 200n26
innovation, 94, 96, 166, 168, 170–2, 180n4, 191, 196–7, 202–3, 208, 211–14, 218, 219n51, 220–3, 230, 233, 237–9, 256
interjurisdictional competition, 245
internal point of view
  and explanation of law, 150–2
invariant restrictions, 97, 180
invisible-hand process, 74, 90, 93–4, 97, 99, 108, 113, 118, 125, 140, 144
invisible-hand explanation, 74n9, 93, 102–3, 120

judgmental strategies, 36

"knowing how," 30–1, 77, 116, 120, 218–19, 225, 236, 238
"knowing that," 30, 218, 236
knowledge spillovers, 225, 231

learning by imitation, 32
losses, 205, 207–8, 210, 219
loss aversion, 207

market-preserving federalism, 243, 245–6
methodological individualism, 3, 80, 257
mind as an instrument of classification, 24, 25, 90, 182
monopoly view of the state, 139
moral behavior, 115, 116
moral network, 109, 113
moral stages, 111–12, 154

Nash equilibrium, 101
natural categories, 25

Ontogenetic knowledge, 17
ontogenetic learning, 16
open markets, 238, 240–1
oppression, 136, 137, 140
organizations as corporate actors, 83, 161

path dependence

cognitive, 214, 224–5, 254–5
institutional, 254
technological 255
pecuniary external effects, 171, 205–8, 211
phenotypes, 70–1
phylogenetic knowledge, 17
phylogenetic learning, 16
political regimes and economic growth, 242–3, 247
political stability vs. political credibility, 248n18
population thinking, 174–7
practical knowledge, 34, 39, 73, 77
practical problems, 30–1, 35–6
precommitment, 14, 59
price-making process, 215, 217
principle of the cognitive creation, 46
prisoner's dilemma, 86, 106, 126–7, 131, 139
prisoner's dilemma with an exit option, 106–8, 115
profit, 165–6, 179, 186, 194–6, 205–7, 210, 213, 216n47, 218–20, 230–1, 237–8
property rights, 66, 95–6, 127, 147–9, 156, 163, 167–8, 182, 205n29, 240–2, 245–8, 250, 256
protective agencies, 136–9, 143
protective state, 140–1, 143–4, 146
public goods, 115

radical subjectivist approach, 192
rational choice theory, 4, 40, 48, 50–4, 58–9, 89, 95, 119, 124, 257
rationality, 4, 12, 14, 21, 40, 53–4, 58, 97

reciprocity, 110–11, 113–14, 121, 127
reflection, 37–9, 43–4, 53, 55–6
relationship between formal and informal institutions, 153, 250, 252
rent-seeking, 194n15
retributive emotions, 110, 113
routine, 29, 38, 40, 42–3, 47, 56–7, 60, 120, 123, 201, 224
rule of law, 243–8, 252
rules-as-tools analogy, 81
rules of thumb 36, 37

scaffolding, 88n8
self-reinforcing mechanisms, 104, 255
social capital, 127, 249n20
social exchange theory, 111
sociobiology, 19, 72
subjectivism, 7, 59, 61, 188, 198

tacit knowledge, 30, 33–4, 225
technology, 221–5, 230
theoretical knowledge, 34, 73, 75
theoretical problems, 30–1, 36, 39
trust, 133, 135, 250

ultimatum game, 155n30
unconsciousness, 29
unconscious routines, 30, 34–5, 43, 60, 87, 186, 254

variation, 177, 190, 211
variety, 175, 192–5, 214, 229
vertical distinction between social rules, 154

weakness of the will, 14
well-defined problems, 51

Other books in the series
(continued from page iii)

Anna L. Harvey, *Votes Without Leverage: Women in American Electoral Politics, 1920–1970*

Murray Horn, *The Political Economy of Public Administration: Institutional Choice in the Public Sector*

John D. Huber, *Rationalizing Parliament: Legislative Institutions and Party Politics in France*

Jack Knight, *Institutions and Social Conflict*

Michael Laver and Kenneth Shepsle, eds., *Making and Breaking Governments*

Michael Laver and Kenneth Shepsle, eds., *Cabinet Ministers and Parliamentary Government*

Margaret Levi, *Consent, Dissent, and Patriotism*

Brian Levy and Pablo T. Spiller, eds., *Regulations, Institutions, and Commitment*

Leif Lewin, *Ideology and Strategy: A Century of Swedish Politics* (English Edition)

Gary Libecap, *Contracting for Property Rights*

John Londregan, *Legislative Institutions and Ideology in Chile*

Arthur Lupia and Mathew D. McCubbins, *The Democratic Dilemma: Can Citizens Learn What They Really Need to Know?*

Mathew D. McCubbins and Terry Sullivan, eds., *Congress: Structure and Policy*

Gary J. Miller, *Managerial Dilemmas: The Political Economy of Hierarchy*

Douglass C. North, *Institutions, Institutional Change, and Economic Performance*

Elinor Ostrom, *Governing the Commons: The Evolution of Institutions for Collective Action*

J. Mark Ramseyer, *Odd Markets in Japanese History*

J. Mark Ramseyer and Frances Rosenbluth, *The Politics of Oligarchy: Institutional Choice in Imperial Japan*

Jean-Laurent Rosenthal, *The Fruits of Revolution: Property Rights, Litigation, and French Agriculture*

Charles Stewart III, *Budget Reform Politics: The Design of the Appropriations Process in the House of Representatives, 1865–1921*

George Tsebelis and Jeannette Money, *Bicameralism*

John Waterbury, *Exposed to Innumerable Delusions: Public Enterprise and State Power in Egypt, India, Mexico, and Turkey*

David L. Weimer, eds., *The Political Economy of Property Rights*